THE HOME FRONT AND WAR IN THE TWENTIETH CENTURY

THE AMERICAN EXPERIENCE IN COMPARATIVE PERSPECTIVE

Proceedings of the
Tenth Military History Symposium
October 20-22, 1982

Edited by
James Titus

United States Air Force Academy
and
Office of Air Force History
Headquarters USAF

1984

Library of Congress Cataloging in Publication Data

Military History Symposium (U.S.) (10th : 1982)
(United States Air Force Academy)
The home front and war in the twentieth century.

Sponsored by: The Department of History and The Association of Graduates.
Includes index.
1. Military history, Modern—20th century—Congresses. 2. War and society—History—20th century—Congresses. 3. War—Economic aspects—Congresses. 4. War—Economic aspects—United States—Congresses. 5. United States—Social conditions—Congresses. I. Titus, James. II. United States Air Force Academy. Dept. of History. III. United States Air Force Academy. Assocation of Graduates. IV. Title.
D431.M54 1982   303.6'6   83–600203
ISBN 0–912799–01–3

For sale by Superintendent of Documents,
U.S. Government Printing Office, Washington, D. C. 20402

THE TENTH MILITARY HISTORY SYMPOSIUM

October 20-22, 1982
United States Air Force Academy

Sponsored by

The Department of History
and
The Association of Graduates

* * * * * * *

Executive Director,
Tenth Military History Symposium: Lieutenant Colonel James Titus

Deputy Director,
Tenth Military History Symposium: Major Sidney F. Baker, USA

Professor and Head,
Department of History: Colonel Carl W. Reddel

President,
Association of Graduates: Lieutenant Colonel Thomas J. Eller, USAF, Retired

Symposium Committee Members:

    Captain John G. Albert
    Captain Mark L. Dues
    Captain Bernard E. Harvey
    Captain Vernon K. Lane
    Captain Robert C. Owen
    Captain Michael W. Paul
    Captain Christie C. Peacock
    Ms. Nellie Dykes

United States Air Force
Historical Advisory Committee
(As of December 1, 1983)

Lt. Gen. Charles G. Cleveland, USAF
Commander, Air University, ATC

Mr. DeWitt S. Copp
The National Volunteer Agency

Dr. Philip A. Crowl
Annapolis, Maryland

Dr. Warren W. Hassler, Jr.
Pennsylvania State University

Brig. Gen. Harris B. Hull,
USAF, Retired
National Aeronautics and Space
Administration

Dr. Alfred F. Hurley
Brig. Gen., USAF, Retired
North Texas State University

Mr. David E. Place,
The General Counsel, USAF

Gen. Bryce Poe II,
USAF, Retired

Lt. Gen. Winfield W. Scott, Jr.
Superintendent, USAF Academy

Dr. David A. Shannon *(Chairman)*
University of Virginia

CONTENTS

	Page
In Memoriam: Major Donald R. Backlund	xi
Preface	xiii
Introduction *James Titus*	1

TWENTY-FIFTH HARMON MEMORIAL LECTURE IN MILITARY HISTORY 3

"United Against: American Culture and Society During World War II" 5
John Morton Blum

SESSION I:

THE QUEST FOR NATIONAL UNITY IN THE GREAT WAR ... 17

Chairman: *David F. Trask*
Introductory Remarks by the Chairman 19

"For King and Kaiser: British and German Mobilization in World War I" 24
Dennis E. Showalter

"Rallying Americans for War: 1917-1918" 47
David M. Kennedy

"The Collapse of the Central Powers in World War I:
The Case of Austria-Hungary" 57
Gunther E. Rothenberg

Commentary 67
Allan M. Winkler

Discussion and Comments 71
David F. Trask (Moderator)

SESSION II:

THE SINEWS OF WAR:
ECONOMIC MOBILIZATION IN WORLD WAR II 79

Chairman: *Russell F. Weigley*
Introductory Remarks by the Chairman 81

"Some Aspects of German Mobilization Under the National Socialist Regime" 83
  Wilhelm Deist

"Warfare and Power Relations in America:
Mobilizing the World War II Economy" 91
  Paul A. C. Koistinen

Commentary 111
  Robert D. Cuff

Discussion and Comments 119
  Russell F. Weigley (Moderator)

BANQUET ADDRESS 121

"Hollywood Goes to War" 123
  David H. Culbert

SESSION III:

SOCIAL EFFECTS OF TOTAL WAR 125

Chairman: *Richard H. Kohn*
Introductory Remarks by the Chairman 127

"Total War and Social Change in Great Britain and Other European Countries" 130
  Arthur Marwick

"American Blacks in World War II:
Rethinking the Militancy-Watershed Hypothesis" 147
  Harvard Sitkoff

"War is Not Healthy for Children and Other Living Things:
Reflections on the Impact of Total War on Women" 156
  Leila J. Rupp

Commentary 170
    Richard Polenberg

Discussion and Comments 176
    Richard H. Kohn (Moderator)

SESSION IV:

LIMITED WAR AND THE PROBLEM OF HEARTS AND MINDS ON THE HOME FRONT 183

Chairman: *Allan R. Millet*
Introductory Remarks by the Chairman 185

"Keeping Algeria French: The War on the Home Front" 187
    John E. Talbott

"A Comment on the Vietnam Crisis in America: Tet 1968" 197
    Peter Braestrup

Commentary 202
    David MacIsaac

Discussion and Comments 206
    Allan R. Millett (Moderator)

SUMMARY 213

Introductory Remarks 215
    Carl W. Reddel

"Beyond the Battlefield" 216
    Edward M. Coffman

Notes 223

Participants 251

Index 265

AVAILABLE MILITARY HISTORY SYMPOSIUM PROCEEDINGS

1st The proceedings of the first symposium *were not published*

2nd *Command and Commanders in Modern Warfare* (2nd ed, 1971)
Stock Number 0874-0003

3rd *Science, Technology, and Warfare* (1971)
Stock Number 0874-0002 (out of print)

4th *Soldiers and Statesmen* (1973)
Stock Number 0870-00335

5th *The Military and Society* (1975)
Stock Number 008-070-00367-8

6th *The Military History of the American Revolution* (1976)
Stock Number 008-070-106109

7th *The American Military on the Frontier* (1978)
Stock Number 008-070-00432-2

8th *Air Power and Warfare* (1979)
Stock Number 008-070-00441-1

9th *The American Military and the Far East* (1980)
Stock Number 008-070-00474-7

THE HOME FRONT AND WAR IN THE TWENTIETH CENTURY: THE AMERICAN EXPERIENCE IN COMPARATIVE PERSPECTIVE

Views or opinions expressed or implied in this publication are those of the authors and are not to be construed as carrying official sanction of the Department of the Air Force, the U.S. Air Force Academy, or the institutions with which the contributors are affiliated.

IN MEMORIAM: MAJOR DONALD R. BACKLUND

The Department of History gratefully acknowledges the generous support given the Tenth Military History Symposium by the Major Donald R. Backlund Memorial Fund.

Major Donald R. Backlund, a member of the Air Force Academy Class of 1971, was a man who possessed special qualities as a leader, a scholar, and a human being. As a second classman he wrote an original research paper which won an Air Force Historical Foundation prize and subsequently was published in *Aerospace Historian*. In his final year at the Academy he received the Outstanding Group Commander Award and was named the Outstanding Cadet in Military History.

After graduation and commissioning, Major Backlund continued his formal education and received a Master's degree in history from Indiana University in 1972. During the next seven years he made his mark as a pilot in a series of demanding operational assignments. He won the Air Force Cross in 1975 for his part in the military operations undertaken at the time of the *Mayaguez* incident. His heroism in that episode also resulted in his joining the small and very select group of Academy graduates who have won the Jabara Award for Airmanship. Major Backlund's unbroken train of distinguished professional accomplishments led to his selection in 1978 for early promotion to the rank of Major.

Major Backlund died in an aircraft accident in 1979. He left behind his parents, Dr. and Mrs. Donald F. Backlund, two sisters, and a host of devoted friends and admirers.

THE MILITARY HISTORY SYMPOSIA SERIES OF THE UNITED STATES AIR FORCE ACADEMY

1. Current Concepts in Military History (May 1967)

2. Command and Commanders in Modern Warfare (May 1968)

3. Science, Technology, and Warfare (May 1969)

4. Soldiers and Statesmen (October 1970)

5. The Military and Society (October 1972)

6. The Military History of the American Revolution (October 1974)

7. The American Military on the Frontier (October 1976)

8. Air Power and Warfare (October 1978)

9. The American Military and the Far East (October 1980)

10. The Home Front and War in the Twentieth Century (October 1982)

PREFACE

The essays and commentaries which form this volume originally were presented at the Tenth Military History Symposium which was held at the United States Air Force Academy on October 20-22, 1982. The Military History Symposium is a biennial event sponsored jointly by the Department of History and the Association of Graduates, United States Air Force Academy. The purpose of this series is to provide a forum in which scholars may present the results of their research in military affairs. We hope in this way to encourage interest in a vital subject among civilian and military scholars, members of the armed forces, and the cadets of the United States Air Force Academy.

Any undertaking of the magnitude and scope of the Tenth Military History Symposium accumulates many debts. Primary thanks are owed to the superb group of scholars who gathered at the Academy to deliver papers, offer commentaries, and moderate the various sessions. Such value as this volume may possess is due entirely to their vigorous scholarship and willingness to share their erudition with the rest of us.

Even historians in uniform belong to a wider community of scholars whose members exchange ideas and information as they pursue a common objective of understanding the past. Many friends of the Department of History offered suggestions and critical insights which contributed significantly to the success of the Tenth Military History Symposium. In that regard, special thanks are owed to Dean C. Allard, Edward M. Coffman, Alfred Goldberg, Robin Higham, I. B. Holley, Jr., Michael Howard, Richard H. Kohn, Allan R. Millett, and Russell F. Weigley.

Thanks are due as well to a number of individuals and organizations here at the Academy. The generous support of the Association of Graduates once again played a vital role in making the symposium possible. Major General Robert E. Kelley, the Superintendent of the Academy, and Brigadier General William A. Orth, the Dean of the Faculty, were constant sources of encouragement. Indeed, those who planned the tenth symposium received unfailing support from virtually the entire Academy community. The wide-ranging administrative and logistical requirements of the symposium exacted substantial demands on the time and organizational skills of the members of the Department of History. As always, their performance surpassed what their duty required. Ms. Nellie Dykes of the Department of History presided over the typing of the manuscript and much more. Mr. Lawrence J. Paszek of the Office of Air Force History oversaw the preparation of the printed volume.

Any editorial blunders are mine alone.

J.T.
USAF Academy
January 1983

INTRODUCTION

James Titus

The decision to organize a symposium around the theme of the home front and war was rooted in two reciprocal ideas: first, that the impact of armed force is not confined to the battlefield; and second, that few governments can hope to wage protracted war successfully without strong domestic support. Although the truth of both propositions seems borne out by the past century or so of warfare, their pertinence often is overlooked by scholars and military professionals alike. Reason enough, it seemed, to subject the interconnections between the home front and war to scholarly scrutiny in the Tenth Military History Symposium.

This volume begins with the Twenty-Fifth Harmon Memorial Lecture which was delivered by Professor John Morton Blum of Yale University. As one of this country's most respected and best known historians and, more specifically, as the author of the much admired *V Was For Victory: Politics and American Culture During World War II*, Professor Blum was uniquely qualified to keynote a symposium on the home front. In a lecture entitled "United Against: American Culture and Society During World War II," Professor Blum took issue with the conventional wisdom that the Second World War was a great source of cohesion among the people of the United States. On the contrary, by exacerbating prewar social divisions, the strains triggered by mobilization intensified racial and class conflict and encouraged a generally squalid brand of politics. The nation stood firm against the foreign foe, but Blum's World War II America was internally discordant; its people were united against their foreign enemies, but they also were united against each other.

At this point the writer of an introduction to a volume of symposium proceedings normally would turn to the chore of discussing the remainder of its contents in some detail. Happily, that task has been handled with perspicuity and grace in Professor Edward M. Coffman's masterful summary analysis. What remains to be said here is that Professor Blum's theme of discordance was taken up by a number of the speakers who followed him. Others saw the domestic consequences of war in terms that were less bleak, but shared a presumption that, for good or ill, war left a significant mark on home front society. Still other participants pursued a different tack and questioned the importance of war as a stimulus for social change. Whatever their individual points of view, all of the participants probably would agree that the domestic stresses produced by total war can be immense.

Precisely because they were predicated on mass mobilization of human and material resources for total war, the military strategies pursued by the major powers throughout most of the twentieth century were also fraught with enormous social implications. The papers presented in the first three sections of this volume deal with some of the problems and consequences of mobilization for total war: the task of forging national unity and mobilizing public opinion; the mobilization of men, money, and materiel; and the various social effects of total war. Most of the papers focus on the home front experience of the United States, but each section includes papers on the experience of other nations as well. A comparative approach was adopted in order to help us see the American experience in a new light, test traditional assumptions, and bring a wider perspective to the subject.

The advent of nuclear weapons effectively undercut the strategy of mass mobilization as practiced in the two world wars. After 1945, the twin concerns of strategists turned on deterring general nuclear war and improving capabilities for fighting limited wars. There are obvious differences of scale between the total wars of the first half of the twentieth century and the limited wars of more recent years. Nevertheless, limited wars create significant tensions and difficulties of their own, especially when waged by democratic states. The interplay between limited war and domestic politics is the common theme of the papers which appear in the fourth section.

Taken individually, the papers and commentaries that follow consider rather specific, and in some cases even narrow, aspects of the complex nexus between home fronts and battle fronts in the twentieth century. When viewed collectively, however, the papers possess a certain thematic unity for each is addressing one or another aspect of the same basic question: the many-faceted relationship between war and society.

Writing almost thirty years ago, the journalist-scholar Walter Millis argued that the study of military history properly includes an exploration of all the factors—social, political, economic, and ideological—that have influenced the existence, organization, and employment of military forces. This volume represents an affirmation of Millis' view and seeks to contribute its own mite towards advancing our understanding of the intricate web of relationships between military systems and the human societies of which they are a part.

TWENTY-FIFTH HARMON MEMORIAL LECTURE IN MILITARY HISTORY

UNITED AGAINST: AMERICAN CULTURE AND SOCIETY DURING WORLD WAR II*

John Morton Blum

The United States fought the Second World War against ruthless and implacable enemies who had to be defeated and deserved to be defeated. Franklin D. Roosevelt felt just as did his countrymen when he condemned the Japanese attacks of December 7, 1941, as dastardly and infamous, and later, as victory approached, when he wrote, with reference to Germany, of retribution. During the war the American people united against those enemies in a measure greater than they united for any other wartime or postwar purpose. That unity was never complete. Periodic exhortations to refresh it drew, as one cabinet officer put it, on "nothing inspirational," nothing "Wilsonian." Rather, the American people responded to their visceral hatreds. Wartime intensification of emotions on the home front in their impact at home ordinarily whetted rather than dampened antecedent divisions within American culture and society. In their ethnic rivalries, class conflict and political partisanship, Americans continually united against each other. To be sure, Churchill was right for Americans, too; war did demand blood and sweat and tears. Obviously in battle but also at home, the tribulations of war again and again called forth courage, sacrifice and selflessness. But war did not alter the human condition, and among Americans, as among other peoples, the war at once aroused and revealed the dark, the naked, and shivering nature of man.

Commercial radio, in the observation of one analyst in 1942, ordinarily provided a twisted treatment of military news. "The war," he wrote, "was handled as if it were a Big Ten football game, and we were hysterical spectators." He should not have been surprised. All social units, nations included, ordinarily achieved cohesion largely by identifying a common enemy against whom all their members could unite. Sensitive to that phenomenon, Franklin D. Roosevelt, while an undergraduate at Harvard, had attempted to whip up school spirit for the Yale game. In the Ivy League as well as the Big Ten, the cohesion of each university community had long reached a peak during the annual contest with a traditional rival, a peak in which a sense of common identity in a common cause imbued not undergraduates only but also alumni and even faculty, dedicated though the last constituency theoretically was to an unemotional pursuit of truth.

---

*This paper was delivered as the Twenty-fifth Harmon Memorial Lecture.

Within the federal government, during the period before American entry into the war, the Office of Facts and Figures (OFF) had a large responsibility for achieving a similar national unity. In that time, Americans were divided about the war. A significant majority came to believe in helping to supply the victims of Axis aggression, but a considerable minority opposed that policy as needlessly inviting direct involvement in the war itself. The head of OFF, the talented poet and Librarian of Congress, Archibald MacLeish, attempted initially to let the facts tell the necessary story. That tactic failed. Several eminent authorities about public opinion advised, as one of them put it, that the agency would have to employ "a large element of fake," the proven technique of American advertising. MacLeish continued to hope that the splendid goals embodied in the Atlantic Charter, from which he drew inspiration, would also inspire the public. After Pearl Harbor, that hope, already fading, surrendered to the banalities and hoopla of commercial practice. The resulting propaganda struck some veterans of Madison Avenue as unpersuasive. One of them called openly for a propaganda of hate. MacLeish balked. He stood, he declared, in accordance with the Christian doctrine of hating sin but forgiving the sinner, not for hatred of the enemy but for hatred of evil. That laudable distinction made few converts, and soon MacLeish resigned.

MacLeish had overlooked a different distinction, one made by Walter Lippmann in his classic study of 1922, *Public Opinion,* a book hewn by its author's experience with propaganda during the First World War. An understanding of "the furies of war and politics," Lippmann wrote, depended upon the recognition that "almost the whole of each party believes absolutely in its picture of the opposition, that it takes as fact, not what is, but what it supposed to be fact." Indeed the adjustment of people to the environment in which they lived occurred "through the medium of fictions." The product of both acculturation and manipulation, those fictions served as facts, albeit counterfeit facts, and determined a large part of behavior.

No counterfeit was required to bring together for a time the factions which for two years had confronted each other about the question of whether the United States should go to war. The Japanese attack on Pearl Harbor ended that debate, as did the ensuing declarations of war on the United States by Germany and Italy. "The suddenness of the . . . attack," in the words of Isaiah Berlin, the British official in Washington charged with informing the Foreign Office about American conditions, " . . . came as a great shock to the nation. . . . The immediate effect has been to make the country completely united in its determination to fight Japan to the end. . . ." Formerly dissident elements, he added a week later, recognized that the country was "in the war for good or ill, and that all should unite their efforts to bring about the defeat of the totalitarian powers. It is also gradually felt that Hitler is the ultimate enemy. . . ." Those were sound analyses, but as the initial trauma of the Japanese attack subsided, Americans at home yielded to habitual sentiments. In the United States the same observer later recalled, "political and economic life to a considerable degree continued as before, and . . . some of the pressures and internecine feuds between individuals and . . . blocs, inherited from the New Deal and even earlier times, continued." In the spring of 1942 surveys indicated that some seventeen million Americans "in one way or another" opposed the prosecution of the war. That summer, after a series of American defeats in the Pacific, public morale sagged. It would turn around, Isaiah Berlin predicted, only with the broad engagement of American troops in the fighting.

That forecast contained a telling insight. As Gordon Allport, a master of the study of prejudice, later demonstrated, "the presence of a threatening common enemy" cemented the loyalties of aggregates of people. There was to be no attack on the United States, but when American troops in large numbers did meet the enemy, they united against their foe with less need for artificial stimulation than was the case with their countrymen at home.

Whether or not there were atheists in American foxholes, there were few men in combat in any of the services who did not know danger and fear and a resulting hatred. Bill Mauldin, writing in Italy during the long campaign there, spoke to the essential condition of every front: "I read someplace that the American boy is not capable of hate . . . but you can't have friends killed without hating the men who did it. . . . When our guys cringe under an SS barrage, you don't hear them say 'Those dirty Nazis.' You hear them say, 'Those goddam Krauts.'" So also in their expletives about the Japanese with the crews in P.T. boats in the Solomons, or the Marines on Iwo, or the airmen over New Guinea.

The common cause each combat unit joined owed much to the shared danger of a group of men fighting side by side. As Ernie Pyle noted about the air corps, "basically it can be said that everything depended on teamwork. Sticking with the team and playing it all together was the only guarantee of safety for everybody." In that respect the aviators were no different from the doggies. The GI fought at once against the enemy and for his buddies. Robert Sherrod phrased it well: "The Marines . . . didn't know what to believe in . . . except the Marine Corps. The Marines fought . . . on esprit de corps." The services deliberately inculcated a sense of unit—of platoon and company, of ship and task group, of pilot and crew and squadron. Training exercises in themselves required a quick responsiveness and spontaneous cooperation that fostered a needed togetherness. But danger provided the strongest cement.

In the backwater of the fighting, behind the lines, esprit was therefore harder to sustain. Like the marines, most soldiers and sailors had little awareness of the Four Freedoms. They were young Americans prepared to defend their country but eager to get it over with and go home. For the supply service in the Chinese-Burma-India theater or the garrison in Greenland, the enemy was far away. They found substitutes in their hatred of the natives, or the heat or cold or dirt, or the inescapable unfamiliarity of their stations. John Horne Burns described that phenomenon as it affected GIs in Naples, Italy; J. D. Salinger as it operated on Attu. In the tragi-comic novel, *Mr. Roberts*, the men of a ship assigned to dull errands in the South Pacific expressed their cohesion in their common detestation of their irascible captain. The officer hero of the novel, who understood the crew, deliberately defied the captain before obtaining the release he wanted, assignment to a combat ship, on which he later was killed. That fiction was rooted in fact, in the coming together of real crews or platoons far from danger in their dislike, sometimes persecution, of a tough drill sergeant or CO, or of an outsider in their ranks, a teetotaler or a socialist, a black or Hispanic or Jew.

American civilians behaved in much the same way. Few doubted that the war had to be won or that they should do their part in contributing to victory. But that commitment often flagged as individuals, impatient for the fruits of victory, shopped in the black markets for consumer goods the government was rationing. Others, tense because of the absence of a husband or brother, or because of long hours on the job or long lines awaiting cigarettes, spent that tension by blaming neighbors or politicians or even phantoms whom they had never liked. But civilian morale was much sustained in a vicarious battle, a hatred of the enemy informed, not without cause, by the malign characteristics attributed to the Germans and Japanese. American civilians characteristically described the Germans as warlike and cruel, though also misled and probably amenable to postwar cooperation. American racism, spurred perhaps by Japanese fanaticism in the field, produced a more negative picture of the Japanese, who were usually viewed as treacherous, sly and fierce, and probably a poor risk for postwar friendship.

Those attributions of generalized national characteristics, those counterfeit facts, emerged, as in all wars, both from prior prejudice and from current propaganda, public and private. So it was that American blacks harbored less animosity toward Asians than did American whites. Yet even whites during the war had a benign opinion of the Chinese, the nation's ally, though few Americans could easily differentiate on sight among different Asian peoples. Indeed at other times, earlier and later, as one authoritative study showed, the American image of the Chinese alternated between the villainous figure of Fu Man Chu and the amiable symbol of Charlie Chan. *Time* magazine endeavored to help its readers tell friend from foe. The Japanese, the journal asserted, with no basis in fact, were hairier than the Chinese; "the Chinese expression is likely to be more placid, kindly, open; the Japanese more positive, dogmatic, arrogant. . . . The Japanese are hesitant, nervous in conversation, laugh loudly at the wrong time. Japanese walk stiffly erect . . . Chinese more relaxed . . . sometimes shuffle." Comic strips drew a similar picture, and even the War Production Board called for the extermination of the Japanese as rats. As did the Germans with the Jews, so did Americans with the Japanese, and to a lesser extent the Germans, enhance their own sense of unity by hating an outside group to which, in each case, they applied stereotypes sustained, as Allport wrote, "by selective perception and selective forgetting."

Though officially the federal government did not consider the United States a party to a racial war or a war of hatred and revenge, official rhetoric sometimes conveyed those feelings. The responsible spokesmen were genuinely angry and more gravely concerned about spurring civilian participation in wartime programs. So it was that the Treasury Department, adopting a tactic which its analysts recommended after extensive study, endorsed advertisements for war savings bonds that depicted the Japanese as "ungodly, subhuman, beastly, sneaky, and treacherous," in one case as "murderous little ape men."

So, too, the War Department in its preparations for the trials at Nuremberg pursued retribution at a large cost to Anglo-American law. The attorneys who worked out the trial procedures proposed from the first to charge the Nazi government, party and agencies with "conspiracy to commit murder, terrorism, and the destruction of peaceful populations in violation of the laws of war." The conviction of individual Nazi leaders would implicate Nazi organizations that had furthered the conspiracy, and lesser German officials would then be convicted in turn if they had been associated with those agencies. That proposal, with its presumption of guilt by association, ran directly counter to the Anglo-American tradition of presuming innocence until guilt was proved. No such thing existed, moreover, as an "international crime of conspiracy to dominate by acts violative of the rules of war." Indeed conspiracy law had no place at all in European practice. Recourse to the conspiracy doctrine made the Germans targets of an *ex post facto* proceeding, even a bill of attainder of a kind. The British Lord Chancellor, unlike the American Secretary of War, preferred to hew to the "Napoleonic precedent" which called for political rather than judicial action to resolve what was essentially a political rather than a legal problem. But the Americans prevailed even though, as one critic later wrote, "the whole of the war-crimes policy planning was shot through with excess . . . combined with . . . overmoralizing." Those were precisely the qualities that marked wartime American reportage, fiction, propaganda and public opinion about the Germans.

Those qualities also characterized the language and behavior of various groups within American society which, throughout the war, united against each other with venom and occasional ferocity. Like troops behind the lines, they found familiar targets close at hand for antagonisms that predated the war but drew new force, often with official sanction or indifference, from wartime developments. In the name of wartime necessity, racial prejudice sparked the most blatant official violation (except for chattel slavery) of civil liberties in American history—the confinement of Japanese-Americans, American citizens as well as immigrants, in barren camps in the interior western states.

The Japanese-Americans, of whom the overwhelming majority were loyal to the United States, were innocent of any proven crime, but after the attack on Pearl Harbor, anti-Japanese sentiment, especially on the west coast, reached hysterical proportions. Within weeks the noxious counterfeits of the Native Sons and Daughters of the Golden West had become official doctrine. The congressional delegations from the Pacific slope and the Attorney General of California demanded the evacuation of the Japanese-Americans from the area, with internment the predictable sequential step. General John L. DeWitt, commanding general there, announced that a "Jap is a Jap. . . . It makes no difference whether he is an American citizen or not." Secretary of War Henry L. Stimson backed DeWitt. The "racial characteristics" of the Japanese, he held, bound them to an enemy nation and required their evacuation. The Attorney General of the United States, after some hesitation, supported Stimson, as also vigorously did President Roosevelt. Almost universally the American press endorsed the policy. The head of the War Relocation Authority, charged with administering the internment camps, attributed a few, rare protests to "liberals and kind-hearted people" who did not understand wartime necessity.

That argument proved barren after the war when returning Japanese-American veterans met open hostility in Washington state and California. The whole policy disregarded the experience of Hawaii where Japanese-Americans, too numerous to be incarcerated, remained, with insignificant exceptions, exemplary citizens throughout the war. Yet even the Supreme Court in the Hirabeyashi case upheld the constitutionality of the evacuation on the ground that "residents having ethnic affiliations with an invading enemy may be a greater source of danger than those of different ancestry," though neither German nor Italian-Americans were locked up. Two later wartime cases resulted in only inadequate modifications of the ruling, which was effectively overturned only many years later. The court's record, its disregard for the wholesale deprivation of liberty without due process of law, provoked just one contemporary rebuke from a distinguished member of the bar, the stinging retort of Eugene V. Rostow. The treatment of the Japanese-Americans, he wrote in 1945, "was in no way required or justified by the circumstances. . . . It was calculated to produce individual injustice and deep-seated maladjustments. . . . (It) violated every democratic social value, yet has been approved by the Congress, the President and the Supreme Court."

The attack on Pearl Harbor afforded a partial explanation for the persecution of the Japanese-Americans but not for its counterpart, the "truculent anti-Negro statements" that "stimulated racial feeling," as Isaiah Berlin observed, in the South and in northern cities. He also reported a less but growing anti-Semitism and mounting hostility, not least among servicemen, toward Hispanic-Americans. The movement of blacks into industrial areas to find employment in war industries, the shortage of housing, schooling and recreational facilities in those places, the resulting rivalry of whites and blacks for various kinds of space, those and other wartime conditions intensified historic prejudices and, just as Allport postulated, sparked episodes of violence. Major race riots occurred in Mobile, Alabama, in Los Angeles (where the victims were largely Chicanos), in Harlem and, most destructively, in Detroit. The motor city, as a Justice Department investigation disclosed in 1943, was a "swashbuckling community. . . . Negro equality . . . an issue which . . . very considerable segments of the white community" resisted. Among whites and blacks, truculence was growing. There had been open conflict in 1942 between Polish-Americans and blacks over access to a new federal housing project. There followed sporadic episodes of fighting, often involving alienated teenagers. In the deep heat of a June weekend in 1943 a clash between blacks and whites in a park escalated into a riot that for two days rocked the city where thirty-four people, mostly blacks, were killed. Federal troops, summoned by the Michigan governor, restored a superficial quiet, but blacks and whites remained united in their suspicions of each other.

Predictably the press in Mississippi blamed the riot on the insolence of Detroit's blacks and on Eleanor Roosevelt for proclaiming and practicing social equality. The NAACP pleaded for a statement from the President to arouse opinion against "deliberately plotted attacks." Roosevelt did condemn mob violence in any form, but he ducked the racial issue as he did generally during the war.

Those developments conformed to the pattern of that issue in that period. The South opposed any threat to segregation. The presumed threats arose from the continued efforts of American blacks, during a war directed in part against Nazi racism, to fight racism at home, too. The federal government moved reluctantly, when it moved at all, under political pressure from black leaders. Only the imminence of a protest march on Washington persuaded the President to establish the Fair Employment Practices Commission which thereafter made small and erratic progress toward its assigned goal. Blacks did obtain jobs in war industry but less because of federal action than because of a shortage of workers, and then usually in semi-skilled positions and as members of pro forma affiliates of segregated labor unions. Worse, no protest succeeded in stirring the armed forces to desegregate the services. Secretary of War Stimson supported segregation, as did Army Chief of Staff George C. Marshall, partly because they would not, in Stimson's words, use the army in wartime as a "sociological laboratory." But Stimson also believed that blacks lacked courage, mechanical aptitude, and the capacity for leadership. Consequently, though Roosevelt now and then scolded the army, black troops served primarily under white officers and in service or supply assignments. There were token exceptions, such as a black fighter squadron, as also within the navy, where almost all blacks performed menial duties. Those policies gave the lie to the government propaganda showing happy black workers at lathes in model factories or contented black soldiers poised for combat. The persisting inequality and humiliation of blacks impelled their leaders to unite their fellows, along with some sympathetic whites, against bigotry and official indifference. The war years saw the founding of CORE and the first modern freedom rides and sit-ins, some of them successful, all portentous, all fraught with interracial tension.

Like ethnic animosities, class conflict persisted during the war. In his reports about American morale, Berlin referred most often to industrial unrest. "Anti-labour feeling," he observed in November 1942, "has risen to a considerable height. Public indignation at . . . strikes in war industries . . . comparisons between industrial workers' wages and those of soldiers and farmers, all continually whipped up by predominantly Republican and anti-labour press." In June 1943 he noted a "rising tide of anti-labour feeling among armed services . . ." stationed within the country. Several months later, as he wrote, that feeling reached the top when General Marshall, during an off-the-record press conference, "struck the table and said with genuine anger that the behavior of the labour leaders . . . might easily prolong the war at a vast cost in . . . blood and treasure." That outburst was not typical of Marshall, though the opinion may have been, as it surely was among almost all business managers, most Republicans and conservative Democrats, and many senior officials in the federal bureaus and agencies responsible for the conduct of the war, particularly those involved in production, manpower, and wage and price control. Their biases led them to exaggerate the satisfactions of working men and women and to resist and overestimate the power of the unions.

The wartime growth of the economy did carry with it significant gains for industrial workers. Demand for labor pulled into the factories previously ostracized blacks, displaced rural workers, and unprecedented numbers of women. Real wages rose, full employment at last returned, and government fiscal policy under those conditions effected a considerable redistribution of income downwards. The War Labor Board's adoption of its "maintenance of membership" policy assured a substantial growth in the unions. But workers nevertheless continually expressed their legitimate discontent. Only a part of rising wages reached weekly pay envelopes which were reduced by deductions for union dues, an unaccustomed charge for the recently unemployed; for the federal income tax, for the first time collected on a pay-as-you-go basis; and for war bonds, which social pressure induced almost everyone to purchase. In crowded industrial cities even rising wages could buy only squalid housing. Rationing limited the availability of choice foods. "To the workers it's a Tantalus situation," a *Fortune* reporter observed: "the luscious fruits of prosperity above their heads—receding as they try to pick them." Other frustrations characterized the work place—the unfamiliar discipline of the assembly line, inequities in job classifications and, especially for women, in pay and in the extra burdens of domesticity. The resulting anxieties and alienation took the form of recurrent absenteeism, particularly among women, and of wildcat strikes, particularly in the automobile, steel and railroad industries. Yet those activities seemed like sabotage to business managers and harassed federal officials, few of whom had ever known the daily burdens of industrial life.

That imperception, a manifestation of both a cultural difference and a latent hostility between social classes, informed angry editorials, provoked military table-pounding, and fostered repeated demands within Congress, among middle-class voters, and ironically, among communists in the labor movement, to discipline or to punish or even to conscript striking workers. Often labor union leaders were the objects of that animosity, though the workers in the troubled industries were usually more restless than were their representatives. Indeed, almost all the leaders had made a no-strike pledge in return for the maintenance of membership policy, and they had thereafter continually to strive to restrain the workers while they negotiated with responsible federal officers for increased wages to match the rising cost of living. In that mediating role they confronted the growing power within government of captains of industry and finance who had been brought to Washington to staff the war agencies and the Navy and War Departments. Among those recruits labor had few friends.

In the circumstances, most labor leaders moved with caution, but not John L. Lewis, the head of the United Mine Workers (UMW), whose militancy made him the despised symbol of establishment hostility. Lewis had never believed in the no strike pledge, disliked the President, and did not trust the government to effect a significant melioration of the still wretched conditions of work in the mines. Yet Lewis was no radical. He remained committed to business unionism, to the traditional objectives of collective bargaining. At least one cabinet member, Harold Ickes, who had a special responsibility for fuel, understood as much. Lewis seemed radical because his wartime tactics, often clumsy and usually strident, appeared to his opponents and were made to appear to most Americans, to be unpatriotic and unreasonable.

During 1942 and 1943 Lewis orchestrated a series of strikes and wildcat strikes to advance his purpose, the unionization of all mines and the improvement of wages, benefits, and safety conditions. In considerable measure he succeeded. But his ventures, colliding with the intransigence of the mine owners, did threaten necessary coal supplies for industry and therefore inspired a temporary government take-over of the mines. They also made Lewis and the UMW the undesignated but identifiable targets of the Smith-Connally bill which Congress passed in 1943. Roosevelt vetoed the measure because he recognized its ineffectuality, but immediately Congress overrode the veto. Essentially useless as a device to impose industrial stability, the act increased the President's power to seize plants in war industries, made it a crime to encourage strikes in those plants, and outlawed union contributions to political campaigns, long an objective of Republicans and conservative Democrats. Its political influence challenged, organized labor could take no solace in Roosevelt's veto message which recommended drafting workers who took part in strikes in plants in the possession of the government. In 1944, prodded by the War Department, the President went further and urged a national service law which, he said, would prevent strikes. Though Congress did not approve that expedient, Roosevelt's recourse revealed how little influence labor had in Washington. Lewis had united his miners against the owners, but in the process, he galvanized opinion at home and among servicemen against himself. The actual and the emotional imperatives of war produced a retaliation potentially damaging to the entire labor movement.

In 1944 the leadership of the CIO, eager to retrieve their losses, had no one to turn to but the President who still stood for most of the causes they embraced. The Republicans, in contrast, had a long record of hostility to unions and to progressive measures. Denied the ability to contribute union funds to the Democrats, Sidney Hillman and his associates formed the Political Action Committee to raise money from workers and their liberal friends, and to get out the vote. Even so, the influence they exerted was too small to effect the renomination of their most outspoken champion in Washington, Vice President Henry A. Wallace. Indeed, the class and ethnic enmities of the war years underlay the rejection by the Democrats of Wallace, and by the Republicans of Wendell Willkie, his counterpart within the GOP. Both men had attacked business management for its narrowness of vision; both had endorsed the aspirations of American blacks.

Divisive issues affected politics throughout the war years. A coalition of Republicans and southern Democrats rolled back the New Deal, opposed progressive taxation, forced Roosevelt to move to the right. Those developments had begun before the war and might well have occurred without it. But politics was never adjourned; political rhetoric was, as ever, intemperate; and both parties stooped to a contentious meanness during the campaign of 1944. Governor Thomas E. Dewey of New York, the Republican nominee, exercised a patriotic generosity in excluding from his campaign any reference to MAGIC, the American compromise of Japanese codes which, had he chosen to mention it, would have assisted the enemy and raised with refreshed force the question of the Administration's culpability for the surprise at Pearl Harbor. Dewey also kept foreign policy out of the campaign in order to avoid premature controversy about the structure of the peace. Nevertheless, the Democrats gave him no quarter; identified him in spite of his record as governor, with the reactionaries in his party; mocked him for his small physique and little moustache. Early and late, the Republicans, including Dewey, identified the Democrats, often openly, with communism, and employed anti-Semitic innuendos to attack Hillman and through him, Roosevelt. Meanness often emerged in national campaigns. In 1944 the form it took again reflected class and ethnic issues.

The war did not create those issues but neither did it subdue them. In one sense, the remoteness of the battle fronts permitted the expressions of divisiveness that might otherwise have militated against victory. In a larger sense, Americans behaved much as they always had and in a manner not markedly different from other peoples, even those exposed to immediate danger and defeat. Social and political factionalism crippled Italy and France where outright treason, as in Norway and the Netherlands, contributed to German victories. Even in Germany, apart from the victims of genocide, hundreds of decent men and women spent the war in concentration camps, dozens in clandestine subversion, and a group of disenchanted officers, good soldiers all, attempted to assassinate Hitler. In Great Britain the government interned German Jews, civilians grumbled far more than official propaganda admitted, and the Labour Party prepared to win the political triumph it enjoyed before the end of hostilities against Japan. The Soviet state imprisoned or killed many ethnic Germans and dissident Ukrainians, systematically murdered Polish soldiers who were allies but not communists, and stood aside while the Germans demolished the resistance in Warsaw. Thousands of Chinese collaborated with the Japanese, more thousands engaged in civil war, and factionalism vitiated the Kuomintang.

In every warring nation, whatever the degree of its unity against the enemy, men and women also united against their fellows, often with the ferocity of prejudice and hatred. In their dealings with each other, Americans at home exhibited a moderation at least equivalent to that of any other peoples. No inherent superiority of the national soul accounted for the difference. Rather, the intensity of internal strife within the belligerent nations correlated strongly with the proximity of attack, invasion and occupation. Defeat, or the close prospect of defeat, excited a search for scapegoats or a scramble for survival of an intensity Americans were spared. In the years after the war, when Americans first came to recognize their national vulnerability to devastating attack, they united against each other much in the patterns of the war years but more savagely and with more lasting damage. Then, as during the war and at other times, the city on the hill, to the sorrow of some of its residents, did not rise much above the plain.

SESSION I

THE QUEST FOR NATIONAL UNITY IN THE GREAT WAR

THE QUEST FOR NATIONAL UNITY IN THE GREAT WAR

INTRODUCTORY REMARKS

David F. Trask

The topic we are dealing with here generally, that is to say the home front in the twentieth century, falls within a larger chronology established earlier for us by Professor Ted Ropp in his stimulating essay entitled "War as a National Experience." The broader chronological focus for our study has to be at least the 200 years stretching from about 1789 to 1982. Let me now make three rather broad and rather unsurprising generalizations about that span of history.

The first generalization or observation I would make is that we, of course, are dealing across that span of 200 years with a constantly escalating pattern of violence, one of greater and greater capability for destruction on the battlefield as a consequence of technology, indeed an unsurprising generalization.

The second generalization I would make is that civilian populations showed unexpected and indeed remarkable durability or staunchness, even in the face of constantly expanding violence in periods of warfare. Now why was this? I would suggest that, as does Professor Ropp, that the explanation for these two phenomena reside in the same general study, namely, in the study of the impact of three great revolutions: the industrial revolution, the national revolution, and the democratic revolution.

The nineteenth century developed the technological capability that undergirded the capacity to make war on hitherto unprecedented scales. In addition, political development across the nineteenth century strengthened the legitimacy of the nation state, giving the nation state standing with people that it had lacked before. On the other side of the coin, the modern nation state developed a tremendous power to coerce. For reasons both of attraction and coercion there was a potential for support of warfare, even of the most destructive sort, as the result of the larger forces operative in modern history. And yet, there is a third generalization, one that seems in the perspective of the 1980s a more logical one than we might have thought earlier. If at the outset of the 200 years with which we deal, there was a strong tendency to glorify war as a human enterprise, or at least to condone it as an extreme reaction, a practical and ethical reaction under certain circumstances, we note a constant and irreversible trend since then in the opposite

19

direction, one pointed out most notably, I suppose, by Bernard Brodie, a shift away from the glorification or condonation of warfare to a revulsion, an intellectual, ethical revulsion, that clearly runs parallel with that rising arc of violence.

What I am trying to suggest is that while populations have responded in a remarkable way in support of modern warfare, there has been a parallel development that undermines such support. That's where we are, I would suggest, today. Increasingly, the intellectual and ethical revulsion of mankind to violence challenges the elan of the modern nation in arms.

This observation brings me to today's concern, namely the First World War. That struggle stands as an especially portentous manifestation of the three generalizations that I have just covered. It exemplifies the extraordinary destruction that modern technology can bring about. It exemplifies amazing civil endurance in the face of unprecedented privation. It exemplifies burgeoning antiwar sentiment especially in its latter stages and in its aftermath.

Let me dwell briefly on the latter subject, the role of the Great War in the history of burgeoning antiwar feeling. One of the most intriguing aspects of that struggle is that the most innovative theorists from both the political sector and the military sector began with comparable estimates of modern warfare. Both groups, especially in the aftermath, reacted strongly against the destructiveness of modern warfare. Both groups decided that its destructiveness was unacceptable. The war had been so devastating that it brought into question, as a central concern almost really for the first time, the question of whether triumph in modern warfare might be so crushing as to be as dangerous to the health of the victors as to the health of the vanquished, perhaps even more so. Many would argue that the First World War wrought more destruction among the victors than among the vanquished. This general insight of 1918 and after, that modern warfare might become so lethal as to outmode it as a means of settling great international questions, is what separates the experience of the First World War from prior conflicts that had occurred after 1789. And yet the seeds of that insight are traceable across the entire nineteenth century. Now, let us look a bit further at the reactions of political and military thinkers in the wake of the great war, the lessons of that war as perceived at the time.

The most innovative political thinkers of the time, the Wilsonians, drew from their contemplation of the destructive conflicts just passed, the presumption that warfare had become obsolete. For this reason, they concentrated on the creation of a just and lasting peace, that is, a reformed world order capable of resolving international conflicts and sponsoring international progress by means short of war. Here was indeed the apotheosis of the nineteenth century faith. National military forces would be reduced to a level required to insure domestic tranquillity. A permanent and universal peacekeeping institution, based on the premise of collective security, would exercise an international police power to control those who dared violate the terms of selective security covenants.

What about the other group, the military thinkers? The most innovative military thinkers of the age departed from exactly the same point, a stark vision of the unacceptable destruction that had just passed, but they reached a different conclusion. The conclusion they reached was that the war just past, although violent, would not have undermined the very foundations of civilization, if it had been possible to get it over with in reasonable time. The key then was the means of restoring decisiveness to modern warfare, bringing necessarily violent encounters to an end before they became unduly expensive of one's own blood and treasure as well as the enemy's resources. Theorists of air power and armored warfare, for example, acted on the assumption that civil populations could withstand the shock of modern warfare only for a limited period of time. How ironic then, that military theory during the interwar years rested in great part on an urgent desire to get wars over with promptly, the means of avoiding an untenable blow to civilization in general, a shock like the one of 1914-1918.

Americans, including American historians, have been slow to grasp much of what I have said even if, in a somewhat different form, this analysis is common coin in Europe and elsewhere. We came late to the fray of 1914-1918 and we emerged largely unscathed by comparison to the apocalypse that overwhelmed Europe. What Europeans deemed a catastrophe was to most Americans a disturbing but transient experience. The national relaxation during the 1920s reflected not only a certain weariness from both the domestic and foreign exertions of the past generations, but a perception of success, of a job well done, something no intelligent European could muster.

American historians managed largely to bypass the war itself; rather, they concentrated on the before and the after. Why had the United States entered the war in 1917? What had caused the failure of the peace settlement? Many scholars do not realize that they cannot hope to find answers to either of these questions unless they hearken to the information now available to them concerning the waging of the war, the clash of arms itself. Even my friend, Russ Weigley now understands that interesting point, if I read the preface to his latest book correctly. What I am trying to suggest is that the failure to recognize the central importance of the First World War in the subsequent history of this century, by far the most violent and barbaric century in the history of humankind, flaws many American perceptions of events at home and abroad since 1918. For those who adopt a European, or better, a global perspective, the Second World War, which loomed so large in American consciousness, however destructive, appears as a logical, expectable extension of the earlier struggle, a second phase in a long, modern, fierce war.

What then, to move on, is the significance of the Second World War in terms of the comments I made earlier concerning that triad of trends across modernity—destructive warfare, civilian sturdiness, antiwar sentiment? The struggle of 1939-1945 resolved certain doubts that survived the hecatomb of 1914-1918. In the aftermath of the Second World War, consensus emerged among both political thinkers and military thinkers concerning the future of general warfare. Note, I say general warfare on a global, total scale, presumably a nuclear war. The advent of nuclear warfare, not only the latest development in destructiveness but also a truly climactic one, led to a broadly shared conclusion. Peaceful methods must be found to preclude further passages at arms on a scale comparable to that of the thirty years' war just past. After 1945, creative political thinkers returned to the search for viable means of resolving fundamental international controversies by means short of war. After 1945, creative military thinkers concentrated on the search for a credible deterrent to nuclear war, a means deemed the only practical and ethical course for military establishments given their vision of a nuclear battlefield. This outcome did not mean that military establishments would never fight. There remained a rational if constrained area for warfare, namely, the controlled conflict for limited stakes as against the general conflict aimed at total victory. The new problem was not simply how to wage and win such contests but how to prevent them from escalating into unacceptable general nuclear warfare. Even limited modes of warfare might encounter increasing resistance on the part of home fronts, given the destructive nature of even the most carefully controlled non-nuclear war.

We therefore arrive at one, at least, of the critical items on the existing agenda of those who study war and most particularly the home front. The prior presumption that there would be strong national support for international wars has come increasingly into question across the 200 years or so since the beginning of the Napoleonic Wars. Most of this reaction, however, has taken place at a rapidly accelerating pace from the time of the First World War. This circumstance has played no mean role in drawing the attention of a small band of American historians to the First World War, especially to the waging of the war as against its origins and consequences. If we hope to comprehend the evolution of attitudes on the home front, as these attitudes stand today, and as they may evolve in the future, we have no recourse but to return, at least, to the First World War, if we wish to understand where we have been, so that we might exercise some modicum of control over where we shall go.

Chairman Trask's Introduction of Professor Showalter
Let us now turn to the first of the papers to be delivered this morning. I feel bound to say immediately that this paper does not appear to fit very well into the theme of this conference or into the subject of this session. This paper is a contribution to the enduring question of what caused the First World War rather than directly to the study of the home front during 1914-1918. This is hardly unsurprising either. How many conferences can boast of another outcome? I might worry more than I do about these circumstances were this paper not a very stimulating and useful effort. The author explains at the outset the reasons why he shifted from the study of belligerency to the study of prewar developments. Perhaps later during the discussion he could be prevailed upon to draw connections between his study of causation and developments on the home front as the war ran its course. Professor Dennis E. Showalter received his doctorate in history at the University of Minnesota in 1969. He then joined the faculty of The Colorado

College, located in Colorado Springs, where he still serves as associate professor of history. He has been the recipient of important scholarly honors, among them a Fulbright fellowship and a Humbolt fellowship. He takes an active part in the organizational life of the profession, presently serving as a trustee of the American Military Institute. The author of numerous scholarly articles and essays, he has among his major publications a book entitled *Railroads and Rifles: Soldiers, Technology and the Unification of Germany,* published in 1975. Professor Showalter's presentation is entitled "For King and Kaiser: British and German Mobilization In World War One."

FOR KING AND KAISER: BRITISH AND GERMAN MOBILIZATION IN WORLD WAR I

Dennis E. Showalter

Three-quarters of a century after the fact, World War I continues to engage intellects and emotions alike. A continent which bestrode the earth turned on itself with a berserker's fury. With the opening rounds of the guns of August, things were indeed changed—changed utterly. But few would agree that a terrible beauty was thereby born. The young were torn to pieces; the old died of typhus. Women made shells as malnutrition crippled their babies. Tolstoy's Pierre Bezukhov, set down anywhere in Europe between 1914 and 1918, might well have cried out "Surely they will stop it. Surely now they will see what they have done and make peace." Yet the carnage continued. Societies described as on the verge of collapse by pre-war critics withstood suffering and deprivation on a scale that paralyzed imaginations.

Endurance under stress is not in itself a remarkable phenomenon. From Thebes and Carthage to Hitler's Germany and Ho's Vietnam, people and their governments have demonstrated incredible powers of resistance when motivated by ideology or faced with a worse alternative. But Europe rushed into Armageddon in 1914 for reasons that hindsight presents as obscenely frivolous relative to the results. It is in particular the gap between cause and effect that inspires the study of World War I's home fronts. We ask ourselves not merely *how* they endured, but *why*.

In this context the transition from war to peace is particularly important. Events once initiated—even wars—tend to develop their own momentum, especially when sustained by a modern administrative apparatus. Initially I proposed to examine the details of this transition, the process of mobilization in Britain and Germany. The two countries seemed ideal for a comparative case study. Both clearly belonged to the European mainstream. Generalizations about social structures and climates of opinion need not be modified out of existence to be applied, as is often the case with Russia or Austria-Hungary. On the other hand, few obvious points of comparison between the Germany of William II and the England of George V suggest themselves. Any underlying religious, ethnic, or cultural ties had been significantly weakened by economic and ideological competition. By 1914, it is the contrasts that come to mind: authoritarianism versus parliamentarism, land power versus sea power, have-not versus status quo.[1]

A reasonable subject and a useful working model: thus far, so good. Then the paper assumed a life of its own. Students of 1914 speak almost universally of a will to war, a climate of belligerence at all levels of European society. I expected to make the same point in two or three paragraphs. But in doing the preliminary research for those paragraphs, I was impressed by the deep ambivalence towards the issue of war in Britain and Germany alike. The same men who spoke of its inevitability spoke at other times and places of its impossibility. Until the actual declarations were exchanged, no one seemed to believe that the worst would happen. Sir Edward Grey's visions of lamps going out all over Europe were matched by Bethmann-Hollweg's gloomy references to Germany's leap in the dark. Similar inconsistencies appeared wherever I looked. Generals and admirals, journalists and politicians, said "yes" and "no" with equal intensity. Even Alfred von Tirpitz, that epitome of the fire-eating navalist, did his best at the crisis point to persuade William II that he was fighting the wrong war at the wrong time against the wrong combination of enemies.[2]

The pattern seemed too general, too deeply rooted, to dismiss in an introduction. What became increasingly significant about the home fronts of Germany and Britain was not their mutual rush to arms in August, nor even their respective adjustments to the demands of a long war. It was rather the ambivalence, the dissonance, which dominated and conditioned attitudes and behavior. The Western mind seeks coherence. More than any intellectual subgroup except perhaps clergymen, academicians are conditioned to explain away contradictions. The historian in particular sees his task as structuring information, establishing the connections and relationships that make history more than one damn thing after another. Thus the events of 1914 are packaged, footnoted, and presented in terms of a Long Fuse, a Third Balkan War, or even a Galloping Gertie effect—but always as a process with at least an underlying order, if not always one clear to the participants.

Today the historian who begins his work without establishing a model runs the risk of dismissal as a professional anachronism. In the process we tend towards the uncritical use of more theoretical disciplines, borrowing and applying their concepts almost at random. Yet despite the caveats implied in the above statements, psychological theory offers a useful alternate framework for interpreting the outbreak of World War I. Cognitive dissonance involves a perceived gap between beliefs and behavior, between what one thinks and what one does. Dissonance generates discomfort. Individuals in turn seek to reduce that discomfort. They may alter one of the poles, modifying either their thoughts or their deeds. They are far likelier to develop patterns of rationalization, avoidance, and denial which reduce ongoing discomfort without eliminating the dissonance which is its underlying cause. A person, for example, concerned with the amount he drinks might reduce his intake. He might also decide that he is somehow better off at his present rate of consumption. Or he might argue that a few drinks before dinner never hurt anyone, that beer is not the same thing as hard liquor, and that he is driven to drink by job stress.[3]

This essay contends that the governments and societies of Britain and Germany faced the challenge of 1914 in a state of what amounted to cognitive dissonance. Positive images of war were balanced by fears of its consequences to an extent that planning and decision-making were inhibited. Instead of either preparing for war or seeking peace in a consequent manner, both countries drifted from crisis to crisis, and ultimately into disaster.

The argument is made in three sections. The first is a general survey of the rise and the simultaneous inhibiting of the martial spirit in Britain and Germany. The second focuses on Germany to describe the influence of this dissonance on the general development of foreign policy. The third section moves to the lesser world, using the evolution of Great Britain's German policy as a case study in inability to draw conclusions and act on them.

Conference papers fall into two general categories. The first, laden with archival references and focusing on a limited topic, is an exercise in scholarly virtuosity. It is intended to be understood by a relatively small proportion of the audience, and correspondingly designed to impress everyone else. The second kind of paper deals in hypotheses and generalizations. It encourages its auditors to pick it apart, to find the loopholes, the faulty reasoning, the weak connections—and hopefully to reconsider their own assumptions about a broad scholarly issue. This conference in particular, with its mixture and overlap of uniforms and business suits, classrooms and flight lines, is an ideal forum for presenting an alternate interpretation of the intellectual and emotional structures underlying the home fronts of Britain and Germany in 1914.

As the nineteenth century progressed, Germany and Britain alike seemed dominated by the martial spirit. In both countries preindustrial attitudes remained influential. The European bourgeoisie was never as triumphant as its supporters believed; the European aristocracies proved far more resilient than their critics expected. Arno Mayer eloquently describes the persistence of a traditional elite, a nobility of land and service, continuing to dominate politics and administration by its skill in co-opting the middle class. This establishment in the years before 1914 was actually working to enhance its political control, and ultimately was willing to risk and wage a war rather than sacrifice jot or tittle of its power. The traditional value systems of the European upper class, with their theoretical emphasis on the heroic and the warlike, had been revitalized by the challenges of the French and Industrial Revolutions. In the process they had become more open—at least in image. As in societies whose very flexibility generated and exacerbated status anxieties, a certain degree of militarization came to be seen not as selling out, but as buying in. The industrialist and the academic sealed their membership in the new synthesis by putting sons in uniform. It was, hopefully at least, less expensive than buying a country estate. It took less time than acquiring a title. And—a point not to be overlooked—it was a far more acceptable subject for boasting, a symbol of social integration, of patriotism, and of conspicuous consumption that could be openly discussed without risking condemnation for vulgarity.[4]

British schoolboys absorbed the vocabulary of militarism while their respectable elders donned volunteer uniforms. German businessmen dressed their children in sailor suits; German professors flaunted reserve commissions. The army was the Second Empire's most visible and most popular institutional symbol, while the Imperial navy seemed to incorporate the essence of a dynamic world power. Britain looked to the Royal Navy for visual as well as diplomatic confirmation of the island empire's strength. And if Queen Victoria's common soldiers remained outcasts in practice, Tommy Atkins in the abstract was cheered in the music halls, copied by toymakers, and fictionalized in many a bestseller.[5]

The martial spirit of the nineteenth century was also fostered by anxiety. In Britain, invasion by a continental power taking advantage of railroads, steamships, and an easily mobilized conscript army was a recurrent bogy. Publicized in popular fiction from Sir George Chesney's *The Battle of Dorking* to William Le Quex's *The Invasion of 1910*, it was given a serious dimension by politicians seeking office through rattling sabers and by generals challenging the navy's share of the defense budget.[6] Germany for its part had found no peace since its emergence as a great power. Bismarck's perception of the implacable hostility of a France deprived of Alsace and Lorraine was reinforced by growing anxiety over the Slavic threat spearheaded by and embodied in Tsarist Russia. The Austrian connection, the oldest and firmest diplomatic alliance in Europe, came increasingly to be perceived as much a liability as an asset. Measures taken to increase Germany's security produced their counter-effects; the construction of a battle fleet generated a Copenhagen complex, the rough equivalent of English fears of a bolt from the blue.[7]

Tension encouraged serious, long-term considerations of the nature of war on intellectual and technical levels. On both sides of the channel, however, the process involved accepting violence as an instrument of international relations. War was the continuation of politics by other means to many German and English decision-makers to whom Clausewitz was little more than a name.[8] Imperialism, with its images of cheap victories over lesser breeds without the law, contributed to positive evaluation of the role of force as an arbiter of diplomacy. Experience closer to home further reinforced the connection. The conflicts of the mid-nineteenth century in Italy and the Crimea, Bohemia and France, were almost universally regarded as cost-effective. Their results, for the victors, at least, were considered acceptable relative to the human and material outlays. American experience from 1861 to 1865 could be discounted as an aspect of a society as yet too undeveloped to conduct its wars in an efficient, modern fashion.[9]

Intellectual developments also affected thoughts on war and peace. Darwinism should not be too directly equated with militarism. Nevertheless, the radicalization and vulgarization of Darwin's ideas did provide an academically respectable underpinning for the theory that war was man's natural state, and seeking its abolition was fruitless. Treitschke's argument that force expressed a nation's will to life found echoes on the other side of the channel in such works as J. A. Cramb's

Germany and England, which described these "sons of Odin" as eventually fated to clash for world mastery. Economists contributed to the process; Werner Sombart was not the first to assert structural links between war and capitalism, or war and modernization. And one deduction from those links was that war could be beneficial to society, a major force for economic and moral growth. The "natural" struggle for existence ultimately meant progress and happiness for all those engaged in it, even the vanquished—who would benefit by their exposure to the higher civilization of their "superior" enemies.[10]

Rhetoric contributed its share to a climate of belligerence. The language of diplomacy became increasingly hostile as the nineteenth century gave way to the twentieth. In part this reflected the growth of a self-conscious, influential public opinion. Ever since Napoleon III, statesmen perceived a need to play to galleries of elected representatives, journalists, and intellectuals, seen as demanding public shows of assertiveness.[11] This tendency, while owing much to conservative distrust of the masses and their spokesmen, did not entirely reflect vivid imaginations. Nationalism was a major force of integration at a time of drastic and rapid change. In the process it provided a rooting interest whose vocabulary and attitudes, particularly in Britain, were directly borrowed from the world of sport.[12] Britain and Germany had the highest proportions of literate, conscientious citizens of any European countries. On both sides of the channel, grass-roots pressure groups, often in tacit or overt alliance with sections of the popular press, could create impressions of strength often at sharp variance with reality, but difficult to test at a time when opinion analysis was a discipline in its infancy.[13]

The debasing of diplomatic intercourse also owed much to changes within the craft itself. The emergence of constitutional states, whether *de jure* or *de facto,* limited the personal element that historically had tended to modify tones, if not always substances. Individuals might be cordial; the governments they served were institutional. The diffusion of power endemic in the modern state meant corresponding diffusion of responsibility. Statesmen tended increasingly to see themselves as the captives of policies they implemented rather than made. Here again, perceptions were more important than *post facto* analyses of realities. It is much easier for historians to determine where the buck stopped than it seemed to the men actually involved in the process.[14]

A personal element was added by the legacy of Otto von Bismarck, who combined his skills with a willingness to use a much broader spectrum of instruments and techniques than were familiar or congenial to his rivals and contemporaries. Bismarck was the first master of crisis management, designing and controlling diplomatic controversies, encouraging public anxieties or mollifying them, partly to test his own virtuosity, partly to demonstrate his indispensability to the system he both served and mastered.[15] There may have been only one Bismarck. There were many imitators--not the least being William II, whose mugger's approach to foreign policy owed much to Bismarck's model.

The martial spirit was focused by the growth of military professionalism. After 1871 planning replaced improvisation throughout military Europe—even Britain. One result was the systematic consideration of neighbors as enemies. This in turn generated institutional momentum difficult to refocus or adjust. The development of short-service conscript armies on the continent played a specific role in the process. However fierce might be the patriotic rhetoric about the abstract concept of one's homeland, rank and file enthusiasm was best sustained by describing tangible enemies. As early as 1869, the Prussian army suffered some embarrassment when a party of French officers visiting an artillery range discovered that the targets had been unofficially repainted with red trousers, blue coats, and pointed beards.[16]

Such attitudes were by no means confined to enlisted draftees. Eighteenth century concepts of the freemasonry of arms faded before the growth of nationalism. Sir John Fisher was by no means the only British admiral who dreamed of destroying Germany's navy by surprise. Sir Henry Wilson placed a map of the BEF's projected concentration area as an offering at the base of a French memorial to the Franco-Prussian war.[17] Such mind-sets were not likely to change at the behest of diplomatic developments. No more were German generals likely to challenge the presumptions of the Schlieffen Plan, or German admirals to modify operational doctrines and construction programs focused on a North Sea Armageddon. Instead, military planning generated its own momentum. The uniformed experts, in turn, exercised an increasing influence over civilian statesmen whose understanding of the data and hypotheses so blithely presented at planning conferences was at best limited. Ignorance, or unwillingness to admit it, often played a far greater role than conscious warmongering.[18]

The image thus far presented is of a Europe ready to tear itself apart at the slightest provocation. Yet considered more closely, significant contradictions emerge. Scholars conditioned by the twentieth century are prone to take an earlier era's homicidal rhodomontade at something very near its face value—to establish a cause-effect relationship. This tendency is enhanced by another result of two world wars and a host of minor ones: the development of a rhetoric of benevolence. Since 1918, few statesmen have felt comfortable loosing the dogs of war without the accompaniment of whipped-cream phrases justifying their action in terms of pure and altruistic humanitarianism. This pattern has become so familiar, and its contradictions so obvious, that it has generated a universal cynicism, a tendency to seek the self-interest, the hypocrisy, underlying the fustian. It is one of the great ironies of the twentieth century that the motives of states and statesmen for going to war have become not merely automatically suspect, but automatically subject to worst-case interpretations. To do otherwise is to risk branding as a naif.[19]

Prior to 1914, however, it seems reasonable to assert the existence of a reverse pattern. The militarization of societies and diplomacy involved more sound and posturing than substance. The belligerence of pre-1914 Europe was a set of gestures, a playing both to public opinion and personal self-images. At bottom, it was a belligerence of the drawing-room. The aristocracy which set so much of its tone had long since ceased to be anything resembling a true warrior caste in its attitudes and behavior. The typical German Junker, a symbol of rampant militarism in so many scholarly works, might pass through a cadet school in lieu of a more expensive educational institution. He might spend his early twenties as a subaltern in a socially suitable regiment. But rather than risk negotiating the choppy waters at the major's corner, he was far more likely to resign his commission and assume management of lands inherited, or purchased with a dowry lured by the uniform. And for those aristocrats who sought a career in state service, the civil service proved increasingly attractive as the nineteenth century progressed. Uniforms might be desirable or even necessary on certain social occasions. Fewer and fewer noblemen wanted to wear one for a living.[20]

The warlike posturings of the bourgeoisie tended to fade even more quickly when translated into money or lives. It is significant that the music hall ditty which gave jingoism its name was sung and shouted during a war scare that ultimately failed to materialize. From Afghanistan to South Africa, Britain's imperialists demanded victory on the cheap. The longer and costlier became a given campaign, the sharper grew the questions in press and parliament, the more could principled anti-imperialists count on support from the pragmatists.[21] Germany's colonial ventures were even less popular once the bills began to come in. A large part of conservative support for the government's policies in Southwest Africa in 1906-07 reflected a desire to thwart domestic political foes—Catholics, socialists, and progressives—rather than positive affirmation of a forward policy in the Kalahari Desert.[22]

Reluctance to translate rhetoric into action was pronounced when relations between the European powers were seriously and directly threatened. During such crises newspaper headlines and parliamentary speeches in Britain and Germany resemble a fever chart. Initial stirrings of anxiety zigzag to a peak of martial enthusiasm—then comes a sudden drop in belligerence when the war hysteria seems on the point of explosion. Peace feelers are featured on front pages. Second thoughts arise from back benches. Nationalism gives way to panic. Theoreical arguments that the state must sustain its interests in arms if necessary begin emphasizing "necessary" instead of "arms." The fatalism so often described as characteristic of European society before 1914 was also a form of camouflage—an acceptable means of papering over the wide gaps between rhetoric and anxiety. In practice, moreover, this fatalism was accompanied by a commitment to a kind of brinkmanship. If one's own state stood up and asserted itself, so the argument ran, opponents would back down rather than risk actually going to war, and the cause of peace would ultimately be served.[23]

The popular enthusiasm so often described as a factor in the outbreak of World War I was in fact a *post facto* phenomenon, surprising not a few who anticipated, like Sir Robert Walpole, that the ringing of bells would soon be succeeded by the wringing of hands.[24] But while public opinion may be important in preparing wars, and is arguably decisive in sustaining them, the actual process of initiation requires governments. Gunpowder proved, however, an even more complete antidote to chauvinism among the policy-makers than among the gun fodder. And nowhere was this pattern more obvious than in Germany.

This assertion seems almost perverse in the context of massive evidence that the Second Empire's international policy represented at worst a deliberate thrust for world power, at best a random antagonizing of her neighbors. Inconsistencies in this approach are usually explained either in terms of tactical conflicts within a policy-making elite, or more generally as manifestations of an intrinsic structural anomaly between aggressive posturing on a world stage and an even deeper commitment to European stability.[25] What the argument lacks, however, is the smoking gun of planning. The most diligent efforts of Fritz Fischer, Adolf Gasser, Immanuel Geiss, and a score of other scholars have failed to turn up significant planning and preparation for a *Hegemonialkrieg*. What they present instead is a pattern of advance and retreat, bluster and back-down, whose principal internal consistency is a profound and deliberate refusal to begin the war for which everyone has just been clamoring.[26]

The Moroccan Crisis of 1905 has been frequently described as illustrating the worst features of a mindlessly bellicose German diplomacy, with Chief of Staff Alfred von Schlieffen championing preventive war, Friedrich von Holstein of the Foreign Office seeking to incite it by diplomatic maneuverings, and the plot failing only because of Chancellor Bernhard von Bulow's inability to understand its nature.[27] The most recent reconstructions of German reactions to the crisis, however, show that when it came to the crunch, neither the government nor any other identifiable interest group was particularly anxious to translate words into deeds. Diplomats suddenly decided the time was not right. Generals suddenly discovered that they needed more men and equipment. Journalists discovered their readers' response to the rhetoric of violence did not extend to a willingness to get themselves shot. The few fire-eaters willing to draw consequences from conclusions found themselves suddenly leading one-man parades to nowhere.[28]

Seven years later, on December 8, 1912, William II summoned his military advisors to a Crown Council. This meeting has achieved semi-mythical status as the occasion when Germany finally decided to go to war, only delaying the outbreak for tactical reasons.[29] But while it is clear that the option of a preventive war was seriously discussed, and vehemently advocated by Chief of Staff Helmuth von Moltke, the concrete results of the council were minimal. An army bill, which had been in preparation well before December in response to French and Russian developments, was accelerated. But Chancellor Theobald von Bethmann-Hollweg, who had not even been at the meeting—and how seriously can a council of war be taken if it excludes the head of the civil government and the Foreign Secretary, even Hitler invited Neurath to the Hossbach Conference—quickly choked off such effusions as a navy bill and a propaganda offensive.[30]

Nor can the 1912 Crown Council be shown to have significant secondary results. Consultation between the government on one hand, and the captains of industry and agriculture on the other, remained minimal. Cooperation among public and private agencies involved little more than vague debates about the best ways of storing forage, or how Germany might best be fed in case of a British naval blockade. Administrative routine dominated the discussions. Memoranda were passed from bureaucrat to bureaucrat and office to office with no particular urgency. The army itself seemed hardly in the process of preparing for an ultimate struggle for world mastery. In 1912 the General Staff and the War Ministry finally responded to the massive consumption of material in the Russo-Japanese War by instituting an expanded program of shell production. Two years later, business as usual had left the program still unfulfilled. Even at calculated consumption rates, Germany had an average stock of raw materials sufficient for no more than six months. Supplies, the argument ran, would be replenished through conquest.[31] Was this an ultimate expression of predatory capitalism, the insouciance of a short-war illusion, or perhaps a manifestation of something else—like an inability to think beyond the first few weeks?

Illustrations might be multiplied; the point remains the same. For a state dominated by the rhetoric of belligerence, a state constantly in diplomatic conflict with her neighbors, Germany was surprisingly unready to prepare or implement the ultimate contingency of a major war. There are, to be sure, intellectual risks in demanding excessive documentation of events with complex causations. Yet the lack of such evidence has generated some startling intellectual gymnastics. In the words of one sympathetic doctoral student, the absence of plans for war, as opposed to war plans, is explained by critics "searching for logical continuities in actions, regardless of the words which were used to cloak them. They subject the written evidence to minute scrutiny which translates code words into their real meanings. Or they focus attention upon the silences, the things not mentioned."[32]

Without denying the importance of reasoned inference to historical research, similar comments written on the margins of an undergraduate paper would have quite different implications. A weak argument may be camouflaged by multiplying footnotes. But this approach is at best an invitation to an historian's theory of epicycles: when a simple answer does not support a complex general theory, explain away the inconvenient points in eight or nine hundred learned pages. At worst, it opens the door to analyses based on preconceived realities, a variation of the conspiracy theory of history. Emperors and generals, Junkers and industrialists, bourgeoisie and aristocrats, must behave in ways ultimately determined by their relationship to the means of production. If they do not seem to behave appropriately, the scholar's task is to strip away their camouflage. When this process brings no obvious results, that only proves the cleverness of the conspiracy.

Golo Mann, Gerhard Ritter, and Egmont Zechlin are only the most familiar scholars who have used the absence of planning as an offensive weapon to defend the Second Empire against what they regard as irresponsible charges of warmongering.[33] This essay, however, does not deny the existence of dangerous warlike tendencies in German society before 1914. It does not deny the irresponsible expression of those tendencies at the highest levels of government. Nor does it deny the strength of an official will to extend Germany's influence by force of arms. It only suggests that all of these were checked, if not balanced, at policy-implementing levels by an emotion: fear. It was neither the rational anxiety accompanying the decision-making process in the mind of any responsible statesman, nor the kind of moral concerns Shakespeare puts in the mouth of Henry V on the eve of Agincourt. It was rather a soul-wrenching panic generated by perceptions of consequences.

German chancellors since Bismarck had made sharp, pragmatic distinctions between rattling the saber and drawing the sword. More than any of his predecessors, however, Bethmann-Hollweg argued in and out of season that the scope and the horror of a future conflict would be immeasurable. Even threats of war were "criminal" unless Germany's honor, security, and future were involved. Conflict undertaken without the most urgent reasons set crown and country alike at peril. In June 1914, Bethmann suggested that resorting to arms might set Germany back to the Thirty Years' War, and, once the conflict began, made significant efforts to restrict its parameters.[34]

William II's career offers an even clearer example of a pattern of belligerence suddenly stifled, then reasserting itself once the flash point was safely past. His current biographers portray a man significantly emotionally disturbed, seeking to hide his basic weakness behind martial posturings, repeatedly insisting that "this time" he would not "fold up" in whatever crisis he had helped provoke.[35] In this context it is worth recalling the colloquial definition of a neurotic as someone who knows two and two are four, but is terrified by the fact. William's instability was checked, if not always balanced, by flashes of perception. He saw more clearly than he understood the perils of a general war. By constantly drawing back from its brink, he exposed himself more completely to charges of indecisiveness. But he also postponed a general crisis he lacked the ability to avert.

To dismiss these attitudes as reflections of incompetence or mendacity involves reducing German foreign policy to the level of a Mack Sennett comedy. The Kaiser and his advisors, for all their grotesqueries, were not quite the historical counterpart of "The Gang That Couldn't Shoot Straight." Their anxieties were in fact generated and reinforced by a most frightening source: the professional soldiers. Germany's mainstream military theorists had moved a long way from Alfred von Waldersee's ebullient advocacy of preventive war. By the turn of the century they were extremely pessimistic about their country's prospects in a future war.

This pessimism reflected to some extent Germany's increasingly unfavorable diplomatic situation—the *Einkreisung* German diplomats had done so much to generate. But it also reflected growing concern about the changing nature of war itself. Often derided for their shortsightedness in failing to predict a war of attrition, the generals were if anything even less correct in evaluating the pace of destruction in modern war. Far from being technological illiterates, the soldiers were well aware of what modern weapons—the rapid-firing field gun, the machine gun, the magazine rifle—could do in theory. The admirals had calculated the destructive potential of heavy guns against armor plate down to centimeters. What they were expecting was not a gentleman's war, not a repetition of 1866 or 1870, but an Armageddon in quick time, events at best proceeding at the outer limits of comprehension and control. I. S. Bloch's *La guerre future* was not only discounted because of its pessimistic predictions of indecisive mass war—more and more experts agreed that the rates of loss under modern conditions made a war of attrition a contradiction in terms.[36] Similarly, the emphasis on heroic vitalism in infantry training which engaged the scorn of so many later critics was not based on ignorance of the nature of modern war. It had proved difficult enough a half-century earlier to keep presumably highly motivated Prussian troops under control on the battlefields of Bohemia and France. The Kaiser's army anticipated S. L. A. Marshall in considering and evaluating problems of straggling, of failure to fire in combat. Tactical theorists increasingly made proposals based on the implication that the wastage in future battles would be so high, the destruction so horrible, that only iron discipline combined with artificial emotional exaltation could sustain the individual combatant until he too was put out of action.[37]

It is commonly asserted that military planners underestimated the resilience of their war machines and the societies sustaining them. What they did rather was to *overestimate* the rates at which men would be killed and machines destroyed. They saw vulnerabilities more clearly than durabilities—and it was the latter which gave Europe time to adjust to the initial casualty rates of 1914-15. Given the nature of prewar anticipations, it by no means indicated lack of faith in one's people to assume that countries facing such a catastrophe might collapse from psychic shock and physical stress. Schlieffen was by no means alone in his assertion that the armed forces available to modern nations could be maintained for any length of time only at the expense of the economic, social and political institutions they were supposed to serve.[38] Financiers and politicians, diplomats and industrialists were similarly pessimistic.

Thus a dichotomy emerged: belligerence inhibited by widely-circulated expert opinions on the results of translating it into decisive action. A Nietzchean breaking of the sword, a search for new patterns of international order, was hardly likely to recommend itself to the statesmen of a country priding itself on its realism. Pacifism was weaker in Germany than anywhere else in Europe, its principles more hedged with ifs and maybes.[39] Fatalism, an acceptance of what Wolfgang Mommsen calls the *topos* of inevitable war, was an increasingly-important rhetorical flourish among Germany policy-makers.[40] Yet in retrospect it emerges as less a faith than an attitude—a mixture of *Weltschmerz* and *fin de siècle* despair. It might be fashionable alike in diaries and drawing rooms. It might be given an extra edge through postwar hindsight. It hardly dominated the working days of men who remained too completely the children of an age of progress to wait for disaster. Instead they did their best to avert the worst.

This approach could be illustrated by Bethmann's constant efforts to limit and localize both prospective conflicts and the actual war which began in 1914. But it can be applied even more usefully to the short-war illusion: the assumption, not to say the faith, that a future European war could be limited at least temporarily to an extent making victory meaningful.[41]

The concept usually is interpreted in terms of caste. The aristocratic establishment which incompletely dominated Germany was unwilling to risk losing its special place by relinquishing its control of the armed forces. Twentieth-century war, this argument runs, demanded rationalized administration. It demanded the positive integration of all elements of the nation behind the military structure. It demanded, in short, the increasing radicalization of a militarism which had spent decades sustaining itself as part of a traditional, autocratic state structure. Faced with this choice, the military establishment preferred to place its faith in a short, decisive struggle whose structure prefigured the Blitzkrieg and whose results would hark back to the cabinet wars of earlier centuries.[42]

In fact, the German army was attempting to lead from strength. At the risk of defying conventional wisdom on the subject, the Kaiser's generals were not bloodthirsty savages delighting in wholesale butchery for its own sake—or even for the sake of caste pride.[43] As professional soldiers, they reasoned that the best way to preserve the social and political position of the military class was to win any future wars as decisively and as cheaply as possible. War, moveover might be the province of chance, but it was the responsibility of professional soldiers to diminish its incalculable elements. Through the nineteenth century Prussian and German military theorists had been essentially concerned with retaming Bellona, with avoiding the unlimited wars of the Revolutionary-Napoleonic era—not least because they had ultimately proved so indecisive, so costly relative to their results.[44]

This search for control influenced force structures as well as attitudes. Scholars conditioned to seek class interest as a motive, particularly where generals and similar moral lepers are concerned, are fond of citing the War Ministry's periodic reluctance to sanction the army's expansion on the grounds that it could not find officers of suitably conservative background and ideology to staff the new units. Professional, technical arguments against numerical expansion are dismissed as window-dressing.[45] But an alternate reading of available evidence suggests that the issue of quality over numbers was in fact important. Germany's military budget was not infinitely expansible, and the General Staff's constant protests of weakness tended to translate into demands for more of everything. In establishing priorities, however, a strong opposing case could be made for technical, material improvements as more necessary than simple increases in troop strength, particularly since Germany had no hope of matching her prospective continental rivals in sheer mass. The professionals of the Empire wanted a rapier, not a bludgeon. The problem lay in justifying this position to the army's conservative social and political supporters in an era when military strength was measured by counting bodies in uniform. What were better, more defensible grounds than questioning the reliability of the new officers needed to command the prospective new army corps? It is not necessary to invert accepted wisdom to suggest that efficiency was vital for an army attempting to transform worst-case expectations into best-case possibilities.[46]

The unpleasant ultimate consequences of military planning also influenced doctrines. The essence of strategy is the calculating of relationships between ends and means. Let calculation obscure relationships, let means become more important than ends, and the result is not bad strategy, but no strategy.[47] The German army in the years before 1914 became increasingly concerned with processes, with methods and techniques. Arguably, Schlieffen's essential flaw as a strategist was his acceptance of Germany's international position as defined by civilian political authority. He responded to it by a desperation move representing a turn away from Russia as much as a turn towards France. His grand plan was a staff college *tour de force*, but a military myth requiring everything to go impossibly right to have a chance of succeeding. "Everything" included political and diplomatic factors, which between 1902 and 1914 were increasingly subordinated to this gambler's gambit.[48]

The Schlieffen Plan, however, had one supreme psychological virtue. It offered hope through diligence. If everyone did his bit and played his part, the Empire might have a chance. The plan's rapid evolution into dogma certainly owed much to the increasingly narrow perspective of German military thinking. But that development in turn represented in large part a response to a paradox. The imperial army was given—and accepted—the task of planning for a war which its own calculations suggested would be so destructive as to be unpredictable, uncontrollable, and ultimately unwinnable. In this context, a withdrawal into procedures, a concentration on mobilization schedules and corps-level tactics, was natural if not exactly inevitable. The Schlieffen Plan was a sophisticated security blanket. Had it not existed, its equivalent would almost certainly have been designed.

The professionals, at least, did not entirely deceive themselves. Schlieffen's prognostications grew darker year by year after his retirement. Erich von Falkenhayn, Prussian War Minister from 1912 to 1914, was convinced long before becoming Chief of Staff that Germany's diplomatic situation was not to be solved by military measures, and instead advocated seeking first a rapprochement, then a separate peace with Russia.[49] But the best example of official anxiety remains Schlieffen's successor as Chief of Staff, Helmuth von Moltke the Younger. He has become the principal villain in the Fritz Fischer school of historical melodrama. In monograph after monograph he emerges as a consistent force for war, a German Cato repeating his call to battle at every likely and unlikely opportunity. Gentler critics describe a sensitive man, a cello-playing dabbler in the occult, whose intellect enabled him to see at least four sides of every three-sided question but who lacked the force of character either to stop a war or prepare for it properly.[50] Yet even from the limited sources available, Moltke's gloom emerges as in large part the result of sober, careful reflection. He was deeply concerned with what he perceived as the coming struggle for Europe between Germans and Slavs. He was deeply disturbed by what he perceived as the growing and uncheckable strength of Germany's rivals. But his advocacy of war was negative, not positive. Germany must fight in order to prevent worse things from happening to her. His case for a prompt war in the December 1912 Crown Council, for example, was based on a mixture of anxiety and desperation, and certainly not followed by any behavior designed to strengthen the German army for all-out aggression against its neighbors.[51] Like his master William II, Moltke seemed paralyzed by conflicting visions. The coming war was necessary, indeed inevitable. Yet the accompanying destruction and dislocation made systemic planning a case of thinking about the unthinkable.

Imperial Germany, aggressive yet afraid, conducted its foreign policy like Wilkins Micawber approached his life—hoping that something would turn up. The anxieties which pulled the German government back from brink after brink in 1914 were theoretical. Their basis was prediction and expectation, not experience. They were strong enough to modify attitudes and behavior, but not to change them. The concrete results promised by belligerent rhetoric, and belligerent behavior just short of war, consistently overrode the uncomfortable process of drawing logical conclusions and acting on them. Accepting the position of a sated, status quo power was as unacceptable as wholeheartedly preparing for the war risked by Germany's behavior. Not until the summer of 1914 was this uneasy status quo destroyed. Even then it gave way not to a tangible reality, but to a fear that finally outweighed the fear of war. The Habsburg Empire's malaise had long been plain in Germany and Europe. Her decline had in fact been assisted by an entente insouciantly indifferent to the consequences of Austria's disappearance from the map.[52] Germany's concern, however, remained rhetorical—until Austria decided against going quietly. Her decision to maintain what was left of her position by force confronted Germany with an emotional as well as a diplomatic challenge. The German response was not an implementation of policy, but a *flucht nach vorne*.

Britain's eventual mobilization against Germany similarly reflected significant patterns of inconsistency. Diplomatic historians are increasingly concerned with the apparent weakness of concrete points of friction between the two countries. Colonial rivalries had always involved more rhetoric than substance. After 1900 they had faded into the background. By 1912, indeed, the bitter imperial rivals proved well able to collaborate on a proposal to divide Por' 'gal's African empire.[53] As for economic hostility, Germany's burgeoning productive and marketing capacities disturbed the repose of British businessmen from Manchester to Buenos Aires. Yet oratorical flourishes about unfair competition were juxtaposed to and undermined by a growing acceptance of the idea that an imperialized globe offered ample opportunities for both industrial giants, and growing recognition of the fact that the bulk of Germany's export trade was with her continental neighbors. Trade and flag might still be profitably linked, but the bumptiousness of a Cecil Rhodes was bad business in the context of 1914: the pith helmet was giving way to the briefcase.[54]

What of the naval race? Germany's fleet programs may have had domestic implications. There is no question that they were also designed to coerce and challenge Great Britain by creating a fleet whose strategic position and internal efficiency would give it a good chance to overcome any numerical weakness. Nor is there any question that the German navy ultimately posed a threat at once perceived and real to British security, if for no other reason than Germany's rapid and triumphant industrialization, which bestowed a corresponding theoretical capacity to match, and perhaps exceed, British construction.[55] The naval question needed to be resolved as a condition for any long-term rapprochement between the two powers. Yet at the same time, among the plethora of military, diplomatic, and political problems facing the declining British Empire, the German naval challenge was the only one that British policy-makers were confident they could match. Even in the limited terms of naval strategy, Japan in the Far East, the United States in the Atlantic and the Caribbean, created problems insoluble except at a price in ship and base construction that made diplomacy the only feasible response. Germany, on the other hand, was seen as a danger to be met within familiar and acceptable parameters. Redeployment, better ships, institutional improvements in gunnery, staff work, or training—these would enable the Royal Navy to deal quite nicely with the German upstart. Indeed in certain particularly salty circles, the Germans were welcomed as the kind of worthy opponent any champion needed to preserve "the eye of the tiger," the kind of foe regrettably absent on British horizons since the French navy's abandonment of the contest during the 1890's.[56]

The discrepancy between demonstrable points of conflict and the increasing depth of hostility between Britain and Germany is frequently presented in psychological and ideological terms. Germany's exhuberant and comprehensive challenge to the status quo in Europe and the world was seen by many Englishmen as an insult to the natural order—an insult compounded by German ill manners. Whatever William II might be to historians, to his British contemporaries, he was a mere bounder. His countrymen appeared similarly lacking in grace, tact, and a sense of their proper place in the world.[57] German xenophobia, while arguably even more vitriolic, tended to be diffused by the nature of Germany's political situation. England might inspire the rage of rejected admiration; France and Russia generated direct fear. In England, on the other hand, fear and dislike became increasingly focused on the same target: Germany. The anxiety sold books and newspapers. It furnished election issues. It provided a means of arousing enthusiasm in schoolboys. Eventually it overrode the many links, ethnic, cultural, and dynastic, between the two societies to the point where right-thinking Englishmen from the highest to the lowest orders rushed to arms against the perfidious Hun as though going to a festival.

Here again, as so often when evaluating the origins of World War I, the problem of finding a smoking gun remains unsolved. A strong case can be made that in Britain even more than in Germany, ideological hostility remained abstract and theoretical. Jingoism was likely to be strong in an island with an independent competitive popular press, defended by the world's most powerful navy. Yet it is also true that states, not citizens, declare wars. The genesis of the Crimean War stands as proof that British governments were not immune to popular pressure. Many another patrioteering outburst found, however, no significant echo in the Cabinet or the Foreign Office. War scare after war scare came and went in the headlines. But Britain's foreign policy, arguably more than any other aspect of her government, remained dominated by a small elite and was kept isolated from popular pressure. From Salisbury to Grey, successive Foreign Secretaries might seek to justify their policies in terms of the public will, but the process remained a sophisticated form of window-dressing.[58]

This in turn leads to the thesis that domestic crises generated a will to war. By 1914, so the argument runs, "Liberal England" faced three interrelated crises that its existing political and social framework could not overcome. In Ireland, guns were beginning to supplant rhetoric. The Ulster Unionists were openly arming and drilling, proclaiming in and out of season their readiness to fight rather than accept Home Rule. Leaders of His Majesty's loyal opposition appeared to be overtly sanctioning this armed resistance; even the political reliability of the officer corps was questionable for the first time since the Glorious Revolution. At home, bourgeois fears of organized labor and red revolution had been sharpened by the newly-formed alliance of miners, railroaders, and transport workers. Long-voiced threats of a general strike which would permanently shift the balance of power in Britain appeared for the first time to have substance. Finally, the British male establishment was facing a significant psychological attack from within. The suffragette movement challenged long-held, often unconscious assumptions about the appropriate structure of the family, about the very nature of men and women. With the movement's cutting edge provided by women of the middle and upper classes, an English gentleman could feel safe neither in his drawing room nor in his bedroom. Everywhere civility was giving way to bellicosity; the first shots fired by the guns of august simply provided an opportunity for Britons to direct their pent-up frustrations against a target on which all could agree, however, temporarily.[59]

Seen in this context, the Anglo-German rivalry becomes essentially an aspect of domestic conflict projected outwards, whether accidentally or by design. But this line of argument is vulnerable on three levels. One is structural. It interprets the industrial revolution as beginning early enough and progressing slowly enough for Britain to be able to develop a political and social system strong enough to postpone or resolve internal conflicts without violence. Almost by definition, tension was endemic in the structures but the tension was at the same time an ultimate guarantee of stability.[60]

A second critique of the internal-crisis thesis turns it on its head. If Britain's traditional elites were being challenged, they were also expanding, incorporating new groups, appealing to new men—and even women. The sense of desperation so often described in German society was simply not present across the channel. Prophets of domestically-generated doom found audiences only with difficulty. With Ireland as a possible exception, no significant interest or pressure group in British society threatened the existing order enough to generate more than *frissons*—the kind of cheap thrills that might send good citizens home with a shudder, but hardly inspired fears of displacement strong enough to inspire consequent action. Certainly diligent research has failed to show any causal connection between domestic tensions and the British cabinet's decision for war in 1914.[61]

The third approach to the assertion that England's role in 1914 was inspired, consciously or unconsciously, by internal anxieties demonstrates that British policy-makers, rather than seeking war as a solution to domestic problems, regarded its predictable consequences as potentially disastrous. Such economic planning as occurred in Britain in the decade before war's outbreak was dominated by fear: fear of blockade, fear of commerce-raiders, fear of invasion. The military results of these contingencies were seen as far less important than their social implications. A future war, even of short duration, might well be lost on the home front while the armed forces were winning it on the battlefield. Planners and policy-makers might not fear revolution and entropy within existing frameworks. But let shipowners refuse to risk their property on the high seas, let food supplies be disrupted, let business close for lack of markets, and the situation could change rapidly. In the summer of 1911 a relatively minor series of strikes had threatened the country's distribution system. High prices, unemployment, and anxiety were an unstable mixture, particularly in large cities with their polyglot, transient populations. Far from counting on public enthusiasm once the trumpets sounded, defense planners prior to 1914 were wondering what to do if the projected side effects of a major war triggered a social explosion. "Business as usual" was less a strategy than the absence of one. It represented not a principled addiction to laissez-faire economics and the liberties of Englishmen, but a response to two articles of belief. First, if it came to a war, France and Russia would do most of the fighting on land. Second, Britain's role in the entente was as an economic prop, supplying material assistance to the continental powers. This in turn put maintaining economic stability at the top of wartime requirements.[62]

Let us overlook the obvious discrepancy between Britain's self-designated mission as an arsenal of democracy and the general expectation that the coming war would be won or lost with supplies on hand. The assumption that continental allies would carry the burden of a land war might have been valid had Britain's anti-German policies represented a commitment to sustain a threatened balance of power. In such circumstances, since the days of Louis XIV her coalition partners had normally been desperate enough to take whatever the island kingdom offered. In fact, as the relative weaknesses of the substantive antagonisms between the powers indicated, Britain's anti-German position was sustained by a different set of impulses.

By 1900 the world's foremost economic, imperial, and naval power was principally concerned with meeting threats to her own frontiers. Far from initiating challenges, Great Britain essentially sought to keep what she had from rivals whose relative increases in strength were internal, and correspondingly unsusceptible to British checks. This in turn explains the halfhearted nature and the ultimate failure of Britain's attempts to achieve an understanding with Germany at the turn of the century. If the two powers had nothing to fight about, neither did they have anything to bring them together.[63] Germany's navy was insignificant. The British army might have been in theory an effective instrument for projecting Britain's influence on the continent. But Britain no more than Germany was interested in a holocaust whose prize would be hegemony over a rubbish heap. Logically, therefore, she increasingly pursued policies of retrenchment and rapprochement. And equally logically, she pursued them relative not to the enemy of her enemies, but to her primary direct rivals, France and Russia.

The Boer War and its aftermath demonstrated that even in a narrowly military sense the British Empire was vulnerable to an external challenge from a major power. A Britain unwilling, arguably unable, to arm to meet such a challenge directly sought cooperation instead. And the ultimate price of that cooperation, of the ententes with France and Russia, was support—direct and indirect, diplomatic and moral—for their ongoing disputes with Germany and Austria.[64]

This did not make Britain a catspaw. Her new relationships might have been generated by imperial considerations but were also intended to prevent war, not provoke it. British statesmen in the years before 1914 counselled restraint on her partners in and out of season. Ententes, moreover, were not alliances, and Britain was at pains to emphasize the difference. Britain's final acceptance of the Franco-Russian connection was neither automatic nor based on moral factors. The decision to go to war in 1914 rested on political and strategic grounds.[65] But the unceasing tendency to perceive Britain's vital interests as requiring preserving and strengthening her ties with France and Russia both increased the entente's cost and structured the nature of its payment. France and Russia perceived England's needs far too clearly to be fobbed off with ships and shells.

To maintain the diplomatic relationships she required, Britain had to do more than commit herself against Germany. She had to justify that commitment and its implications in view of the absence of issues directly worth fighting over—and in view of the Royal Navy's continued hostility to a continental war. On one level, this requirement encouraged a form of mind reading. Concrete antagonisms focus hostilities. Germanophobia in France was based not so much on hatred of the Boche as Boche, but as the violator of Alsace-Lorraine, the military menace which had beaten France twice in a century.⁶⁶ Without equivalent foci, the hostility originally institutionalized as part of a policy of imperial rapprochement tended to become abstracted and universalized. Britain before 1914 was less and less inclined to mirror image perceptions of Germany.

Since the Congress of Vienna, Europe's great powers had regarded each other as pursuing similar general ends by similar general rules. Napoleon III's France or Bismarck's Prussia might stress the system, might even distort it, but were nevertheless considered part of it by their rivals. In Britain, arguably more than anywhere else in Europe, policy-makers had by 1914 come to regard Germany as "not-like," as essentially different from the diplomatic game's other players. A familiar illustration of this attitude is Sir Eyre Crowe's 1907 memorandum. Germany, he argued, was pursuing a policy of European and world hegemony. Whether this approach was conscious or unconscious was less important than the fact of its existence. Germany was ultimately a revolutionary state in its desire to create a new international order. This made her an irreconcilable threat to Britain's vital interests—a threat ultimately impossible to conciliate. The only possible response was "the most unbending determination to uphold Britain's rights and interests in every part of the globe.⁶⁷

These were not entirely counsels of paranoia. Germany's erratic pursuit of an ill-defined *Weltpolitik* often cast her in the role of ants at a picnic: always *there*, always demanding compensation and consideration for merely existing, or to avert what she might do if she only decided to do it. At bottom, however this was more irritant than vital threat. And paradoxically the relative weakness of concrete Anglo-German conflicts generated a corresponding optimism in Whitehall. For all the gloomy predictions of war as an abstract inevitability, it appeared a practical improbability—not from any positive will to peace, but from a lack of definite motives for a final grapple.

This survival from the days of cabinet diplomacy significantly inhibited planning for, or even reacting to, the logical conclusion to be drawn from the nature of Britain's ententes with France and Russia: war with Germany, on terms largely determined by the friends Britain perceived herself as needing. Until recently, general histories of the British army described the years before 1914 in terms of a systematic overhauling of equipment, doctrine, and organization in order to fit the army into Britain's new diplomatic patterns. From a collection of draft-finding regiments and battalions emerged six superbly trained regular divisions, poised for immediate service against Germany.⁶⁸

Reality is less tidy. The British army's structure of linked battalions was reasonably suited for imperial commitments. It provided for no functional higher organizations and meant that most units stationed in Britain itself were essentially training formations. Nevertheless, for a quarter-century, worst-case expectations that Britain might have to face a major military opponent on the continent, in the empire, or even on her own soil gave way before the day-to-day realities of imperial policing. Then the Boer War conclusively demonstrated Britain's inability to field a significant expeditionary force without stripping empire and home islands alike.

Secretaries of State for War St. John Brodrick and H. O. Arnold-Forster sought to create a stable field force while at the same time sustaining an effective imperial presence. The purpose of such a force, however, remained debatable. Advocates of the Indian connection argued that Britain's essential military responsibility was to secure the defense of the subcontinent. Other critics argued for the "British way" of war—attacking colonies, ports, bases, and any other targets vulnerable to relatively small forces transported by sea.

Both approaches presented problems. The first was essentially passive—and Britain was too weak militarily to afford the luxury of passivity. The second might be theoretically effective against France, but France was an increasingly unlikely enemy after 1904. Germany and Russia were virtually invulnerable to it, particularly if the next general war was as short as the experts predicted. Operationally, moreover, imperialism's palmy days were over; the buffer zones were gone. Future conflicts anywhere were likely to be against great powers: perhaps in the Far East against Japan, perhaps in Canada against the United States. No longer could improvised task forces be dispatched around the globe with the vague sense of all coming right on the night as long as the navy was there. Imperial security would from now on require the ability to deploy large forces in a wide variety of operational environments.

This fact was the genesis of the Haldane reforms. It is, indeed, more appropriate to speak of the Haldane rearrangements. The units stationed in Britain were formed into six divisions, with supporting troops—but not to implement that continental commitment which was more and more at the logical center of British diplomacy. Instead, they were planned as general-purpose forces, able to apply efficiently-structured military power anywhere in the world that British interests might require it, from Central Africa to China. They represented at least as much of a warning to Britain's new allies as to Germany.

The rationalization of Britain's home forces was long overdue, but unaccompanied by the deeper changes which might have given point to foreign policy. National service remained politically unthinkable despite the rhetoric of Field Marshall Roberts and Rudyard Kipling. The Territorial Force remained a home guard of Saturday-night soldiers, dismissed by the professionals as dog-shooters. Batteries and battalions on home service were still essentially training units, depending on reservists in order to take the field, with no systematic provision for replacing the ruinous casualties everyone expected. To be sure, the experts predicted a short war. But those same experts calculated that a continental expeditionary force of 100,000 men would lose over half its men in the first seven weeks. And since most of the casualties would be suffered by the combat arms, the infantry and artillery, a British army in Europe was likely to prove not merely a wasting, but a disappearing, asset.[69]

The army's development of continental strategy had not been an institutional response to a change in national policy. It began in part as a turn away from imperial commitments—specifically the defense of India against a major Russian invasion—impossible to fulfill with existing or projected force structures. Germany was at least an adversary which could be war-gamed, and the historical limitations on the British army's size and responsibilities made British planners less influenced than their German counterparts by the apocalyptic possibilities of a future general war.[70]

Attitudes also played a significant role. The British army had never accepted the argument that it was essentially an imperial police force. It may have done most of its fighting on the Northwest Frontier and its equivalents, but it did so with an eye on broader spheres and a greater game. The repeated fiascoes of the Boer War had been humiliating enough to act as a catalyst. The British army of the twentieth century was increasingly institutionally committed to achieving first-line status. Drills and maneuvers in the empire's far-flung garrisons were oriented as far as possible toward *la grande guerre*. The Indian army began changing from an instrument of internal and regional security to a force with projected European responsibilities. And since no matter where a British army might fight in the future, it could reckon with up-to-date opposition, continental models were also important because they set the standards copied elsewhere.

The British army rapidly overtook and outstripped its teachers. Only the British in 1914 used trucks as the principal means of transportation between railheads and divisional supply columns. Only the British had both a first-rate modern field gun and light howitzer. Only the British stressed both rifle markmanship and automatic fire-power. Military Britain's interest in machine guns had been noted by foreign observers as early as 1905: the often-cited Blimpish admonition to "take the damned things to a flank and hide them" is actually sound tactical advice for a weapon most effective in concealed enfilade positions.[71] But these internal improvements were not a response to the continental commitment. They were rather a parallel development, one which encouraged Britain to pursue a forward policy for which she was ultimately unprepared, against an enemy whose role in British diplomacy was instrumental, a means to an end rather than a strategic end in itself.

This process was further encouraged by Britain's growing institutional and personal connections with the French army. Inter-service rivalry and professional calculation blended to convince the General Staff that the only feasible European deployment of the newly-formed field force was in northern France. Any other targets were too risky, and made the army too much an auxiliary of the navy, which would deliver, supply, and probably evacuate it. Deployed on the French left flank, however, the BEF could have a decisive impact on any future conflict.[72] This viewpoint was encouraged by the growing readiness of French soldiers to give first-team status to their British counterparts, at least for purposes of public consumption. To a France historically suspicious of perfidious Albion, and heavily outnumbered by her more populous neighbor, a concrete British commitment would be worth any amount of honeyed words.[73] Sir Henry Wilson, Director of Military Operations after 1910, was a political soldier, the kind of careerist whose highly-charged emotional commitment to France and its cause seems sharply out of character, particularly in view of the consistent reluctance to keep him informed of French strategic intentions. To what extent was it fostered by the close personal contacts in the French army which Wilson found so flattering?[74]

At the cutting edge of Britain's continental commitment, planning tended to determine, as opposed to merely influence, policy. A general purpose expeditionary force evolved into a single-mission instrument. But this was not a reflection of the army's political strength. It was rather a manifestation of fundamental confusion. The B.E.F. became for Britain what the Schlieffen Plan was for Germany: a means of rationalizing dissonances. Questions of its role and its value were constantly raised—but the answers were too uncomfortable to be heard. It grew even easier to become absorbed in "conflict-as-a-game." The fact that no one at policy-making levels challenged effectively the military assumptions of a continental commitment cannot be ascribed entirely to the secret nature of Anglo-French conferences, or the ability of Machiavellian staff officers to manipulate the information they supplied.[75] Haldane's six divisions protected British statesmen from making ultimate decisions about their country's relationship with Germany on one hand, and France and Russia on the other.

The hysterical enthusiasm accompanying the outbreak of war in 1914 is usually explained either positively or negatively. On the one hand, it becomes a manifestation of collective and individual relief from overwhelming tension, or a response to the boring routines of everyday life. On the other, it is presented in terms of a generation "taught to howl" for war, or of a virtuous proletariat temporarily led astray by its class enemies.[76] The material consulted for this paper suggests, however, that the war fever of July and August 1914, was a manifestation of the dichotomies underlying the issue of a general war. Doubts and certainties, affirmations and negations, were so closely balanced in Britain and Germany that they inhibited preparation for the war regarded as inevitable. As the specific stresses of the July Crisis overloaded more and more of the diplomatic system's safety mechanisms, everyone worked correspondingly hard to suppress ambivalences, to resolve the dissonances at least enough to present a firm public face. The adaptive value of such behavior for generals or statesmen is obvious. But it is hardly coincidence that mobilization was enthusiastically supported by intellectuals and the young—the social groups which would probably be most likely to be reluctant to admit their mouths had bought more than their hands could pick up. The challenge for the warring states would be harnessing, institutionalizing, and sustaining a zeal with such ultimately shaky foundations.

Chairman Trask's Introduction of Professor Kennedy
Professor David M. Kennedy received his doctorate in American Studies at Yale University in 1968. He joined the faculty of Stanford University in 1967 where he attained the rank of full professor in 1980. He has been awarded a number of honors, among them fellowships from the Guggenheim Foundation and the American Council of Learned Societies. His book entitled *Birth Control In America: The Career of Margaret Sanger,* published in 1970, received the Bancroft Prize. In 1980 he published a book directly related to his appearance here. It is entitled *Over Here: The First World War and American Society.* His paper today is styled: "Rallying Americans For War, 1917-1918".

RALLYING AMERICANS FOR WAR, 1917-1918

David M. Kennedy
Stanford University

The Great War exploded with terrible vastness over Europe in the summer of 1914. Within a few frenzied weeks all the great powers had become belligerents, and millions of men were under arms. A serpentine battle perimeter soon girdled Europe, from the Adriatic in the south to Flanders in the west and Russia in the East. As the weeks stretched to months and to seemingly endless years, and as the death toll climbed into many millions, there was scarcely a corner of Europe not washed by this colossal bloodletting.

Contrast, now, the situation of the United States. The journalist Mark Sullivan aptly described it some years later:

> The war did not come to America as it came to Europe. No Oregon rancher working in his field of a peaceful afternoon was disturbed by an odd whirring in the sunny air, and looked over Mount Hood to see an airplane spitting fire upon his neighboring village. In no New England town did children huddle in the windows and peer at exultant Uhlans prancing down the maple-shaded street. No Maryland farmer from his hilltop field saw a thing that sent him hurrying to the house to gather his children into his cart and take to the road in fear. No city of ours walked for days in anxiety, listening to the rise and fall of a fateful cannonade. . . . . It was not in the shape of violence of any sort that the war . . . came to us. Its coming took a form hardly physical at all; it came as newspaper despatches from far away, far away in distance and even farther away in spirit.[1]

Sullivan concluded that "the most accurate and comprehending reflection of the American attitude" toward the outbreak of the war was voiced by the Wabash, Indiana *Plain Dealer,* which editorialized: "We never appreciated so keenly as now the foresight exercised by our forefathers in emigrating from Europe."[2]

"Far away in distance and even farther away in spirit. . . ." Sullivan properly emphasized these simple truths about the conflict that Americans persisted in calling the "European" War. Its destruction never directly touched America; it made no demands on American resources comparable to the exactions it levied upon the treasuries of the Old World powers; and the reflexive response of most Americans, at least in 1914, was simply to regard the war as none of their business. These homely facts help to explain much about America's role in the Great War of 1914-1918: the long-enjoyed luxury of neutrality; the confusion surrounding President Wilson's request for a declaration of belligerency in April 1917; the singular

47

methods the United States employed to place the economy on a war footing; and, not least, the techniques adopted by the Wilson administration to rally public support for the war effort.

Woodrow Wilson's war address to Congress on April 2, 1917, vividly illustrated America's peculiar relation to the war she was about to enter. Perhaps the most significant fact to be noted about that address was the date of its delivery—more than two and one-half years after the fighting had erupted on the old continent, two years after the sinking of the *Lusitania* (which many bellicose Americans had regarded as a more than adequate *casus belli*), and two full months after the German announcement of unrestricted submarine warfare.

Wilson cited the submarine campaign as the fundamental reason for America's belligerency. But the President, perhaps seeking to deflect criticism of his belated response to the U-boat challenge, also attempted to make a broader case for American entry into the war. He proclaimed that America must enter the fray because "the world must be made safe for democracy." Wilson here revealed both his own reservations about the adequacy of the submarine attacks as a justification for the abandonment of neutrality, and his effort, sometimes desperate, never fully successful, to make the waging of war purposeful to his largely indifferent, even militantly isolationist, people. The President instinctively emphasized ideas about democracy and self-determination. Those ideas always held sacred meaning for Americans. They had particular power in the atmosphere of 1917, charged by two decades of Populist and Progressive preachment of precisely those principles. But their concrete application to the war that Wilson now urged his countrymen to embrace remained obscure.

"I am not voting for war in the name of democracy," declared Ohio Senator Warren G. Harding during the Congressional debate on the war resolution. "I am voting for war tonight for the maintenance of just American rights."[3] Wilson himself contributed to the confusion when in his war address he maintained that "We have no selfish ends to serve. . . . We are but one of the champions of the rights of mankind. We seek nothing for ourselves . . .," but then declined to ask for a declaration of war against Germany's ally, Austria-Hungary, because "We enter this war only where we are clearly forced into it because there are no other means of defending *our rights*."[4] Were America's purposes disinterested or self-interested, universalist or nationalist? Wilson's listeners had no agreed answer at the time, and history has not settled the question.

Wilson further revealed the problem attendant on American entry into the war when in his war address he frankly raised the question of "disloyalty" and threatened that "it will be dealt with with a firm hand of stern repression." Almost simultaneously with his request for a declaration of war, the President caused to be introduced in Congress bills empowering the federal government to control the expression of opinion about the war (the so-called "espionage" bill) and providing for forced military conscription. Both the President's warning and the proposed legislation suggested the degree of doubt in Wilson's mind that a united American people would follow him willingly into the distant European conflict. The espionage bill and the conscription bill, Wisconsin Senator Robert LaFollette pointedly noted, furnished "the complete proof that those responsible for this war fear that it has no popular support. . . ."[5]

So Woodrow Wilson took the country to war—uncertain of public commitment to the enterprise, appearing confused even in his own pronouncements about the rationale for his action. During the nineteen months of America's belligerency, Wilson continued to insist on the necessity of American intervention on the side of the allies. Yet many aspects of his administration's diplomatic, military, and mobilization policies indicated a persistent tentativeness in the American war effort. The United States fought as an "associate" of the allies, deliberately signifying its political distance from them, and particularly its refusal to be implicated in their various plans for organizing the post-war international economic order. Despite the passionate importunings of British and French military men, the Americans rejected all proposals to amalgamate American troops into Allied units. That decision deprived the Allies for many months of the benefit of American manpower in the fighting line; and men were second only to money on the list of assets that the Europeans needed from the United States.

But it was with respect to domestic mobilization, both economic and psychological, that the qualified character of American belligerency was most tellingly revealed. Again, timing is significant. Only in late 1915 did Wilson openly advocate a program of limited "preparedness," to be directed by a toothless agency, the Council of National Defense. On paper, the Council elaborated a complex administrative apparatus whose utter disutility was instantly demonstrated when it was called upon to perform in April 1917. The Council's record of almost unrelieved irrelevancy constitutes perhaps the best evidence that the administration genuinely sought, until the last minute, to avoid American involvement in the war. Yet even when involvement eventually came, and the Council's plans for economic mobilization proved grossly inappropriate, the administration did not move decisively to put new mobilization machinery in place. (Agricultural mobilization was a partial exception; Wilson named Herbert Hoover to head the Food Administration in the month following the American declaration of war.) Yet even that agency had sound statutory authority only after passage of the Lever Act in August 1917. The administration undertook its boldest measure of economic mobilization, nationalization of the railroads, in December 1917, nearly at the midpoint of American belligerency. And the War Industries Board, the supposed centerpiece of economic mobilization, did not emerge until mid-summer 1917. It limped along without strong direction from two successive chairmen through the following autumn and winter, and finally assumed a modicum of effectiveness (and congressionally defined authority) only when Bernard Baruch took over the chairmanship in March 1918, just eight months before the war's end.

Even at the height of its influence, the War Industries Board never attempted to place the American economy fully on a war footing. Though some major economic sectors were declared "non-essential," most notably the young but already booming passenger automobile industry, they were not absolutely curtailed or totally redirected to production for military use. In large part, the explanation for this partial mobilization lay outside the United States. America was permitted the unique privilege of such a policy because Allied productive facilities remained substantially intact, even after several years of war. The paramount needs of the Allies were troops and credits, not materiel. The American Expeditionary Force ultimately purchased more of its supplies in Europe, including artillery pieces and aircraft, than it shipped from the United States.

The policy of less than total economic mobilization was also purposeful, a deliberate course of action that served some of the Wilson administration's highest political objectives. Prominent among these was the opportunity, glimpsed in 1914 and fixed firmly during the years of neutrality in the vision of men like Treasury Secretary William Gibbs McAdoo and Shipping Board Chairman Edward N. Hurley, to improve America's international economic position while the Europeans were wholly absorbed in war. Accusations flew between British and American representatives on the Allied Maritime Transport Council that one side or the other was holding back, for commercial use, precious ships needed for war service. When the United States Department of Commerce finally commissioned a study of the issue, it concluded, with some mortification, that it was not the British but the Americans who should have felt themselves "in an embarrassing position before the British because of the relatively uninterrupted service of our merchant marine to the West Indies and Central America."[6] By war's end, the British merchant fleet had shrunk nearly 15 percent from its pre-war strength, while the American merchant marine had grown some 60 percent. This was but one of the several entirely anticipated results of America's peripheral engagement in the "war to end all wars."

No less purposeful, and still more indicative of the somewhat tenuous character of American belligerency, were the methods employed by the War Industries Board, and cognate bodies like the Food Administration, to accomplish their goals. One word summarily describes the techniques of virtually all the American mobilization agencies: voluntarism. American war managers shunned the exercise of formal power. In part they made a virtue of necessity, as Congress and the President withheld from them the kind of sweeping authority that their European counterparts wielded. But to a greater extent, as Robert Cuff has cogently argued, Wilson's war mobilizers were guided by a conscious, articulate ideology. That ideology comported well with the official rhetoric describing the war as a struggle between autocracy and democracy, an antinomy popularly conflated with the folk tradition that contrasted Europe with America. Europe represented the political culture of authoritarian regimes; America the opposing principles of individualism and free choice. American war organizers repeatedly invoked that familiar polarity when they described their preferred methods. "The food administrations of Europe," Herbert Hoover explained, "are of the nature of dictatorship," but he intended that American policy should be "based on an entirely different conception from that of Europe.... Our conception is that we should assemble the voluntary effort of the people.... We propose to mobilize the spirit of self-denial and self-sacrifice in this country."[7] Similarly, George Creel, head of the American war propaganda agency, the Committee on Public Information, sneered at his European counterparts, panoplied with heavy authority to censor and punish. "We had no authority," Creel later declared in a typically American boast. "Yet the American idea *worked*. And it worked better than any European *law*."[8]

Hoover was as good as his word. To stimulate increased agricultural output, his Food Administration set no production quotas, but instead relied on high prices, partly supported by the American government, partly squeezed out of hungry (and resentful) Allies, to induce American farmers to do their duty. To dampen domestic consumption, he rejected any suggestion of food rationing, by then a long-familiar practice in the European belligerent countries. He chose instead to launch a massive publicity campaign, aimed at persuading American housewives voluntarily to introduce "wheatless" and "meatless" days into their families' diets. The Food Administration, one of its official pamphlets explained, relied upon "cooperation rather than coercion, upon the compelling force of patriotic sentiment as a means to be tried before resort to threats and prosecutions."[9]

Analogous techniques characterized the operations of the War Industries Board, even after it came under Bernard Baruch's energetic leadership in March 1918. Despite the sweep of the Board's mandate—nothing less than the harmonious orchestration of all war-related industrial production—its formal powers were few. It possessed no legal authority to set prices, nor even to enter into binding purchase agreements with suppliers. The Board's most potent instrument, one observer concluded, was Baruch's personality. He flattered, exhorted, occasionally intimidated—but avoided the threat of legal sanctions that he had not the power to invoke. The Board's official historian, though sensitive to charges of illegitimate wartime collusion between government and industry, nevertheless conceded that the Board's price setting procedures "always took the form of negotiations, and the results were, strictly speaking, agreed rather than decreed prices." All the Board's operations, the same observer concluded, proceeded "by request rather than by mandate.... Compliance was based as much upon the compulsion of reasonableness and the pressure of opinion as upon fear of governmental power." In one notable application of the pressure of opinion, Baruch warned a balky lumber supplier that failure to honor the Board's requests would make him "such an object of contempt and scorn in your home town that you will not dare to show your face there. If you should, your fellow citizens would call you a slacker, the boys would hoot at you, and the draft men would likely run you out of town."[10]

Even the most frankly coercive measure that the Wilson administration adopted—the military draft—was wrapped in the rhetoric of voluntarism, as when the President declared that the draft simply constituted a mechanism of "selection from a nation which has volunteered in mass."[11] The officials responsible for administering the draft in fact believed no such thing, and even feared riots on the initial registration day, June 5, 1917. Characteristically, they sought to avert that unwanted development by appealing to the force of public opinion, urging citizens to ensure that their draft-age male neighbors were cajoled or shamed into compliance with the registration procedures, endeavoring, as Secretary of War Newton D. Baker put it, "to make the day of registration a festival and patriotic occasion."[12] Most ingeniously, Baker and Provost Marshall General Enoch H. Crowder placed the day-to-day administration of the draft in the hands of some 5000 local draft boards. They thus strengthened the image of local control and voluntary service that the President had tried to summon up when he spoke of the nation volunteering "in mass." The local boards also served, as Crowder noted, to divert and ground "at 5000 local points . . . the disturbance that might have been caused by the concentrated total of dissatisfaction" focussing upon a single, centralized, administrative organ.[13]

Several threads run commonly through these various aspects of American mobilization in World War I. Together, they weave a fabric of discernible pattern that marks the distinctiveness of America's way of war-making in 1917-18. That pattern repeatedly reveals the uncertain, attenuated degree of American commitment to the Allied cause; the undismissable anxiety that public support for American participation in the war might not be sufficiently forthcoming; the strenuous, even occasionally contorting, efforts to refrain from nakedly applying the power of the state to the tasks at hand; and the consequent reliance on appeals to patriotism, on "public relations" campaigns, and on propaganda, to get the job done.

The principal agency for propagandizing the American public, of course, was George Creel's Committee on Public Information. Though officially dedicated only to providing factual information about the war, the CPI rapidly evolved into a remarkably effective instrument for playing upon a wide range of public emotions. In speech and in print, in posters and in music, in dramatizations and even films, its basic themes were three: that the war constituted a struggle between democracy and autocracy; that loyalty to America must be unalloyed; and that "Huns" were bestial sub-humans (one of the CPI's most notorious films was entitled "The Kaiser: The Beast of Berlin.").

Responsive to the President's expressed concerns as well as to the sometimes seething fears of old-stock Americans, the CPI gave a high priority to guaranteeing the loyalty of America's abundant foreign-born residents (15 percent of the American population in the census of 1910, and, with their children, nearly 40 percent of the total). The CPI's Division of Work with the Foreign Born organized "Loyalty Leagues" in ethnic communities, fed war news to foreign-language newspapers, and promoted gigantic rallies and pageants around the theme of "100 percent Americanism." Overall, the CPI distributed 75 million copies of more than thirty pamphlets in several languages, explaining America's role in the war. It deployed some 75,000 "Four-Minute Men" as a kind of human broadcasting network, primarily to urge cooperation with the draft. It flooded the news services with press releases, and sponsored travelling war expositions attended by an estimated 10 million people.

In short, the CPI had a more pervasive effect than virtually any other American agency spawned by the war. Its techniques of publicity, persuasion, and propaganda were duplicated, to be sure, in the Food Administration, the War Industries Board, the Selective Service Administration, and even in the Treasury Department's bond-selling campaigns. But the CPI was the pure, undiluted article, and may be taken as the summary example of the style that characterized American mobilization: the appeal not to the majesty of the laws nor even to the concrete discipline of felt necessity, but to high abstractions like "democracy" and "loyalty" and to the base emotions of hatred and fear. The consequences of invoking those abstractions and emotions are infamously documented in the record of anti-radical hysteria, vigilantism, and violence that stained the history of World War I America.

Less well documented is the linkage that connects those sorry domestic effects of America's belligerency to their causes in the over-all context of mobilization, and in the still larger context of early twentieth-century American political culture. American mobilization in the First World War illustrates what is perhaps a general principle about the domestic implications of war-making. Where popular consensus about the necessity of a war crisis is broad and deep, governments may apply with impunity measures that are intrinsically coercive—precisely because compliance need not be forced. Food rationing in World War II provides an example. But where such a consensus is absent, as it assuredly was from World War I America, then governments must employ the methods of indirection. They must somehow stimulate voluntary alignment with policies they dare not formally enforce.

This is perhaps an overly complicated way of stating the obvious. But the point merits emphasis that an inverse relationship exists between the exercise of sovereign political authority and the resort to propaganda. Unwillingness or incapacity to pursue the former strongly compels the latter. Seen in this light, the hyperagitated atmosphere of American society in World War I did not derive from the spontaneous enthusiasm of the people for the war. It was, rather, in significant measure a direct function of the administration's willful avoidance of formal instrumentalities to effect its mobilization program.

From what sources did that distaste for such instrumentalities proceed? It derived, first, of course, from the President's original inability to make a coherent, concrete case for the necessity of American involvement. Woodrow Wilson understandably hesitated to make more than minimal demands on a people that he justifiably feared were not entirely convinced of the wisdom of his course. And the brevity and relative marginality of American involvement permitted that approach to persist substantially unmodified until the Armistice.

Yet in no smaller degree the pattern of American war mobilization was woven from strands that ran back in time well before the declaration of war, deep into the fabric of peacetime society. Despite the expectation, even the hope, of many Americans in 1917 that the war might instantly transform American culture, and despite the tendency of historians to emphasize the mutating power of dramatic events, the prosaic truth remains that the basic structures of any society have a deep durability, even in the face of massive disruptions like war. The best clues as to what drove mobilization, then, are surely to be found outside the confines of the period of belligerency itself.

Two features of American society in the years immediately before 1917 must figure prominently in any effort to explain wartime behavior. First was the unusually active debate, focussed especially sharply in the presidential election campaign of 1912, about the proper relationship between government and business. This issue dominated the agenda of a generation of reformers, known as progressives, and they were themselves sharply divided over it. Some, like Theodore Roosevelt, favored active government intervention in the workings of the market, with the state exercising continuous micro-economic controls over business. Others, most notably Woodrow Wilson, advocated a far more limited program of government intervention, with state power confined to a few macro-economic matters such as regulation of the money supply and the general configuration of discrete but broadly defined markets through anti-trust legislation.

Both progressive camps represented challenges, of a sort, to the American religion of laissez faire, which was regnant economic doctrine in early twentieth century America, and has uniquely persisted in this country, almost alone among industrialized nations, down to the present day. Yet also common to both schools of progressive political economy was a willingness to settle for what Richard Hofstadter once called "ceremonial solutions"—morally comforting but substantively empty reforms of a capitalist system that was sufficiently functional, and powerful, to discourage attempts at radical restructuring.

Wilson clearly stood with that wing of progressives who preferred a minimal expansion of state economic power, a preference powerfully reinforced by the predilections of his constituents in the Democratic party, still heavily a regional party in that era, suffused with the states' rights, anti-federal ideology of the South. It is still more important to recognize the comparatively attenuated character of the *entire* progressive challenge to the tenets of laissez faire. Again, almost uniquely among modern states, the United States had no history of strong centralized government, and progressivism represented but the most modest of challenges to that tradition. It followed naturally, therefore, that in wartime, especially under Woodrow Wilson's direction, the United States would hesitate to embrace statism.

It moved in that direction, and then only grudgingly, only as far as necessity compelled.

The second notable feature of prewar society was, in significant ways, a corollary of the first. Unwilling to tamper drastically with the institutional structure of their society, yet disturbed by its manifest ills, progressives sought remedies in publicity—in the muckraking expose, and in the appeal to people's better selves, to their consciences, as the keys to social change. These techniques received encouragement from the presumption prevalent in turn-of-the-century American culture that men and women were, in the main, rational beings who would behave predictably and reasonably when presented with "the facts." That kind of thinking informed much of the progressive educational movement, with its emphasis on the child's innate capacity for logical thought and moral growth, rather than his or her need for rote instruction and discipline imposed by others. It also, not incidentally, informed the Wilson administration's approach to war mobilization, depending as it did more on the cultivation of right thinking that on the compulsion of naked government power. It was scarcely accidental that the Committee on Public Information drew many of its key personnel from the ranks of the pre-war muckrakers.

Thus in many ways the shape of prewar America determined the contours of wartime policy. To cite one final but revealing example: the CPI undertook almost no propaganda work among American farmers, though they were concentrated heavily in those regions, especially in the Midwest, that were presumably most isolationist and therefore most in need of convincing about the war's purpose. The CPI focused its concern, rather, on nurturing the loyalty of urban immigrants whose alienness had been at issue long before 1917. No strict logic of the war's necessities dictated that policy emphasis. Quite the contrary. It can be explained only by recognizing that the society's prewar agenda persisted tenaciously beyond the declaration of war.

Permitting that persistence, of course, was the deeply underlying fact of America's far removal, in distance and in spirit, from the European battlefront. The unique dispensations of geography and history inoculated Americans, perhaps for the last time, against the afflictions that modern warfare brought to other peoples.

When Woodrow Wilson shattered ancient precedent and led his countrymen into a European war, they went about it in a typically American way, a way charted over three centuries of insulated experience that had molded the character of the republic. In the last analysis, they could do no other.

Chairman Trask's Introduction of Professor Rothenberg
Professor Gunther E. Rothenberg received his doctorate in 1958 at the University of Illinois. He taught at Illinois State University, Southern Illinois

University, and the University of New Mexico before joining the faculty of Purdue University in 1973, a wise choice given its technological affluence, where he is now professor of military history. A recipient of a Guggenheim fellowship, he is well known for extensive studies of European military history. Among his most recent works are *The Army of Francis Joseph*, in 1976, *The Art of Warfare in the Age of Napoleon*, 1977, and most recently, *Napoleon's Great Adversaries: The Archduke Charles and the Austrian Army*, published in this very year. His subject today is "The Collapse of the Central Powers in World War I: The Case of Austria-Hungary."

THE COLLAPSE OF THE CENTRAL POWERS IN WORLD WAR I: THE CASE OF AUSTRIA-HUNGARY

Gunther E. Rothenberg

When, in November 1918, revolutions toppled the governments of Austria-Hungary and Germany, their armies still held lines deep in enemy territory. Therefore a few historians, numerous politicians, and many senior officers have charged that "treason" and not military defeat were the real causes of collapse. This view, albeit one stressing national revolution, was promoted by many writers in the succession states, notably in Czechoslovakia and Yugoslavia, in order to show the effectiveness of their resistance to Habsburg rule. Yet, these claims are, at best, only partially true. There was a close correlation between the military events and, especially in Austria-Hungary, the cohesion of the empire. Morale and loyalty were reasonably high until 1916. After that date, when victory no longer seemed likely, these feelings declined and finally plummeted in the early summer of 1918 when, after the failure of the final offensives, the Central Powers no longer had offensive capabilities or reserves to block enemy thrusts. Only when the war was lost, and both the German and the Austro-Hungarian high commands demanded an immediate end to the fighting, did revolutions erupt to end the rule of the Hohenzollern and the Habsburg.

This does not mean that internal difficulties and dissensions had not contributed to the ultimate defeat. There were, however, very significant differences between Germany and Austria-Hungary. The populations of both empires suffered extremely high casualties, hunger, and deprivation. Social-political discontent also existed in both empires. But in Austria-Hungary the additional critical factor was the existence of separatist national movements. In fact, nationalism had already weakened, fatally in the opinion of some observers, the Habsburg Empire before the war. At that time, curiously, the major difficulties had been with the Magyars, one of the two dominant nationalities.

The Dual Monarchy of Austria-Hungary combined two sovereign states—Austria, "those lands and provinces represented in the Vienna *Reichsrat*," and Hungary, "lands of the Crown of St. Stephen" with a government and parliament in Budapest—in a personal union under a common ruler, Emperor of Austria and King of Hungary. As additional links there existed certain "joint" ministries—war, foreign affairs, and finance—all dependent on appropriations from the two parliaments. The basic formula for the joint budget had to be renegotiated every ten years.[1]

This arrangement, the *Ausgleich* of 1867, had conceded much to Hungary, but there remained dissatisfaction with the joint military establishment. Adoption of universal conscription in 1867-69 required that the masses of the people accept the essential legitimacy of the governments; to achieve this, the emperor had made military concessions to Hungary in 1868.[2] But these had not sufficed, and from 1886 to 1906 a bitter fight ensued in which the Magyars demanded both a larger national army as well as more control over the joint army (i.e., the imperial-royal army) considered vital to preserve the national and social structure of the kingdom. Although this dispute was eventually settled by another compromise, the Right starved the military budget and weakened the army.[3] In 1914 the Austro-Hungarian army was prepared for a "campaign against Serbia, but not for a major European war,"[4] and this situation, one historian charged, was largely owing to the "intransigence of politicians in Hungary."[5]

Moreover, Hungary's success in obtaining the rudiments of a national army fanned the aspirations of other national groups. And because the joint army accurately reflected the multi-national composition of the empire, including, for every 1,000 men, 267 Germans, 223 Magyars, 135 Czechs, 85 Poles, 81 Ruthenes, 67 Croats and Serbs, 64 Rumanians, 38 Slovaks, 26 Slovenes, and 14 Italians, Hungary's incipient national army caused great concern among senior officials, both military and civilian.[6] Many authorities believed that national conflicts made it impossible for Austria-Hungary to fight a major war. In 1895, Count Kasimir Badeni, Prime Minister of Austria, asserted that a "multi-national state cannot make war without endangering its existence."[7] In 1911, Conrad von Hötzendorf, Chief of the Imperial and Royal General Staff, wrote that "all preparations for war are in vain as long as our internal problems are not resolved."[8]

In particular, there were worries that national antagonisms would disrupt swift and orderly mobilization and that socialist workers might sabotage industry and communications. However, to the surprise of Austria's enemies and the relief of the Habsburg authorities, mobilization in July 1914 went without a hitch. Fears that the Magyars would rebel, a nightmare that had haunted senior officers, did not materialize.[9] On the contrary, Magyar regiments remained loyal to the end. Unsuspected reservoirs of dynastic loyalty emerged, even among the Czechs and Serbs. "The army," one scholar concluded, "on the whole remained an effective instrument until the summer of 1918."[10] And the same was true of the socialists. Until 1918, there were no strikes or sabotage, and while the limited industrial capacity of the empire could never furnish the range or quantity of weapons available to the major belligerents, it managed to reequip the army and provide for some twenty-five new divisions.[11]

But all this apparent cohesion could not conceal the major problems of the empire, which were so great that many historians, albeit in retrospect, believe that even victory would not have saved the Dual Monarchy.[12] The gravest problem was nationalism; the need for a fundamental revision of the *Ausgleich* to give greater voice to the various nationalities in both Austria and Hungary. Here, the mechanics of dualism did not make the outlook very hopeful. Hungary repeatedly used its leverage to block concessions to the other nationalities, and even during the war, Budapest, jealously guarding its status as a sovereign state, frequently pursued policies at odds with Vienna and the military high command, the *Armee Oberkommando* or *AOK*. The existence of two separate governments with different and often opposed policies constituted a complication unknown in Germany or, for that matter, in any of the other belligerent nations.

Any discussion of Austria-Hungary during World War I falls rather neatly into two periods—from 1914 to the death of Emperor Francis Joseph in November 1916; and from November 1916 to November 1918. The first period, which coincided with hopes for victory or a compromise peace, was relatively quiet on the home front. During the second period, however, hopes of victory and peace receded, contributing to greater unrest, strikes, small-scale revolts, and finally, revolution. Efforts at conciliation made by the new emperor, Charles I, can be regarded as well-meaning, but too late.

The outbreak of war gave greater powers to the military leadership. As with every continental power, the Austro-Hungarian constitutions provided for an extraordinary expansion of executive controls in the event of war. These laws culminated in the War Service Act of 1912, passed after stormy debates in the *Reichsrat;* similar legislation was enacted by the Budapest parliament. The War Service Act provided for the conscription of manpower and materials to be enforced by military courts if necessary—and for censorship and supervision of suspected subversive elements as well. Procedures for the actual implementation of these measures were worked out in a number of conferences between the military and concerned civilian authorities.[13]

With mobilization, the *AOK* (with Archduke Friedrich as titular head and Chief of Staff Conrad as actual decision maker) assumed command and control, and implemented the War Services Act. As a first step, the *AOK* established the *Kriegsüberwachungsamt,* the War Supervisory Office, headed by a senior general and including officers as well as officials from the interior, commerce, justice, and finance ministries.[14] There was no parliamentary opposition in Austria because in 1913 Prime Minister Count Stürgkh, facing obstruction mainly from a combination of Czech and socialist deputies, had prorogued parliament. In Hungary, where parliament continued to sit, Prime Minister Stephen Tisza refused to recognize the competence of the War Supervisory Office, though legislation for limited cooperation with the military in such matters as treason, and subversion was passed.[15]

In contrast to the situation in Germany, the Austrian military never eclipsed civilian government; indeed, the enforcement of war emergency powers led to conflicts with the Austrian civilian authorities. During the opening phases of the war, the army had introduced martial law within the zone of operations; that is, in Bukovina and Galicia, and in the fall of 1914, the *AOK* attempted to extend a modified form of military jurisdiction to Bohemia, Moravia, Silesia, and Croatia. At issue was not only authority, but also two conflicting philosophies regarding the treatment of civilian dissent. The soldiers favored a harsh line, whereas the civilians were more tolerant toward the political opposition. The civil governor of Bohemia, Baron Thun, stood firm against military incursions, supported in this stance by Stürgkh.[16] For that matter, some of the traditionalist senior officers did not like the idea of the army's entering politics; even General Bolfras, the head of the emperor's military chancery, grumbled that the *AOK* was overstepping its competence.[17] Therefore, when Conrad took his complaints directly to Francis Joseph, he had but limited success. Thun, considered too soft, was replaced by Count Coudenhove in March 1915, but there would be no military government in Bohemia.[18] As for Croatia, part of the Crown of St. Stephen, Tisza refused to listen to Conrad, and though he shared Conrad's aversion to Slavs, Tisza brutally repressed any political agitation there with Hungarian police.[19]

In May 1915, the exasperated military took the law into its own hands and arrested two leading Czech opposition politicans, Kramar and Scheiner. The military justified this action by pointing to the mass defection of the 28th Infantry, a regiment that in its home garrison in Prague had been the target of much socialist and nationalist agitation, and by the clear intention of Italy to enter the war against Austria-Hungary.[20] The emperor tolerated the arrests but refused to sanction military rule. Early that summer, however, a German-assisted offensive cleared the Russians out of Galicia and Bukovina, and a general was appointed to govern the liberated territories; but, even as the Italians were held in the southwest, Kramar and Scheiner remained in jail, despite repeated protests by Sturgh. Basically, however, the *AOK* had failed to supersede civilian government in Austria.[21]

Even so, the *AOK* had forced both the Austrian and the Hungarian governments to adopt a heavy-handed attitude, one certainly no worse than measures adopted in other states at war, but not likely to be taken as an argument for the good will of the Habsburg rulers. Yet during that first two years of the war, there was little evidence that even the most radical of the anti-Habsburg movements were seriously at work to disrupt the monarchy. The Magyars, though obstreperously insisting on further concessions, provided excellent troops; the pro-Russian movements among the Ruthenes in the Bukovina had not survived the Russian invasion, and the population had turned to the Ukrainian independence movement sponsored by Vienna and Berlin. The Croats were loyal, the Serbs cowed, and most Poles still looked to the Central Powers for a restoration of their state. The Rumanians, Slovenes, Slovaks, and Italians either still hoped for improvements under Habsburg rule or were too weak to count for much. As for the Czechs, they were most active abroad. At home, despite the many post-war claims and the rather misleading picture of the "good soldier Schwejk," the population cooperated with the authorities.[22] The all-important Skoda works and the rifle factories at Brunn (Brno) and elsewhere continued to turn out substantial quantities of war materiel.

To be sure, the Czechs were sullen, but they also were cautious: they were waiting for a clear signal about how the war would end. Abroad, Thomas Masaryk and his Czech National Council in Paris prepared for the contingency of an allied victory; at home, the Czechs were making plans based on cooperation with the authorities and eventual demands for Bohemian state rights.[23]

Thus, military events and the retention of the loyalties, or at least the acquiescence of the peoples to Habsburg rule, were closely related. By 1916 the military horizon was clouded. On the Isonzo, the front held firm against the Italians although a grandiose offensive from the Tyrol had failed. Serbia had been conquered and Rumania, which entered the war in August 1916, was soon overrun. The picture was worse on the Russian front where in June 1916, the Brusilov offensive had broken the Austro-Hungarian lines and reached the Carpathians. As for the German ally, there now was a bloody stalemate on the western front, but adequate forces were still available for future operations. In short, by 1916 defeat was by no means certain, but victory seemed equally elusive. And so was peace. The failure of the peace initiative by the Central Powers as well as through the mediation efforts of President Wilson had been bitter disappointments; moreover, in both Austria and Hungary the enormous casualty lists had shaken public morale. Food and fuel had become critically short on the home front; even the army was on short rations. Although the Entente had not yet made the break-up of the Habsburg Empire an official war aim, the unresolved conflicts both between the nations and between the nations and the crown, muted for two years, were becoming more pronounced.[24]

It was at this point that Emperor Francis Joseph died on 21 November 1916, in his eighty-seventh year of life and the sixty-eighth year of his reign. His death removed an important cohesive element and loosened national restraints. Even the Austrian socialists, long derided as "His Majesty's imperial and royal Socialists," became more militant. "Every class and every nationality," observed C. A. Macartney and A. W. Palmer, "was preparing for a struggle to enforce change or to resist it."[25]

The old emperor's successor was his nephew, Charles I, a well-meaning young man, twenty-nine years old, with humanitarian inclinations, but lacking experience and unable to stick with his decisions. Even worse, his outlook and that of his main advisors, aristocrats and some aging liberal professors, was unrealistic; he still believed, for instance, that some academic schemes of internal reconciliation would halt the disintegration of the Dual Monarchy.[26] From the outset, such hopes were limited by the Magyars who feared that Charles I might try to appease the Slavs at the expense of the dualistic system and the Kingdom of St. Stephen. To prevent such an occurrence, Tisza rushed to Vienna to assure the young monarch of Hungary's continued allegiance, and in return obtained the promise of an early coronation in Budapest, a promise which committed Charles to uphold dualism.[27] Thus from the outset, Hungary forestalled any change from above in the structure of the Dual Monarchy.

But the emperor's most urgent objective was to make peace. To this end he personally assumed command of the army, removed Conrad, and brought the *AOK* from its headquarters in Silesia back to the outskirts of Vienna. At the same time, between February and April 1917, he attempted to negotiate directly with the French government, using his brother-in-law, Prince Sixtus of Parma, then a Belgian officer, as intermediary. The attempt failed. Nothing Charles could offer would have been acceptable to Italy; major territorial concessions, a confession of military defeat, would have been opposed by the Germans in the *Reichsrat* and a majority in the Hungarian parliament. Such a move, moreover, could not remain hidden from Germany, but would eventually force the Habsburg Empire into even greater dependence on its powerful ally.[28] On the home front, Charles faced three interlocking problems: the food situation, Hungarian demands, and the ever-growing militancy of the nationalists. The food problem was the most pressing and immediate.

Since the 1880s Austria had to import a considerable portion of its food supply, ordinarily from Hungary, but, when the harvest there was poor, from Russia and Rumania. The Austrian grain harvest of 1914 had been below average, and the Russian invasion of Galicia had cut off one of the major sources of supply. Lack of manpower, draft animals, and fertilizers aggravated the situation; the harvests of 1915 and 1916 were even worse than that of 1914. By 1916 the situation in the Austrian urban and industrial centers, as well as in the less fertile areas such as Istria, Dalmatia, Moravia, and other places, had become difficult, even desperate. Bread rations were down to 200 grams a day; meat, milk, and fats were almost unobtainable. Hopes that the conquest of Rumania would alleviate shortages did not materialize.

It had been expected that with the existence of the Dual Monarchy at stake Hungary would do its best to help Austria, but nothing of the sort happened. On the contrary, in April 1915, Hungary closed its borders to the export of grain and would make deliveries only in return for Austrian goods or political concessions.[29]

In this near catastrophic situation, Emperor Charles appointed General Ottokar Landwehr to head a joint Austro-Hungarian food commission in the spring of 1917. But with negotiations for a revision of the *Ausgleich* in Hungary's favor then underway, the commission spent most of its time in bureaucratic squabbles—and very little additional food reached Austria.[30] To complicate the difficulty, the internal Austrian machinery was also unequal to the pressures of wartime. Rationing had been introduced in 1915, and when Hungary later closed its borders, the authorities took over the entire process of marketing, milling, baking, and distribution. But the critical food situation hardly improved. There was not enough food, and in Austria, as in other countries under pressure, the sense of civic duty and cooperation vanished. There was much profiteering and black market activity—and little effective action to halt it.[31] The *AOK* repeatedly urged draconic penalties, pointing out that a well functioning food supply was vital for the war effort. Military courts, it was urged, should try offenders. But the emperor would not listen. On the contrary, he relaxed military controls and granted amnesty to political offenders, including Kramar and others. The gesture had little effect, and some observers considered it counterproductive.[32] The hardships in Vienna, by far the largest city, had become so great by the fall of 1917 that one German journalist reported that for "the Viennese the war is finished."[33]

That fall a German-Austrian offensive defeated the Italians at Caporetto and revolution swept away the Russian government. The outlook for the Central Powers temporarily appeared much improved. But the entry of the United States into the war had changed the real balance of power beyond repair. President Wilson's Fourteen Points, published on January 8, 1918, called for the dismemberment of the Habsburg Empire and encouraged the nationalities to seek independence instead of the federal solution they might have accepted earlier. But negotiations with the new Bolshevik rulers of Russia at Brest-Litovsk dragged on. An *AOK* memorandum on the "Possibilities of our lasting through the Winter of 1917/18" recognized the critical situation. Replacements and weapons might last until spring, but, the writer of the memorandum declared, increased rations for industrial workers would be essential.[34]

Finally, in October 1917, Austria established an agency dealing with all aspects, civil as well as military, of food supply—the *Kriegsernährungsamt*. In January 1918, this agency found it necessary to reduce the bread ration in Austria to 165 grams a day. A few days before, the Brest Litovsk negotiations had broken down, leaving the impression that Berlin, abetted by Vienna, had sabotaged an opportunity for peace. The Austrian socialists, including the Czechs, had become more militant since the death of Francis Joseph, and under their leadership strikes involving over half a million workers broke out in and around Vienna and soon spread to Styria and Bohemia. The Vienna garrison appeared unreliable, the police powerless. The *AOK* had to respond with operations Mogul and Revolver, rushing seven reliable divisions from the front.[35]

In the end the strikes were broken by a mixture of coercion and political concessions—including the reopening of the negotiations with Russia. When these talks failed in February 1918, Austro-Hungarian forces participated in a limited offensive designed to occupy the Ukraine. "The most important task," Charles wired the commander, "is seizure and shipment of food, not only for the army but even more importantly, to alleviate distress at home."[36] Again, results were disappointing, and the episode merely served to estrange the Poles from the Habsburg state. Indeed, in the early months of 1918 there was considerable political activity—though little to comfort the emperor. There was a tentative renewal of the *Ausgleich* with Hungary, though on terms that would have made the kingdom completely independent. At the same time, a radical anti-Habsburg swing occurred among the Czechs and the South Slavs. Finally, there were politically motivated mutinies in the armed forces—a large-scale naval mutiny at Cattaro (Kotor) and minor, if worrisome, outbreaks among the army units. The authorities believed that some of the mutinies were led by indoctrinated POW's returned from Russia, but were unable to isolate these men.[37]

Against this background there was political maneuvering in Vienna, Budapest, Zagreb, Prague, and many other provincial capitals. In Vienna, Charles had reconvened the *Reichsrat* early in 1917. Few of its members wanted the dissolution of the monarchy, though the Czechs and South Slav delegates, uniting in national committees and parliamentary unions, demanded during May and June the reorganization of the empire along federal lines.[38] But this restructuring was blocked again by the Magyars. During the preliminary negotiations for a renewal of the *Ausgleich,* the Magyar ruling class in Hungary, which governed with a very limited franchise, remained adamantly opposed to Austria's having any voice regarding the future status of the nationalities in the kingdom. On this stand all Hungarian parties, including the opposition radicals led by Count Mihaly Karolyi, were united. Talks were suspended at the end of 1916 but resumed in February 1917. By this time Charles had undercut Tisza's position by opening negotiations with the opposition, and Tisza was forced to resign in the spring of 1917. His successor, Alexander Wejerle, was willing to make limited reforms in the franchise but tried to bolster his position by reopening the army issue. With the balance tilting against the Central Powers, Magyar politicians of all shades were determined to safeguard the future of the kingdom by a separate military establishment.[39]

Senior military officers opposed such proposals, but in the end a compromise was cobbled together. Hungary's share of the joint expenses was reduced, and its armed forces were to be completely separate and independent. In return, the agreement was to run for twenty years. When terms of the deal leaked out, an uproar arose in Vienna and Budapest. Habsburg loyalists objected because the agreement left the monarchy no more than a personal union, and Hungarian champions of independence were dissatisfied with the twenty-year term. In November 1917, the two prime ministers agreed not to seek ratification of the agreement but to allow the existing Compromise of 1907 to remain in force until the end of 1919.[40]

Taking their cue from the Magyars, the other nationalities became bolder in their demands. While still recognizing the monarchy, the Czechs called for a greater Bohemia, a Czecho-Slovak state including Bohemia, Moravia, and Silesia; the South Slavs called for the unification of the Ukraine. All these schemes, of course, were totally contrary to the wishes of the Magyars, who let it be known that any such developments would be countered by a total food embargo. Neither would the Germans, the largest national group, but not a majority, accept these proposals. So the situation deadlocked early in 1918.[41]

Of course, much of this controversy was a charade played out while the real decisions were made on the battlefield and in the allied capitals of the West. After considerable wavering, Italy and France committed themselves to national independence for the Czechs and South Slavs, a move that for the first time gained the self-exiled politicians a mass following at home. These commitments, however, were made in the wake of the last German offensive in the West and were primarily based on military rather than on political considerations.[42]

The Central Powers played their last military card in the summer offensives of 1918 and failed. Austria-Hungary opened an ill-conceived offensive across the Piave on June 6 that managed to gain a shallow bridgehead, but her troops were contained by superior forces and withdrew with heavy losses two weeks later.[43] Following the Piave offensive, the *AOK*, short on reserves, no longer possessed offensive capabilities. A few weeks later, the German drive in the West petered out; on August 8, British and French tank-supported forces tore a great hole in the German front. The German *Oberste Heeresleitung*, having assumed control over the entire conduct of the war in 1917, then decided that it had to be ended, and by September 1918, called on a hastily reconstituted civilian leadership to negotiate for an immediate armistice. The much maligned, belittled, and basically less effective Austro-Hungarian army and state had managed to hold on just as long as its more powerful ally.

But the end had come for the Habsburg. In Vienna, Emperor Charles made desperate attempts to save his inheritance. An appeal for peace on September 14 had gone unanswered; a second appeal on October 4 asked for an armistice on the basis of Wilson's Fourteen Points. That day Hungary unilaterally accepted Wilson's program, in effect endorsing the dissolution of the Dual Monarchy in an effort to safeguard the kingdom. But it was too late for that. On September 3, 1918, the United States had recognized Masaryk and his National Council as the *de facto* government of Czecho-Slovakia, the Serbs were making contact with figures in Laibach (Lubljana) and Agram (Zagreb), and in Cracow there was talk of a Polish state guaranteed by the Allies. National Councils, no longer looking toward autonomy but toward independence, were forming in the various provincial capitals. In a last-ditch effort to preserve a role for his dynasty, the emperor issued a manifesto on October 16 promising to reorganize Austria into a federal state. Of course, the manifesto did not apply to the South Slavs—even now Hungary refused to permit this; in fact, the manifesto promised not to "touch the integrity of the lands of the Crown of St. Stephen." It also was far too late to satisfy either the Czechs or the Poles.[44]

The manifesto did destroy the remaining legitimacy of the Habsburg Empire, absolving soldiers and civil servants from their oaths. When Wilson announced on October 21 that he no longer could accept mere autonomy, he merely recognized an established fact. By the end of October, in city after city—in Prague, Zagreb, Ljubljana, Budapest, Cracow, and even Vienna—the nations of the empire had abandoned the Habsburg and established functioning governments of their own. A few local commanders contemplated resistance, but Charles refused to sanction it. The Dual Monarchy had already disintegrated, but the Habsburg army continued to fight on Italian territory.[45] On October 24 a British-French-Italian offensive, Italy's much celebrated victory at Vittorio Veneto, opened. The Austro-Hungarian troops already had taken oaths of allegiance to their new governments, but resistance, nonetheless, continued until on November 3 an armistice was signed near Padua. At that, the last units, a corps in Albania, did not cease fighting until three days later.[46]

All that remained of the ancient monarchy was the emperor and his cabinet of elderly civil servants—a few rooms full of ghosts and papers. On November 11, 1918, Charles renounced all share in the government of Austria; two days later he did the same for Hungary, though he would not formally abdicate. He left Vienna for a retreat in the countryside and within weeks went into exile in Switzerland.[47]

There is, after all, no clear answer about the causes for the disintegration and defeat of the Dual Monarchy. Clearly the problems of the home front, antedating the war by many years, played a major role. At the same time, only military defeat could rally the opposition into a determined action. The most remarkable thing, however, was that an ancient empire, shackled by a complicated and unsteady political and social structure, had held out so long against a combination of internal tensions and a superior foreign enemy. In the end, a multi-national empire lacking strong central controls could not maintain itself in the world of the twentieth century. Whether its ultimate dissolution really brought advantages to the various nations and peoples may, in retrospect, be doubted.

Chairman Trask's Introduction of Professor Winkler

I now turn to our commentator. Professor Allan M. Winkler received his doctorate from Yale University in 1974. I might have said 1984 because he looks ten years younger than he really is. At any event, after receiving his degree he taught at Yale University and more recently joined the faculty at the University of Oregon. Like his colleagues he is full of honors for one so young, having received a Mellon fellowship and having served as a visiting professor at the University of Helsinki. The author of a series of articles on the problem of "demon rum" in the mid-nineteenth century, he went on to a work that qualifies him for his commentary this morning, namely a book in 1978 entitled *The Politics of Propaganda: The Office of War Information, 1940-1945*.

COMMENTARY

Allan M. Winkler

I'd like to follow Professor Rothenberg's lead and be suggestive rather than exhaustive and open the way up to you, the audience, for commentary on the papers and the issues that have been raised. I would like to single out a number of themes which have come through in the three papers we've heard this morning, to grapple with a number of points presented in those papers and then to tie up the session very briefly. First, a comment about the general theme of the symposium and this session in particular. I'd simply like to underscore from my perspective the absolute importance of studying the interplay between internal and external events, the impact of war on home front society, and its corollary, of course, the impact of society on what happens in terms of the outcome of the war. Some scholars have noted that time and again. Richard Ullman and Arno Mayer are among the most perceptive historians confronting that issue, but others have dealt with it too. I think the papers given today contribute towards an understanding of that vitally important theme and that's a step in favor for all of them. All three of the papers we've seen deal with that interplay to different degrees, arguing in different ways about how the interplay occurred.

Let me begin by talking about the connections raised by Dennis Showalter in the first paper dealing with British and German preparation for World War I. In a paper that Professor Showalter acknowledges assumed a life of its own, he focuses on "dichotomies" and "dissonances," as he terms them. He talks about militarism in both English and German society. He talks about the rhetoric of preparedness. He talks about a variety of forces impelling both of those nations toward ultimate intervention and involvement in a war when it occurred. On the other hand, in spite of the rhetoric, in spite of the militarism, in spite of those positive forces, he talks about a corollary negative force, fear of the war that might come, a hesitation to become totally involved, and he tries to understand how ultimate involvement in the war finally took place. I think it's important for me to raise a notion that he argues more aggressively in the written version of the paper that I received, one which he didn't deal with in as great detail in the spoken version, because I think it provides a kind of coherence to the argument.

The term "dissonance" arose a number of times in the presentation this morning. In the written version, Professor Showalter speaks much more specifically about the psychological term, "cognitive dissonance," as his analytical

67

framework, and uses it to pull the different strands together. That, I think, was his justification for making a bold and conceptual leap into an area that other historians might have left alone. Very briefly, he declares "cognitive dissonance" to mean "a perceived gap between beliefs and behavior, between what one thinks and what one does," and argues that people need to make accommodations to reconcile the different and sometimes contradictory notions which they may embrace. This, he argues, is what was going on in both Germany and Britain on the eve of World War I. My question, very briefly, is how useful is that construct, how important is it? What does it give us in terms of trying to understand the themes that have been raised. He has dealt a good deal with the problem of ambivalence in those two societies. Yet I must confess to an ambivalence of my own with regard to psychological model building. I studied psycho-history as a graduate student and I've read a good deal in the field. I firmly believe that William Langer was right when he urged historians to consider that area. And yet, I'd simply like to voice to you my questions about whether one can effectively apply micro-psychological notions, if they can be so called, to a broader field, a broader discipline, the study of society as a whole. I think I'll leave it at that. I simply would like to voice a skepticism that perhaps the audience can follow through on, as we move into the discussion in a few moments.

David Kennedy, in his paper "Rallying Americans for the War: 1917-1918," speaks of a different kind of ambivalence as he explores American society during its involvement in the war itself. He argues, on the one hand, that while there was an inexorable movement of the United States toward war, as indeed there was after 1914, there was firm resistance to that on the part of most other Americans at the same time, and he contends that the same ambivalence persisted and continued after the United States became involved in the war in April of 1917. I think he does an admirable job of describing the qualified character of American belligerency, of showing the limitation of the American war effort, and of helping us understand why the nation therefore had to resort to propaganda to draw Americans better into the fold. What do we make of this? It seems to me that in his argument Professor Kennedy is at his very best in his assessment and analysis of the tentativeness and ambivalence that was inherent in the American response to war. He is persuasive in showing the constraints of the American past, particularly as he focuses on the legacy of progressivism and the limits imposed on a real embracing of the notion of statism during the war years. That framework helps us understand the implications of that ambivalence for the larger effort in the war, for the larger external involvement of the United States, once it had chosen to join the struggle.

Gunther Rothenberg's presentation moves us beyond the period of mobilization into the war years themselves, particularly with regard to the Austro-Hungarian empire. Once again, questions of national unity, questions of national sentiment, and questions of ambivalence are present as well—perhaps to an even greater degree given the fragmented nature of Austria-Hungary during the First World War. In a crisp and well argued paper and presentation, as given off the cuff, Professor Rothenberg argues that mobilization at first went very easily. Despite the incredible centrifugal forces that might have been expected to have torn the empire apart in 1914, a cohesion was maintained until the war began to go more poorly, until after the death of the emperor. It was this conjunction of factors—the war itself, as well as the internal fragmentary forces—which ultimately culminated in the empire's falling apart. I think the real importance of this paper, and what I'd like to draw out of it most specifically, is that sense again of the crucial interplay of internal and external forces. We can follow the development of national aspirations, not in a vacuum but as they pertained to the question of unity, our theme for this morning, during the course of the war. We can explore the developments, parallel and often involving one another, as internal forces had an external effect, and vice versa, throughout the years of the war. That tension between the different nationalities is, in a way, very similar to a tension within American society, and a tension within British and German society at the same time. All of which leads us again to underscore the importance of dealing with all areas in the study of World War I.

The papers taken together give us a comparative focus on important questions in the First World War. One could and should pursue the notion of comparative study. At the very outset of his very brief essay in C. Vann Woodward's *Comparative Approach to American History,* Arno Mayer observes that not simply were there severe internal tensions in Britain and Germany, but in France and Italy as well. One simply needs to glance at the example of the Russian empire and the Soviet experiment that began in the war years to be aware of the same kind of tension there. By looking at several different kinds of societies, as we have this morning, we can begin to understand the broader dynamics of the war, the similarities and connections between events in different lands, as a monumental military struggle unfolded.

I'd like to close this morning by exploring one last theme, by providing one more perspective, particularly with regard to American involvement in World War I. I would like to offer a chronological perspective, to compare events of this time to those of the Second World War, to tie into some of the themes that John Blum spoke about so well last night, to give us a sense, again, of that interplay between internal and external forces and how we can assess it. A short while ago, David Kennedy spoke about the tensions in American society. There was hesitation over involvement in World War I, even though there was at the same time, of course, a mobilization on behalf of the struggle. Songs like "Over There" provide one small bit of evidence of that exuberance that some Americans felt. But the fragmentary forces were far more important. During World War II much the same thing was true. The nation was unified after the attack on Pearl Harbor. But as John Blum indicated last night, there were certainly severe fragmentary forces that were at work for the duration of the war. David Kennedy argued that propaganda in a society where there isn't a firm commitment or a firm consensus behind the issues and aims of the war is often necessary. And one can argue that much the same kind of thing held true in the second major war of the century, precisely because of the centrifugal forces that did exist then too. A propaganda network arose during the

Second World War, as the Office of War Information became the successor to the Committee on Public Information. One sees many of the same forces at work. One sees the same issues being developed. There were disagreements about the nature of the war, troubles and tensions at home. And all contributed to the same kind of effect in World War II that there was in World War I.

Very briefly, by way of conclusion, what do we make of all of this? I think one can argue that in the twentieth century, particularly in the last fifty years, total war, modern war, is absolutely impossible to consider without regard to the question of national unity. A society that hopes to wage war as it was waged in World War I and then in World War II and in the aftermath as well, has to be concerned with questions of national unity. That throws us once again to the question of the interplay of internal forces with foreign and military affairs, a question that I think we need to continue discussing, both this morning and for the duration of the conference as well.

DISCUSSION AND COMMENTS

David F. Trask (Moderator)

Robert J. Watson (Historical Division, Joint Chiefs of Staff): I would like to ask Professor Kennedy, you contrast the American approach to relying largely on propaganda with the European approach of relying on the authority of the state. But is it possible to show that the European governments thereby relied less on propaganda? My impression is that they drove the propaganda in just as hard as we did, while at the same time using state power. Is that correct?

Kennedy: The question is excellent. I wish I could give a proportionately excellent answer. What I think is clear is that in European belligerent states, coercive measures such as food rationing and so on were resorted to early on, or relatively early on, while they were willfully avoided in the United States. One could easily sustain the argument that there was a greater degree of centralization of state power, in the European belligerent governments. Whether or not there was, therefore, a proportionately lesser degree of reliance on propaganda in those European belligerent governments, I don't know. I would call upon some of our colleagues here with greater knowledge of those developments to comment on that.

Showalter: A useful reference in this context for the German experience certainly would be the two volume edition of *Militär und Innenpolitik* by Professor Wilhelm Deist who's up this afternoon. The thing that struck me working through that, and working through other literature on German military censorship in World War I, was the tremendous concern which the German army had for propaganda, both affirmative and negative. By that I mean that their concern with censoring Munich pacifist groups, for example, would match just about anything that you saw coming out of Bernard Baruch's office. I was struck more by the parallels between at least the German experience and some of the things that David Kennedy cited in his paper. Certainly the authority was there in the European states, but I think even the most Prussian of Prussian officers tended to remember Tallyrand's axiom that one can do everything with bayonets except sit on them. I mean they much preferred coercion and affirmation to a simple use of blind force, although there were, of course, some very serious debates between hard and soft liners. This is not something I've looked into in depth, but as far as Germany is concerned, I am impressed by the willingness of leaders there to use propaganda and to favor propaganda as opposed to simple force.

Kennedy: I think Arthur Marwick is here someplace. Maybe he would like to comment on activities in England.

Marwick: The problem in addressing this question to me is that I basically disagree with the whole thesis that David Kennedy was putting forward. However, he's right to get me to speak about Britain because that is where this polarity between America and Europe falls down since Britain, in fact, comes somewhere in between. The same reluctance in Britain to abandon laissez faire that David Kennedy was talking about in regards to the United States, was not inspired by a lack of enthusiasm of the war. It was simply that laissez faire principles were thought to be good principles and something which you could defend at the same time as, in the early stages, rather ineffectually waging war against Germany. What I find striking is the similarity between what happened in America and what happened in Britain. You simply went through the same processes a bit later than we did. I have to say David Kennedy, I think you're wrong to use your point about American propaganda having to be "hepped up" as an argument to demonstrate both a lack of enthusiasm for the war, and the war's limited impact on American society. If the war had gone on longer what would have happened in American society? I don't want to anticipate my own oration tomorrow morning, but what I will be arguing for is the tremendous similarity of the war's impact on all of the societies involved in it, regardless of whether they won or lost. It seems to me that the similarities are more important. I had to say all that to explain why I'm not answering the question which David Kennedy has put to me as directly as he would wish. I think the answer is that in Britain and the other European countries the propaganda effort was just as strong as it was in the United States. In Britain it was characterized by the extent to which, for a long period of the war, it was very much in the hands of voluntary agencies, very much the same sort of thing that was happening in the States. Well, perhaps there was some difference in that regard since there was no need in Britain for the government to force propaganda on people because the intellectuals, the newspaper editors, were all enthusiastic for the war anyway. At any rate, it only became necessary for the British government to step in in a big way in 1917 when food shortages began to affect the country. I would like to say to Professor Rothenberg that okay, it was worse in Austria-Hungary, but you also had the same kind of discontent there as in Britain in 1917, and that's when propaganda has to take over. I'm sorry for taking so much time, but in my view the answer to your question is that the propaganda effort in all of the European countries, including Great Britain, was just as strong as it was in the United States.

Kennedy: Can I add just one quick coda to that? I think we are not engaging the question properly if we just compare relative strengths to propaganda efforts. I think a closer examination would have to look at the content of the propaganda and the internal audiences to whom it was particularly directed. Part of my argument earlier this morning was that American propaganda showed a very strong coloration of items that were on the prewar agenda and had only marginal relationship to the war itself.

Robert Buchanan (Adams State College): Regarding the question which the commentator raised about Professor Showalter's analytical framework of cognitive dissonance, there is actual documentary evidence to support this argument. Between 1888 and 1914, Germany was not yet, really, a unified nation state. Various opposing groups, rooted in the new industrial technology, were competing with one another to establish a central government in Germany with a popular base of support. I have worked primarily with the naval interests in this struggle, and they were using war scares, armaments and armaments races to win domestic political battles. Domestic victories were often far more important than foreign war. If you move over to the other side, to the foreign office and the Kreuzzeitung working with Army interests, they were also doing this. So I think there is factual basis to support the argument set forth in Professor Showalter's paper.

Ron Cole (Center of Military History): I think Professor Kennedy made a very interesting case that the geographic and psychological distance between the United States and Europe made it necessary, after the war began, for Wilson, Baker, and Creel to drum up support for the war effort. But I have a couple of problems with this thesis. First of all, I think the widespread fear of radical labor and political movements in the United States stemmed in large part from what was going on in Europe, fear of Marxism and syndicalism to be specific. And this fear, which was quite extant in the American West in the period 1917-1918, led to extralegal, if not occasionally illegal, suppression of aliens and dissenters and the IWW [International Workers of the World], the subject which I am now researching. Such suppression, it seems to me, could only have been made possible because of a widespread public fear of European radicalism, and great concern that it might take root over here. That's my concern with your thesis. I would also like to know, if you can answer this, how President Wilson and George Creel reconciled a war for democratic principles abroad while they were so vigorously suppressing peaceful strikers at home?

Kennedy: I'm not sure I take the point of your first observation. But let me try to answer the second part of your statement. You are, of course, echoing a proposition that was certainly part of public discourse in 1917 and 1918: the apparent hypocrisy of a war to make the world safe for democracy in the face of egregiously anti-democratic procedures at home. I think I can do no better than to agree: it was hypocritical. I don't know if it was all together 100 percent consciously so, but certainly in practice there was a highly objectionable degree of contradiction between stated policy goals and actual behavior at home, no doubt about it.

Cole: I will be glad to clarify that first part of the comment. You made a big case of the fact that the separation of the United States from events three thousand miles away made people in the midwest, for example, feel as though they were not part of what was going on over there and why should they get involved. Yet, my study of the radicals and the use of federal military forces in the 1880s, 1890s, and 1900s shows that there was a very real concern, even in the midwest, as isolated as it was, for what was going on in Europe. So I maintain that there was very much concern about European matters, and that that had a great deal to do with the rise of a need to repress radicals in order to get economic solidarity or labor solidarity, in full support of the war effort.

Kennedy: If your point is that, as part of the attack on radical labor groups in the United States, the charge was made that they were somehow connected with, or took their inspiration from, European radical movements, yes, I agree. But I'm not sure how that could have translated directly into some kind of conscious notion that the war in Europe interested anti-labor groups in the United States. The war was just a very distant affair. For people in in the American West, where the greatest labor difficulties were experienced, the relationship to the European conflict was especially distant and tenuous. Smearing radical labor organizations with all kinds of charges, including one of being directed by the Second International and so on, was a very common tactic. But I think it was a rhetorical ploy more than it was something translated into a concrete sense of connection with the European war. It was only in the aftermath of the war that the issue of radicalism, as one of the war's products, really became focused as a conscious issue. There, I think, in the case of the Red Scare in 1919 and 1920, your point is much more cogent because there was a quite conscious idea that this Red wave that had washed up over the ruins of Europe was about to wash all the way across the Atlantic to the United States. But during the war itself, I don't think there is much evidence to support the existence of a fear of war-inspired radicalism.

Cole: I have seen some documentation to the effect that, at the beginning of the war, the connection made with Europe was that the IWW was really working somehow in connection with the Kaiser or the Austro-Hungarian empire.

Paul Koistinen (California State University, Northridge): I think we can tie in both what Professor Kennedy was saying and the comments made here about the IWW. First, quite clearly in terms of "establishment orientation," I think more than European radicalism, it was the war effort at home that was used as a "convenient" means "to get" the IWW. It is a pre-war condition that is involved. Second, the AF of L was in on the "getting" of the IWW. Again, a pre-war trend. So both the points that are being made, I think, have validity.

Dick Hallion (Air Force Flight Test Center): I'd just like to address a remark made by one of our commentators concerning mobilization activities in the field of industry and business, and by implication, in the field of science and technology, in the years prior to the First World War. I think if we take a look at the application of science and technology to military affairs in the years prior to the First World War, we see many times that the champions of these developments were less concerned with saving or restructuring their governments and more concerned with bringing an increased awareness to government of the potential of the new technologies. This is especially true in the case of hydrodynamics, which has direct application to naval architecture, and aerodynamics, which was becoming of increasing importance as the various European nations and the United States recognized the potential of the airplane. Particularly if we take a look at Germany and the activities at Gottingen University under the direction of Felix Klein in the years prior to the First World War, we see what one historian of science, Paul Hanle at the Smithsonian Institution, has referred to as the beginning of what we now commonly accept as the military-industrial complex. In Klein's championing of the work of such individuals as Ludwig Prandtl in the field of hydrodynamics, and Prandtl's disciple, Theodore von Karman who, of course, developed a very special and significant relationship after the First World War with the U.S. Army Air Corps, we really see the reshaping of a military approach to technology. It is also very interesting to note the way in which professional military engineers and members of the academic community in the United States, during the years prior to the First World War, started championing the cause of developing aeronautical research laboratories. As early as 1909 they pointed to the work in European laboratories—first, to the National Physical Laboratory in Great Britain and then to Prandtl's work in Germany—as having the potential to contribute meaningfully to the capabilities of the American military. This resulted in the emergence of the National Advisory Committee for Aeronautics in 1915. Dr. Alex Roland of Duke University is doing a very excellent job in researching early NACA history. I think in questions involving the mobilization spirit of various societies in the years prior to the First World War, we must consider these aspects, the aspects of science and technology, and also that they reflected largely social concerns. For example, in the United States, the drive for a National Aeronautical Laboratory system was directly connected to the ongoing progressive request for economy and efficiency. These, in fact, were the terms that were used over and over in congressional debates.

Trask: A very interesting comment.

Robin Higham (Kansas State University): I'd just like to make two quick comments. It seems to me one thing that nobody has looked at, although you have mentioned comparative history here, is that the United States before the First World War was really almost a multi-national society. This was the period right after our great immigration. That is something somebody might like to comment on. The other thing that people might like to comment on would be the impact of air attack on civil populations. Air attacks in World War I were just beginning to reach over the battlefield and get at the population on the homefront. It certainly had some rather dramatic effects in England with long-term consequences. There also were attacks on Germany, and, I believe, some attacks on Austria.

Kennedy: I'll just comment very briefly on the first point. I absolutely agree with you. I tried to allude briefly to the fact that the percentage of foreign-born in the American population at the time of World War I was in the 15 percent range, the highest it has ever been historically. And I think it is quite plausible, conceptually, to think of the United States as a multi-national society, more so than ever at that stage of its development. I would go further and say that is but one aspect of the general character of American society in the early twentieth century, something which was rapidly and rather painfully discovered as mobilization started to get under way. American society was just terribly disarticulated, it was not organized, it was not "centralizable,"—if I can coin that word—in a way that I think some people rather naively expected it to be. When the economic mobilizers went out and tried to find, for example, basic production figures, how many automobile manufacturers there were and so on, they found that basic statistical data like that just did not exist. Trade organizations didn't exist. The mechanisms by which impulse is put into a system from a central administrative point and through which it might travel efficiently to the periphery, weren't there.

Showalter: Relative to air attacks, certainly a lot of popular fiction, H.G. Wells', *War in the Air* and a lot of the material discussed by I.F. Clarke in *Voices Prophesying War,* projected the impact of air power. There is a book in the Colorado State University library up at Fort Collins that discusses battleships being sunk or crippled by aircraft which operated very much like the Harrier, aircraft that were able to take-off from ordinary converted merchantmen. The title escapes me, but the book was written in 1906. However, I think these sorts of apocalyptic concerns were of less importance to at least the German planners than what we might call the straight line projections they could make based on the destructive potential of weapons that they actually had at hand. They were less concerned with what was likely to happen because of aircraft or Zeppelins dropping bombs than they were with what was going to happen in the front lines. For example, a good deal of the heroic vitalism that characterized German infantry training before 1914 reflected the conviction that the ordinary rifleman was going to need every resource he had if he was going to make any kind of contribution in the few minutes before he was knocked out. They were expecting a massive casualty rate, a very high rate of destruction, and they could manage to accomplish that quite well without bringing in the potential of destruction from the air. There is a gap here, perhaps I might say a dissonance, between the writings of popular authors and the expectations of military planners, at least in Germany. I think England was about the same, although there are people here who are better equipped to speak to that.

CONCLUDING REMARKS

David F. Trask

May I now, in the interest of having a happy ending, bring this session to a conclusion with a very few brief remarks I've been asked to make that might help us understand where we are now and where we might go this afternoon. Here again I begin with another unsurprising generalization: historians, in dealing with past processes, concern themselves with two grand categories. One of those categories is change. The other is continuity. I now turn to the study of twentieth century American history by American historians. There is a great dichotomy in that study. There is a group of historians whose work is confined largely to the study of domestic events. They represent by far the larger group. They have concentrated primarily on the study of peacetime America. Only recently have people from this group began to give serious attention, for reasons I think are quite evident, to the war period of American history in the twentieth century. This group, then, is drawn to continuity. David Kennedy's study here is only the latest example of the strong, dominating tendency of people who approach the American twentieth century from the domestic point of view to emphasize elements of continuity. The other side of the treatment of American history by American historians in the twentieth century is that which comes from those studying military and international questions. That group, highly concerned with warfare as such, emphasizes change. That is to say, what alters as against what continues. This is, I think, where we are now in terms of historiographical approaches to this field. It is clear that a whole new agenda of concern with regard to home fronts has arisen, and that it is going to be a most important subject for the rest of the twentieth century. David Kennedy, for example, is going to attempt in his next work to cope with this question once more. What I'm trying to suggest here is an endorsement of the statement Professor Winkler made, that we must think both in terms of continuity and change, and must approach these questions both from an internal, or domestic, and an external, or international, point of view. We must realize that this is indeed a great and important question. And that's why this conference is so much needed and why it can be so helpful in sorting out the future. Let me give one example of a recent study which, in fact, approaches questions of the sort we are talking about from this dual point of view. I refer to Colonel James Abrahamson's book, *America Arms For a New Century,* which, if you are looking for a beginning guidebook on how to do it, I strongly recommend.

SESSION II

THE SINEWS OF WAR: ECONOMIC MOBILIZATION IN WORLD WAR II

THE SINEWS OF WAR: ECONOMIC MOBILIZATION IN WORLD WAR II

INTRODUCTORY REMARKS

Russell F. Weigley

As my friend David Trask reminded us this morning, some of us old timer military historians have difficulty learning new things. But the Air Force Academy tries to help us out through its military history symposia which have explored one after another aspect of the "new" military history, the military history that seeks to place the history of armed forces in its social and political setting. But even the Air Force Academy has been somewhat chary of taking up the economic dimensions of military history. This afternoon's program on economic mobilization in Germany and the United States seeks to remedy that deficiency so that again, the Air Force Academy, through these symposia, is educating all of us.

I suspect that one of the reasons why even the new socially broad military history has been slow to explore the economic relationships of military history is because economic history is so specialized a subject with such specialized problems. Probably economic history is even more isolated from the main stream of the historical profession than military history, which is saying a great deal. As we will find out, though, from this afternoon's papers, the slowness of military historians to deal with the economic dimensions of their subject is somewhat mitigated by the fact that before and during the Second World War, in Germany and the United States at least, the armed forces themselves were slow to relate their military needs and even their industrial mobilization needs to the economies of their countries at large. Instead, the military both in Germany and the United States were content for a long time with ad hoc, short run, sorts of expedient relationships with business and the economy, hoping that such ad hoc relationships would suffice. We are going to find that not only in that way, but in another respect as well, the German and American economic mobilization experiences in the Second World War were similar to each other. Both Germany and the United States were slow to invoke all their economic strength for the waging of the Second World War. But although both were slow to do so at the outset of the war, we shall find that the two experiences diverged, and our two papers this afternoon will diverge, in that Germany much more than the United States eventually did enlist its economy in the war effort. This despite the fact that we Americans have been inclined since the Second World War to take pride in so-called miracles of productivity that we've come to imagine our economy accomplished during the Second World War. One of our papers this afternoon will show how much those miracles of productivity were a myth. The other paper, on Germany, will show something of a contrast.

Even though, as I stated a few minutes ago, military historians may have a kind of excuse for a relative neglect of the economic dimensions of our study, I think we'll find too as the afternoon goes on that the excuse is not adequate, that linking economic and military history offers a means to illuminate all sorts of problems of military history. Not only that, but I think we'll find this afternoon that linking economic and military history offers us some illuminating insights into the whole history of great powers in the modern world and particularly into the present economic predicaments of the United States that perhaps even threaten its superpower status in the modern world.

Chairman Weigley's Introduction of Wilhelm Deist

With those general observations, let me proceed to introduce the first of this afternoon's speakers. Wilhelm Deist is a member of the Militärgeschichtliches Forschungsamt in Freiburg, the Federal Republic of Germany. He studied at the University of Tübingen and received his Ph.D. from the University of Freiburg. He is co-editor of the *Militär-Geschichtliche Miteilungen* and the *War and Society Newsletter*. His publications are numerous. They include a work that was referred to in the discussions this morning on the First World War, *Militär und Innenpolitik im Weltkrieg, 1914-1918*. He is also the author of *Flotten Politik und Flotten Propaganda*, a book which concerns the German Naval Information Office from 1897 to 1914. In English he has written *The Wehrmacht and German Rearmament*. I'm happy to introduce and to welcome to the United States, Wilhelm Deist.

SOME ASPECTS OF GERMAN MOBILIZATION UNDER THE NATIONAL SOCIALIST REGIME

Wilhelm Deist

On the morning of September 1, 1939, as Hitler made his way from the Reichskanzlei to the Reichstag, he heard virtually no applause from the onlookers gathered behind the closed rows of SA men. The correspondent of the *Neue Züricher Zeitung* observed only a small row of spectators who, according to the Swedish businessman, Birger Dahlerus, watched the events without expression. This scene in Berlin mirrored the reaction of great parts of the German population to news that war had begun. The many reports describing popular feeling in those days suggest a frame of mind ranging from apprehension and depressed silence to gloom and uneasiness. In any case, this reaction stands in clear contrast to the overwhelming national enthusiasm with which Germans of almost all classes had greeted the declaration of war in August 1914. On the other hand, one must note that—again in contrast to events during the First World War—domestic unrest, industrial actions, and mutinies comparable to those of 1917-1918 did not occur during the course of the Second World War, despite its much greater psychological impact on the German population. However sharply popular feelings in September 1939 contrasted with those of August 1914, there were parallels in Germany's economic situation at the outset of both World Wars I and II. Consider the comparative analysis contained in an Army High Command (*OKH*) report of April 1939:

> The present situation resulting from steel shortages is to a certain extent comparable with that prior to the World War. At that time the three army corps which would have helped decide the war quickly in its first year did not exist because of parliament's refusal to grant funds. Today, the army is refused the quantities of steel needed to equip it with modern offensive weapons. The results could be comparable to that of 1914.

General Georg Thomas, Chief of the Wehrmacht's economic section, shared these views and criticized both Hitler and the regime's most powerful political and military representatives for refusing to implement more than an "improvised economic mobilization." It was largely because of this improvisation, reinforced in its negative effects by the inefficiency of the bureaucratic steering system, that the Wehrmacht faced an ammunition shortage in late autumn 1939—exactly as had occurred in the First World War. The parallels between crises in the war economy in the first stages of both wars are even more striking when one takes into account the military literature of the inter-war years. This literature had stressed—as a result of the First World War—the decisive importance of economic factors in modern industrialized warfare.

A comparison of a few aspects of the early mobilization periods in both wars is especially interesting, because in many respects the so-called "lessons" of the First World War determined German rearmament from 1928 onwards. The first industrialized war on European soil had added new dimensions to the concept of "war." Mobilization of the economy and of public opinion had become major factors in armed conflict. It thus was not surprising that leading Reichswehr officers, men who had studied the problems of national defense intensively, came to realize that a comprehensive mobilization of Germany's material, human, and moral resources had to be the basis of any future war. Furthermore, these officers realized that one must plan and prepare in the greatest detail in peacetime if one wished to achieve a total mobilization early in any war. But the Versailles Treaty, which had been incorporated into German law, and which determined the size and structure of the Reichswehr down to the details of equipment, prohibited any preparation for mobilization.

Historical research on the Reichswehr until now has stressed the veiled and illegal connections of the Reichswehr leadership to right-wing paramilitary organizations in the Weimar Republic and the political importance of those connections. In my opinion, one must also note as equally or even more important the first steps taken in 1927 towards an initially modest but systematically planned, comprehensive rearmament program. Such a rearmament program could only be implemented with the cooperation of industry and the republican government itself. The connections between industry and the military had never been completely severed. Those connections took on even greater economic significance during the years of the Great Depression and were highly valued by German industrialists, the very limited financial resources of the Reichswehr notwithstanding. As rearmament depended on regular government financial support, the vital question was whether the Reichswehr leadership could succeed in obtaining the governmental approval for this illegal program. In October 1928 the cabinet of Reich Chancellor Hermann Muller, a Social Democrat, expressed its approval. Henceforth the Reichstag's constitutional right to control the budget was by-passed by means of executive decrees. Not surprisingly, since it had to put up with only minimal formal supervision, the Reichswehr expressed a general willingness to cooperate with the civilian executive. What Carsten has called a jump to the Left by the Reichswehr was, in fact, only an unpremeditated by-product of the Reichswehr's rearmament policy.*

In its rearmament programs for the periods 1928-1932 and 1933-1938, the Reichswehr sought to modernize and modestly increase its weaponry and equipment. More important, the programs also were aimed at facilitating a switch to

---

*Ed note: The author is referring to the conclusions reached by Professor F. L. Carsten in his *The Reichswehr and Politics, 1918-1933* (Oxford, 1966).

mass-production of weapons and equipment in case of war. This led to a variety of measures and demands which in some portions of industry introduced state intervention in peacetime. Included in this respect were certain precautionary measures to assure the supply of raw materials, and the placement of orders which influenced the infrastructure of both the state and the national economy. These were areas that required careful attention and detailed planning in peacetime in order to lay a basis for efficient mobilization during the first decisive weeks of a future war.

Thus the lessons of the First World War strengthened tendencies towards mobilization of important sections of the nation's industrial base. These tendencies existed not only in the economic field. In 1926 the Minister of Transport, Dr. Rudolf Krohne, a member of Gustav Stresemann's *Deutsche Volkspartei* categorically stated in a memorandum: "There is no field, which is not to be used by the state for the preparation and implementation of a future war." In fact, under the influence of General Kurt von Schleicher as Chancellor and Reichswehr Minister, Germany was slowly evolving towards a military state even before the end of the Weimar Republic.

In one field the Reichswehr nevertheless ran into nearly insurmountable barriers. All the military, organizational, economic, and technical measures and plans for a gradual rearmament designed to restore Germany's European position would be decisively hampered if the integration of the entire population into this military and political program foundered. The traumatic experience of the 1918 breakdown and collapse of the Kaiser's army was an ever disquieting warning to the Reichswehr. A memorandum of March 1924 discussing the "psychological preparation of the people for war" is an indication of the importance of this issue to the Reichswehr. Citing the supposed failure of republican governments and parties to provide support, the memorandum demanded that the Reichswehr, with the help of the right wing paramilitary organizations, institute a program of systematic propaganda to strengthen the popular will to arm. In spite of various initiatives and some successes, until January 1933 the Reichswehr never received much sympathy from the Left which, during the pre-Hitler years, formed a sizeable percentage of the political spectrum. With Hitler's appointment as Reich Chancellor and the seizure of power by the National Socialists, the basic political premises changed in favour of an effective Reichswehr propaganda campaign to strengthen the will to arm, while at the same time the Reichswehr's position within the state and society received a new definition.

This change was underlined to the generals on February 3, 1933 when Hitler spoke to them in the home of the Commander-in-Chief of the Army about the fundamental pattern of his future policy. At the outset Hitler announced that "regaining political power" was his sole aim, and that this depended upon a complete change of existing domestic political circumstances. More especially, he emphasized a "strengthening of the will to arm" employing all possible means. Using several dramatic examples, Hitler enlarged on his plans for "rearming," and promised that he would overcome the politically motivated opposition to the organization of national defense, opposition which the Reichswehr previously had been unable to overcome. He asserted that the Reichswehr, as it then existed, was "the most important institution in the State." Both this statement and his program of "rearming" provided a firm basis of cooperation between the Reichswehr and Hitler's National Socialist movement. For the first time the opportunity seemed ripe for organizing Germany's material and human resources to meet military needs and thus to create—in accordance with the perceived lessons of the First World War—the decisive preconditions for an effective national defence. Hitler expressed this incisively when he argued that success at the disarmament conference in Geneva would be "pointless . . . if a nation (did not) possess the will to arm." From the generals' viewpoint, the fact that the Reichswehr would be more firmly anchored in the population under the new regime and that conscription would expand the small professional army was of decisive importance. An atmosphere of optimism now emerged. The early February 1933 dictum of Colonel Walter von Reichenau which held that the Wehrmacht had "never before" been "so identical with the State," was in fact wishful thinking, but it nevertheless described the exact goal that the army hoped its alliance with the new regime would achieve.

The program to strengthen the will to arm was pushed forward by the National Socialist state and the Wehrmacht with all possible means and considerable success. After the elimination of the political opposition and the *Gleichschaltung* [i.e., "coordination"] of all public and private organizations, the new Propaganda Minister, Josef Goebbels', and the *OKW* made every effort to enhance the relationship between the German people and the Wehrmacht. The tactics of Goebbels' propaganda machine are well known, and they were all fully employed in this case. The aim and content of the propaganda appeared as early as Hitler's speech on February 3, 1933: "Strengthening of the will to arm employing all possible means. . . . Youth, the population as a whole, to be recruited to the belief that only a struggle can save us and that everything must be subordinated to this belief. . . . Strict authoritarian government. Removal of the cancer of democracy." The propaganda, of course, resulted from Hitler's social Darwinistic ideology which extolled military virtues and emphasized pride in German military traditions. Slowly but surely the growing power of the new Wehrmacht became the basic theme of propaganda, with Goering's Luftwaffe especially highlighted. The Wehrmacht's march into the Rhineland in 1936, its maneuvers in 1937, and above all, the army's occupation of Austria in 1938, were successful tools to rally popular sentiment to the Wehrmacht. In comparison with the Reichswehr, the Wehrmacht thus gained a broad and solid basis of public support during the peacetime period of rearmament.

Nevertheless, Hitler and his propaganda chief faced a dilemma. Hitler's social Darwinistic conviction that a continuing struggle for survival determined not only the life of individuals, but also the development of nations, was a basic axiom of his policy, which thus is to be understood as a policy of preparing for war. In his speech to the Reichswehr's generals in 1933, Hitler expressed this viewpoint explicitly. Yet he also added that the period of the Wehrmacht's build-up would be extremely dangerous because of the external risks. This phase, he added, would show whether France really possessed "statesmen." If this were the case then it was to be expected that France would regard German rearmament as a reason for "attacking us (probably with [the help of] their allies in the east)." But Hitler was correctly convinced that in the first phase of rearmament, the risks of isolation or of sanctions, whether political or economic in nature, could be circumvented by skillful diplomacy. Hitler avoided direct confrontation with France and Great Britain in favour of a policy of deception as outlined in his "Peace Speech" of May 17, 1933.

In general Hitler succeeded in deceiving foreign powers with the help of a skillfully presented peace propaganda, but these tactics had highly undesirable domestic consequences. During the Czech crisis in 1938 there was virtually no enthusiasm among the German population for a military adventure. The opposite was true. Himmler's SS (Security Headquarters) described popular feelings and attitudes with words like "depressed" and "in a psychosis." The peaceful solution of the crisis at Munich in late September 1938 was greeted not only with relief but enthusiastic approval. Hitler naturally was aware that such sentiments were inconsistent with his political and military aims and thus he mounted a major effort to influence popular attitudes. On November 10, 1938 he declared to approximately 400 German journalists and publishers:

> Circumstances have forced me to talk for ten years only about peace. . . . It is obvious that such peace-propaganda employed in the recent past has had a pernicious impact. It can easily make the people think that today's regime has identified itself with a decision and will to preserve peace under all circumstances. . . . It was therefore necessary to transform the German people psychologically and to make clear that there are policies and national goals that can only be achieved through force. To effect this change we must not only propagate power as such, but to explain events in foreign policy to the German population in a way that our people's inward conception makes them long for force and power.

In the course of this secret speech Hitler spoke of the "pacifistical record" which now had to be "scrapped." Propaganda directions and strategy, of course, could be altered easily and quickly, but in the summer of 1939 Hitler was to learn that it was not so easy to achieve the desired results. The national enthusiasm of August 1914 could not be recreated even with the aid of Goebbels' propaganda machine.

The regime had doubtlessly succeeded in organizing the population into a militarized community *(Volksgemeinschaft)* and in inculcating the population more or less with a very heterogeneous National Socialist ideology. The regime had made the masses pliable, sometimes by intimidation, and if necessary, by terror. However, in spite of enthusiastic approval of Hitler's performance in foreign policy, and for his success in overcoming the severe economic crisis, he could not succeed in creating enthusiasm for war. Thus the propaganda mobilization, the "psychological preparation of the people for war," failed. For many Germans the misery and the horror of the First World War were too recent a memory, and the danger to their modest living standards too obvious, to allow them to follow Hitler's war policy with enthusiasm.

In spite of this relative failure of the regime's propaganda, one can assert that the Wehrmacht, with the help of the National Socialist movement, had broken free of its isolation and was, as a result, regarded with sympathy by nearly the whole population. What a difference from the situation in the winter of 1932-33.

In regard to economic preparation for war, the Reichswehr had thought through the basic premises of mobilization even before the seizure of power by the National Socialists. Accordingly, one would expect that rearmament would be executed in the way the Reichswehr had already begun; i.e., by comprehensive rearmament programs that tried to balance military and economic factors, and attempted to adjust demands by the Wehrmacht's three services. In a cabinet meeting of February 8, 1933, Hitler demanded that all measures concerned with creating employment—the most important political task considering six million unemployed—should be closely coordinated with the idea of "rearming" the nation, i.e., with rearmament itself. Hitler held firmly to this principle throughout the following years and did in fact regard the economy purely as an instrument for creating the military forces necessary for his expanded policy. A consequence of Hitler's decision was a marked acceleration in the implementation of the Reichswehr's Second Armaments Program. The program, which originally was targeted for completion on March 31, 1938, in fact was accomplished by the end of 1934.

The officers who had been working on the rearmament program since 1927 believed that what was important for the Wehrmacht's "operational readiness" was not the number of weapons available by a particular date, but rather the availability of raw materials and the capacity of industry to reach a wartime level of production in the shortest possible time. In particular, General Thomas, later the head of the War Economic Staff, endeavored to use the opportunity created by Hitler's basic policy decisions to propose comprehensive economic preparation for war. Given the complexity of economic affairs and the technical problems of industrial production, the economic program devised by Thomas was a very ambitious one. Thomas initially received support from the Reich Defense Minister Werner von Blomberg, especially on questions of organization. Ironically, it was not the intrinsic economic problems involved which were responsible for the failure to organize the economy and armaments production according to "defense economy" criteria. The failure turned instead on the refusal of the services themselves to subordinate their own armament programs to the authority and direction of a single Wehrmacht administrative department. Thus from the outset Thomas never managed to exert a decisive influence on essential decisions regarding armaments.

Severe opposition to unified direction of rearmament came in particular from the newly founded Luftwaffe. Secretary of State for Air Erhard Milch worked in close cooperation with the President of the Reichsbank, Hjalmar Schacht, on creating a financial basis for air force armament and also on the successful expansion of the industrial base for aircraft production. But Milch, with the backing of the number two man in the Nazi regime, Goering, energetically opposed all attempts by the Wehrmacht and the army leadership to guide air force armament into a comprehensive program. In fact, Milch succeeded in further extending his own sphere of autonomy by having his long-term armament program of July 1934 approved by Hitler personally. In contrast, the Commander-in-Chief of the Wehrmacht, Blomberg, played a much more subordinate role.

The Navy, like the Luftwaffe, sailed on unimpeded in the lee of these disagreements. It also insisted on the right to carry out its own armament measures independently. From the outset, Grand Admiral Erich Raeder sought to establish personal contact with Hitler in the interests of his own armament plans. At the end of June 1934, by completely by-passing the Wehrmacht's Commander-in-Chief, Raeder extracted Hitler's approval for considerable changes in the planning of ship construction. The result of this state of affairs was that Blomberg's attempt to organize a unified build-up and expansion of the armed forces had failed utterly by as early as the fall of 1934. The individual chaotic expansion of the services thus not only resulted from unresolved organizational problems, but was also a consequence of the military's incapacity to take due account of the relationship between the economy and rearmament, a relationship which had radically altered since the First World War.

Since rearmament held absolute priority within the framework of Hitler's policy, one might imagine that the Füehrer himself would have coordinated Wehrmacht rearmament. Apart from occasional and very general comments, Hitler, as far as is known, never issued any directive dealing with overall Wehrmacht rearmament prior to the war. Nor, it seems, did he suggest that there were limits beyond which the economy could not go, a stance which would have forced at least a loose coordination of armaments measures between the individual services. Rather, decisions on armament programs seem to have been reached with reference only to those aspects relevant to the individual service concerned. Moreover, Hitler considerably increased inter-service competition for resources by demanding that armament be accelerated and by continually establishing new institutions with responsibilities in the field of armament. The fact that this approach to deciding armament questions continued unchanged after Hitler assumed supreme command of the Wehrmacht early in February 1938, shows how little the expansion of the individual services was influenced by problems in the structure of the Wehrmacht command.

Thus the extent and structure of German rearmament was defined solely by the armament programs of the individual services. The only factors that limited this otherwise unrestricted process were the marked shortage of raw materials that first appeared in the second half of 1936, the more general economic problems evident from 1937 onwards, and finally the growing financial crisis after the end of the Mefo-Bills early in 1938. In short, from 1936-1937 onwards even the concept of "armament in breadth" (as opposed to "armament in depth") had reached the limits of economic possibility. The most acceptable solution to the problem thereafter seemed to be short predatory wars for the benefit of the armaments economy. The reversal of the relationship of means to ends was almost total. It was no longer only necessary to rearm in order to wage war but also necessary to have war in order to continue rearming.

In sum, German rearmament was not, as some still believe, a comprehensively planned, systematically organized, and centrally directed process. Moreover, Hitler had not, as he claimed in his speech to the Reichstag of September 1, 1939, worked for six years "to build-up the German Wehrmacht." On the contrary, as Reich Chancellor and Commander-in-Chief of the Wehrmacht, he had neglected the idea of a unified Wehrmacht and promoted the uncoordinated expansion of the separate services. Thus, General Thomas, who always had favored armament in depth, was quite correct when he stated there was only an improvised economic mobilization at the beginning of the war. The process of mobilization in the German Reich—economic as well as psychological mobilization—had started as early as 1933. Ironically, by 1939 it had developed to such an extent along the lines described above as to preclude a total mobilization corresponding to the so-called "lessons" of the First World War. Total mobilization was attempted under vastly changed premises and conditions only in 1942-1943 when defeat loomed as a real possibility.

Chairman Weigley's Introduction of Professor Koistinen

Our next speaker is Professor Paul Koistinen, professor of history at California State University at Northridge. Professor Koistinen is probably our leading authority on the twentieth century origins of the military-industrial complex in the United States and on this country's military-economic mobilization for the world wars. His Berkeley dissertation was published in 1979 under the title, *The Hammer and the Sword: Labor, the Military, and Industrial Mobilization, 1920-1945*. He has also published numerous articles in many journals; a number of these were brought together under the title, *The Military-Industrial Complex: A Historical Perspective*, published in 1980. I should add too that, unfortunately, until the proceedings of this symposium are published, you will miss one of the strongest parts of Professor Koistinen's paper: his footnotes. Professor Koistinen himself, early in his footnotes, describes his citations and references as comprising a sort of subpaper. They are indeed extremely rich. By all means, buy the proceedings volume when it is published in order to share in the bibliographical references and the general wealth of information in the notes which accompany this paper.

WARFARE AND POWER RELATIONS IN AMERICA: MOBILIZING THE WORLD WAR II ECONOMY

Paul A. C. Koistinen

I

Scholars are increasingly turning to a form of determinism in order to explain economic mobilization for World War II. "Necessitarian" conditions—a term coined or made prominent by John Morton Blum—it is claimed, shaped the wartime effort. The nation's leadership, the fighting forces, and the general population all gave primacy to winning the war as quickly as possible and favored the most practical means for achieving that goal.

Necessity dictated that "available institutions" be used in order to harness the economy for hostilities. Those institutions ultimately produced a rough sort of equilibrium through the countervailing power of big government, big business, big labor, and big agriculture. In looking to the postwar world, modest, not grandiose, views prevailed. Security against more wars abroad and more depressions at home was what counted. Throughout the war years, leaders and led alike believed that for the interim, reform—the New Deal's quest for a better, more just, and a more equitable society at home—had to be shelved in order to achieve most effectively and efficiently the primary goals of victory and security. But not a great deal of choice at any level actually existed. "The managers of the war did not use the war . . . to achieve set purposes," Blum observes. "The war used them. They accepted the necessities that then prevailed."[1]

The necessity concept is inadequate for explaining wartime economic mobilization for two basic reasons. First, it provides ready-made explanations about exceptionally complex events. *Why* events occurred is already known. Scholars need only relate *what* has taken place. Second, the necessity interpretation assumes that agreement on ends produced agreement on means. No doubt the vast majority of Americans accepted victory and security as primary goals during the war. But they divided acrimoniously along interest group and class lines about how those aims could best be achieved.

When the focus is kept on means, not ends, much of the necessity thesis appears questionable. At the root of the intense and ongoing conflict of the Second World War were matters of power. Elitist, not pluralist, modes of economic mobilization emerged in which a collection of awkward, makeshift agencies made decisions in an often haphazard fashion. A more rational form of full-scale planning was practically impossible to achieve under elitist power patterns because too many interest groups were excluded. The clumsy mobilization structure got the job done, but only adequately, not exceptionally, so. What that system could not do was satisfy the population's almost desperate quest for security by preparing the economy satisfactorily for the risky transition from war to peace.

What occurred during World War II was neither inevitable nor purposeless. The President and his chief assistants, by selecting the wartime managers and by making certain decisions and not others, set the general outlines for economic mobilization. From the outset of war, they had real options. The most important involved the military. Practically overnight it was transformed from a relatively weak institution into a power center of enormous strength. If so inclined, Roosevelt could have used the armed services as vehicles for facilitating significant change. Instead, he proceeded in a way which ensured that the military acted as an agent for supporting the nation's power elite.

The following pages will explore the themes briefly outlined above. First, the evolution of the mobilization system from 1940 to 1945 will be traced. The dominant trend was the constant narrowing of the decision-making base until by 1943 the giant corporations and the military services were fully in control of the mobilization apparatus. Second, America's economic performance during the war will be compared with its prewar potential and with the accomplishments of other belligerents in order to point out that what occurred at home was not extraordinary. Third, the possibilities of comprehensive planning under a war council, including the now powerful armed services, will be examined. Finally, in the conclusion, Roosevelt will be characterized as a leader who deliberately obscured the extremely sensitive matters of power in a corporate capitalist system, instead of simply as a sloppy administrator or as an executive intent upon keeping control in his own hands by consistently dividing responsibility and authority among his subordinates.

II

The process of mobilizing the economy for war went through roughly three phases. First, between 1940 and 1942, weak mobilization agencies and a recalcitrant corporate community forced the President to rely upon New Dealers, labor representatives, and others to prod the civilian structure to perform. The armed services played an ambiguous role of both advancing and retarding the economic mobilization process. Then, with war declared, economic mobilization began in earnest with a potentially strong civilian agency, but a weak leader at the top. Eighteen months of extended and bitter bureaucratic battle ensued before control over production became centered in the civilian mobilization administration through an alliance of corporate leaders and the military. Last, a virtual assistant president for domestic events was appointed in mid-1943 to hold a shaky mobilization apparatus together until the war's end.[2]

Economic mobilization got off to a slow and divisive start in the first phase. The National Defense Advisory Commission (NDAC) and the Office of Production Management (OPM), created in May and December 1940, respectively, proved to be ineffective. The two agencies made little head-way in converting industry to munitions production. Until after the nation entered the war, most defense output was accomplished in addition to normal civilian production and through new or enlarged facilities. The basic industries like steel, aluminum, and magnesium, however, were not expanded. Desiring to exploit growing civilian markets, fearful of creating excess capacity or disturbing intra-industry power patterns, and doubtful or distrustful of the President's foreign and domestic policies, industrial America set the terms for cooperating with the Roosevelt Administration. That was possible because the NDAC and OPM, despite a facade of broad interest-group representation, were actually dominated by industry. Officials from the large corporations and trade associations, serving for a dollar-a-year or without compensation, filled key executive positions and staffed the crucially important Industry Advisory Committees. They made decisions which reflected the attitude of their firms and organizations.

The mobilization agencies also failed to exercise any real control over military procurement despite being granted the right to do so. Contracts, including the burgeoning facilities program, were let without any effective review and the armed services were even allowed to administer their own priorities system. The consequences for the future were grave. Invariably, the Army and Navy turned to the nation's largest corporations, whose plants were located principally in the Northeast, for meeting their munitions needs. Since what began before the war continued after the nation entered hostilities, a relatively few urban areas became overloaded with contracts far beyond the capacity to produce in terms of facilities, power, labor force, and the like. Moreover, unreviewed military procurement placed the overwhelming percentage of defense and war contracts in the hands of the nation's giant corporations.

The NDAC and OPM did manage to get the Army and Navy to raise somewhat their extremely low demand, or requirements, figures for dealing with various defense and wartime threats. But those calculations still remained inconsistent and unreliable. The armed services operated on the assumption that the economy could meet any level of demand, making accuracy on their part unnecessary.

The defense years witnessed the growth of strange and contradictory alliances. Insisting upon the urgent need for greatly strengthened civilian mobilization agencies and chafing under the refusal of industry to covert or expand facilities for defense purposes, the War and Navy Departments still lined up with corporate America and its representatives on almost every major issue. For example, in late

1940 as the Roosevelt Administration was hammering out a legislative program on the economics of munitions production, the War Department carried industry's banner for the most generous terms possible on plant amortization, profit limitations, and excess profits taxes. It also led in the drive to end anti-trust action. Curiously, the armed forces sided with industry on what turned out to be very low projections of the economy's manufacturing potential and the percentage of existing capacity convertible to arms output. Industrialists and their representatives in the NDAC and OPM, who were resisting the drive for greater munitions production and strong mobilization agencies, still looked with favor upon the military services. Big business was willing to encourage the military services to adopt more realistic procurement goals but unwilling to press the armed services at any point or overtly oppose the policies they advocated.

In terms of issues alone, the natural allies of the military would have been the so-called "all-outers," who included New Dealers like Leon Henderson, labor spokesmen like Sidney Hillman, and small business and consumer advocates. Considerations of ideology and power as perceived by the military services, however, made this group an adversary. While favoring maximum preparation for economic mobilizaton, the "all-outers" believed that that goal could best be achieved through careful, widely representative planning in which defense contracts would be distributed systematically throughout the nation. Additionally, existing plants, including those of small business, would be utilized fully before new facilities were built, less essential civilian production would be concentrated in a few facilities within an industry as curtailment of those industries became necessary, and so forth. Such policies, according to the War and Navy Departments, inhibited rather than facilitated mobilization because they alienated and antagonized corporate and financial America. Hence, those proposals and their advocates were to be opposed.

With industry and the military supporting each other but, in effect, pulling in different directions, stalemate constantly threatened the prewar economic defense effort. Some momentum was maintained by the President's creating new agencies in which the "all-outers" had more influence and by the military continuing to build its own mobilization systems. The overall result was movement but with increasing fragmentation, instead of concentration, of mobilization authority and activity.

In April 1941 the President established the Office of Price Administration and Civilian Supply (OPACS). It was headed by Henderson and staffed primarily by civil servants, attorneys, and academicians. This agency was intended to begin working for price stabilization as inflationary forces mounted and to ensure that civilian needs were protected as military requirements grew and industrial conversion accelerated. Whether priorities over civilian production would be exercised by the OPM or the OPACS was not settled, and this produced a long and bitter feud between the two agencies which highlighted the differences between the industrialists and the "all-outers" who staffed the competing agencies. The conflict came to a head during July and August 1941, when the OPACS, exasperated by the OPM's solicitude for the corporate elite, took the initiative by ordering drastic cutbacks in future production schedules for automobiles and other consumer producer goods which were lavishly consuming steel and other basic supplies as well as delaying the conversion to munitions production. This action generated so much controversy that in late August 1941, the Office of Price Administration was separated from Civilian Supply and the latter absorbed by the OPM. The authority of the OPM, however, was curbed by placing it under a new coordinating body, the Supply Priorities and Allocation Board (SPAB) which, while including the top members of the OPM, was weighted in favor of "all-outers" by awarding seats to Henderson, Harry Hopkins, Donald M. Nelson, and, the chair, Vice President Henry A. Wallace. Although an administrative nightmare in terms of lines of authority, the SPAB managed to make some headway in terms of requirements, priority and allocation systems, means for protecting the civilian economy against overbearing military demands, curtailment of less essential civilian production, and the expansion of basic industries like steel.

While the OPACS and the SPAB pushed the mobilization forward from a liberal civilian direction, the Army-Navy Munitions Board (ANMB) exerted pressure from the conservative military side. The board, created in 1922 as part of the War Department's attempt to include the Navy in its interwar industrial mobilization planning, began to be reorganized late in 1941, and was ultimately placed under the chairmanship of Ferdinand Eberstadt, a prominent Wall Street investment banker. Eberstadt was well known to Under Secretary of the Navy James V. Forrestal and had the confidence of Secretary of War Henry L. Stimson and his Under Secretary, Robert P. Patterson. Unable to get the type of civilian mobilization administration they favored, the armed services gradually began building up the ANMB which partly paralleled and competed with the civilian mobilization agencies. It was through the board that the armed services started to coordinate their procurement operations, including the granting of priorities, the distribution of contracts, the construction and financing of facilities, and the like.

America's entry into World War II forced Roosevelt to try centralizing control over the badly fragmented economic mobilization structure by creating the War Production Board (WPB) in Janurary 1942. In retrospect, the President acted half-heartedly. James F. Byrnes, a close political ally, had warned Roosevelt that the success of any new mobilization chief depended upon the full confidence and support of the White House. Yet, Donald M. Nelson, who was picked for the post, was neither well known to the President nor viewed as a strong leader. He appears to have been selected for his availability: most of the interest groups vying to shape the industrial mobilization program did not oppose him. Three immediate tests faced Nelson if he were to establish WPB dominance over the wartime economy. First, he had to get tough with the industrialists who were coming over from the OPM and who had looked to the mobilization agency more to protect industry's interests than to harness the economy for war. Second, he had to bend the military, which had grown powerful and practically independent, to the board's will. Last, he had to give labor, New Dealers, and small business a meaningful voice in mobilization matters so that the WPB involved broad-based, not simply big business, planning, and thus, tapped the nation's full economic potential.

Before the year was out, Nelson had failed all three tests and, consequently, had begun to lose control of the WPB and the mobilization program. Throughout 1942 and into 1943, decisions were made less by orderly process than by infighting, machinations, confrontations, and explosions. Nelson could not manage the big industrial elements dominating the board. Some continued to resist converting facilities to war as late as March 1942. Only dramatic resignations, accusatory headlines, and an inquiry by the Senate Special Committee to Investigate the National Defense Program (the Truman Committee) got the economy on the way to full conversion by June 1942. The chairman of the WPB was even less successful with the armed services. In March and April 1942 the War and Navy Departments persuaded the well intentioned Nelson to sign agreements on spheres of operations that left the military largely free of WPB authority. Finally, in case after case involving economic mobilization, interest groups other than the corporate structure were ignored, shoved to the periphery, or isolated within the WPB. The World War II mobilization program went forward much like the prewar effort but with the industrial and military communities now preparing to cooperate fully in order to attain shared and mutually beneficial goals.

Before the economy could be mobilized effectively, however, Nelson had to modify his March and April agreements with the armed services. Between August 1942 and March 1943, as a result of a series of intensely acrimonious struggles which had actually begun in late 1940, the military was gradually integrated into the board's structure. The first step in that direction grew out of the requirements muddle, in what has come to be called the "Feasibility Dispute." When the nation entered the war, the armed services suddenly dumped over $100 billion dollars of new contracts into the economy and maintained that their needs, not the economy's potential, had to be the gauge for future requirements. The WPB's Planning Committee—composed of Robert R. Nathan and Thomas C. Blaisdell, Jr., scholar-civil servants, and Fred Searls, Jr., a construction engineer, and assisted by the eminent economist-statistician Simon Kuznets and his staff—had been arguing for months that unless military requirements were set and contracting carried out within a framework of feasibility, the entire economic mobilization program and economy could be disastrously dislocated. To facilitate balance, the Planning Committee recommended the creation of a supreme war production council, a broadly representative body superior to all departments and agencies, for establishing, monitoring, and enforcing military, production, social, and political strategies. Late in 1942, after months of virtual bare-knuckle brawling, the services finally agreed to allow the WPB to set the maximum limits for their requirements. The Planning Committee's larger goal of a war council went without high-level support within the Roosevelt Administration and, therefore, never stood a chance, since it threatened power relations in the wartime economy. Many industrialists, for complex reasons, were as antagonistic to economic mobilization based on feasibility as was the military. Facing hostility from all sides for its unpopular advocacy, the Planning Committee was soon downgraded to a position of insignificance within the board.

Feasible requirements were only a start in devising a workable mobilization program. Next was the need for alloting materials so that contracts could be completed in their order of importance; then, production had to be scheduled to synchronize the flow of components and end items for balanced programs. The first goal began to be achieved in September 1942 when Eberstadt moved over from the ANMB to the WPB as the Program Vice Chairman in charge of materials and requirements. His appointment was also intended to placate the armed services as the WPB reclaimed some of its functions and power. Eberstadt's principal task was to replace a cumbersome and failing priority-allocation system with a new allocation approach labeled the Controlled Materials Plan (CMP) in which basic materials like steel, aluminum, and copper would follow contracting and force all other inputs of production into the same channel. Block grants of materials were made to the procurement agencies which distributed them to their contractors, the contractors to the subcontractors, and so forth. Since the armed services were the main claimants on the economy and relatively few corporations controlled the lion's share of prime contracts, the CMP served to increase the hold of the military and the corporate giants on the WPB and the economy.

The CMP could work only if production was properly scheduled. Consequently, in September 1942, Nelson also brought in Charles E. Wilson, president of the General Electric Company, and a leading production expert, to serve as the Board's Production Vice Chairman and to head a Production Executive Committee (PEC) composed principally of representatives from the procurement agencies. Wilson's appointment was partly intended to offset that of Eberstadt, who was identified with the military. The two executives almost inevitably became rivals. Eberstadt directed the Industry Division and control groups in charge of facilities, tools, shipbuilding, aircraft, and the like. These were the principal subdivisions of the Board which Eberstadt needed to solve problems of material shortages. With the CMP beginning to work well, such shortages became less urgent. Now Wilson required the Industry and Material Divisions and other staff bureaus to fulfill his production responsibilities. Nelson, accordingly, began transferring the divisions and bureaus to Wilson's domain in late 1942 and early 1943. This alarmed the military. Wilson, after an almost three-month battle, had just succeeded in having the resistive and suspicious armed services recognize the existence and authority of the PEC. Nelson's act of shifting the centers of power within the WPB from Eberstadt to Wilson was looked upon as an attempt to undermine further military influence within the Board. Therefore, the War and Navy Departments combined their political power with that of Byrnes, Director of Economic Stabilization, to persuade Roosevelt to replace Nelson with Bernard M. Baruch, whom they viewed as sympathetic to their cause. Nelson saved his job in February 1943 by uncharacteristically attacking instead of retreating. He quickly fired Eberstadt and elevated

Wilson, a strong executive whom he still trusted, to Executive Vice Chairman with practically full control over the WPB's operations.

By early 1943, the WPB had fairly well taken on its final shape. Nelson remained as chairman, but Wilson had the real power. He commanded the Industry and Material Divisions and other subdivisions which represented the corporate muscle of the nation's economy. Wilson also directed the PEC in which all claimant agencies were represented, but with the military dominant. Gradually, he dispelled the latter's suspicion of the Board and won the full cooperation and respect of the armed forces. Through Wilson's office the industry-military production team which dominated the WPB and the economy began to grow.

Despite many false starts and intense controversy, the Roosevelt Administration had eventually managed to center wartime production controls in one agency. That was not the case with financial management; it remained the one area of the wartime economy without a governmental body responsible for its execution. Ideally, one administration should have determined policy for wartime revenue (taxation and borrowing), price and wage controls, rationing, and like policies. All were closely related and interacted to shape economic conditions during the war years. The Office of Price Administration (OPA) controlled price and rationing programs, the War Labor Board (WLB) wage determination, but no administration set revenue policy. That was left to internecine struggles between the Treasury Department, the Bureau of the Budget, and various Roosevelt advisers, with the President often acting as final arbiter. Consequently, policy-making and execution, especially as it involved relations with Congress, was awkward, chaotic, and ill-advised. Despite these conditions, the administration's revenue policies compared favorably with the record of past American wars but unfavorably with the achievements of the nation's allies such as Great Britain.[3] Nonetheless, this was too vital an area for casual policy-formulation and remained the major omission in the economic mobilization apparatus.

The closest the administration came to having a body to devise and administer general economic policy was the Office of Economic Stabilization (OES) created in October 1942 by an Executive Order based on the Economic Stabilization Act of the same month. Roosevelt chose Byrnes to head the new office. His principal assignment was to control inflationary pressures. While Byrnes had some voice in revenue measures, he faced stiff competition from Secretary of the Treasury Henry Morgenthau, Jr. and Director of the Bureau of the Budget Harold D. Smith. Byrnes' impressive knowledge of and ability to work with Congress on revenue matters, regrettably, was never exploited to the fullest. He fared much better in the area of price, wage, and rationing controls. According to the figures of the Bureau of Labor Statistics, which were probably low, the cost of living had risen by 24.3 percent between January 1941 and April 1943. The President's Hold-the-Line Order of April 1943, however, effectively capped further increases with only an additional 4.8 percent rise registered at the war's end.

Wartime stabilization clearly was accomplished principally by squeezing mass purchasing power. Although the working population experienced a substantial growth in income, that came more from full employment and overtime work than from increased wages. The farmer and corporate America did much better. Supposedly, the agricultural population experienced the greatest increase in income, but that is questionable. When calculation of corporate gains includes the extensive plant acquired at the government's expense, industrial America unquestionably benefitted more than any other interest group in the economic system. Again, however, this proposition holds principally for the giant corporations, whose grip on the economy increased during the war years, not the small-to-medium sized firms. The former received the lion's share of all war production benefits including contracts, plants, subcontracts, research and development funds, and the like. Also, the nation will never fully know corporate America's wartime gains because the industrial establishment, in significant areas like the operation of government-built plants, largely ran, audited, and policed itself during the war years. There are now and will always be better figures on the income and assets of the working population and the farmer than on corporate America.[4]

From the outset, Byrnes became involved in much more than economic stabilization. As separate administrations were set up for manpower, rubber, petroleum, and food, conflict inevitably grew and added to the power struggles which continued to wrack the WPB and other agencies. With less time and energy to devote to domestic matters, Roosevelt turned more and more to Byrnes to mediate, coordinate, and direct the mobilization effort even though his office was not intended for that role. Byrnes' authority came much closer to matching his growing responsibility when, in May 1943, Roosevelt by Executive Order created the Office of War Mobilization (OWM) to oversee the home front and made the South Carolinian its director. The President had acted in 1943 to head off legislation in Congress designed to bring order to the increasingly chaotic mobilization scene. In October 1944, Congress expanded the scope of Byrnes' office, now called the Office of War Mobilization and Reconversion (OWMR), to quell the growing discord over reconversion policies.

Heading the OWM-OWMR, Byrnes came as close as any individual to being the assistant president for domestic affairs, He had been tapped for the OES in 1942 and the OWM in 1943 because he had the President's confidence in a close political relationship reaching back to World War I. Between 1939 and 1942, first as an influential senator and then, after June 1941, even as a member of the Supreme Court, Byrnes had advised and acted as a trouble-shooter for Roosevelt on war mobilization matters. As a broker of power and as a Southern conservative, Byrnes, with the obvious approval and most likely the encouragement of the President, devoted himself to making the existing mobilization system work.

Byrnes' most important task became that of guarding the industry-military production team that had come to dominate the WPB. This protective role was clearly evident in two areas: the mobilization of manpower and the controversy over reconversion. By mid-1943, manpower, no longer materials or facilities, became the principal limiting factor for production. This situation could have placed the War Manpower Commission (WMC), created in April 1942, in a key position for shaping the mobilization program. Industry and the military had no intention of allowing a manpower agency, and particularly one in which organized labor had a strong voice, to play such a part. During the infighting that ensued in mid-1943 and continued practically until V-J Day over meeting manpower problems, Byrnes used his authority to ensure that control over labor supply was determined largely by the WPB's Production Executive Committee and the procurement agencies and to minimize the WMC's influence over the raising of military forces.[5]

Byrnes also played an instrumental role in shaping plans and preparations for peace in ways acceptable to the industry-military production team. Between late 1943 and mid-1944, Nelson initiated WPB preparations for reconverting the economy and began to take modest steps toward easing the transition from a war to peacetime footing as war orders began to be cut back. By then, Nelson's base of support within the WPB was indeed weak. It consisted principally of his own staff, the labor and small business offices, and the Office of Civilian Requirements. The big industrial interests and the military vehemently opposed Nelson's position: the former because they wanted to protect postwar market positions by holding civilian production to a minimum until all firms could resume peacetime pursuits simultaneously; the latter because they feared that any increase in civilian production could set off a stampede detrimental to munitions output.

At crucial points between July and December 1944, Byrnes used his power first to delay and later to halt the implementation of Nelson's very limited and cautious program. This turned out to be Nelson's last battle. Because of it, he was finally driven from office. The federal government approached peace ready to terminate and settle contracts quickly and dismantle the mobilization structure once hostilities were over; it was not prepared to handle a crisis. As a result, although the postwar depression anticipated by many did not materialize, accelerating and destabilizing inflation did, a situation which contributed to a very tumultuous labor scene and a generally disillusioned and divided nation.[6]

Nelson and the interests he represented in the WPB had constant support from the Truman Committee and the Senate Special Committee to Study and Survey the Problems of American Small Business (Murray Committee) and the House Select Committee Investigating National Defense Migration (Tolan Committee). These Congressional committees consistently advocated centralized, broad-based, and progressive planning by drafting and/or backing legislation for incorporating all mobilization functions, including production and procurement, in one agency staffed by civil servants and advised by a board made up of representatives from industry, labor, agriculture, and the public. With such a mobilization structure, committee members argued, conflicts of interest would be reduced substantially and the contribution of all interest groups maximized. While the proposed legislation never even approached passage, Truman and his Congressional colleagues played an instrumental role in forcing the Roosevelt Administration to coordinate the mobilization program better through the OWM-OWMR.

The Truman, Tolan, and Murray Committees, and especially the first, won the respect and trust of Congress and the nation because of their responsible, reliable, and reasonably objective investigations, findings, and recommendations. The alternate mobilization scheme they favored was intended to further the cause of efficiency rather than reform. But the two ends, after all, are not antithetical. The widespread support the committees enjoyed indicated, at a minimum, general discontent with how the economy was being mobilized for war. Nonetheless, the Roosevelt Administration never encouraged the committees' work or attempted to use their popularity to counter the conservative opposition. When the President chose to challenge effectively a recalcitrant Congress on an issue which had popular appeal, the nation's legislators usually backed down. Such was the case with the Economic Stabilization Act of October 1942 which led to the creation of the Office of Economic Stabilization. The Roosevelt Administration's methods for mobilizing the economy appear to have helped strengthen the conservative elements in Congress as much or more than those elements shaped the mobilization programs.[7]

III

Viewed in gross figures and in isolation, the American production effort during World War II appears impressive. The GNP in 1939 dollars grew by 52 percent between 1939 and 1944; 124 percent in unadjusted dollars. Munitions production went from about 10 to 40 percent of total output between 1940 and 1943-1944. Manufacturing industries trebled their output from the period 1939 to 1944. All of that was accomplished while consumer expenditures in 1944 were 12 percent above the 1939 mark. Going from national to international calculations, the United States in 1944 produced in excess of 40 percent of total world munitions output and around 50 percent more than either all of its allies or all of its enemies combined.[8]

From these or similar figures has grown the notion of wartime "miracles of production," "prodigious production," and like characterizations.[9] Such observations hold up only if the nation's prewar production potential and the achievements of other belligerents are ignored. To approach the World War II record from such a narrow perspective not only limits understanding of the event greatly, but also strengthens the concept of American Exceptionalism—a mode of thought that encourages parochialism on the part of both the general public and the scholar.

When placed in the proper context, the American production record appears neither exceptional, miraculous, nor prodigious, unless such characterizations apply equally to all other belligerent nations. Gauged by the "Percentage Distribution of the World's Manufacturing Production" for the period 1926-1929, the United States in the peak year 1944 was producing munitions at almost exactly the level it should have been. Great Britain is modestly high; Canada low; Germany high; Japan very high; and the Soviet Union spectacularly high. If the 1936-1938 period is taken instead, the United States and Great Britain are reasonably high; and Canada is still low; Germany and Japan are both high; but the Soviet Union is now somewhat low.[10]

Of course, these measures are crude. But they are corroborated by Raymond W. Goldsmith in what is the best available study on the general topic. Goldsmith served as an economist on the WPB's Planning Committee with an assignment which included analyzing worldwide munitions output. His principal conclusion is as follows:

> The munitions production of the major billigerents at full mobilization was roughly proportional to the size of their prewar industrial labor force combined with the prewar level of productivity in industry. This is hardly an astonishing result, but one which confirms the belief that basic economic factors rather than accidental developments or sudden changes in elementary economic relationships—more familiar under the names of "secret weapons" and "miracles of production"—have determined the course of munitions production.[11]

Goldsmith also found that about two years were required to convert fully from peace to wartime production even if a nation started from scratch. Finally, he observed that in 1944, all belligerents except for the United States, and perhaps Canada, had stretched themselves to the ultimate with a drop off imminent for both Great Britain and Germany. For the United States, full mobilization had not been achieved, and an additional 10 to 20 percent increase of munitions production could have been implemented within a short period of time and without excessive strain "through some curtailment of civilian consumption even if only down to the prewar level, through a labor draft, and through a tighter control over the efficiency of munitions production."[12]

What Goldsmith did not state, although he at times implied it, is that the United States economic mobilization program was carried out under ideal circumstances compared with all other major belligerents except Canada. Great Britain, the USSR, Germany, and Japan all met, exceeded, or came close to their prewar production potential even with the homeland being attacked, the population in every way under much greater strain, fewer resources available, and, Britain apart, extremely volatile political circumstances. If the spectator of the World War II munitions scene insists upon the awesome, he would be advised to look past the United States to Germany upping its productivity by 25 percent between 1943 and 1944; to the Soviet Union steadily increasing output while transferring its industrial plant eastward to the Urals and Siberia; to Japan grinding out more products each year despite growing calamity everywhere; and to Great Britain making annually more munitions while subject to the physical and psychological trauma of new and heinous weapons of war. In spite of, perhaps because of, such extreme adversity, other belligerents, as noted earlier, achieved a better record than the United States in financing the war out of current income. A close examination of other critical statistics and information might make the United States war production effort appear more modest by comparison.[13] All of this is intended to make a simple, though important point: When viewed in terms of prewar potential and when compared with other belligerents, America's World War II munitions production effort was not outstanding.

IV

The performance of the economy during the Second World War is not simply an academic matter. Assuming prodigious production, scholars and other analysts have maintained either that the endless conflict of the war years was part of the price of progress, or they have viewed it as unimportant.[14] If the record was not exceptional, then the negative aspects of economic mobilization take on greater significance and among other matters raise the question of whether there were meaningful alternatives for mobilizing the World War II economy.

Another and attainable way did exist and it relates to the Roosevelt Administration's methods of commanding the armed services. During the war years the services emerged as the new power group of great significance, and how they were managed would have an enormous impact upon any program of economic mobilization. A fairly good guide to military thinking about that subject on the eve of World War II is available in the Industrial Mobilization Plans, written by the Office of the Assistant Secretary of War in the 1920s and 1930s. Those plans, and the planning, are loaded with ambiguity. Nonetheless, after a long and intense controversy within the War Department, the Industrial Mobilization Plans also proposed the careful distribution of contracts to maintain economic balance, the utilization of most existing facilities, including those of small business, before new or expanded plants and equipment were built, the efficient use of manpower, the proper allocation of resources to ensure the health of the civilian economy and adequate community facilites, and the preparation of programs for reconversion. This approach resembles that which was constantly proposed and pursued by the Truman, Tolan, and Murray Committees, and among Nelson's advisers. Like those advocates, the army planners were not supporting reforms, but rather were seeking effective and practical programs for mobilizing the economy for war.

In order to marshal the military's strength in behalf of rational economic planning for war, the United States required something comparable to the British War Cabinet with its secretariat for directing overall wartime policy. Such a council or staff would have included, at a minimum, the Secretaries of State, War, and Navy, the military chiefs, and the directors of the wartime economy. The idea of a war council is not idle speculation. Throughout the twentieth century various civilian and military leaders had favored a similar agency under the title of a Council of National Defense; the Industrial Mobilization Plans provided for an Advisory War Council; and, before and after the nation entered the war, support for such a body came from Congress, members of the Roosevelt Administration, and other sources.[15]

From 1939 through 1942, Roosevelt had several excellent opportunities for establishing a war council. Indeed, for a time he appeared to be heading in that direction. In July 1939, by military order, Roosevelt placed the Joint Board, created in 1903 to coordinate military strategy between the Army and Navy, and the Army-Navy Munitions Board, which by this time issued the Industrial Mobilization Plans under its imprimatur, directly under his authority. Here was a skeletal structure for establishing and coordinating military strategy and supply. With the organization of the War Resources Board in August 1939, the President appeared to be seeking a civilian counterpart to the emerging military coordinating system in order to have a balanced overall mobilization structure. For complex reasons, this particular administrative approach did not work, with the result that thereafter defense policy was formulated in a confused, unclear, and often contradictory fashion, and the economic mobilization bureaucracy became fragmented.

Roosevelt never again came as close to organizing a war council as he appeared to be in mid-to-late 1939, despite new opportunities and strong pressure on him to act. Instead, the President proceeded in a way that undermined coherent direction of the war effort. In June 1940, Roosevelt selected Stimson and Frank Knox as Secretaries of War and Navy respectively, and shortly thereafter Patterson and Forrestal were chosen as Under Secretaries for those departments. While in the short run the appointments may have been politically expedient, in the long run they had several negative consequences. First, much of the benefit of the interwar economic mobilization planning was simply lost, at least at the top echelons of the departments, and especially so for the War Department, the principal planning agency. New Secretaries brought in new staffs who ignored most of the past planning or considered it to be irrelevant. This helps to explain, along with other developments, why the War Department, which went through such agony in the 1920s and 1930s learning the hard lesson of the indispensable need for feasible requirements to protect the economic base which supplied it, resisted ardently the concept of feasibility from 1940 onward.

Second, numerous representatives from corporate and financial America, serving both in and out of uniform, entered the armed services' procurement and economic mobilization structures. The War Department at times did not even know the economic affiliations of the executives it took on. With changed staffing, the orientation and attitudes of the military services had a different character after 1940 than it had before. For example, the Army planners had harbored a certain reserve about, if not suspicion of, corporate America prior to 1940. After that date, such doubts simply vanished or were no longer evident. Last, and most important, the new Secretaries and Under Secretaries left much to be desired. Stimson was a narrow, zealously class-conscious conservative dedicated to military, even martial, values. He acted more as chief lobbyist and aggressive advocate for the Army than as a strong leader viewing the department he headed as part of a larger war mobilization whole. Patterson responded similarly. Knox was largely inconsequential. Of all four, Forrestal came closest to being a true statesman, but Navy Department politics, a subordinate position, and certain personality traits prevented him from exercising fully his leadership abilities.[16]

The creation of the Joint Chiefs of Staff (JCS) in February 1942, complicated even further economic mobilization matters. Roosevelt began using that body to plan and manage the war abroad. This placed the JCS in a unique position. It had continuous and direct access to the Commander-in-Chief. The civilian secretaries of the military departments, along with representatives from the economic mobilization structure, were excluded from all deliberations. Yet, the JCS's decisions involving strategy set the overall military requirements which vitally effected the WPB and other agencies. By example the President encouraged the JCS to act arbitrarily in determining its material needs. With the nation's entry into the war, the President, in a very casual way, publicly announced production goals which were most unrealistic. Following Roosevelt's lead, the JCS, with no check upon it from the civilian secretaries and lower echelon officers, set requirements in an equally capricious manner. Out of these circumstances grew the "Feasibility Dispute" of mid-to-late 1942. Only the WPB's Planning Committee forced the nation's power structure to face reality.[17] The JCS and Roosevelt's relationship with it, constituted a war council of sorts, but one that was truncated, that added to the fragmentation of the war effort, and that created confusion and antagonism throughout the fractured war mobilization system.

Actually, about the time the JCS was organized, Roosevelt had another opportunity for creating a war council, had he been so disposed. With Pearl Harbor silencing practically all Administration critics, the President had virtually a free hand in putting together the governmental system he wanted for directing the war. Additionally, within a few months between late 1941 and early 1942, almost every major agency for conducting the war effort was either established or was reorganized. The WPB was created in January 1942 and the JCS in February; in March both the Army and Navy completed streamlining their systems of command and administration;[18] and in February the armed services put the finishing touches on the rebuilding of the ANMB. Here were all of the administrative parts for a war council. The need for such a council was emphasized in January and February 1942, when the United States and Great Britain put together organizations designed to advance planning and execution of the war effort on an Allied basis. These included the Combined Chiefs of Staff, the Munitions Assignment Board, the Combined Raw Materials Board, and, in June 1942, the Combined Production and Resources Board, along with other combined agencies. The Combined Chiefs of Staff worked reasonably well, but the combined economic boards never really got off the ground.

The President passed up the opportunity within the nation and between it and Great Britain for rationalizing the mobilization programs. That greatly exacerbated the problems plaguing the WPB. As head of the Board, Nelson lacked the JCS's direct access to the President, and he was not a ruthless bureaucratic infighter like Stimson and Patterson. Yet, early in 1942, Nelson and his aides concluded that they required close collaboration with the JCS on miltary requirements in order to fulfill their job adequately. This led to the proposal of the Planning Committee for a supreme war production council and, when that was rejected, other more modest proposals for cooperation between the WPB and JCS. With even these efforts failing, Nelson rather desperately looked to the Allied combined boards as a way of achieving indirectly what he could not get directly from the recalcitrant military. Of especial importance were the Combined Production and Resources Board and the Munitions Assignment Board. The first consisted primarily of Nelson and his British counterpart, who were expected to work with the Combined Chiefs of Staff for integrating economic mobilization programs so that they were consistent with Allied strategic and production requirements; the second, chaired by Harry Hopkins, who was also a member of the WPB and the President's chief assistant, had the responsibility for assigning munitions output to various nations according to need and priority. Since these boards never worked well, they did not serve to strengthen Nelson's hand as he had hoped would be the case.

If the President did not want a war council, then a coordinated war effort through collaboration between the WPB and the JCS could have been attained. This would have avoided the institutional upheavals advocated by the Planning Committee and supported throughout the war years by the Truman and other Congressional committees. Nelson and his assistants did not stand alone in their drive for a cooperative approach with the military heads. They were supported by such highly placed officials as Hopkins and his assistant, Isador Lubin, who was also Commissioner of Labor Statistics, Leon Henderson, OPA price administrator, and others. The President failed to be moved, and without prodding from him, the JCS had no reason to share its access to the principal seat of political power. The most the Joint Chiefs agreed to do in October 1942, was to appoint officers to keep the WPB informed of the military's material and manpower needs. But that was more a gesture than a serious proposal for solving a real problem.[19]

Collaboration between the civilian and military mobilization systems was ultimately resolved when, for all intents and purposes, the WPB came under the domination of Wilson, and industry and the armed forces synchronized their efforts largely through the Production Executive Committee. Once that pattern was underway in 1943, the mobilization struggles that wracked the economy were no longer essentially civilian versus military; instead they involved interest groups: giant corporations and the armed services as opposed to New Dealers, academicians and civil servants, labor, and small business. Byrnes, in his various posts, did not restore "civilian" balance to the home front, but rather served to protect the decision-making of the industry-military production team.

While no one can be certain of how a war council would have functioned, the subject is worth some examination. To have worked well, strong executives, capable of focusing upon the entire war effort, would have been essential for the military departments and the major mobilization agencies. Among the first and ongoing tasks of such a body would have been setting and adjusting military requirements. Practically every major conflict that shook the Washington establishment just before and during the Second World War either directly or indirectly involved the armed forces' demand for munitions and manpower. With requirements set at the highest levels of government and under conditions of broad, informed, and responsible review, the major source of contention could have been settled with authority and finality and not left as a matter of continuing rancor and dispute.

Under the right conditions and leadership, a war council established at the outset of hostilities would most likely have been acceptable to the armed services. The idea of careful, broadly conceived planning had become part of the military ethos largely as a result of the twenty years of procurement and industrial mobilization planning conducted by the Office of the Assistant Secretary of War. From that effort came the Industrial Mobilization Plans, which resulted in the Army, and to a degree the Navy, adapting its war plans in the 1930s to the nation's industrial potential.

Unquestionably, the greatest obstacle to a war council would have been the corporate community, not the military. Industry was not opposed to planning per se. The indirect planning of the Republican Administrations in the 1920s, although it turned out disastrously after 1929, had the enthusiastic support of the business community. The more direct planning by an enlarged state in the 1930s, which corporate America did not fully control, and proposals for the same in the defense and war years are what created suspicion and opposition on industry's part.[20] Nonetheless, industrial statesmen like Charles E. Wilson, who were also strong executives, could have been selected from the outset for top leadership positions in the defense and war mobilization systems not only to lead forcefully, but also to try and persuade industry to rise above its parochial concerns. As it turned out, the civilian mobilization agencies became dominated by industrial representatives who too often narrowly concentrated upon short-run corporate interests instead of the long-run benefits of the business community and the nation.

The structure of power within the WPB meant that when the military services faced the necessity of integrating their procurement system into the board in late 1942 and early 1943, they allied themselves with big business out of self-interest. Hence, the World War II industry-military production team was probable under existing circumstances, but not inevitable. Indeed, the armed services participation in World War I economic mobilization and their interwar procurement and industrial mobilization planning indicate a strong measure of doubt about close relations with industry and a concern on the part of some officers that such conditions could undermine military professionalism.

A properly organized and managed war council had many possibilities. It could have offered the military the opportunity to work with industry without becoming involved in an alliance which served the long-run interests of neither. Certainly a war council could have devised a mobilization program which incorporated in a meaningful way more interest groups than was the case during the Second World War. Ideally, such a council could have served to elevate the sights and the aspirations of the business community. Surely a rational mobilization program, formulated by a high level council and defended in the name of military and strategic necessity, would have put the more short-sighted members of the business community and the obstructionist conservatives in and outside of Congress on the defensive. At the least, mobilization by a war council could not have been worse than that which evolved during World War II; at the most, such an approach could have served orderly, reasonable, and even progressive ends, instead of haphazard, careless, and conservative-to-reactionary goals.[21]

Enough historical evidence now exists to indicate that the general population was deeply disturbed about the nature of the economic mobilization program. That disturbance may have caused or contributed significantly to the serious Democratic setback in the mid-term election of 1942 which served to embolden the growing conservative Democratic-Republican Congressional coalition.[22] If that was the case, Roosevelt helped to create the very conservatism that supposedly trapped him.[23] Whatever the case, the impact of the misguided means for harnessing the economy reached far beyond the election of 1942. Polls point up the fact that public opinion appeared not only confused and contradictory during the war, but also manifested a callous, selfish, and uncaring streak.[24] Such attitudes are not surprising. War was catapulting the nation from a decade of depression into quite sudden and robust prosperity. Such a transition—leaving aside the need for raising the perspective of the people from the national to the international level—would be difficult under the best of circumstances. That it occurred at a time of inattentive and ineffective domestic leadership could only bewilder and bring out in many people their worst, not their best, instincts.[25] The New Deal as symbol and reality had offered Americans more than recovery; it had pledged a more just, equitable, and humane society. For the President to tell the masses in December 1943 that "Dr. New Deal" had to give way to "Dr. Win-the-War" was to imply that New Deal promises stood in the way of military victory or were inconsistent with it. If such was the case, then something was lacking either in the New Deal or in the war effort. The public was left with a riddle bound to cause worry and generate resentment.

V

Economic mobilization for World War II demonstrated Roosevelt's genius for mastering the intricacies of power in American society. Political success depended upon handling an elitist reality within the context of a populist ideology. The President constantly finessed that blatant contradiction with great skill. His penchant for decision-making through conflict and competition stemmed less from an animus towards clear lines of authority and planning, and more from an instinctive and/or calculated tactic of obfuscating the elitist contours of power in America which he both accepted and supported.

A pattern existed beneath the surface confusion of economic mobilization for war. Conventional knowledge notwithstanding, the President was willing to delegate authority over domestic events, and recognized the need to do so. But before that could take place, two crucial conditions had to be met: first, the mobilization apparatus had to reflect the true power patterns of the social system; and second, a leader capable of protecting that apparatus had to be groomed.

Before Pearl Harbor, the nation was too divided over foreign and domestic policy to create effective agencies for harnessing the economy. Organizations like the NDAC and OPM had the advantage of appearing to balance interest groups and placing the talented advocates of economic preparedness in a position to push the reluctant corporate community and the confused military in the right direction. With war declared, the time was right for a strong agency, but not a strongman. Nelson was perfect. He genuinely believed in and articulated the prewar idea of broad-based, interest-group planning without in any way demonstrating the determination to implement it. By consistently dodging the tough decisions and avoiding confrontation, Nelson allowed power in the WPB to pass gradually to the large corporations working with the military. By late 1942-early 1943, with the board in elitist hands, Roosevelt could safely appoint a general director and coordinator for the home front so that he could concentrate on events abroad. Byrnes was first tested in the position of economic stabilizer. Once he had proven his executive abilities, his responsibility and authority were expanded to include the entire mobilization and reconversion process. Unlike Nelson, Byrnes made the hard choices. They were almost always on the conservative side, but with Byrnes rather than the President now held responsible for what was done.

Contrary to the analysis of the necessity school and the interpretation of other scholars, economic mobilization for the Second World War grew out of, rather than varied from, the basic patterns of the New Deal. Recovery was always the Roosevelt Administration's primary objective during the Great Depression, with relief and reform used to buy time and make the minimal changes necessary to keep the system going. The first major effort for ending the depression came with the National Recovery Administration (NRA). When that experiment failed and the restive masses threatened to get out of hand, only then did the President switch to the more liberal tactics of the so-called Second New Deal. With defense and war production from 1940 onward bringing about full recovery and requiring some form of planning, the Roosevelt Administration gradually and logically returned to the NRA, in effect, the World War I approach.[26]

Roosevelt's consumate ability to manipulate the realities and images of power in America was both his greatest strenght and weakness. During the Great Depression, his leadership was instrumental in guarding the system against its gravest threat since the Civil War. With the Second World War he managed to rally a very divided people behind a common cause. While substantial, those accomplishments met immediate crises without resolving deep-seated and fundamental national problems. The crash of the economy in 1929 and the ensuing depression laid bare the severe limitations, even bankruptcy, of the nation's elite leadership. To secure the nation's future, restructuring the operations of power was essential. That did not mean socialism or a huge and permanent bureaucratic planning apparatus, but rather broadened and rationalized economic decision-making along the lines of the indicative planning practiced by every major modified capitalist country today with the exception of the United States.

Since the opportunity created by the crisis of the depression and the planning of the war was not seized upon to implement coherent economic policies, the chances for doing so in the postwar years were practically nil. Prosperity gave the illusion of security. Actually, the nation began drifting towards trouble. It turned to military Keynesianism as an easy means for stimulating the economy and in doing so aided the growth of the Military-Industrial Complex. Those were only the most blatant signs of spreading difficulty. More subtly, the nation gradually became uncompetitive internationally as most other nations of consequence adopted some form of economic planning. Blatant or subtle, the results of an economic system only haphazardly directed have produced the current comprehensive crisis engulfing the nation.[27]

Although the Roosevelt Administration did not cause the manifold problems of today, it also did not help create the institutions for avoiding or solving them. Purposefully manipulating power to handle emergencies in the short run is no substitute for restructuring power to produce more effective policies in the long run. The war, not the New Deal, ended the depression; mobilizing the economy for hostilities was patterned after the NRA, the New Deal's most glaring failure. Increasingly, the perspective of time reveals the weaknesses rather than the strengths of the Roosevelt leadership.

Chairman Weigley's Introduction of Professor Cuff

Our commentator this afternoon is Robert Cuff, a professor of history at York University in Toronto. Professor Cuff has also taught at Princeton and Rochester. His publications include *American Dollars, Canadian Prosperity: Canadian-American Economic Relations, 1945-1950*. By way of background for his commentary this afternoon, and also for linkage of this afternoon's session with that of this morning, he is also the author of *The War Industries Board: Business-Government Relations During World War I*.

COMMENTARY

Robert D. Cuff

In these remarks I want to focus primarily on Professor Koistinen's paper, since it is closest to my own interests. I will refer to Professor Deist's work for comparative perspective on the American case.

Let me begin with a summary of Professor Koistinen's paper.

Professor Koistinen judges American economic mobilization during the war as a chaotically administered, poorly organized, and less than optimal production performance. He also finds it anti-democratic in its political and economic implications. Top policy-makers functioned essentially—and intentionally—to preserve private corporate capitalist power.

Franklin Roosevelt is held chiefly responsible for these negative outcomes. According to Koistinen, Roosevelt took a casual approach to economic policy making; he deliberately refused to push powerful military institutions toward fundamental structural change; and, most significantly of all, he failed to challenge patterns of private corporate power. To that end Roosevelt purposely obscured institutional power relations so as to diffuse and confuse political potential for democratic challenge. The war, then, like the New Deal before it, Koistinen argues, is best understood as an episode in America's long-term decline, as an opportunity missed, for example, to institute the kinds of comprehensive planning mechanisms the country currently requires, in his view, to combat deepening economic crisis.

Professor Koistinen offers here, of course, a decidedly revisionist analysis. Fascinated with the question of what-might-have-been, he implies as a counterfactual proposition that the United States could have, and should have, fundamentally restructured economic power relations during the war, and that the White House could have, and should have, laid the basis for postwar national economic planning.

In the context of American historiography, the paper reminds me of the provocative perspective that Gabriel Kolko took to the Progressive Era some years ago in *The Triumph of Conservatism*. He too speculated on what might have been, and he too found that a synthesis of corporate capitalism and executive branch

111

politics short-circuited progressive social and economic change. One thinks too of Barton Bernstein's earlier analysis of the New Deal in peace and war. There the task was also to account for the limited consequences—the weaknesses rather than the strengths—of Rooseveltian policies. In each instance the author directs us to important and difficult questions about power, class, and institutional relations. These are among the major contributions of critical history to recent American historiography.

In trying to come to grips with Professor Koistinen's particular variation on a revisionist theme, I want to do three things. I want first, to qualify a number of his specific historical judgments; second, to take up the issue of Roosevelt's motivation, which is central to his overall thesis; and third, to outline three structural conditions that I believe we need to consider in understanding both FDR's behavior and the overall form of American industrial and economic mobilization.

On the first point, I want to replace Professor Koistinen's critical point of view with a less morally-charged, less-demanding perspective and have another look at several issues. First of all, it is worth noting that the United States was not unique in bureaucratic confusion. All belligerents passed through administrative experimentation on the road to total war. Professor Deist reminds us, for example, that Hitler also practiced the arts of economic improvisation; that a comprehensively planned and centrally-directed economic program also failed to emerge in early German mobilization.

Furthermore, it can be argued that the American output of munitions and troops is perhaps even more impressive in the light of the confusing, ad hoc central administration that Professor Koistinen describes. The United States did, after all, supply 60 percent of all combat munitions of the Allies in 1944. At home, economic and social gains did reach less privileged groups swept up in industrial mobilization, and organized interests among agricultural producers and industrial workers consolidated the gains they had made during the 1930s in relation to central state administration and to the Democratic Party. Their representatives did enter war administration and they did influence the shape of mobilization policies. Both farm and labor groups played a role in the politics of manpower mobilization, for example. So a variety of interests influenced industrial and economic policies to their benefit, even if they did not offset major business corporations in general economic power and administrative influence.

And finally, within the narrower realm of industrial-military administration, a war council did not emerge, it is true, but the war experience did provide an important source of administrative knowledge, and participants later sought to remedy the institutional weaknesses of wartime when they drafted the National Security Act of 1947, the administrative charter of postwar defense organization. For example, under that Act, a National Security Resources Board (NSRB) was established and charged with the coordination of military, industrial and civilian mobilization, and its chairman, in order to coordinate more effectively economics and strategy, acquired a seat in the National Security Council. Which is not to say that serious problems did not remain; but only to suggest that managers did try to learn from their wartime experiences. In sum, then, we can make a more positive evaluation of a number of specific outcomes that Professor Koistinen cites negatively in his paper.

This is especially the case when we consider the limiting circumstances, especially political constraints, outside and inside the Roosevelt administration, as well as the complicated nature of the problems requiring a solution. Professor Polenberg shows in his work, for example, how in the realm of finance executive initiatives for steeper tax and revenue policies ran afoul of Congressional politics, how the Farm Bloc fought price controls, how national service legislation went down to defeat, and how an anti-New Deal political coalition lunged after New Deal symbols such as the National Resources Planning Board. The wartime fate of NSRB is a telling example of the obstacles in the path of national economic planning, since it was the closest the administration ever came to sponsoring a comprehensive planning approach to national economic problems. Within the administration itself, vested bureaucratic interests, both civilian and military, obstructed central political discipline. And again, Washington was not unique in this. Professor Deist shows that bureaucratic rivalries also plagued German rearmament. These then are some of the counterjudgements one can make of American economic mobilization from a different—and obviously more charitable—evaluative perspective.

I realize, however, there are difficulties with this kind of response to a revisionist challenge. For one thing, the polemical tone of the revisionist critique frequently throws the respondent on the defensive—especially the moral defensive—and Professor Koistinen's paper is no exception. One can end up sounding like an apologist for the Roosevelt administration—or for capitalist elites, or for capitalism—and unsympathetic to social democratic aspirations. These are not my intentions. More seriously, one can also fall into a philosophical trap—and that is of yielding up the realm of freedom in history for the realm of necessity; of saying that what happened had to happen; that in this case wartime events defied the control of even powerful corporate elites and the White House. Professor Koistinen criticizes Professor Blum and others, and I think rather ungenerously, on just this point.

Moreover, the response so far does not come to grips with Professor Koistinen's central claim: that the situation, even granting limited achievements and political constraints, could still have been very different—better administered and organized certainly, probably more democratic as well—if only FDR had acted differently. For example, he argues that conservative attacks on liberal economic initiatives succeeded in part because Roosevelt refused to fight persistently against them. Roosevelt embraced "Dr.-Win-The-War" too willingly.

113

Perhaps this is true. Perhaps FDR could have done more for social democratic change in wartime. To support Professor Koistinen's point we could speculate on the situation in later 1945 had Henry Wallace succeeded to the presidency. In that case, there probably would have been more White House support for the policies Professor Koistinen favors. Washington observers in the British Embassy would have agreed, for example. They believed that Wallace entertained a "view of the New Deal as the New Islam."

The person in the White House obviously makes a difference. Moreover, Koistinen shows that FDR did consider, if only to reject, real options in mobilization management. There was some freedom of choice, in other words. For example, in 1939 Roosevelt scuttled the Industrial Mobilization Plan (IMP) that military and business representatives had fashioned during the 1930s, only to be driven back to its essential form by 1943 after years of wasted administrative motion. Similarly, he rejected proposals for closer collaboration between military and civilian planning systems. Professor Koistinen obviously has a significant point here.

But why did Roosevelt do these things—or fail to do other things? On this point I find Professor Koistinen surprisingly vague, beyond his attribution to Roosevelt of an underlying motive to protect the status quo in power relations. I say "surprising" because so much of the paper's argument turns on Roosevelt's behavior. In general, Professor Koistinen measures the Roosevelt performance against two criteria: coherent economic planning and the transformation of power relations, and Roosevelt naturally fares badly on both counts because he never gave high priority to either. But in justice, I think we can add a third criterion—and one closer to Roosevelt's intentions— and that is the criterion of rallying and sustaining a New Deal political coalition for reelection and a nation for a united world war effort. In this context it becomes common sense and not deviousness to avoid, where possible, confrontation with major power groups, both inside and outside of Washington.

As Professor Koistinen illustrates in his own writing, Roosevelt rejected the IMP in part because he could not afford politically to be seen to support a plan that organized labor and agricultural spokesmen and influential New Dealers opposed, even if he had wanted it himself. The Plan included the representatives of none of these groups so central to his political base. It is important to note too that we have here an example of FDR obstructing, not appeasing, corporate spokesmen, insofar as we can identify them as supporters of IMP. So if a key question rests on Roosevelt's motives for action or inaction in economic mobilization, there is far more to consider than his relation to military and business leaders. Industrial and economic policies were fashioned in relation to concerns for national morale and for partisan political consequences.

Moreover, it would be difficult to prove in every instance that altered planning structures would have improved economic mobilization. For example, it might have been the case that a disruption occasioned by a major reorganization at any one point—such as elimination of procurement authority from the military services—would have brought more costs than benefits. Woodrow Wilson accepted this argument against a Munitions Ministry in World War I, for example. He gave authority to Bernard Baruch in the War Industries Board partly to avoid that more radical institutional option. Nor is it necessarily the case that more systematic economic planning would have solved the problem— if it is a problem—of concentrating munitions production in large-scale enterprise. Nor, finally, was Roosevelt unique among American war presidents in failing to establish a single, administrative center of economic and industrial control. Wilson and Truman established competing authorities in their respective mobilizations. Perhaps the issue is less the president than a structure of government that compels him to husband his personal power and protect his personal autonomy in a competitive political and bureaucratic environment. Thus the fear of yielding to superagencies.

But let us suppose that FDR had been motivated to transform the American economic power structure and to institute permanent forms of democratic national planning. It seems to me there are three structural contexts we need to consider in judging the potential for this change before subscribing to Professor Koistinen's harsh judgment of Roosevelt's failure to bring it about.

The first of these, and one that Koistinen himself has done much to inform us about in previous work, is the power of private corporate decision-makers in industrial mobilization. Private business decision-makers in the United States had already demonstrated unparalled ability to retain prerogatives notwithstanding economic and wartime crises. And they continued to exact a price for their private performances. Charles Lindblom has speculated on the contemporary implications of this continuing phenomenon in his *Politics and Markets,* and Secretary of War Henry L. Stimson caught the essence of it in the early stages of American war mobilization: "If you are going to try to go to war or to prepare for war in a capitalist country, you've got to let business make money out of the process or business won't work." Roosevelt in the so-called defense period had to adapt to the reluctance of producers to convert to munitions production. Continued production of private aircraft in the face of rising military demand annoyed military circles, including Stimson. Yet Washington's obvious dependency on the cooperation of private power-holders remained. Washington had to bargain, and bargaining means joint decisionmaking and shared power.

In addition, those with governmental authority did not possess relevant knowledge and control in technical matters, while those with technical knowledge and industrial control did not possess governmental authority. The goal, in a crisis, was to bind them together, not drive them apart, and yet to do this in a nation divided on the very issue of war itself. And here policy middlemen—investment bankers and corporate lawyers—men like Ferdinand Eberstadt played important roles. A similar pattern of gradual rapprochment had occurred with the Wilson administration in World War I, and Bernard Baruch played shrewdly the role of policy middleman between private and public powerholders. For Stimson, Patterson, and the rest the issue was how to overcome economic and political obstacles to cooperation both in government and in the economy. Private managers occupied strategic bargaining positions in the process. And not only because of their ultimate control over the production means and familiarity with technical processes, but also because of their influential positions as policy-makers in emergency agencies. The probable implications of business influence and bargaining within emergency political administration in wartime was already evident in the NRA experience, and in the War Industries Board experience before that.

The second fundamental structural condition a president devoted to national planning would have had to confront in the 1940s was the comparative underdevelopment of the administrative capacity of the central state, including the absence of a permanent higher civil service at the heart of government. This is a dimension that Professor Koistinen does not comment upon but one that is central to American mobilization dilemmas. It is true that the scope of federal government increased immeasurably in the 1930s. It is unnecessary to subscribe to James Burnham's managerial revolution thesis to acknowledge the growth of the regulatory apparatus, the creation of TVA, the Budget Bureau, the Executive Office of the President and so on. Public administrators regarded the war mobilization as a brilliant opportunity to vindicate their New Deal accomplishments. Some even hoped to go forward with essentially New Deal agencies and personnel. This, I suspect, was a restraining force on cooperation between the President and various business interests in early mobilization as the rejection of IMP suggests.

Yet the legacy of the thirties in administrative personnel and central coordinating machinery was rudimentary at best, as Otis Graham and others have pointed out, and a cadre of political appointments loyal to the President is not the same as a higher civil service. Economic mobilization demanded far more, and so Washington turned to private organizations and to private managerial elites—to academics, scientists, lawyers and other professionals, as well as businessmen—for personnel and administrative support, much as it had done in World War I. Professor Funigiello describes how in the area of federal-state relations, for example, the absence of a federal bureaucratic apparatus made reliance upon local officials likely even if there had been enthusiasm for an alternative. A central war administration that relied heavily upon private voluntary personnel did not provide a stable basis for presidential control or for coherent administration. Wartime Washington was awash with competing centers of administrative decision-making. Lester Pearson, the Canadian Ambassador, observed one of the consequences: "Commitments to other governments made on one level in Washington were not or could not be fully implemented on another. This is not due to bad faith, but to the lack of coordination of the activity and authority of so many unrelated decision-makers."

Some commentators tried to put the best face on these developments by suggesting that in the United States bureaucracy itself was representative, just as in

Washington "czars" were democratic. In the United States, it was believed, hoped, that democracy and efficiency combined in exceptional ways. Private groups were admitted to the administrative game in areas that concerned them, so the argument ran: agricultural groups in farm policy; labor groups in manpower and labor policy; industrialists in industrial mobilization policy; scientists in scientific policy; military in military policy, and so on—a variant of pluralist theory, and a promise of intense jurisdictional conflicts. Such a view, of course, is simply making a virtue of necessity from the perspective of a coherent national administration and a permanent higher civil service, even when it is not misleading as a complete picture of political reality. Some liberal critics hoped to find in an expanded managerial presidency a source for administrative coherence and control; others, like James Forrestal, longed for a cabinet form of government and for the British civil service tradition.

The point here is that political structures can help to explain how patterns of conflict were likely to develop in war administration, as diverse groups struggled for position and power, irrespective of a particular president's intent. And it is also to caution against trying to explain what was in effect a collective institutional enterprise in terms of a single individual's behavior.

The third structure to consider in estimating the potential for national planning to emerge from the war is a structure of ideas—a political culture or set of cultural norms—in which the administration of economic mobilization and demobilization was embedded. Professor Koistinen makes the important point in his paper that Roosevelt had to negotiate a tension between an elitist reality and a populist ideology. He concentrates on the elitist realities, but we should not overlook the populist or democratic ideology. This is not easy to characterize. However, I think we can say that under the press of wartime crisis and the cultural pressure to distinguish American democracy from its fascist, Nazi, and eventually its Communist counterparts, that this democratic ideology did not promise support for departures in peacetime national planning.

In American social life, this cultural pressure seems to have strengthened the hold of possessive individualism on middle class life, a major theme of Professor Blum's book. With its enthusiasm for images of market success, and its compulsion for competitive emulation, this set of private-orientated values held little promise for those who hoped for more collectivist efforts toward democratic planning. If the populist ideology Professor Koistinen mentions feared aggregations of economic power, it is also feared aggregations of state power, despite the New Deal, indeed in some circles because of the New Deal. It was an ideology as well that remained suspicious of the very forms of close cooperation between private interests and the state that the haphazard, ad hoc American form of interventionism required in the absence of a coherent national bureaucracy. There were contradictions between elitism and democratic ideology in American economic mobilization and demobilization, but there were contradictions in the ideology itself.

These then are three structural patterns—in political economy, politics and culture—that wove their way through American industrial and economic mobilization. And they are institutional patterns in which a president encountered *both* freedom and necessity. Recognition of these patterns does not automatically answer the difficult questions that Professor Koistinen poses: why did certain changes not occur; what motivated Roosevelt? But I do believe they are worth considering in trying to comprehend the institutional field in which Roosevelt and corporate elites pursued their converging and diverging goals. Ultimately, of course, a more definitive answer to such difficult questions will gain from a comparative institutional perspective that a reading of Professor Deist's work encourages us to consider.

DISCUSSION AND COMMENTS

Russell F. Weigley (Moderator)

Weigley: We're really up against the clock. I'm going to give Professor Koistinen an opportunity to respond if he wishes to Professor Cuff's remarks because those remarks have so much focused on his paper. I know that the few minutes I can offer Professor Koistinen won't be adequate. I also regret that we must defer any kind of participation on the part of the audience until the summary session tomorrow. Paul do you want to say anything?

Koistinen: Yes, I would like to say a few words. I don't want to take up Cuff's three points specifically, but I do want to make a comment which I think embraces all three.

In a sense, what we have encountered in the twentieth century is the corporate community attempting to work out a system in which it will deal with modern industrialization in a way that does not violate America's individualistic, and in a sense, even populistic, ideology. It has done that through various organizations, starting around the turn-of-the-century with the National Civic Federation. It pursued that quest in the 1920s with the associational activities promoted by Herbert Hoover. The search continued in the 1930s with the organization of the Business Advisory Council and the National Planning Association, and in the 1940s with the Council of Economic Development and the like. Together with other major interest groups, particularly labor, and to some degree the consumer and the government, these institutions attempted to work out a system capable of operating a modern industrial state. We reached some point of fruition in this effort with World War I.

The First World War presented a situation in which a planned economy was needed, and a sort of system was created in which one couldn't tell where private started and public stopped and vice versa. There was some effort immediately after the war years to perpetuate this system. That attempt failed. But the planning effort did continue through things like the associational activities and trade associations. What was encountered during World War I, however, was a very recalcitrant military. The military obstructed. In effect, the military was not ready to integrate itself into, and participate in, the twentieth century. In contrast, what we had during World War II were ideal circumstances for change. We had ideal circumstances in that the military was no longer the obstructionist element. You don't need what Cuff is speaking about in terms of the civil service if what the so-called business liberals had been preaching since the turn of the century was true: that business can be responsible, that it will work out relationships with labor, that it will be responsible to the larger commonwealth, that it will work with consumer groups. Business liberals had their golden opportunity during World War II. But yet when we look at some of the major representatives of this very business liberalism we see men like Donald Nelson. Nelson would not confront, he retreated. Another case in point is William Batt* who sided continually with the more traditional elements such as the National Association of Manufacturers and the Chamber of Commerce. In effect, it wasn't just Roosevelt who failed. What I am speaking of is the corporate community. The corporate community has promised something throughout the twentieth century and has not delivered. What I am saying is that since the corporate community had failed, the Roosevelt Administration had a new opportunity: it could have employed the military, a very new power group, to force the corporate community to live up to its promises. Roosevelt demonstrated what very few American commanders-in-chief have demonstrated: he would use his powers as commander-in-chief. Accordingly, he could have used the military to persuade corporate America to assume greater responsibility than it did.

Weigley: Thank you. I am sorry that I must cut off this lively debate.

---

*Ed note: Among his other wartime posts, William L. Batt was Vice Chairman of the War Production Board.

BANQUET ADDRESS

BANQUET ADDRESS

Hollywood Goes to War

David H. Culbert

The banquet address at the Tenth Military History Symposium took the form of a visual analysis of selected World War II propaganda films. The banquet speaker, Professor David H. Culbert, assembled and edited clips from a variety of motion pictures ranging from Walt Disney cartoons to Army information films. Much of the footage was rare; all of it was very interesting. Professor Culbert introduced and commented on the film clips and shared his ideas on the use of motion pictures as instruments of propaganda in war.

SESSION III

SOCIAL EFFECTS OF TOTAL WAR

SOCIAL EFFECTS OF TOTAL WAR

INTRODUCTORY REMARKS

Richard H. Kohn

Yesterday we studied in broad essentials the heart of the home front in war: mobilizing the human and material resources to prosecute conflict, a problem that has increasingly expanded as war has expanded in the nineteenth and twentieth centuries. The stress and strain produced in society is often immense, as John Blum persuaded us. He questioned the conventional interpretation, which I still perceive as current in American society if not among scholars, that the United States was truly unified in World War II. David Culbert showed us one of the key mechanisms by which the state, itself a product, in many respects, of the expansion of war-making in western society, attempted to dampen dissent and unify and motivate the population, at heart, the fundamental precondition for prosecuting a war.

Today, we study the results: first, by probing some of the social effects of war; then by looking for contrast, and I think in some ways for a very enlightening contrast, at two limited wars, since we have spent virtually all of the conference to this point studying the home front in total war.

These effects of total war at home on societies have long been felt by historians to be immense. However, we have usually assumed, rather than concluded, that there was change, in part because change seemed to make such sense. Over fifty years ago, for example, J. Franklin Jamison, in a little book called *The American Revolution Considered as a Social and Economic Movement,* focused on various effects of the Revolution, and in the process, of course, confused the Revolution with the war. One single aspect, such as the confiscation of Tory estates, set in motion processes that led downstream to immense social, political, or economic change. Later, R. R. Palmer compared the effects of revolution on French and American society by comparing the number of refugees that each movement created. And as recently as the last ten years, John Shy has looked specifically at the War of American Independence and at the effects that mobilization and service had on individuals and groups. This approach has continued. We have looked at war after war in broad context and simply posited the fact that there was change: in World Wars I and II, the movement of people, the effect on the black population of service in France in World War I, and the acceleration of the great migration from the South; the movement of people in World War II, stimulation of science and technology, the introduction of atomic power, the introduction of far greater numbers of women into the labor force in non-traditional roles; even one single facet, the GI Bill of Rights, and how education might have transformed American society.

Thus there are problems in exploring this topic. When we deal with the effects of total war, we are dealing blindly with an elephant, feeling the sides of it. We know that it is immense, but we don't really quite know how to deal with it. If you were to take the Soviet Union alone, in World War II, and step back using some of Arthur Marwick's organizing ideas about the effect of the disruption, the destruction, the participation of individuals, the psychological experience of it—if you look at the Soviet Union in World War II, you say, "What must have happened?" Here was a huge nation. About half of its inhabited areas were occupied. Vast armies traversed it for four years. Perhaps 1,700 towns and 70,000 villages were leveled, cities reduced to rubble, perhaps 20 million people died, and another 25 million rendered homeless. A vast guerrilla war was fought behind the lines. Three million Russians, Byelorussians, and Ukrainians went to Germany as slave labor. What indeed must have been the social effects? How do we probe this? How do we deal with this problem?

One way is to produce microscopic studies, as was thought in World War I, at the time when the Carnegie Endowment for International Peace commissioned many studies, some 144 volumes of them. But we have trouble philosophically dealing with these issues, with showing the linkage of change and war, and avoiding the post-hoc fallacy. Are these direct or are these indirect effects? How much time must pass before factors other than war, other than the disruptions and destructions and the psychological effects, can be said to have caused change?

Historians are only beginning to come to grips with many of these questions in a systematic way. Arthur Marwick, Harvard Sitkoff, and Leila Rupp will deal with these questions this morning. They are themselves questioning much of the conventional wisdom on what war created or how much change war caused. I see another problem in this scholarly effort. Two of our speakers this morning come at the problem from the continuity of the study of particular groups in American society, and one of our speakers comes at it directly from the standpoint of assessing war's effect. The results are, I think, rather interesting, and I think will stimulate you to consider one of the major questions in dealing with war and the social history of any society.

Chairman Kohn's Introduction of Dr. Arthur Marwick
Our first speaker is Arthur Marwick, who studied at Balliol College, Oxford, and Edinburgh University, from which he received the Doctor of Letters degree. He was appointed the first professor of history at the pioneering Open University when it was founded in 1969, and he has been Dean of Arts there since 1978. I

counted on his resume some eleven books authored or edited, many of them centered on the question of the effects of war and the social history of society at war. Three of his books alone have focused on Britain, war and social change; another of his works has examined women at war from 1914 to 1918. But I think for our session this morning, he is probably best known for his *War and Social Change in the Twentieth Century: A Comparative Study of Britain, France, Germany, Russia and the United States*. He will speak to us this morning on "Total War and Social Change in Great Britain and Other European Countries."

TOTAL WAR AND SOCIAL CHANGE IN GREAT BRITAIN AND OTHER EUROPEAN COUNTRIES

Arthur Marwick

Recently British historians have been saying some arresting things about the First World War. Ross McKibbin has insisted that the transformation of the Labour Party as between the Edwardian era and the 1920s had nothing to do with the war; the basic factor was the reform of the franchise in 1918.[1] Briefly allowing himself a more generous glance round British society, McKibbin further argued that there had been little change in the structure of Britain as a result of the war: "The towns were no larger than they had been; there were few new industries; there was no increase in the mobility of the population; despite fashionable forms of social dissent there was little of that political disorientation so noticeable on the Continent."[2] In this contention, McKibbin was joined by Paul Thompson, respected author of an excellent work on *The Edwardians,* who ventured sufficiently far out of his time to deny any significance to the war in bringing about social change.[3] On the much discussed subject of women's suffrage, Martin Pugh has claimed that there is no evidence that women's war work materially affected the issue, and that, indeed, women gained less in 1918 than they would have done had there been no war.[4] Feminist writers, too, have maintained that, since women are still downtrodden today, they could not possibly have made any real gains during the First World War.[5] It is, of course, traditional to stress the negative effects of war. W. J. Reader, in his history of Imperial Chemical Industries, writes, with perhaps more cleverness than illumination: "The Great War, in the world of the chemical industry as in the world at large, shattered the old order, set a great many questions about what would replace it, and provided answers to none of them."[6] Philippe Bernard's volume in the most up-to-date general history of modern France is called *La Fin d'un Monde 1914-1929.*[7] Marxists have had problems, wanting to see the war as fostering revolutionary tendencies, yet having to admit that it often seemed to create national solidarity.[8] The German historian Gerd H. Hardach has preferred to stress the continuities across the war period, and has joined with the distinguished French historian Marc Ferro in pointing to the Russian Revolution as the single most significant consequence of the war.[9] However, there have also been some more complex attempts to situate the war within the general development of twentieth century society. Keith Middlemas in Britain has seen it as marking a critical stage in the reallocation of power as between government and unions and employers, taking society a long way towards, as he sees it, the corporatist society.[10] Similar arguments have been presented by the Americans, Gerald Feldman and Charles Maier, and Feldman, concentrating on Germany, has seen the war as prologue to the first era in which statesmen had to wrestle with the very contemporary economic problems of inflation, and the balance between government and private spending.[11]

Perhaps, even in the most complex and subtle analyses, there is a too ready tendency to look in a direct, one-to-one way, for war's "effects" or "consequences"—often, of course, for the very purpose of denying their existence. We do not really have war as one independent variable to be added to another, society, to produce "consequences." What we really have is a complex interrelationship—best pinned down by the phrase "society at war"—wherein there are many reactions, interactions, and mechanisms of both destruction *and* change, that change being of many different orders. Thus, I prefer to speak of "war and social change." Social change, of course, is taking place anyway. It may, indeed, help to bring about a war; it will certainly determine the means by which the war is waged. It is with such considerations in mind, that I offer my own form of analysis of the relationship between war and social change. I do not offer a set of common generalizations about war and social change, but rather a means towards exploring particular relationships in different wars and in different societies. In the last few weeks I have examined a University of Malta thesis in which the method was successfully applied to the experience of Malta during the First World War; and the method was also effectively used in the well-known book by Neil Wynn, *The Afro-American and the Second World War.* History is, of course, very much concerned with the particular and unique. In any study we must be careful to establish the nature of the society we are examining, and the forms and extent of change already taking place in that society. We must make an assessment of the social "size" of the war: how total? how limited? And, thirdly, we must be clear about the degree of physical impingement of the war: invasion of all, or part, of a country's territory? Heavy civilian bombardment, or considerable geographical isolation from actual theatres of war?—all this, naturally, is finally bound in with the question of whether the nation is on the winning or the losing in turn, is by no means as simple as it sounds. These matters taken care of, the intricate relationship between war and social change can then best, my argument is, be teased out by taking in turn the four "dimensions" within which war interacts with society. These are: the destructive and disruptive dimension; the "test" dimension; the participation dimension; and the psychological dimension.

When I speak of destruction-disruption I am referring to the most obvious aspect, the catastrophic face of war, and in working out its implications I have drawn both upon historical observation of what has actually happened in wars and upon the disaster studies of social scientists. The destruction of war can certainly, as many liberal commentators have stressed, put a stop to peacetime social progress. In looking at any particular society in any particular war it is necessary to see first whether the total destructive effect outweighs any positive results accruing from the destruction. Because positive results there often are. Again and again—in face of natural disaster as well as in face of war—we see the desire within human societies to rebuild, and to rebuild better than before. That apart, the disruption of war forces people into new life-styles and patterns of living and behaviour and offers new opportunities; it is necessary, of course, to scrutinize these very carefully to see whether they are long-lasting or merely temporary.

To talk of the "test" dimension of war is perhaps to stray too far into the realm of common wisdom, or even cliche. Certainly studies of war of all types are full of references, overt or covert, to the way in which war tests social organizations, institutions, ideas, as well as personal qualities. In my view there is validity in this idea of "test"—provided we handle it with very great care—and my argument is that through the test of war, ideas, institutions and so on are destroyed, or reinforced or altered, but that anyway there is social change, whether backwards, forwards or downwards. The trouble with the word "test" is that it seems to imply a kind of value judgment (perhaps conjuring up a vision of the hard-working little swot who passes his examinations), and perhaps even suggests that it is an important function of social organization to be prepared for war—that well-prepared societies are reinforced and perhaps in some cases moderately and beneficially altered, while ill-prepared societies collapse. This is not the argument at all. The word test should be taken to include also the connotations of stress and strain (perhaps I should coin a new word "strest"). The argument is not that it is good that societies from time to time should be submitted to the "challenge" (for there is an element of challenge in this too) of war but that, historically, it has in fact been in the nature of human society that wars do occur. These wars submit social institutions to a combination ot test, stress, strain and challenge, in turn producing changes which may well seem to be highly undesirable—such as the creation of autocracy or a secret police. But, my argument runs, such is the irony of human events, and such the power of greater complexes of social and human circumstances over the mere aspirations of individual humans, that often the changes are in a direction which many would hold to be beneficial—as, for instance, in the democratization of institutions, or the abandonment of purely laissez-faire doctrines.

The idea that there is some correlation between the extent to which different groups in society participate in a war and the social gains which these groups make is also, as all the best ideas are, fairly obvious. It was first fully developed in Stanislav Andreski's famous and seminal work *Military Organisation and Society (1954)*, and elements of this idea have appeared implicitly or explicitly ever since in various different works. Andreski actually coined the term "MPR" (Military Participation Ratio). I prefer to stick simply to "participation" since it is participation in civilian employment in time of war which often seems to be the more potent force for social change than actual participation in the armed forces. And this brings me to the point that in using this concept one has to analyze very carefully the nature and extent of the participation involved. I have no quantitiative tools for doing this but it seems clear, both in nature and in consequence, that there is a qualitative difference between, say, the participation of the black American conscript in the Vietnam War, and the participation of women volunteers in the Women's Land Army in Britain during the First World War. Here, as with all of the first three of my dimensions, we begin to overlap with the fourth dimension, the psychological; at any rate, among other relevant issues, it is of importance to know something of the extent to which the individual himself *feels* that he is a participant. But in broad outline participation has two major aspects. First, it can involve the conscious decision of the ruling elements in society that since underprivileged elements have participated in the national effort they should be directly rewarded. However, the second and more important aspect is that, irrespective of the wishes and actions of the country's leaders, participation directly touches off mechanisms of social change and levelling, through, in particular, the operation of supply and demand within the market, and through the prestige and status accumulated by the participants in the war effort. In my view, historians who persist in seeing social change as something done by "us" (the upper and middle class) to "them" (the lower classes) have gone sadly wrong in concentrating on, and then usually dismissing, the first aspect. Thus, many years ago now, Philip Abrams was able to write about "The Failure of Social Reform: 1918-1920"[12] because he was looking solely for guided, conscious reform brought about by the government to reward the working classes; he ignored totally changes brought about irrespective of the direct actions of government. More recently Henry Pelling, in discussing World War II, has fallen into the same error, phrasing the theory exclusively in the following fashion: "Modern wars have called for an increasingly large participation by the people as a whole, and as a price for their support the people in one way or another secured compensation in the form of increased social welfare." Pelling then continued: "Unfortunately for the supporters of the theory of the military participation ratio, in neither of these two periods [the two world wars] was it assumed by the government that war if it came, would require the active participation of the bulk of the population."[13] Actually, it is not a question of what governments assumed but of what actually happened when thousands of individuals found themselves in possession of new economic and political strength and heightened social prestige. Dr. Pelling then goes on to misrepresent the arguments of Professor R. C. O. Mathews in developing his case that participation in the Second World War was not relevant to the change from a mass unemployment economy to a full employment economy. In fact, Professor Mathews very properly indicates the effects working-class participation had had in bringing about a significant "change in entrepreneurial attitudes"—in other words an end to the "hire 'em fire 'em" attitudes of the thirties. (A major part of Mathews' explanation of full employment falls under what I would call the test dimension of war—the war giving the economy "a once-for-all hoist upwards.")[14]

To talk simply of the psychological dimension of war is both to seem to beg many questions, and (as already noted) to overlap with points touched on in regard to the other three dimensions. Again, there is a distinction to be made between the responses triggered off in various parts of the community irrespective of government action, and the deliberate moves of the government to maintain morale. Once more it is my view that historians, in keeping with the traditional rather overpersonalized view of historical processes, have put too much emphasis on the latter to the exclusion of the former. The "unguided" psychological responses can be fairly precisely designated under two main headings. First there is the intensification of "in-group" feelings and a heightening of hostility to "out-groups," which can mean a great loyalty to one's nation, and a canalizing of hostility towards enemy nations, but can also mean an intensification of loyalty to one's immediate community or social class, with an intensification of hostility towards other social classes, or minority and immigrant groups within the society. The second aspect is the way in which war produces an expectation of, and therefore demand for change. This is in part related to the disruption of war which projects people into new roles and provides them with new reference groups, and that, in turn, is partly related back to government attempts to maintain morale.

As I have most unwisely undertaken to deal not only with two wars, but with several countries, I shall fairly briefly outline my main conclusions in regard to British society in the First World War, taking each of my dimensions in turn, before, with even greater brevity, pointing up some comparisons and contrasts from the experience of one or two other European countries. I shall then repeat the same cavalier treatment with World War II.

In Britain the ironic twist to the disruptive effect of war shows itself most obviously in education and in housing. Liberal plans for further educational reform were in fact halted by the war and in the course of the war educational standards for the bulk of the country's children worsened considerably as influential local employers and farmers maneuvered to have children released from school to work "in the national interest"—i.e., in the interests of the local employers and farmers. All normal developments in house building were brought to a stop, and by the end of the war it was quite clear that private enterprise could no longer provide houses at rents the working classes could afford; there was in any case now an appalling short-fall of houses. These immense, and highly visible, gaps in the country's social provision helped (in combination, of course, with the other dimensions of war) to create the political will to pass the Fisher Education Act and the Addison Housing Act at the end of the war. Now, it is of course true that these acts achieved much less in practice than they promised on paper (a point seized on by Philip Abrams in regard to the Addison Housing Act). But, while it is certainly a serious, and very traditional error to write history as if every act of parliament was in itself a concrete social change, it is also an error to underestimate the role of parliamentary legislation in setting new norms for a society. The (completely new) idea of central government subsidies for working-class house building was now the new basic norm in housing policy, and one realized with some success after 1924. Where governments fell behind there was now a legislative standard against which to measure their failings: much of the history of social policy in the inter-war years is the history of the struggles of Labour local authorities to carry out declared (often Conservative) national policies. The importance of the disruptive effects of war in altering working-class reference groups, and therefore creating a continuing demand for further social change, has been well summed up by W. G. Runciman in his standard work *Relative Deprivation and Social Justice*.[15]

The leisure pursuits of both rich and poor were seriously interrupted by the war, but since the various sporting activities were resumed unchanged after the armistice, the long-term effects on British society of these various minor disruptions can be discounted. On the other hand the new tensions and excitements of war undoubtedly gave rise to new leisure patterns in which dancing and nightclubs played a prominent part, creating that hedonistic subculture more often associated with the 1920s. The introduction in 1916 of military conscription was of profound social significance. Conscription meant that first-hand experience of war was brought, not merely to two million volunteers and professionals, but, willy-nilly, to twice as many ordinary unadventurous citizens—one in three of the adult male population.

The test of war is to be seen most obviously in the change in social and economic ideologies and institutions: in the change, crudely from laissez-faire and piecemeal social policy to a situation in which, for example, the state assumed full responsibility for war pensions, and went on to extend the rudimentary unemployment insurance provision of 1911 to the working class as a whole. Certainly the British Government made a pretty determined attempt to put the clock back in the early twenties but it could not succeed everywhere, and it, and the nation at large, always had before it "The Analogue of War"—when the going got tough, the automatic question tended to be "what did we do in the war?"[16] Some institutions, and many people, were beyond the reach of government. The Left, for instance, had no wish to put the clock back; in J. M. Winter's study of *Socialism and the Challenge of War* (1974) the notion of the test dimension of war is very central. Writing of Sidney and Beatrice Webb, R. H. Tawney, and G. D. H. Cole, Winter declares: "The ideas of each of these thinkers were severely *tested* during the war" (my italics), and he shows how in their different ways they pushed towards developing the new ideological consensus which effectively underlay much Labour Party policy in the inter-war years.[17] The extension, particularly in the last years of the war, of state control over major industries, and almost all imports, is well-known. More interesting, is the way in which war tested Britain's woeful inadequacies in the exploitation of science and technology. A white paper issued in July 1915 outlined a form of "permanent organisation for the promotion of industrial and scientific research."[18] After an interim existence as a committee of the Privy Council, a separate government department, the Department of Scientific and Industrial Research (DSIR) emerged, and soon took over the running of the National Physical Laboratory. The Medical Research Committee has its origins in the 1911 National Insurance Act, but it really only achieved significance in response to the necessities of war. Through the Medical Research Committee vital work was carried out on dysentery, typhoid, cerebro-spinal fever, and new antiseptics. Permanence was assured with the change of title in April 1920 to Medical Research Council. In responding to the needs of war, Britain found itself by the war's end equipped for the first time with a motorcar industry, a nascent film industry, a nascent radio industry, and with its electrical generating power doubled.[19] Ross McKibbin has made much of the absence of any striking quantitative change in the structure of British industry: the point is that, though relatively small in size, these new industries had enormous potency for further social change.

The obvious areas in which participation involved social change are those concerning the working class as a whole, and women. In the first place there is the simple question of strengthened market position. Men were required to fill the vast armies in the front line; beyond that they were required to man the factories upon which the entire war effort depended. As men were sucked into the trenches they had to be replaced by up-grading unskilled labor, and by bringing women into jobs which women had never done before. Because there was a demand for labor, workers, women and men, were able to exact higher wages. It was simply not worthwhile for the government to allow strikes to take place; better to offer war bonuses than to permit the country's entire war effort to collapse. That labor was in fact willing to use its strengthened bargaining position is clearly seen from the large number of strikes which took place in Britain, particularly in 1917. It is true that the cost of living tended to rise faster than actual wage rates; but family earnings, on the whole, kept ahead of rises in the cost of living, because of the increased number of wage-earners per family, and because of the longer hours of work available to anyone willing to put them in. Overall there was a very clear gain to the working class: they had the chance to purchase goods previously denied to them. And this taste for new standards of affluence was to remain with them as a continuing spur towards demanding further rises in their standard of living. The strengthened market position can also be seen in the growth of trade union membership, which rose from four million in 1914 to eight million in 1920. Stronger trade unions led (in combination with the desire of the government to reward labor for its efforts) to a reduction in the working week, from fifty hours at the beginning of the war to forty-eight in the early 1920s. Without doubt, the economic depression, itself largely a product of the disruptions of war, severely curtailed the gains made by the working class. The labor troubles of the early 1920s were part of the struggle of the workers to maintain the gains which they had made during the war against attempts to return them to pre-war standards.

A second way in which wartime conditions could be turned to the advantage of members of the working class was through their direct participation in government. When the coalition government was formed in May 1915, a post was allocated to the Secretary of the Labour Party, Arthur Henderson, whose general brief was to watch over the interests of labor and to maintain labor support for the government. When the small war cabinet was formed in December 1916, Henderson joined the select few, while a number of other Labour men were given important posts. These representatives of the Labour Party, then, were able to pressure governments into giving special attention to the social issues which were of particular interest to the working class. In the long term, the fact that Labour men were in government and were seen to work efficiently in government, greatly enhanced the claims of the Labour Party to be accepted as a possible party of government. Too much is sometimes made of the point (which is, nonetheless, extremely important) that the government felt it necessary, as it were, to *buy* the support of labor; that it deliberately sought, through social welfare measures, to maintain working-class morale and support for the war effort. The twin notions of boosting morale and of conceding rewards to the working class were an important element behind the major social reforms which took place at the end of the war.

The question of what gains, if any, women made from their participation in the war effort has been subject to much more controversy. While, after a slow start and against much resistance, there was a great expansion in female employment from the middle of the war onwards (a total increase of about one-and-a-quarter million). By the early 1920s there were only about 200,000 more women in employment than there had been immediately before the war. Great stress has been laid by feminist historians on the hostility to women's employment in the first years of peace, and to the way in which women were forced out of their wartime occupations. Again, quantities can be misleading: there were permanent gains in the professions, and in commerce, though these gains make little showing in the statistics. There is general agreement among feminists that women's wartime experience gave them a new self-confidence and a new willingness to assert themselves.[20] In fact, there is plenty of evidence to show that although many women had to go back into the old occupations as domestic servants or shop assistants, they were now willing and able to resist successfully the imposition of the humiliations which these occupations had connoted in Edwardian times.[21] Changes in women's employment opportunities during the war were very closely related to the changing circumstances of men, particularly the imposition of military conscription. The question of votes for women, too, is very closely related to the male experience. Britain before the war was very far from being a democracy: two-fifths of all adult males did not have the vote. The major voting qualification was that of residence; thus many soldiers, and munitions workers, who had formerly had the vote, actually lost it because of their war service. In addition to this, many war heroes came from social groups which had never had the vote in the first place. David H. Colse, in a brilliant article whose title is itself extremely revealing, has cut through Ross McKibbin's absurd efforts to treat the franchise reform of 1918 in artificial isolation from the circumstances of the war:

> The war quickly made a vast expansion of the franchise inevitable, by establishing the claim to vote of new categories of people—especially servicemen and women—and by making intolerable the old difficulties of access to the electoral register, particularly the twelve-month qualifying period.[22]

In detail, when the advocates of women's suffrage, who had curtailed their agitation in the interests of national unity, realized that reform of male suffrage was in the air, they reasserted the claims of women. Now, with the example of women's contribution to the national effort clearly apparent, they were pushing on an opening door (Colse deals effectively with Pugh's contentions in this matter).[23] In the new Representation of the People Act of 1918, which gave the vote to all men over twenty-one (except—and it is a significant point in regard to the participation thesis—conscientious objectors), the vote was conceded only to women over thirty, and a small property qualification was also insisted upon. Nonetheless, Mrs. Millicent Garrett Fawcett, leader of the Suffragist Movement, recognized this as a triumph, and recognized also what it owed to the war experience.[24] Mrs. Fawcett saw the restrictions upon women's franchise as temporary tactical concessions—there were convinced supporters of the principle of women's enfranchisement who had reservations about the possibility of women actually being in a majority in the electorate: but once the principle had been accepted, it was easy in 1928 to introduce voting for women on exactly the same basis as that for men. Winning the vote was important, but it should not divert attention from the (qualified) social and economic emancipation also gained. Undoubtedly the changes for women remained within the framework of a traditional conception of women's role in the family and in society. But we should beware of applying the standards of the later twentieth century to its earlier decades.

If the psychological dimension of war is seen as operating in the way I have suggested then we are in a position to resolve some of the contradictions between the over-romanticized patriotic view of the entire British nation being united in its efforts against Germany, and the clear evidence of working class militancy and, in some cases, hostility to middle-class and upper-class interests. In general, it was the upper elements in society, those in a position to bring about conscious social change, who felt the sense of united patriotic nationhood and identification of interests with the brave working class; it was working-class groups whose sense of class loyalty was strengthened and who were therefore all the more ready to *demand* social change. The two, apparently contradictory, tendencies thus come together to create a strong pressure for social change. With regard to the other major aspects of the psychological dimension of war, I would not wish to disagree with what James Joll says in the preface to his well-received general work, *Europe Since 1870:* "We can now see for instance that the First World War was not such a total break as it appeared to be, and that the movements and ideas which have conditioned the experiences of the later twentieth century had nearly all made their appearance before 1914."[25] The point about the war is that it gave a new currency and a new acceptability to these ideas, and by virtue of the very fact that it seemed like a total break to people at the time, reinforced the strength of these new ideas. The historian W. H. Dawson, writing in late 1916, expressed the whole mood very well:

> We are living at a time when days and weeks have the fullness and significance of years and decades. Who does not feel that since August 1914 England has in many ways broken with her past and entered an entirely new epoch in her history, marked by transformations of every kind, so that when the day of peace arrives, be it soon or late, we shall be confronted at home by an altogether altered situation?[26]

With regard to the arts in particular I can do no better than quote the introduction which the art critic P. G. Konody wrote in his introduction to *Modern War: Paintings by C. R. W. Nevinson (1917):*

It is fairly obvious that the ordinary representational manner of painting is wholly inadequate for the interpretation of this tremendous conflict in which all the forces of nature have to be conquered and pressed into service against the opposing enemy. A more synthetic method is needed to express the essential character of this cataclysmic war, in which the very earth is disembowelled and rocky mountain summits are blown sky-high to bury all life under the falling debris. How could even a faint echo of such things find its way into that species of enlarged and coloured newspaper illustration that continues to represent the art of the battle painter on the walls of the Royal Academy?

I quote, and discuss further, this passage in *War and Social Change in the Twentieth Century,* page 84. Paul Fussel's, *The Great War in Modern Memory* (1975) argues along the same lines in regard to the war's effects on literature.

What of the other European countries? The test of war was particularly devastating for rambling, shambling, Russian society. War brought the first real opportunity for middle-class participation, through the "voluntary organizations." Workers and peasants, even if in uniform, were, with rifles, a formidable threat to an incompetent regime. Revolution, such as it was, took place in Germany under the impact of defeat, but the crucial reallocations of power took place *during* the war, as Gerald Feldman has convincingly demonstrated. Change appears sharper in Russia and in Germany because these societies were more obviously autocratic in 1914. What of France? Here the important point to stress is that, despite optimistic predictions being voiced as early as 1915, women did not get the vote at the end of the war. Partly this was because traditional attitudes about the roles of the sexes was stronger in rural, Catholic France. But two other factors are also relevant: *all* French *men* already had the vote, so in France there could be no question of men's efforts helping to open the door for women; and, secondly, the French labor movement, being weaker than the British, was less able to push anyway. On the other hand, because France was industrially less developed than Britain, and because, indeed, she went through something of an industrial revolution to meet the demands of war, there was a permanent expansion in industrial employment for women.[27] That there is universal validity to the argument about the war experience changing women's own attitudes and enhancing their self-confidence gains further support from this extract from the journals of the American Ambassador to Belgium:

August 17, 1916. - One of the curious things the war has brought to Belgium is a certain liberation of women. They go out alone without chaperones; some of them walk among the poor side streets, and so forth, which many of them had never seen before. Girls ride everywhere on bicycles, there being no automobiles or other form of transport. Van Holder (a well-known Brussels painter) says girls come and pose at his studio for their portraits; girls of the best families, without a chaperone, as they never did before the war. And Count de Jonghe made a similar observation to me the other day. Women seem to have found themselves; they *work,* from patriotic motives, but they work.[28]

With the opening of the archives in the 1970s, there has been a spate of intensive work on British social policy and British social experience during the Second World War. Unfortunately, this has led one of the most brilliant of the younger historians, Dr. Josie Harris, to the tiresome conclusion that we cannot make any generalizations about the relationship between that war and social change till far more research has been accomplished and digested.[29] Again, I would appeal, not to the accumulation of still more evidence, but to the method whereby that evidence is analyzed. A. J. P. Taylor, in the concluding chapter of his final volume of the *Oxford History*, has emphazised the social changes he saw as accompanying the Second World War, as has Gordon Wright in his *The Ordeal of Total War*. Among the new generation of historians, Paul Addison in *The Road to 1945: British Politics and the Second World War*, argued that the war pushed the fulcrum of British politics towards a centre-left position. On the other hand, Henry Pelling very cautiously argued the case against the war having had any significant effects on British society. Angus Calder, in his massive study of the *People's War*, argued passionately that the war simply hastened the country along the old grooves, and the journalist and essayist Anthony Howard bluntly remarked that "1945 brought the biggest restoration of traditional values since 1660." In my view, Calder and Howard are measuring social change against some unreal socialist society of their own: Britain after 1945 manifestly was not such a society, therefore, they argue, the war did not bring about social change.

The great change in material standards for the vast majority of the British people as between the 1930s and the war and postwar period would seem not to be open to question, and certainly Calder seems to agree to this. I believe further that an analysis of the war experience in the light of my four dimensions, particularly that of participation, brings out clearly the central role of the war in bringing about this change. In this short essay, I do not wish to linger longer on this aspect. What I want to do is to concentrate on the question of the gradual change in attitudes towards social policy and social relationships which built up steadily throughout the war period. I believe that where many of those who argue that the war had no significant long-term effects have gone wrong is in posing a false antithesis between a glorious "people's war" in which there was a series of sudden mass conversions from selfishness to patriotism, and from snobbishness to practical socialism, and the postwar period in which all the conversions just as suddenly lapsed. I believe this incorrect analysis arises largely (as with the theory about "the failure of social reform" at the end of the First World War) from too strong a belief in the ability of human beings consciously to alter themselves and their environment. An analysis which brings out how change comes irrespective of the deliberate decisions of individuals, can uncover more realistically the slow build-up of change during the war period leading to lasting change in the postwar period.

Let me first of all take the question of civilian evacuation in face of the threat, and the reality, of enemy bombing, in itself an important segment of the disruptive dimension of the war. Evacuation has had much attention from social historians for, it is argued, it was the sudden projection of slum children into contact with wealthy middle class householders which aroused in the latter the social conscience which fed into the reforms at the end of the war. (Commentators of a different persuasion, of course, have excoriated the evacuation policy for the traumatic effects it undoubtedly had on some evacuees.)[30] To my mind it is better to see the evacuation experience as but a part, though a substantial one, of a much more extensive, forced intermingling of members of the upper and lower classes brought about by the disruption of this war. Thus in place of the rather limited picture of two short evacuations at the beginning of the war marked by many well-documented instances of rich and poor positively refusing to mix, followed by a final evacuation at the time of the V-bomb menace (where, significantly, the evidence does show a much greater, and unforced, mixing of classes), we have a much broader, developing process embracing the Women's Volunteer Service, the Auxiliary Fire Services, the other voluntary services and corps, and such unofficial activities as the establishment of playgroups for slum kids by middle class volunteers.[31]

If we turn to the test of war we find it at its most powerful in bringing about the collapse of local authority services, and in exposing the inadequacy in face of the blitz of the divided hospital services. We find in the Emergency Hospital Scheme the basis of the National Health Service at the end of the war, and we find a new powerful contempt for the style and methods of the old local elites. If any one single document merits quotation here, it is the unpublished report of Mass Observation on the East End blitz in September 1940, which in turn formed the basis of an article entitled, revealingly enough, "A Test for Democratic Institutions" in the *Economist:*

> Alas for Whitehall, it turned out quite differently. Nobody foresaw the tidal wave of refugees who fled all over the country after that first hideous weekend, inundating places like Oxford with homeless people, being decanted in peaceful Essex suburbs from lorries by desperate local authorities who hoped for the best that something would be done about them. Nobody foresaw that everybody would not know all about the official plans for them, that the rest centres would be overflowing, that people would stay there for weeks instead of hours, that people would not be able to be billeted in their own boroughs, that transport would not turn up, so that refugees were bombed to death in the rest centres, that people would flock to the tubes and unofficial deep shelters rather than use the official surface shelters which they regarded as death-traps. In fact, there were rather too many things that nobody foresaw for official democracy to plume itself very much on its efficiency as a wager of war on the Home Front.

But the report goes on to praise the magnificent work of the "mainly middle-class" voluntary workers. There is a wealth of evidence elsewhere of middle class anger over the incompetence of the authorities, and determination to see that in the postwar world the social services would be organized more effectively.[32]

If we turn to the question of participation, we do not find a great heroic surge of uncomplaining enthusiasm on behalf of the patriotic effort. Instead we find morale disturbingly low in the early summer of 1940, we find plenty of examples in the blitz (contrary to the versions published in the press) of people fleeing from their homes and (understandably) in very deep distress over the apparent collapse of their world and all supporting services around them. In the South Wales coal mines the morale was certainly pretty hostile to Government and management: perhaps war doesn't have such "impact" when you're working underground anyway. Yet there is much evidence too of the grim, and sometimes extrovert, determination beloved of in the popular traditional accounts.[33] And as the war progressed a greater optimism about the possibilities of social change, and a greater determination to secure it, begins to manifest itself. (I leave aside, remember, the potent "market" aspect of participation, the way in which workers could effectively demand better wages and conditions—and did; the number of days lost due to strikes went up every year from 1941 to 1944, and in 1945 was still double the 1938 figure.)

What of women's participation, and its consequences? Perfectly properly much attention now is focused on the lack of advances made by women in the twentieth century (Margaret Thatcher notwithstanding). It has been argued (most specifically by Betty Friedan, the American feminist, in *The Feminine Mystique*) that, having had masculine roles thrust upon them during the war, women, just as unceremoniously, had the traditional feminine image reimposed upon them as soon as the war ended. Again this is, to my mind, to fall into the error of positing abrupt change in one direction during the war, followed by abrupt reaction in the other at the end of the war. The evidence clearly indicates that during the war many were simply continuing to fulfill feminine occupations, albeit in a different environment: the women's land army, for instance, advertised for women "who like doing housework." In assessing the gains made by women due to wartime participation one must also consider what it was women themselves wanted: all surveys at the end of the war showed that a majority of women, in fact, wanted to get back to their traditional role in the home.[34] However, a broad base for further steady changes had been laid; new status, new independence, new economic freedom as in the previous war; and, above all, as a government survey showed, a big swing in opinion among employers who were now more prepared to regard married women as perfectly acceptable employees (there was a deeply entrenched tradition before the war that as soon as a woman got married, she got fired).[35]

Here I have spilled over into the psychological dimensions of war—the greater acceptance of change, and the greater belief in its possibility. What I said about evacuation and other aspects of disruption overlap with what I was saying earlier about "ingroup-outgroup" reactions. Let me stress again that these are not all in the direction which could be regarded as progressive. Hostility to Jews long settled in this country intensified in the first years of the war; feeling in favor of locking up all aliens, mostly more recent refugees from the Hitler regime was very strong; and there was not too much sympathy for evacuees from the over-run territories of Europe.[36] About the best that anyone could say on behalf of Belgian refugees, for instance, is encapsulated in these remarks of a lower middle class housewife who ran a sweet shop: "If they are anything like the Belgians in the last war—they're a dirty lot . . . but poor things they can't help it. I mean the Irish are dirty but we don't hate them. That's the only way they've been brought up."[37]

But if the war inevitably intensified xenophobic and sectional feelings, it undoubtedly also fostered a broad, and clearly identifiable, movement of change.

Two Mass Observation documents are again specially helpful here: a summary by Tom Harrisson, the moving spirit, and sharp scientific brain behind the organization, on "The Mood of Britain-1938 and 1944," bringing together a vast range of Mass Observation evidence on, basically, working-class opinion; and the "Report on Changes of Outlook During the War" compiled by the organization's national panel of observers.

The Mass Observation national panel reported that, with regard to temperament, the most frequent changes mentioned were a greater self-reliance and courage, and a greater seriousness which was to some extent offset by an appreciable number of comments about greater frivolity. The two most important social changes were a greater sociability and tolerance, with a decrease in class prejudice. In some cases reported, the change was said to be really great. Political developments were not all in one direction. The most frequently mentioned changes were an increase in cynicism and apathy, on the one side, yet on the other more political interest, but also more hatred of the Germans. However, there was also considerable evidence that more people were taking more interest in politics than before the war. The main broad movement detectable was definitely from the Right to the Left. In the realm of morals, the main changes noted were a tendency to a greater spirit of service and cooperation, and also, inevitably, changes in sexual morals. The panel were finally asked to report on people's interests: here the evidence was that, apart from the political changes already mentioned, people's interests had broadened, usually owing to experiences directly related to the war.[38] Tom Harrisson summarized the mood of 1938 as: bewilderment, uncertainty, insecurity and hope for the best. For the period 1932-42 he recorded the mood as less selfish, but with the main concentration on the war. From 1942 onwards he detected a shift in focus towards the period after the peace, and he saw the publication of the Beveridge Report in December 1942 as a turning point because of its basic concern with security. Very perceptively, Harrisson noted that there was nothing terribly new in the interest in postwar reform, but that people were now able to be more specific and concrete about the sort of reforms they wanted. As I have tried to argue throughout this paper, people do not undergo sudden conversions: as Harrisson saw it, the underlying big values had not changed, but people's *focus* on them had.[39]

Now the publication of the Beveridge Report, as is today too often forgotten, attracted an enormous amount of hostility from the rich and powerful.[40] Within the government and civil service there was a colossal battle over the publication and implementation of the Report: the files of the Lord President's Committee give a clear view of the tremendous fight the Secretary to the Beveridge Committee, D. N. Chester (a wartime civil servant and former university lecturer) put up on behalf of the Report against the Treasury mandarins.[41] However, not all the rich and the powerful were opposed to the Report. In a private letter, W. H. Haslam, landowner and director of several companies, hostile critic of Clement Attlee and believer in the breaking up of the Trade Union system, penned a marvelous piece of full-blooded military participation theory:

The Government in my view have made a great mistake in not endorsing the Beveridge Report to the extent of creating a Ministry of Social Security. Such an institution would be an earnest of their intentions that unemployment and want shall not prevail on demobilization. I feel sure such a gesture would have appealed to the services. Surely the first two calls on the national finances for the future are maintenance of defence and freedom from want. Financial consideration must be subservient to both necessities.[42]

That was a private letter, so we can't accuse it of being propaganda. In fact, I don't think we need worry too much about propaganda. Undoubtedly, in my view, low morale in the early stages of the war is related to the incompetence with which official propaganda was conducted. But in the later stages it is generally fair to say, I believe, that propaganda canalized a deeper feeling within society, rather than creating it (and this view seems to be supported by Ian McLaine's recent important study of the Ministry of Information, *Ministry of Morale* (1979)). No doubt some of the statements about building a better world after the war were simply politicians' hot air, of purely temporary validity. But on the whole the picture is of a broad, and pretty genuine, movement towards the Left among those in influential positions; those who did not share in this movement did not hesitate to speak out against it.

Whatever the substantial defects subsequently revealed, social services of the post-1945 period were qualitatively quite different from the fragmented, means-tested services of the thirties. So too was the whole language and imagery of social class, even if, as is undoubtedly true, the essential class structure of the country remained the same. In the popular cartoon series made just after the war by Harrison and Bachelor for the Central Office of Information in order to summarize Britain's recent history and explain her postwar economic problems, the average Briton at the center of the cartoon, "Robinson Charlie," is played as a black-collar working man;[43] analogous efforts to portray the ordinary citizen of the 1930s would always have given him a white collar. The detail of housing legislation and policy in the thirties is full of argument and discussion over the nature of the working classes for whom housing policy is exclusively directed, including gems such as this:

> In order to constitute a redevelopment area, the area must contain not less than fifty working class houses. At least one third of these houses must be congested, over-crowded or unfit for human habitation and not capable at reasonable expense of being rendered fit. The area must be one which clearly ought to be used to a substantial extent for working class houses, and it must be one which ought to be redeveloped as a whole.[44]

In explicit intention, the Housing Act of 1946 was supposed to apply to the community as a whole, and the Housing Act of 1949 for the first time dropped any reference to the "working classes." Likewise the other social legislation of the forties moves away from the contorted but crystal-clear euphemisms of the thirties: "employed workpeople" (in Holidays with Pay legislation) and "ex-PES" and "non-ex-PES" (in education).[45]

These are brief, and rather fragmentary points, chosen to highlight arguments which I have developed much more thoroughly elsewhere. There is much irony in the way in which social change comes about. Neither in 1914 nor in 1939 did British governments embark on war in order to transform their societies: rather were they forced into war in the vain hope of preserving the cosy worlds they inhabited. World War I brought the British working class and British women within the pale of citizenship. World War II administered severe shocks to continuing upper-class complacencies, and, above all, helped to banish many of the social insecurities which had been the nightmare of the thirties. World War I was the more significant watershed, but World War II revealed a vital glimpse of social, economic, and participatory democracy.

Yet, in comparison with other European countries what stands out in regard to the Second World War is that, in the end, it did not impinge physically upon British society to anything like the degree that it did on France, Germany, or Russia. Much of Britain's poor economic and social performance since the war, compared with that of both France and Germany, can be attributed to the way in which, in the matter of social expectations, Britain had not been reduced to a minimal level as had the two continental countries;[46] in addition, there was a general British complacency over "having won the war." Thus the destructive dimension, in its negative as well as positive aspects, was particularly important for continental Europe. But the participation dimension has particular relevance in connection with the social reform programs of the European resistance movements which, illuminatingly, tended usually to incorporate references to the British Beveridge Report.

What, finally, of neutral countries? Since, overall, they have gone through broadly the same social transformations as belligerent countries does this not suggest that in the end any analysis of the relationship between war and social change is really irrelevant? On closer inspection the problem simply dissolves. In some degree or another, war did impinge on the several neutral countries of the First World War, and on occupied Denmark and neutral Sweden in the Second World War. Even in spheres where the direct impact of war was slight, or nonexistent, as with regard to *participation* within the neutral countries in the Second World War, these countries found that, after the war was over, they were inescapably part of the new social, intellectual, economic and political structures created elsewhere by war. Broadly, this applies to Switzerland, though, revealingly, women did not get the vote there till the 1970s; Spain has remained one of the most socially backward of European countries. Sweden in the First World War enjoyed a boom in the production of her high-grade steel, and endured a blockade more complete than that of any country save Germany. Norway in the same war suffered destruction of her shipping greater, in proportion to her shipping resources, than any other country, and in absolute terms second only to the United Kingdom. In 1921 Sweden *followed* most of the major belligerent countries in granting universal manhood suffrage and votes for women; even though there had been no participation dimension, Sweden was now *joining* a new political and social order created elsewhere by the experience of war. In the Second World War Sweden was inevitably affected by the international dislocations of war; she was subject to severe press control; and she was torn by arguments over where participation in the national interest properly lay.

In the 1960s Western countries moved into a new phase of social transformation which can, without too much bathos, be described as the time of "cultural revolution." In all countries there were striking changes in social relationships, customs, and morals; France went through economic changes probably greater than at any other time in the twentieth century. Wars or no wars, the well-springs of social change are manifold. But the two World Wars do exist as historical facts: horrific and tragic though they undoubtedly were, they still call out for the careful attention of the student of social change.

Chairman Kohn's Introduction of Professor Harvard Sitkoff

Our second speaker this morning is Harvard Sitkoff of the University of New Hampshire. Professor Sitkoff studied at Queens College and at Columbia University, where he received his Ph.D. in 1975. He has taught at Queens, at Washington University, and since 1976, at the University of New Hampshire, where he is currently associate professor. He has been the recipient of many grants, fellowships, and awards, including in 1979-1980, a National Endowment for the Humanities fellowship and a Charles Warren fellowship from Harvard University. He is the author of many articles and essays, but he is perhaps best known for his two most recent books, *The Struggle for Black Equality, 1954-1980,* and his *A New Deal for Blacks: The Emergence of Civil Rights as a National Issue;* Volume I, *Depression Decade,* published by Oxford University in 1978. He will speak to us this morning on "American Blacks in World War II: Rethinking the Militancy-Watershed Hypothesis."

AMERICAN BLACKS IN WORLD WAR II: RETHINKING THE MILITANCY-WATERSHED HYPOTHESIS

Harvard Sitkoff

In the early and mid-1960s, as the civil rights movement seared its way into the American consciousness, most journalists and social scientists writing about the struggle for racial equality and justice depicted it as something new, unique, a revolutionary break with the past. These commentators on the "Negro Revolution" or the "Civil Rights Revolution," after giving a perfunctory nod to the formation of the National Association for the Advancement of Colored People (NAACP) early in the century, and perhaps a glance to the Harlem Renaissance and Garveyism in the 1920s, focused on the 1954 Supreme Court decision on school desegregation, or the 1955 Montgomery bus boycott, or the sit-ins of 1960 as the starting point of the modern black struggle. Not surprisingly, however, as historians grew interested in the movement they searched deeper into our past for origins and antecedents, for the sources and roots of black protest, for a continuing tradition of black struggle. Toward the end of the 1960s, a number of historians, myself included, published essays asserting that the true beginning of the contemporary militant movement, the watershed years of the struggle, were the years of the Second World War. Today, this is virtually a historical truism.[1]

It is now a textbook cliche to follow Richard Dalfiume in seeing the war years as the "forgotten years of the Negro revolution," the time when "a mass militancy became characteristic of the American Negro" and when blacks first aggressively protested the racial status quo. The war is now generally viewed as the turning point in black consciousness and behavior that culminated in the civil rights revolution of the 1950s and 1960s. According to Dalfiume, the discrimination faced by blacks in defense industries and in the armed forces, plus the bitter memories of World War I, led to low morale in regard to the war effort and high morale in race consciousness and determination to institute a revolutionary change in the nation's racial policies. Dalfiume underscores this by stressing isolationist and even pro-Axis sentiment by blacks in the immediate pre-war period and by emphasizing militant protests against discrimination and segregation, as exemplified by the Durham conference of Southern blacks in 1942, the outspokenness of the Negro press, the race riots of 1943, the anger and unity of the black masses, their involvement in protest and political activities, and, most of all, the March on Washington Movement (MOWM).

A quick survey of some recent writings on black history and on World War II reveals how thoroughly the militancy-watershed hypothesis has been adopted. John Brooks' history of the civil rights movement begins with a couple of chapters on the war years whose theme is the militancy of the black masses forcing civil rights to become a central concern of the era. Brooks particularly stresses the significance of both the Congress of Racial Equality's (CORE) nonviolent civil disobedience and the MOWM's mass militancy to the civil rights movement of the 1960s. Histories of the home front by John Blum, Richard Polenberg, Richard Lingeman and Geoffrey Perrett do the same. Each, in varying ways, emphasizes the unique and unprecedented militancy of the black masses, the importance of CORE and the MOWM, and the ways in which pressure from blacks forced white society to grant concessions. As Perrett sums it up: "new techniques, leaders, organizations, race consciousness and militancy" came into being which "launched the modern phase of the struggle for equality." These were the "watershed" years, Perrett continues, "when American Negroes began for the first time to fight for their rights effectively and independently. . . . Here was where the modern civil rights movement began; here was where it scored its first important victories." The militancy-watershed hypothesis also reverberates throughout Neil Wynn's and A. Russell Buchanan's accounts of black Americans in the Second World War, and Lee Finkle goes even further in his treatment of black militancy, claiming that the Negro press lagged behind the temper of the masses. Two recent scholarly articles pinpoint this new consensus. In *The Historian,* Peter Kellogg boldly contrasts the lack of concern for civil rights in the 1930s with the passion for and progress of civil rights suddenly stimulated by the war. And writing in *Prologue,* James Nuechterlein states in his very first sentence: "It is now clear that the period of World War II marked the beginning of the modern civil rights movement in the United States."[2]

It is no longer so clear to me, however. Having published several essays a decade ago which contributed to this watershed thesis, I began research for a full-scale study of the civil rights issue in World War II several years ago as a fervent believer in it. I fully expected my research to uncover much new evidence of the black protest movement building on its experiences in the New Deal era and going far beyond it in attracting mass support and in actively demonstrating against segregation and discrimination. But, to date, my research indicates that the Second World War delayed and stifled black protest activism, that it dampened black militancy. And the more often I returned to Dalfiume's work, and to others who argue similarly, the more flaws I found in the argument that the war marks a sharp break with the past in race consciousness and militancy and activity, and in the conclusion that these so-called new developments led directly to the civil rights revolution of the fifties and sixties.

First, there is the matter of timing, of the dates when things happened. Almost all of the references by the above historians to vitriolic editorials in the Negro press, to angry statements by black protest leaders and organizations, to allegations of black disloyalty or tepid support by blacks for the American cause are dated pre-Pearl Harbor. They should not be confused with *wartime* militancy. Much of this supposed militancy was really opposition to Roosevelt's reelection in 1940 by some Negro publishers and organizations; much of it was really Communist-related opposition to defense mobilization and aid to Great Britain during the Hitler-Stalin pact. Most of it was simply the desire of blacks to share equitably in the gains of the pre-war defense effort. Certainly blacks were angered at the racist military, trade union, and industrial policies which denied them their due. But to assume that what blacks sought to do about these problems was not at all changed by the actual entrance of the United States into the Second World War is fallacious. What Roosevelt called the war for survival affected blacks as well as whites, and as the nation became more fully involved, the belligerence of blacks dramatically decreased. Black soldier violence diminished perceptibly after 1941, as did opposition to the draft. Serious talk of a march on Washington ended. Demonstrations against war industries which discriminated ceased; indeed, racial strikes constituted only .00054 percent of all wartime work stoppages! And the Negro press, as Lee Finkle has demonstrated conclusively, was *not* militant after Pearl Harbor.[3]

This decreased belligerency, moreover, occurred at a time when militancy might have flourished. The war years were a period of black rising expectations and white reaction, an era in which gains by blacks whetted their appetite for further progress and stimulated white opposition. Such a combination should have resulted in an explosion of black protest activity, but it did not. The reason was total war, and all the constraints placed on a protest movement in the midst of a nation's war for survival. However determined and united blacks were to end segregation and discrimination, few flirted with anything that might remotely be considered treasonous to the war effort.

Secondly, in this matter, the militancy-watershed hypothesis greatly overstates the significance, even for the pre-war period, of isolationist or pro-Axis or pro-Japanese black groups. There were a few such groups, not "many" as Dalfiume claims, and their numbers remained miniscule in a nation of 13 million blacks. There were *only* 33 black conscientious objectors in 1941, about *2 percent* of the total number of COs, and *only* 166 for the following four years. Only a tiny handful of blacks was ever convicted of draft evasion, much less sedition, and they and the cults they belonged to were loudly and insistently condemned as "fanatics" and "crackpots" by virtually every major Negro leader, organization and newspaper, even those reputedly most militant like A. Philip Randolph. Typically, black spokesmen stated, as the *Chicago Defender* did in the case of Robert O. Jordan and his four supporters in the Ethiopian Pacific Movement who were charged with sedition, that as "agents of fascism" the court should "convict them all." In addition to their numerical insignificance and the manner in which black spokesmen disassociated themselves from whatever smacked of disloyalty, there is also the fact that not all black opposition to the war was racially motivated. It cannot all be equated with black militancy. There were sincere religious objections, pacifistic ones, and during the Nazi-Soviet pact, ideological concerns that had nothing to do with black advancement.[4]

An enlargement of this point leads to my third objection. There has been an all too facile effort to label any and all black violence, or anti-social behavior, as evidence of racial militancy. The evidence does not support such a view. We simply do not know enough about most of the clashes between black and white soldiers, or between black servicemen and white townsfolk, or between blacks and military and civilian police to ascribe them to militant *protest* attitudes and behavior. Some surely were related to the black quest for equality and justice and dignity, and some just as surely were manifestations of criminality devoid of ideological content. Some were as much evidence of black despair as of assertiveness. Some were caused not by blacks demanding more but by whites irrationally reacting against their perceptions of Negro gains. We need to know far more about racial violence in World War II before we make some of the assertions I did a decade ago. It is wrong, for example, to couple the 1943 Detroit and Harlem riots. Virtually every major black spokesman repudiated the Harlem rioters. The *Pittsburgh Courier* labeled the riot "an orgy of vandalism." A writer in *Crisis* compared the crowd in Harlem "in spirit, ironically, to a Southern lynch mob." "It took a riot in Harlem to teach Negro America that all racial intolerance is not on one side of the fence," Lester Granger stated, "and that a Negro riot in action is every bit as bestial and blindly destructive as a white mob." Indeed, black leaders as diverse as Adam Clayton Powell, Jr., and Walter White joined to praise the actions of Mayor LaGuardia and the New York City police, and a poll showed that fewer than one in three Harlem residents thought the riot justified.[5]

One may well speculate, given the legitimacy of Negro frustration and their presumed militancy, why there were not more riots in World War II? Why Detroit qualifies as the only genuine race riot? Why wasn't the Second World War, in this respect, more like the 1917-1919 period or the 1964-1968 period? Mass racial violence in World War II was the exception, not the rule. It was not a prevailing mood or mode of action. Black spokesmen almost without exception condemned racial violence as harmful both to victory abroad and at home. I find it striking that while some of my early essays are cited and quoted from historians to buttress their hypotheses of black militancy, few have bothered with my conclusions—namely, that these conflagrations frightened the black leadership, made it excessively fearful of further outbreaks, and caused it to turn its attention to reducing black aggressive behavior of any kind. Moderation became the watchword; gradual reform the order of the day. For well over half the time we were engaged in the war, "Good Conduct" campaigns and controlling racial rumors took precedence over actively combatting segregation and discrimination. Furthermore, much of the evidence often considered indicative of civil rights militancy, particularly the mushrooming of hundreds of new interracial committees and organizations including the American Council on Race Relations, the Race Relations Institute, and the National Association of Intergroup Relations Officials, actually demonstrated decreasing manifestations of militancy. Fearing a postwar wave of racial violence like the one which followed World War I, the emphasis of these new groups was racial quiet, not racial justice. Most worked closely with police departments and were funded by conservative philanthropic or municipal agencies. Their primary goal was stopping racial violence—not seeking greater rights for blacks.[6]

Fourth, the militancy-watershed hypothesis suffers from a confusion of elite opinion and mass behavior. Again and again I see assertions similar to Dalfiume's that "The Negro masses simply did not support a strategy of moderating their grievances for the duration of the war," or that "Never before had Negroes been so united behind a cause" or so involved in protest activity, and the footnote reference, when there is one, is to an editorial in the Negro press or a speech or article by a civil rights leader. This is not sufficient as evidence of mass militancy. Militant mass protest activity would constitute such evidence. Militant mass political behavior would constitute such evidence. But such evidence is not forthcoming, and there is no proof whatsoever for Dalfiume's statement that the Negro press "simply reflected the Negro mind." The *Courier* may have had the "Double V" plastered on its masthead, but it had a weekly circulation of 140,000. We have to be careful of making it representative of the feelings of 13 million people, or of similarly utilizing the *Chicago Defender,* the next largest weekly, with a circulation of under 80,000. There is good reason to question, moreover, Dalfiume's characterization of these papers as militant. The fullest study of the Negro press, by Lee Finkle, concludes just the opposite, agreeing with A. Philip Randolph's description of the *Courier* as the "spokesman for the petty black bourgeoisie." And, however unradical the *Courier* and *Defender* might have been, the great bulk of the Negro press, mainly small Southern weeklies, was even less forceful in opposing racism.[7]

The absence of this distinction between North and South is a fifth error commonly made by historians expressing the militancy-watershed hypothesis. There was in the 1940s a tremendous difference between what could be done by black protest, and what was done, in the South as opposed to the North. Southern blacks were not militant during the war—not in demonstrations, not in the activities of the scattered Southern branches of civil rights organizations, not in their support of two new protest groups most historians see as indicative of the new black militancy, CORE and the March on Washington Movement, not even in the editorials of their newspapers or the statements of their leaders. And this at a time when nearly three-quarters of all Afro-Americans still lived below the Mason-Dixon Line. One poll in the Negro press, for example, indicated that only one out of ten Southern blacks felt that segregation should be attacked during the war. Even the supposedly militant statement of the Southern Negro leaders who met in Durham in 1942 needs to be qualified far more than Dalfiume does. True, it criticized segregation; but it did not call for its abolition. Instead, the Southern blacks asked for an improvement in race relations within the existing framework of segregation. They asked for equal education and economic opportunities, but not for integrated ones. Perhaps most importantly, the Durham conference led to no direct actions against Jim Crow. Eventually, it was subsumed in the Southern

Regional Council formed in 1944. No effort was made to make the SRC an organizaton with mass appeal. The Council was a vehicle for Southern white sociologists and newspapermen who desired a liberalization of race relations without fundamental changes. Not until late 1949 would it finally declare itself against segregation.[8]

Even among the quarter of the black population who lived in the North, militancy was neither common nor massive. This is in the sixth and most significant problem with the militancy-watershed argument. The centerpiece of the hypothesis is that blacks, unlike the preceding decades, in huge numbers aggressively combatted Jim Crow during World War II, and the main proof offered is the MOWM. Building on Herbert Garfinkel's work, Dalfiume claims that the MOWM pioneered "the spontaneous involvement of large masses of Negroes in a political protest. . . . Unlike the older Negro movements, the March on Washington had captured the imagination of the masses." John Brooks, asserting that the MOWM "is the granddaddy of all the black protest that proliferated through the 1960's," states: "Randolph ushered the Negro masses onto the stage of history. . . . The march marked a change in the character of Negro protest." The change stressed by all the historians I mentioned earlier is that the MOWM was an all-black mass movement that used direct action pressure tactics to force concessions from white America. Purportedly this is unique, other civil rights organizations being interracial rather than all-black, devoted to pleading rather than pressuring, placing their faith in lobbying, litigation and legislation rather than direct action by the masses.[9]

The extent of the MOWM's break with earlier black protest, its success in enlisting the support of the masses, and its influence on later protests in Montgomery, in Greensboro, in Birmingham, are the critical questions that need to be raised. I have already discussed in detail the first two questions in the first volume of my history of the emergence of civil rights, *A New Deal For Blacks*. Time now permits me only to recapitulate briefly my answers. To the extent that the MOWM was a departure, it was so only in Randolph's extremely militant and nationalistic rhetoric. All the existing civil rights groups, including the NAACP and National Urban League (NUL), agreed with the movement's goals and endorsed the march. None considered the idea of bringing mass pressure to bear on the government particularly novel or radical. Many black leaders had sounded that theme in the depression decade. Talk of "mass action," of "mass power," of "mass marches on Washington," was common in the leftist and labor vocabulary of the 1930s, and numerous black organizations adopted the language. Even for Randolph, the phrases and tactics were not new; he was reiterating in 1941 the themes he had propounded as head of the National Negro Congress (NNC) in the thirties. Nor was Randolph's insistence that the MOWM be an all-black enterprise particularly new in civil rights. During the Great Depression, Cleveland had its all-black Future Outlook League to fight discrimination, Detroit had a similar Civil Rights League, at least thirty-five cities had all-black "Don't Buy Where You Can't Work" organizations. Moreover, despite some recent accounts of the MOWM which take

Randolph's rhetoric and turn him into an early version of Malcolm X, Randolph and the MOWM had integrationist goals and welcomed all possible cooperation and collaboration with white liberals and white labor. Randolph's all-black posture was primarily designed to avoid a Communist takeover of the MOWM, as white Communists had previously taken over the NNC. It was not to foster separation. That was understood at the time and so, not surprisingly, the MOWM drew support from white church, liberal, and labor groups and from all the major civil rights spokesmen and organizations opposed to separation and nationalism. In addition, the MOWM gained this support because its aim was to arouse white America to the plight of blacks for the purpose of influencing the political system to make necessary reforms—a common goal for race advancement organizations in the thirties.[10]

The amount of Randolph's mass support is problematic. No one knows for sure. The march never took place. But some guesses are in order. If 100,000 blacks were ready to march, as Randolph said, or even if 50,000 blacks were so mobilized, or 20,000, why did Randolph accept such a weak and tarnished compromise from Roosevelt? If as many blacks were militant, why didn't another leader take up where Randolph left off? If his support was so massive, why did the March on Washington Committee have a budget of less than $3,000 in August, 1941, about half of it coming from Randolph's own Brotherhood of Sleeping Car Porters and much the rest of it from the NAACP? If the MOWM was indicative of such mass militancy, why did it wither away after the NAACP and NUL ended their support in 1942? Why did a *Courier* poll in October 1942 show 71 percent of the blacks in Washington against the idea of a March on Washington? Why did no support materialize when Randolph called for mass marches on city halls in 1942? Why did no blacks march? Why, given such purported mass militancy, did all the major civil rights spokesmen and Negro newspapers shun and denounce Randolph's 1943 call for civil disobedience to protest Jim Crow schools and railroads? And why didn't mass numbers of blacks engage in such actions? Why, indeed, considering what historians have written about Randolph and the MOWM as being representative of the new wartime mood of black militancy, did the MOWM convention at the start of the summer of '43, held in the city of Chicago, attract virtually no blacks other than a handful of Sleeping Car Porters? Indeed, in the light of most of what has been written about the MOWM, I find it ironic that the bulk of Randolph's energies for *over* half the wartime period was directed to his leadership of the National Council for a Permanent Fair Employment Practices Commission (FEPC), a traditional legislative lobby which never talked of direct action or of mobilizing the masses, and which was controlled by a small group of mainly white New York labor leaders and Socialists.[11]

As to the MOWM's much-heralded influence on later direct action civil rights campaigns, as well as CORE's, I am persuaded by Meier and Rudwick's exhaustive survey of protest that the history of direct action and militancy has been episodic and marked by sharp discontinuities. "We would argue," they conclude, "that such tactics and strategies were continuously reinvented by blacks in response to shifting patterns of race relations and the changing status of blacks in American society." Most civil rights participants have been ahistorical, knowing little of earlier protest techniques. Both the sit-in students and Martin Luther King, Jr., and his associates thought they were inventing new forms of protest. Neither thought they owed anything to Randolph, or even, initally, to CORE. The Gandhian ideology introduced by CORE during the Second World War did not enter the mainstream of black protest until King articulated it, well after the Montgomery bus boycott was underway. CORE, during World War II, remained a tiny, little known, interracial group, attractive mainly to A. J. Muste's pacifist and socialist followers. It sought to involve large numbers of blacks, and failed. CORE, and its Gandhism, was not even known to blacks at Howard University and in St. Louis who, independent of each other, thought they were inventing the sit-in. Moreover, CORE's direct action tactics are not nearly so novel as often pictured. Most came directly from the CIO experiences in 1930s; CORE even called its first sit-in a "sit-down" after the famous CIO strikes. Considering their leadership, it is not at all surprising that both CORE and MOWM owed much to the Marxist and labor union activities of the thirties.[12]

Finally, given my short time remaining, I would like to cite Meier and Rudwick again on the critical questions of the uniqueness and magnitude of black militancy. "The era of the Depression," they write, "marked a watershed in Afro-American direct action." It was in the 1930s that blacks for the first time massively marched, picketed, boycotted, and sat-in for the goal of racial equality. "Indeed," they state, "direct action during the Depression contrasted sharply both quantitatively and qualitatively with the history of such tactics during the entire preceding century, and achieved a salience in black protest that would not be equalled or surpassed until the late 1950s and 1960s." Meier and Rudwick continue: "there was less actual use of direct action tactics during World War II than in the 1930s." Because the wartime emergency created a milieu unfavorable to such militant protest, blacks did not employ it as a major weapon. They conclude that "despite the publicity which Randolph gave to direct action and the diligent work of the CORE chapters, demonstrations had declined sharply during World War II compared to the 1930s. . . . Overall, the amount of direct action was minor compared to the Depression era."[13]

However, even if the Second World War does not mark a sharp break in civil rights thinking, leadership and militancy, and even if it was not the direct progenitor of the movement that burst onto the American scene a dozen years later, the war era is still critically important in the development of the struggle for black equality. It is so primarily because World War II changed the United States, deeply, fundamentally. And these unanticipated consequences of our involvement, in the realms of demography and our economy, in the scope and nature of our federal government, and in our place in the world, created the preconditions which made the modern civil rights struggle not only possible, but successful. Objective conditions that had little to do with race in a primary sense created a context in which organizations and leaders could press for racial reforms. And more directly, the experience of war, especially the nation's shocked reaction to Nazi racism, its fear of massive racial violence, and its concern that white racism weakened our security, established a milieu in which blacks could confidently organize for fundamental social change. To the extent that World War II was a watershed for civil rights it was not so because of a new mass militancy, but rather, it was so because of the revolutionary changes in American life that made it impossible for this nation to remain ignorant of, or ignore, the black quest for racial equality and justice.

Chairman Kohn's Introduction of Professor Leila J. Rupp

Our third paper this morning is by Professor Leila Rupp. Professor Rupp received her Ph.D. from Bryn Mawr College in 1976, taught for a year at the University of Pennsylvania, and has been teaching history and women's studies since 1977 at the Ohio State University, where she is currently associate professor. She has published *Mobilizing Women for War: German and American Propaganda, 1939-1945*, and with Barbara Miller Lane, *Nazi Ideology Before 1933: A Documentation*. Currently she is engaged in collaborative research with Verda Taylor on the American women's movement in the post-Second World War period, under a two-year research grant from the National Endowment for the Humanities. A book tentatively titled, *The Survival of American Feminism: The Women's Movement 1945 to the 1960s*, will be published by Yale University Press. Her paper this morning is "War is Not Healthy for Children and Other Living Things: Reflections on the Impact of Total War on Women."

WAR IS NOT HEALTHY FOR CHILDREN AND OTHER LIVING THINGS: REFLECTIONS ON THE IMPACT OF TOTAL WAR ON WOMEN

Leila J. Rupp

A poster so common in the 1960s that it has become an artifact of sixties culture proclaimed that "war is not healthy for children and other living things." I chose to use this slogan in my title for two reasons. First, it suggests the tenor of my conclusions about the ultimate impact of total war on women. Second, the reference to the antiwar movement reminds us that, although war might bring certain kinds of gains to women, it is not a method of social change that women as a group ever have, or I hope ever would, advocate. The question of gains arises because some observers believe that war can liberate women. Anne O'Hare McCormick, an editor of the *New York Times*, expressed this view in 1943: "[M]en are apt to wake up some day and stop wars on the grounds that women win them," she wrote.[1] Those who disagree with such an optimistic evaluation usually point to the temporary nature of women's wartime opportunities and argue that permanent change does not result from the wartime necessity for women's greater participation. It is a debate that most often focuses on the American experience in the Second World War, but one that can be and is extended to other countries and other wars as well.[2]

I would like to look beyond the relatively simple terms of this debate by considering the issue of the impact of total war on women from a broader and comparative perspective. Although the Second World War was a total war—that is, a war that demanded extensive mobilization of the home front—the American experience is not the most representative one for building an argument about the impact of war on women. As the popular wartime query "Don't you know there's a war on?" suggests, the war touched this country less than it did all the other combatants. As Arthur Marwick has suggested in his study of war in the twentieth century and as the case of the Vietnam War makes clear, a "total war" can be total for some combatants and not for others.[3] Given this situation, a comparative perspective is essential for any consideration of the general issue.

Making use of such a comparative perspective, it is important to be precise about what groups of women were affected in what ways. To take two obvious cases, Jewish women in Europe, swept up in the Holocaust, and Japanese-

American women in the United States, sent to internment camps, suffered in particular ways from the experience of total war. On a less obvious level, women of different classes, races, ages, and family arrangements experienced the war in different ways. Maurine Greenwald has shown, for example, in her study of American women workers in the First World War, that even workers within particular industries had quite different experiences during the war: within the railroad industry, clerical workers, common laborers, and skilled workers found different obstacles confronting them and took advantage of different opportunities; within the streetcar industry, women conductors in different cities had widely divergent experiences moving into a previously all-male occupation.[4] Women historians in general warn us not to take traditional rhetoric that speaks of "Woman" as an accurate reflection of reality. Women as a group share certain characteristics, including the potential for bearing children and, perhaps most important, socially-defined roles, but women do not comprise a homogeneous group.

In addition to employing a comparative perspective that recognizes differences among groups of women, it is important to look beyond the most obvious issue of women's wartime employment. I shall consider, first, women's roles in the labor force but shall then turn to women's reproductive, sexual, and childbearing roles; the impact of wartime violence on women; and, finally, public attitudes toward women and women's own self-perceptions. This does not pretend to be a comprehensive and systematic study of women and war, but is rather a series of reflections based on existing research on the Second World War. I offer examples from the German, Japanese, American, British, and Soviet experiences in order to raise questions and suggest new perspectives on the ways that total war affects women.

Turning first to the area most often discussed in histories of the war, the area on which most claims of the liberating effects of war are based—women's role in the labor force—what is immediately striking is how similar the story is in all countries, regardless of government system or prevailing political ideology. A patriarchal ideology that proclaimed a particular "place" for women prevailed in every country involved in the war. All governments realized at some point in the war that it would be necessary to recruit women into the labor force in order to replace men drafted into the armed forces. Important groups in all countries— individual government officials or leaders, employers, male workers—opposed the mobilization of women. Despite the desperate need for female labor, women continued to experience discrimination in wages, promotion, training, seniority, and so on. At the end of the war, all countries made haste to send women either back home or back to their traditional low-status, poorly-paid, sex-segregated jobs. It is a grim scenario, yet it cannot be denied that women moved into jobs previously reserved for men, and in some cases, earned high wages during the war. What did this mean for women? To suggest an answer to that question, we must consider the experiences of different groups of women in different countries. Women moved into new sectors of the labor force, but we cannot ignore the way they got there—that is, what degree of compulsion they experienced in mobilization. Surprisingly, the totalitarian nations of Germany and Japan allowed citizen women more choice than did Britain. Britain, along with the Soviet Union, utilized women's labor most efficiently. British women had to register with the government and those considered "mobile"—without children under fourteen or other significant domestic responsibilities—could be drafted into the armed forces or for work anywhere in the country. By 1943, 90 percent of single women and 80 percent of married women with children over fourteen were working.[5] In the Soviet Union, women served under military discipline in all areas of the economy, comprising 56 percent of the labor force by 1945, and one million of them even served, on a voluntary basis, in the military as snipers, machine gunners, artillery soldiers, tank crewmembers, and combat engineers.[6] In Germany and Japan, on the other hand, the governments reluctantly passed but did not systematically enforce registration laws. In both countries, ambivalence on the part of the regimes about the proper roles of women resulted in a relatively small-scale mobilization. In Germany, the female labor force increased by only 1 percent during the war, despite the desperate need for labor as the war continued. The Nazis imported prisoners of war and foreign workers as a substitute for "Aryan" women, at the same time that they poured enormous amounts of labor power into the extermination of the Jews. "Protection of women" meant only concern for the proper role of "racially-acceptable" women. Women of "non-Aryan" stock helped to make up the contingents of forced and slave labor. At the same time, Hitler spoke of the need to preserve women's place in the home in total disregard of the millions of "Aryan" women already at work under strict regulations. While women already at work could be imprisoned for missing work, non-working women flaunted their leisure at cafes and resorts. Middle and upper class women evaded registration without penalty while less privileged women, whether working or not, bitterly resented the lack of a fairly enforced conscription decree that would spread the burden equitably among the population. By the end of the war, the working class population had come to resent the social injustices of the mobilization program and publicly expressed sentiments of class conflict.[7]

In Japan, too, the female labor force increased very little in the course of the war—less than 10 percent between 1940 and 1944. At first unmarried, later even married, women were supposed to register with the government, but many officials opposed the conscription of women as a measure that would disrupt the family. Nominally volunteer labor associations, which neighborhood leaders hounded women to join, set women to work in factories, but, as in Germany, women evaded work by failing to register, taking easy office jobs, bribing officials, or marrying. By the end of the war, systematic bombing by American forces led to such disruption that the state could no longer control the labor force.[8]

In the United States, success at mobilizing women fell somewhere between the extremes already described. Ultimate victory in the war and, even more important, the absence of fighting and destruction at home, set the American experience apart. Although the government discussed the possibility of registration and conscription throughout the war, it relied instead on propaganda to mobilize women into the labor force. The Office of War Information coordinated large-scale intensive national campaigns designed to "sell" war work to women and recruit women into the women's branches of the armed forces. The female labor force increased by 32 percent from 1941 to 1945, but, in contrast to the situation in Britain, only 36 percent of all women over the age of fourteen worked outside the home at the peak of employment. As was true elsewhere, women moved from traditionally female jobs into war industry at the same time that previously non-employed women joined the work force. Black women found that for the first time they could move out of domestic service and agricultural labor into jobs previously barred to them on the basis of both their race and gender, but they continued to experience discrimination in their new jobs.[9] Industrial wages were high in the United States (although, as in every country, unequal to those of men) and this attracted women to war industries in particular. Propaganda pictured "Rosie the Riveter" as the white middle class housewife in overalls maintaining her glamour and doing her domestic duty for her man by making airplanes. The reality, as the recently released documentary "The Life and Times of Rosie the Riveter" makes clear, was different, but women of all groups—white women and women of color, young women and old women, single women and married women—did seize the opportunities opened to them during the war and thereby contributed to the war effort.[10]

What can we make of all this? We know that work outside the home does not mean automatic liberation, for if it did, the least privileged women in every society would be the most liberated. Even work in previously male jobs did not "free" women, as the avoidance of factory work by German and Japanese women suggests. Japanese women lived in filthy company dormitories, worked an excessive number of hours, and received too little food and low wages based on age, gender, and experience rather than work performed. Women in all countries complained about inadequate social services and the problems of the "double shift," the necessity of working a full day in a factory and doing their household chores at night. Nevertheless, women did move into new roles and sometimes received good pay—"men's pay"—for doing so. So it might be possible to argue that, despite continuing discrimination and bad conditions, women made employment gains during the war. But what about the permanence of these gains?

The situation in the postwar period depends very much, of course, on the war's outcome for each country, but I believe that the evidence shows that postwar patterns of employment were generally a consequence of long-term changes in the labor force rather than a result of the war. This is a point very much in dispute with regard to the United States. The contemporary trend of employment for married women, including middle class women, is one that some scholars attribute to the wartime experience.[11] William Chafe, for example, sees the Second World War as a watershed in women's history; the movement of women into the labor force that the war initiated created the essential foundation, according to Chafe, for the emergence of the women's movement in the 1960s. Others argue, as I do, that the contemporary acceptability of work outside the home is a consequence of structural changes in the labor force, especially the growth of the service sector, and has little to do with the massive influx of women into industry during the war.[12]

The patterns in other countries seem to support the argument that factors other than the war shaped women's labor force participation. In Japan, the female labor force today consists primarily of young women not yet married and housewives with older children, a pattern brought about by urbanization and cultural tradition.[13] In the two Germanies, the patterns differ significantly. In the Federal Republic, about 50 percent of all working-age women are gainfully employed, while in the German Democratic Republic, the comparable figure is over 80 percent.[14] As in the United States and the Soviet Union, whose patterns the two German states reflect, economic necessity and ideology determine levels and patterns of female employment. In general, the changes in women's employment patterns—primarily the increase in women's labor force participation—that emerged by the 1960s seem to have been a consequence of long-term economic, social, and technological developments, in both capitalist and socialist societies, rather than a result of the war.

Nevertheless, an intriguing situation discovered by Karen Anderson in her book on American women in the war suggests that the war might at least have had the potential to bring about real change. The United States Employment Service traditionally classified job seekers into categories based on previous employment and permitted registrants to refuse jobs outside their categories without losing unemployment benefits. In Detroit, large numbers of women registered for industrial jobs while many returning veterans, who had done clerical work in the army, registered for white-collar jobs traditionally considered women's work. Faced with this unexpected situation, the Employment Service warned the men that opportunities in the clerical field were limited and the pay was too low for men, and denied unemployment benefits to women who refused to take jobs outside the industrial category.[15] This experience suggests that war did in fact have some potential for breaking down the traditional division of labor, but makes clear that employers and government had an interest in thwarting that change and used whatever means were necessary to maintain the traditional order. Perhaps war is a potentially liberating experience in the realm of work, but in practice its effects can be subverted.

Turning away from the question of women's work during the war, we enter a realm not often considered in discussions of the impact of war on women. Reproduction, as women's studies scholars have pointed out, plays a central role in women's lives and must be considered alongside production if we want to understand women's experiences. Here I would like to consider what we know about reproduction, sexuality, and childrearing together, although the three areas are not necessarily linked in the experiences of individual women.

From the perspective of the fascist states, the link between sexuality and reproduction was a vital one. Both Germany and Japan maintained, at the same time, that they had to expand territorially in order to provide resources for an overcrowded population and that they had to increase the birth rate in order to keep the nation strong. The Nazis instituted a eugenics policy that had both negative and positive measures: for the "racially fit," the outlawing of contraception and abortion, marriage loans, and medals of honor for prolific mothers; for the "racially impure" and physically or mentally disabled, compulsory sterlization.[16] Although Nazi propaganda glorified the family, the government encouraged the bearing of "racially-pure" children by unmarried women. The rigidity of gender arrangements and the emphasis on reproduction can be seen as well in the intensity of the Nazi leadership's hatred of homosexuality, which dictated the extermination of an unknown number of lesbians and gay men in the concentration camps.[17]

In Japan, too, a national eugenics law forbade contraception for the healthy and required sterilization of the insane. As in Germany, state policy attempted to entice women to marry and bear children with institutions and measures such as matchmaking agencies, baby bonuses, state subsidies for those too poor to purchase wedding clothes, and a program of free higher education for families with ten or more children. At the same time, the government shut down the geisha houses and brothels and sent the women who worked in such institutions to the labor corps.[18] But in neither Germany nor Japan did such measures succeed in raising the birth rate.

No such explicit eugenics policies existed in the U.S., although the government was not all together unconcerned about sexuality and reproduction. The war caused a great deal of social disruption, especially in the boom towns where industry attracted migrants from all over the country. Women who seemed to flaunt conventional morality by sleeping with servicemen out of patriotism or a desire for excitement were dubbed "victory girls," and their appearance awakened fears of a massive challenge to traditional morality. Concern for loose morals and fear of a venereal disease epidemic led to serious violations of women's constitutional rights as citizens. Women suspected of engaging in sexual relations without "sincere emotional" involvement or young women found in places or at hours deemed inappropriate could be detained for mandatory VD testing and held until the results came in. Local officials in Detroit attempted to enforce special regulations for unescorted women entering bars. Needless to say, nothing was done to control unescorted men, and the male partners of women detained for VD testing were not arrested or forced to submit to testing.[19] Despite the persistence of the traditional double standard, the war does seem to have had some impact on the sexual behavior of young married women, but the increase in the incidence of extramarital sexual relations does not necessarily mean that women had taken greater control over their own sexuality. As feminist scholars have shown with regard to the much-vaunted "sexual revolutions" of the 1920s and 1960s, greater permissiveness in sexual relations can mean simply the substitution of one male-defined standard of sexuality for another. On the other hand, the war did seem to bring greater autonomy and security for lesbian women, who found freedom in increased geographical mobility and urban growth, in the relaxed wartime standards of "femininity"—especially the new acceptability of pants for women—and in the opportunity to establish economic independence through wartime jobs in industry or the military.[20]

If the American government did not place much emphasis on increasing the birth rate in the war years, it did express concern for the future of the family. The belief that mothers belonged at home with their young children had, at the outset of the mobilization campaigns, hampered the recruitment of women. The government's reluctance to fund day care centers and the growing concern that the employment of women led to juvenile delinquency created practical and emotional difficulties for many women. Because many of the centers established were of poor quality, overcrowded, and/or inconvenient, most women preferred to arrange for a relative or friend to care for their children while they worked. What day care centers were opened with federal funds were shut down as soon as possible at the end of the war, making it clear that day care was a response to wartime necessity and had nothing to do with oppotunities for women.[21]

War brought even greater disruption to the British family, since children from London were evacuated and sent to the countryside during the bombing and a higher percentage of women with children worked outside the home. As in the United States, however, the end of the war brought a reduction to the number of nursery schools and a burst of psychological propaganda on the importance of full-time mothering.[22] British services for working women were superior to those provided American women, but perhaps that fact says more about the war's threat to British existence than any commitment to equality for women.

While the Nazi regime was clear about its desire for an increased birth rate, its attitude toward the family, as suggested by its encouragement of childbearing by unmarried "racially-pure" women, was more confused. On the one hand, Nazi ideology glorified the traditional family and compared, in true patriarchal fashion, the authority of the state to the authority of the father. On the other hand, Nazi policy disrupted the family by encouraging sex-segregated and age-segregated organizations for leisure time activities and glorifying male bonding at the expense of family relationships. As a means of extending the authority of the state into personal life, children were encouraged to inform on treasonous parents. Thus the family, supposedly the foundation of the state, was also viewed as a potential source of opposition. If, as sociologist Philip Slater has suggested, it is impossible for a government to establish an authoritarian regime at the same time that it destroys traditional authority in a society, then the Nazi regime would have had difficutly maintaining itself even had it not lost the war.[23] Family policy, in any case, was fraught with contradictions. Nazi ideology appealed to some women because it promised them a return to security and status within the family, but the realities of the Third Reich undermined the family and women's "place" with it.

What conclusions can we draw from all this? More research on reproduction, sexuality, and childrearing is needed before any definite conclusions can be reached, but the available research does suggest that the war increased the concern for control of women's reproductive capacities, sexuality, and traditional mothering role. All governments fashion population policies that determine women's access to contraception and abortion. Sometimes those policies allow some groups of women access to the information and technology necessary for reproductive control, but the vital issue is who controls the access. In wartime, government concern for population policy is heightened, so it is clear that war is not likely to bring any increase in reproductive freedom for women. In the fascist states, the government decided which women should bear children prolifically and which women should not give birth at all. Although the war may have opened up sexual opportunities for some American women, the balance sheet shows the losses to be greater than the gains. The war created anxiety about women's roles as mothers, since government interest in women caring for their children at home came into conflict with the need for women in the labor force and, in Germany, the attempt to regiment society. The consequence for women was difficulty juggling roles during the war and exposure to propaganda glorifying motherhood at the war's end. In a total war, people became resources to be allocated along with natural resources and equipment, and the tendency to view women as sexual and reproductive commodities was intensified.

We turn now to a third area of concern suggested by the work of some women's studies scholars: violence against women. Feminist theorists argue that it is impossible to understand women's lives without considering the institutionalized violence that supports the social order by confronting women with actual or threatened rape, domestic violence, and harassment on the street or at work. In exploring the impact of total war on women, we must consider gender-related ways that women experienced the violence of war. Little research has been done in this area to date. We do not know, for example, what percentage of the people killed in Nazi concentration camps and in the bombing of civilian targets were women. As a result, what I shall discuss here is quite tentative, meant only to suggest some of the questions that need to be raised in this area.

We do know something about the prevalence and function of rape in the Second World War. There was, of course, nothing new about this phenomenon—rape in war is as old as human history. Susan Brownmiller, in her classic study of rape, has documented the use of rape by the Germans and Japanese as a means of achieving their ultimate objective, the destruction of "inferior peoples" and the establishment of a master race.[24] Mass rape of Jewish women began even before the war as part of the process leading up to the "final solution" and continued in the ghettoes and concentration camps. At the Nuremburg trials, the Soviets presented careful and extensive documentation of the German practice of raping women as they invaded Soviet territory. In that case, rape served as notice that an area had been conquered. Evidence from occupied France shows that the Germans also raped for military retaliation or reprisal, as evidence shows that outbreaks of systematic rape followed a successful maneuver by the Resistance. The Japanese army, too, used rape as a means of solidifying conquest. The Japanese victory over the city of Nanking in 1937 was not called the "Rape of Nanking" for nothing: evidence that emerged at the postwar tribunal indicated that the Japanese raped 20,000 women within the first month of conquest.

The rape of women was, of course, only one of the horrors suffered by the people under German and Japanese occupation. But the liberation did not bring the end of rape, nor was the use of rape confined to the Axis powers. Soviet soldiers raped German women in retaliation for the same acts by German soldiers. And General George S. Patton, Jr. admitted in his memoirs that he had had to warn the Moroccan sultan during the North African campaign that, "in spite of my most diligent efforts, there would unquestionably be some raping" by American soldiers.[25] Rape in war is a weapon used by men of one side against men of the other, but it is an institution that terrorizes and destroys women.

Rape is a form of violence that affects only, or primarily, women, and its functions of controlling women is not confined to wartime. The second form of violence against women I would like to discuss here—the atomic bombing of Hiroshima and Nagasaki—is quite different. The bomb killed indiscriminately and it was a form of violence confined to wartime. Yet women suffered in gender-specific ways as a result of the bombing, which by the end of 1945 had killed 210,000 people, 35 percent of the population of Hiroshima and 25 percent of the population of Nagasaki. First of all, in both cities, the majority of the population by 1945 consisted of women, children, and old persons of both sexes, so a majority of victims were women. The same was certainly true of the conventional bombings of other cities throughout the war, a fact apparently never considered by those who pondered the connection between bombing and civilian morale. Although men died in huge numbers at the front, women died waiting, passive and defenseless, in the air raids that killed so many civilians. Second, women survivors of the atomic bombings suffered from particular kinds of injuries related to their reproductive capacity. Diseases of the breast and uterus were (and still are) common. Women widowed by the bombs or abandoned because of facial disfigurement eked out a marginal existence in a society that saw no alternative to marriage for women. Perhaps most terrible was the decision whether or not to marry and bear children and, if they chose to have children, the anxiety women felt over the health of their daughters and sons, who suffered from a myriad of health problems and died at an unusually high rate from cancer. In 1967, two Japanese women set up a Women's Section of the Osaka Association of the A-Bomb Victims to provide emotional and tangible support. The Women's Section helped women to find assistance for specific problems, offered understanding and support, and set out to collect the stories of women survivors as eloquent testimony of the necessity for a nuclear-free world. I would like to quote here from one such story as an example of the particular kind of violence war can inflict on women. This is the story of Kazue Miura, who in 1945 was an eighteen-year-old switchboard operator in Hiroshima. She survived within five hundred meters of the hypocenter of the explosion, wrote a memoir published by the Women's Section in 1979, and died in 1980 of cancer of the stomach. She wrote of her daughter, Maki:

> As she grew older, Maki noticed that newspapers in the summer featured stories of the bombings and deaths of survivors. She came to hate all reminders of the bombings because of the pain it had caused me and her fear that I, too, would succumb. When she was 14 she looked me in the face reproachfully and asked, 'Why did you give birth to me, Mom? You are a bomb victim, so you should not have brought me into the world.' I had long anticipated that question, but no amount of emotional preparation could have softened the blow of those few words. I told her that I had thought a lot before giving birth to her and didn't know whether she might get a bad disease, not wanting to mention leukemia. 'And what would you do if it happened to me?' she asked. What could I answer her? In painful honesty I told her there was nothing we could do about it. That was the saddest and most heartbreaking moment of my life.[26]

War brings violence to all people, and men have traditionally borne the brunt of that violence, but we cannot consider the impact of war on women without asking how women experienced violence differently because they were women. Any analysis of "gains" that women made as a result of war must be set in the context not only of losses of family and friends but also in the context of the special horrors war held for women.

The last area I would like to consider here is a particularly elusive one: public attitudes toward women and women's own self-perceptions. William Chafe argues that social change occurs when a new social situation forces people to question and revise old ideas. In the case of the American home front, he suggests, men had to deal with women working competently in "masculine" jobs, which eventually led to the beginning of a change in public attitudes toward women. Using a similar argument, those who believe that war has a liberating effect on women place a great deal of reliance on the self-confidence and independence that women gain from taking over previously male jobs and roles during the war, and this does seem to be the area in which positive change is most likely to occur. The problem lies in collecting evidence of such change.

I would argue that war does not change public attitudes toward women in any significant way. The human mind seems amazingly capable of fitting the most non-traditional activities of women into women's traditional roles. One has only to think of the phenomenon of Nazi women sewing and wearing brown shirts and brawling in the streets on behalf of a system that promised them a secure place in the home. Propaganda in both Germany and the United States conceptualized women's work in war industry as an extension of their traditional roles as wives and mothers. American propaganda films and Nazi tracts compared the operation of industrial machinery to women's familiar work with sewing machines and vacuum cleaners. And propaganda viewed women as simply exercising their concern for their husbands and sons by donning pants and making airplanes. "Earlier I buttered bread for him, now I paint grenades and think, this is for him," one Nazi tract quoted a woman munitions worker as saying.[27] In the same vein, an American newspaperwoman wrote of the "deep satisfaction which a woman of today knows who has made a rubber boat which may save the life of her aviator husband, or helped fashion a bullet which may avenge her son!"[28] In part as a consequence of such propaganda, public attitudes toward women's employment changed little as a result of the war. In the American case, the public rather readily accepted the need for women's labor during the war, but in 1945 only 18 percent of a Gallup poll sample approved of a married woman working if she had a husband capable of supporting her.[29]

There is no evidence of great changes in attitudes in other societies either, although we know much less about the postwar situation, complicated as it was by demographic imbalance, widespread destruction, and changed political systems. In the Soviet Union, for example, the loss of millions of men wrought havoc with the demographic balance. The dictates of population policy led the Stalinist regime to revise the Family Code in 1944 along even more conservative lines than the changes associated with the "sexual counterrevolution" of the 1930s. The new code reestablished the man as head of the household and made divorce extremely difficult. Children born to unmarried women became once again "illegitimate" and lost their inheritance rights, while the state maintained some responsibility for their support out of fear of abortion, which had already become illegal. As in Nazi Germany and Japan, women with large families received special honors and cash awards. While women were able to move into some professional jobs, due to the shortage of men, the overwhelming majority of women remained in unskilled, low-status, and poorly-paid jobs. The population imbalance may have opened up opportunities to a few privileged women, but for the majority of women it meant not only personal loss but pressure to bear children and, perhaps most important, a social setting that substituted pampering of men for equality.[30]

But what about women's own self-perceptions? Is it possible that women took on new tasks and survived the rigors of the war without some major change in consciousness? The documentary "The Life and Times of Rosie the Riveter" tells the stories of five women for whom the war was a confidence-building experience. But what happened to all the women who learned new skills and prized their independence and competence in the 1950s? We still do not know how the wartime experience affected their lives in the period of extreme domesticity labelled by Betty Friedan the era of the "feminine mystique."[31]

Whatever the impact on American women, we might expect more dramatic changes in societies that experienced the war more directly. An article by Ingrid Schmidt-Harzbach which appeared recently in a West German feminist magazine takes up the question of the war's impact on German women. Schmidt-Harzbach argues, first of all, that women experience war quite differently than do men, that German women today do not expect recognition for their heroic acts of survival but view their efforts as an obvious extension of what they had always done. And she suggests that the exceptional situation of the war and postwar period created self-assurance in this generation of women by forcing them to be strong and overstep their limits.[32]

Schmidt-Harzbach goes on to suggest that the strength of women in the war leads women today to wonder why their mothers did not make more of the opportunities open to them at the time to push forward in the economic, political, and social realms. She suggests that we remember that such opportunities grew out of the destruction of the world women knew. And yet the war did force women to think differently about traditional gender arrangements. A woman in Berlin told Schmidt-Harzbach that her feelings about men—that the feelings of all women about men—had changed. Men seemed so pitiful and powerless, the weaker sex. The Nazi regime had stood for male power and masculinity, and it had been destroyed. In the postwar period, the "crisis of marriage and the family" became a public issue. The men who survived came home empty-handed, insecure, with feelings of inferiority, especially those who had believed in victory to the end and had expected to return as heroes. They expected women to be the way they had left them, but found them instead heading their families and coping with the harsh realities of daily life. At the same time, the shortage of men, as in the Soviet Union, increased their value and encouraged deference and service on the part of women. Out of these contradictory realities postwar German society worked out a new, but still patriarchal, balance.

Surely the experience of work, of survival, of self-confidence and independence must have made a profound impact on the consciousness of individual women. At the same time, the war created an artificial situation in which the absence of men created opportunities—as well as anxiety and loneliness—for many women. There seems to be no guarantee that either public attitudes or women's own self-perceptions change permanently as a result of war.

We know, even without further badly-needed research, that the postwar period did not bring a social revolution in the status of women in any country. These reflections are intended to suggest that the question of the impact of total war on women is a complex one that necessitates looking beyond the boundaries of the issue as ordinarily defined. Women moved into non-traditional jobs in the labor force and the military, but the consequences of such changes were neither clearly positive nor permanent. Wartime brought increased control over women's reproductive, sexual, and childrearing roles. Women experienced the violence of war in ways directly connected to gender, and that violence cannot be left out of any consideration of the impact of war on women. Finally, what evidence we have of attitudinal change suggests that traditional ideas about gender persist even in the face of total war.

These reflections perhaps suggest a new perspective on women's historical association with pacifism and the peace movement. The connection between women's penchant for peace and the female capacity for bearing children is one that has been made over and over again. An article in the first postwar issue of the German Catholic women's magazine, for example, insisted that "Men make war—women must endure it. For war is foreign to the essence of woman. She, who carries and passes on life, must hate him, the killer, as her most terrible enemy."[33] But we do not have to assume that women are biologically programmed for pacifism because of their reproductive capacities; it is, rather, a question of social roles and socialization. Public opinion polls show persistent gender difference in American attitudes toward violence as an instrument of foreign policy. In August 1972, 70 percent of women as compared to 54 percent of men, favored withdrawal of American troops from Vietnam. In 1980, 17 percent more men than women favored increased defense spending. In 1981, only 56 percent of women, compared to 73 percent of men, approved of President Reagan's handling of defense.[34] In the last presidential election, in fact, women's lesser support of Reagan emerged as the first significant divergence in male-female voting patterns since women were granted suffrage in 1920. In my own neighborhood, the results of opinion polls distributed by our congressional representative consistently show a gap between women's and men's opinions on only one issue: the desirability of the neutron bomb, a weapon that kills people but leaves property intact. Approximately 70 percent of women oppose it, while the same percentage of men approve it.

What I would like to point out here is that women's historical desire for peace is consistent with the largely negative impact of total war on women. It is perhaps significant that, in the political and legal arena, women gained most after the war in the defeated and occupied nations of Germany and Japan. The American military government in Japan granted women the vote out of the conviction that women could transform Japanese society into a peaceful and democratic system.[35] The 1949 constitutions of both the Federal Republic of Germany and the German Democratic Republic granted women equal rights—something that has not yet been accomplished in this country.[36] The relationship between defeat and the granting of equal rights for women is striking. Legal equality for women was, to a certain extent, imposed as a sort of punishment for militaristic men rather than as any kind of reward for women for a job well done.

Presumably no one really favors war, as long as particular objectives can be achieved by other means, but someone generally benefits from it. Despite the popular notion, it is not women as a group who benefit, and women's attitudes toward violence must be understood in that context.

I offer these reflections in order to suggest that we must look at all aspects of women's lives in any attempt to evaluate the impact of total war on women. Richard Polenberg may be right that historians, who accuse generals of fighting the previous war, themselves write about the most recent one.* I would not deny that

---

*Ed note: For Profesor Polenberg's commentary, see pp 170-175.

the lessons of Vietnam overshadow what I write. But I would argue that those lessons, if used carefully, can help us see more clearly.

Chairman Kohn's Introduction of Professor Richard Polenberg
Our commentator for this session is Professor Richard Polenberg of Cornell University. Professor Polenberg was educated at Brooklyn College and at Columbia University, where he received his doctorate in 1964. He's taught at Cornell since 1966, where he is now professor of history, also having served as chairman of the History Department there from 1977 to 1980. He has been the recipient of grants from the Social Sciences Research Council and the American Philosophical Society, and he is the author of many publications, including *Reorganizing Roosevelt's Government, 1936-1939*, and several works on America at war in World War II. I must say that when I first began to teach military history in 1970, Professor Polenberg's excellent edition of documents on the American home front, *America at War: The Home Front, 1941-1945*, was just extraordinary in helping me to define and teach the subject. In a subsequent book, *War and Society: The United States, 1941-1945*, he drew the key sources together and analyzed them for the elucidation of us all.

COMMENTARY

Richard Polenberg

Thank you, Dr. Kohn, for those very kind remarks about my book, *America At War*. The publishing industry being what it is, that book, of course, is now out of print. However, given the choice of being out of print or out of date, I suppose I prefer to be out of print. And after listening to some of the comments this morning, I'm not sure whether it's not both of them.

In their informative and provocative papers, Professors Rupp and Sitkoff have attempted to turn upside-down many of the things historians have been saying for the last fifteen years about war and society, more particularly about World War II and American society. Of course, Professor Marwick's intent is quite different; nevertheless, even his argument is not wholly at odds with this revisionist view which, simply stated, holds that historians have exaggerated the impact of war on social change, especially its liberating or progressive effect on women, blacks, and workers.

Well, I'm reminded of the story that was told about George Bernard Shaw. You know, the story of the young, aspiring playwright who went to see Shaw and asked him what the secret of his success was, and Shaw said, "Well, it's really quite simple. Every play boils down to the same thing, the plots are all the same. Act I, curtain rises, girl meets boy, curtain falls. Act II, curtain rises, girls falls in love with boy, curtain falls. Act III, curtain rises, girl marries boy, curtain falls." "But Mr. Shaw," the young playwright protested, "what's so exciting about that?" And Shaw smiled and said, "Same girl, different boy."

Listening to the papers this morning I'm tempted to say, same war, different interpretation. And this type of historiographical debate certainly adds dramatic interest, at least, to the study of the social effects of war. Now, of course, we've heard about more than one war, and about more than one country, but my comments will focus on the United States during World War II, the case in which changing interpretations are most clearly evident.

According to Professor Rupp, the war proved about as liberating for American women as a day spent at the ironing board or, perhaps, an evening spent reading the collected works of Phyllis Schlafley. The war, she believes, did "not change public attitudes toward women in any significant way." The gains women made resulted less from the war than from long-term economic trends operating independently of it. According to Professor Sitkoff, the war, far from being a watershed for the civil rights movement, was more like a dry well, for it "delayed and stifled black protest activism." I've always thought the shortest book in the world would be entitled "His Friends' Tribute to George Steinbrenner." However, a book about black militancy during World War II might be even shorter. And we undoubtedly will find out when Professor Sitkoff publishes his next volume. Now, Professor Marwick takes a different view. He holds that World War II was indeed a force for social change in England, but he makes rather modest claims, actually, mentioning the willingness to hire married women and the popularity of the Beveridge Report. And even in the written version of his paper, Professor Marwick concludes that while the language and imagery of social class changed as a result of the war, "the essential class structure of the country remained the same."

So, the interpretation that emerges, at least from Professors Rupp's and Sitkoff's papers, certainly differs from the traditional one. Which leads me to my first question: if World War II was not as significant an agent of social change as is commonly believed, why did historians fall, hook, line, and sinker, for the idea that it was? The first answer is that contemporaries, those who wrote about American life during the war, left all sorts of enticing bait in the form of self-conscious assertions that the war was reshaping the nation. There those juicy statements were, flashing and wriggling like lures on the water's surface. Who could blame historians if we swam up for a nibble? For example, we find Breckenridge Long, a State Department official, writing in his diary just two weeks after Pearl Harbor: "This is the end of an era. It is one of the great moments in history. That which has been shall be no more. A new order begins." And a few months later, almost as if he were worried that some future historian, perhaps in too much of a hurry, would overlook that first entry in his diary, he said it all over again. "The signs all point one way—a changed country with a new schedule of economic, financial, social and political conditions. The World of Yesterday died . . . but that which will then exist will be of an entirely different character than that which was."

When historians read popular journals and travelers' accounts published during the war, what did we find? Articles whose very titles, "What the War is Doing to Us," or "Revolution at Home," emphasized massive change and whose very choice of language—"transformation," "cataclysmic," "profoundly affect," "the lightning of war"—drove home the same point. As one writer put it in 1943: "The whole pattern of our economic and social life is undergoing kaleidoscopic changes without so much as a bomb being dropped on our shores." Similarly, journalists who crisscrossed the country wrote accounts that focused on mobility, metamorphosis, modernization. "The war has brought a long overdue economic revolution" in the South, one observer wrote, "and the changes that have come will outlast the war."

Sober minded scholars in the 1940s echoed this view, grounding it in social science theory and lending it a reassuring aura of respectability. In 1943, a book entitled *American Society in Wartime* was published. Edited by William F. Ogburn, it contained essays by eleven members of the University of Chicago's Sociology Department, including such eminent and soon to be eminent men as Robert Redfield, Robert Park, W. Lloyd Warner, Louis Wirth, and Samuel Stouffer. And what did the book have to say about the very issues of gender, race, and class? An essay on the family noted the newly favorable economic climate for women: "The big increase in the number of working women spells increased economic independence which lays a solid basis for enhancing social status." An essay on race relations, while pointing out the persistence of white supremacist sentiment, commented that "the racial structure of society seems to be cracking." An essay on class structure held that the war "is rapidly destroying many social barriers that separate people." But it was the editor's preface that most clearly set the book's tone. "Note what the application of steam power to handicraft manufacture did to revolutionize the social order. A big modern war is in the same category of influences as steam and its attendant inventions. Hardly an aspect of culture escapes its influence."

That image—of war as a powerful engine transforming and modernizing society—proved irresistible to historians, who, reading these diaries, journals, and books and taking copious notes, were inclined to agree with what they said. But there's a second reason, too, why historians emphasized the impact of war on social change, an obvious reason, perhaps, but one that merits at least a word or two. An impressive amount of evidence showed that tangible changes did occur in all the areas that we've been considering. Four and a half million women, many of whom had never expected to work outside the home, much less earn decent wages, took jobs, often in war industries. Nearly three quarter of a million blacks migrated north and west; many of them were rural southerners who had hardly dared dream they would, in their lifetimes, ever walk into a polling booth and vote. Four and one-quarter million workers, many of whom had not held a steady job in ten years, or seen the inside of a union hall, signed up in the AFL and CIO, acquiring job security and seniority rights.

Now, one might, with Professors Rupp and Sitkoff, certainly ask whether wartime changes were entirely beneficial, whether they proved permanent, or whether they would have occurred if the United States had not entered the war. Yet if the significance of the changes can be contested, the changes themselves cannot be discounted. To return for a moment to the analogy of war and steam power: one might wish to contest the significance of the change-over from sailing vessels to steamships, or from stagecoaches to locomotives, but one wouldn't want to deny that the trip was a whole lot faster.

There's still a third explanation of why historians emphasized the transforming effects of World War II, one I offer somewhat more tentatively. The social changes that the war produced were, on the whole, changes which most historians approved, and so it was natural to emphasize them. The direction in which American society moved during the war was, broadly speaking, the direction in which historians thought it should have moved and hoped it would keep on moving. If you believe in equality and job opportunities for women, or in racial justice and civil rights, or in the reduction of disparities in wealth and class privilege, then the war seemed to serve worthwhile purposes. Further, the war validated these purposes, showing that it was possible to accomplish all these liberal goals and gain public acceptance for them. The war, from this perspective, was almost too good to be true. One might say, with apologies to Voltaire, that if World War II hadn't existed, it would have been necessary to invent it.

Moreover, as historians well knew, wartime changes in these areas did not just happen all by themselves, as if by magic. The federal government, under the leadership of Franklin Roosevelt, encouraged or facilitated them by adopting certain policies respecting manpower allocation, fair employment practices, price control, and rationing. To focus on the social effects of World War II was, in a way, to justify both the exercise of presidential authority and the expansion of the welfare state. And it is probably fair to say that historians who formulated the older view of World War II, one that emphasized its transforming and beneficial effects, were not only responding to what people had written during the war, and to what had actually taken place, but were also justifying their own liberal values and progressive inclinations.

And that brings me to my second question. Why have some historians begun to view the war in a different, less favorable light? Not, I think, because new evidence has suddenly appeared that alters our view of what happened, though new archival materials are opening up all the time. Nor, I think, because history is like some huge grandfather clock with interpretations swinging, pendulum-like, from one side to the other, though, in fact, interpretations do shift with a distressing degree of regularity in just that way. And certainly not because historians have grown any less sympathetic with the goals of social, racial, and sexual equality. Rather, new interpretations of World War II reflect disenchantment with the notion that war can be a means of achieving those goals. Our present values usually shape, in some measure, our perspectives on the past, and the study of World War II is no exception.

I think attitudes towards World War II have been powerfully affected by the most recent war through which we've lived, and the lessons of Vietnam, at least the lessons many historians learned, were that the social consequences of war could be harmful and destructive. World War II had seemed to unify different groups in American society, but Vietnam, as a Defense Department official said in 1967, had sown the "seeds of the worst split in our people in more than a century." During World War II hardly anyone questioned the justification for American involvement or the legitimacy of American goals. "Never in our history," an aide wrote to President Roosevelt in 1942, "have issues been so clear." But never in our history were issues more opaque or murkier than during the late 1960s and early 1970s. As Vietnam produced unprecedented division and bitter discord at home, the editors

173

of *Time* magazine admitted to "the loss of a working consensus, for the first time in our lives, as to what we think America means."

Vietnam demonstrated the dangers inherent in an imperial presidency, and historians began to question whether Roosevelt's use of executive authority in World War II had been wholly benign. The revelation in James MacGregor Burns's biography that Roosevelt had encouraged Adolf Berle, in private, to call him "Caesar," did nothing to discourage such questions. (It is, however, safe to infer that Berle never asked FDR to call him "Brutus.") Vietnam demonstrated that government policies could contribute to the twin evils of unemployment and inflation, and historians began to ask whether economic policy in World War II had accomplished all that much. A recent study of the War Manpower Commission, for example, concluded that far from transforming class relations, manpower policies illustrated "the power of social continuity even during war." An important new study of wartime labor argues that the CIO was converted into a "politically timid" bureaucratic organization whose accommodationism led to a "filial-dependent relationship" with government.

The Vietnam years demonstrated to civil rights activists and to feminists just how little progress they had made and just how far they had to go. Not surprisingly, scholars reexamining the 1940s began to insist that blacks and women had not made the substantive gains it once seemed they had. Or rather, that those gains, consisting essentially of better jobs and higher pay, were partial or short-lived. Some historians continue to reiterate the older view, but their scope is so narrow, or their arguments so qualified, as to leave one wondering. The most recent article to state that World War II was, in fact, a civil rights watershed, written by Thomas Cripps and published in the journal *Prologue* just a few months ago, focuses on the alliance between black activists, white liberals, and federal bureaucrats. And what did this alliance manage to accomplish? Ensure voting rights? Win job equality? No, nothing of the sort. Rather, it persuaded Metro Goldwyn Mayer that its film *Tennessee Johnson,* about President Andrew Johnson and Reconstruction, should portray the radical Republican leader, Thaddeus Stevens, as a man not utterly without some redeeming social value. The film was a commercial flop and an artistic Waterloo, but a resounding political success. Again, Karen Anderson's recent book, which maintains the war profoundly affected women workers, is careful to point out that wartime gains disappeared almost immediately after VJ Day as women on the west coast lost their jobs in aircraft factories and shipyards. The author cites one woman, a columnist for a union publication, who preached a return to domesticity, suggesting that Rosie the Riveter make a beeline for the beauty parlor: "When this war is over—I'll get a manicure, put on the frilliest dress I can find, pour a whole bottle of cologne over my head, and then, I'll be glad to give up my Union chair . . . to some boy who comes marching home deserving it."

Historians had grown increasingly uneasy with the view that war could have a generally positive effect, that it could move society in a liberal direction. Looking back on the 1940s from a post-Vietnam vantage point, the old accomplishments began to seem less impressive, the old failures more prominent. Historians sometimes comment that the trouble with generals is that they're always fighting the last war. Perhaps generals should turn the tables and say that the trouble with historians is that they're always writing about the last war.

And this leads me to a third and final question: where should historians who wish to understand the social impact of total war, go from here? What approaches are likely to be most fruitful? Fortunately, the papers presented this morning make a number of useful suggestions, at least three of which deserve some comment. First, Professor Marwick makes the perfectly reasonable point that historians should be cautious about making generalizations regarding the effects of war, since war is not an independent variable to be added to another independent variable—society—to come up with "consequences." There's no simple one to one relationship, he claims, but rather a complex evolving relationship involving all the things that he talked about. And I think that he's right. While it's necessary to generalize about the past, it's just as important to understand what kinds of generalizations make sense and what kinds of generalizations don't make any sense. Second, as Professor Rupp points out, the most enlightening generalizations are likely to be those made within a comparative framework. Her account of the regulation of women's labor in the United States is sharpened by comparisons with the situation in England and Russia on the one hand, and in Germany and Japan on the other. Third, as Professor Sitkoff indicates, the most trustworthy generalizations do not gloss over differences within particular groups, but take them into account. To make sense of the civil rights movement during World War II certainly requires a willingness to distinguish between southern and northern blacks, blacks who were militant and those who were not, and the black middle and lower classes.

I'm not sure that historians can or should be wholly objective in writing about the past. Our interpretations will, to some extent, always reflect our current concerns. But to revert to the story with which I began, if each new generation is likely to say "same war, different interpretation," historians will be much better off if the interpretations, however they vary, are based on the drawing of careful distinctions, the use of comparative analysis, and a proper caution in the making of generalizations.

DISCUSSION AND COMMENTS

Richard H. Kohn (Moderator)

Kohn: Thank you, Professor Polenberg. We have just a brief time for questions, but first, Professor Sitkoff would like to make a brief comment.

Sitkoff: I would. I think sometimes there's a distressing tendency to lump blacks and women together as minorities and to think that the same things are always happening to each, and what you say about one group you can say about the other. Here, I think, Professor Polenberg's desire for symmetry in talking about Professor Rupp's paper and mine may have caused some misunderstanding. I never sought to deny, and it certainly was not the intent of my paper to deny, that the Second World War caused fundamental changes in race relations that were vital to the development of the civil rights revolution. I do think that the war was a watershed in causing certain developments that would become ever increasingly important to the civil rights revolution. What my paper sought to do was to differentiate between the war as a stimulus to black militancy and the war as a stimulus to social change. David Kennedy, during the break, asked me a question which, I think, summed up the thrust of my paper very well in that direction; that is, what I'm arguing is that changes in objective conditions preceded changes in mass consciousness. In that sense, it was the changed conditions in black life in the United States which preceded mass militancy. Thank you.

Kohn: We have just a brief time for questions so please keep your questions or comments as disciplined and brief as did our presenters and commentators.

James Watson (State Historical Society of Wisconsin): I would like to suggest that perhaps the watershed hypothesis is a kind of a situation where we have an effect that is looking for a cause. As you may remember, in the 1948 national election period, Harry Truman issued an order ordering the integration of the armed services of the United States, which was probably the first great civil rights victory for the black movement. Now this order received surprisingly little resisitance in the army and air force, and the reason why goes back to the First World War experience and an observation made by John J. Pershing: "Due to the disadvantages of their civil condition, it takes long and careful training under the best quality of officers in order to bring out the full fighting ability of the black soldier." Pershing had commanded black soldiers in Mindanao during the Philippine insurrection. He was with the 10th Cavalry. He knew what good troops they could be. He also understood that only in a regular army of long service soldiers could blacks be good soldiers. He learned that in the First World War. Now Pershing had a profound effect upon the general staff officers of the American army during the twenties and thirties, on men like Marshall, Eisenhower, and many others. And these men, as they considered the problem of mobilization for war, realized that within the constraints of the American method of war, it would be impossible to raise effective black combat units. Therefore, in World War II, because they could not integrate the army, due to southern opposition, there was a tendency to form only those black units that the army could use. They had to form two combat infantry divisions, but these divisions were given no priority in training because they were never expected to go overseas. They did form black technical service units, anti-aircraft artillery and field artillery units, transportation, truck, and quartermaster labor units in large numbers, and also engineer units. But the situation changed in 1944 when the army faced an infantry crisis. The army was running out of infantry riflemen. The two black divisions were sent to Italy where it was hoped that they could be kept out of serious combat.

Kohn: Can you sum up your point?

Watson: I'm getting to it. Also in 1944, a very significant thing happened in Europe and that was the formation of infantry rifle platoons of black soldiers in one company of one battalion in the regiments of six infantry divisions. These units fought very well and creditably in the fall of 1944 and into 1945. There was also the black artillery battalion that stood with the 101st at Bastogne. The performance of these units convinced the army that the way to utilize black troops in a war was to integrate, to break up the old black units completely and put the black troops into white units. In 1948, Harry Truman accepted this as military policy and the army began to integrate. Many whites who fought alongside of blacks in World War II did not oppose this. I think that this was one of the things that really helped the civil rights movement get started.

Kohn: Thank you for the point. Do we have other questions or points?

Lt Colonel Vance Mitchell (Office of Air Force History): I would like the panel to respond to the following observation: The status of a group in society is enhanced by its right to serve in the military. Would you please comment on that?

Rupp: I think that that is true and I think that in the American context, probably one of the things that came out of the war that I would see as a gain for women as a group, and that I think is very clearly related to the war, is the integration of women into the armed services. I don't think that would have happened without the war. It might have eventually, but I think it would have come after some of the other gains that women made in the labor force.

Marwick: I think I have some doubts about the statement. One of the funny things about Britain before the First World War was that the argument often used for not giving women the vote was that they could not defend the country and that men could, which would seem to support the contention that was just made. But the actual fact was that the overwhelming majority of men in Britain before 1914 had no expectation of actually serving in the army. It was a nice theoretical point to make. Now, one mustn't forget that large numbers of men did, in fact, volunteer after 1914 out of a sense of duty, love of country, and all the rest. But many others didn't and it was not until the actual imposition of conscription in 1916, as I said in my talk, that many men somewhat reluctantly, and who's to blame them, were forced into the army. So, I think it's one of those statements that sounds very nice in theory, but I think it doesn't quite check out in practice, in all cases at any rate.

Sitkoff: Very briefly, I would agree with Arthur. That is not to deny the very, very significant gains for blacks that flowed from their service in the Second World War, but I think that we also have to face the fact that blacks have fought in the military in every one of our nation's wars and the struggle for equality is still not completed.

Polenberg: Well, I'll make it two against two. I agree with the statement. You know, one of the interesting things is that the army sees itself and the military sees itself as merely reflecting society rather than somehow acting as an agent to transform it. The argument against admitting blacks to full rights in the military during World War II was that the army should not be an engine for social transformation. But in fact that's what the military has turned out to be, and as different groups have won rights in the military, I think that their status has indeed been enhanced.

Robert Kinsey (Golden High School, Golden, Colorado): I'm concerned about the fact that most of the conversation has dealt with minority groups or various sorts of sub-groups in society. I would like to ask a question about the effect that military service on a large-scale might have had on a society which, prior to World War II, did not look on the military with great deal of favor. I also wonder about the effect of secrecy on a democratic society over a long period of time, both in terms of political participation and of the individual citizen's sense of having any sort of influence over government policy.

Kohn: In the absence of volunteers, let me respond. There is an interpretation that military service itself is a unifying and cohering force in society. My own impression, looking backwards three centuries, and after teaching military history for some years, is that the rise of the modern state and its power—the ability of the state and its centralizing power—did unify and integrate societies and nations, and materially through military service. Eugene Weber, in his study of the French peasantry in the late nineteenth century, made that point. Conscription in the nineteenth century helped to make French persons into Frenchmen and Frenchwomen. So I think that cohering process has occurred.

The secrecy question is more elusive. Because of the World Wars, Americans came to see the government itself as a social arbiter almost in the patriarchial sense, they came to look to government as the embodiment of the nation and the institution that spoke for society, and to trust it more than Americans had in the past, particularly the central government. I believe total war had that effect. The trust has dissipated, of course, in the last twenty-five or thirty years beginning to some degree with the Korean War and the politicization of war with limited war or war as an extension of policy. One would expect that.

Kohn: I think we have time for one more question.

Dick Hallion (Air Force Flight Test Center): I have a question for Professor Rupp. In your studies of women in the Second World War, did you go back and examine the experience of women who served in the military and in industry during the First World War to see if there were any conditioning factors that might have played a later role in influencing military and civilian bureaucracies to incorporate women in the mobilization effort during the Second World War?

Rupp: At least in some countries I think that the First World War did serve as a kind of rehearsal for what went on later in the Second World War. I think that's particularly clear in the case of Britain. In part because of their mobilization policies during the First World War, the British were more adept at mobilizing women during the Second World War. I know less about the military mobilization experience elsewhere, although it's something I hope someone will do some more research on soon. However, I do think there is a connection and that in some countries— though not so much in the United States—women's military service in the First World War helped in terms of mobilizing women for military service in the Second World War.

Robin Higham (Kansas State University): Several speakers referred to "the horrors of war". It is true that sometimes there are some, but at the symposium we have been in danger of making that into a myth. Even for civilians, war may have been unfamiliar, and it may on occasion have been bloody and horrible, but the vast majority of the time it was boring. Until detailed studies are undertaken, we have very little precise, as opposed to literary generalities, about the actual minutes or hours of fear that people experienced, even for the First World War. C. E. Carrington's *A Subaltern from the Wars Returning* is one of the few accounts to specify the days actually spent in the front-line trenches. Stouffer, *et al,* in *The American Soldier* do provide an introduction to the subject in some detail. But we still have to be very careful about making statements about the "horrors of war".

The other point which none of the speakers mentioned was that in World War II, as opposed to World War I, there is a considerable case to be made that those on the home front, especially wives and mothers, faced a much harder life than did their husbands and lovers in the services. The latter had everything "found," to use the British expression, while the former had to cope with queues and ration books and heating and the blackout and firewatches, and all those other intrusions into family life in which they were also both father and mother. In this respect, after the war one of the London dailies published some statistics coordinating the monthly birthrate with embarkation leave and the beginning of overseas campaigns and showing that there was about a similar nine-month lag that culminated in action on both the hospital and battlefront.

CONCLUDING REMARKS

Richard H. Kohn

In summation, while this century has been the century of total war, historians still disagree about war's effects. But I think no one, no matter what side he or she takes of any interpretation, disagrees that potentially, possibly, the social and political and economic effects of war can be massive. Until we find out more, until we begin to dissect the various issues and problems and take a hard look, with the connective research between action, activity, and change, we will still be far away from explaining the development of society in the twentieth century.

SESSION IV

LIMITED WAR AND THE PROBLEM OF HEARTS AND MINDS ON THE HOME FRONT

LIMITED WAR AND THE PROBLEM OF HEARTS AND MINDS ON THE HOMEFRONT
INTRODUCTORY REMARKS

Allan R. Millett

I think it is appropriate on the twentieth anniversary of the Cuban missile crisis to end a symposium discussing home fronts and total wars with a session on limited war. Twenty years ago this very day, I was standing on a runway at the Naval Base, Guantanamo Bay, loaded down with more hand grenades and ammunition than I should have been carrying for my own and my troops' safety. And I can tell you from having that one brief brush with the possibility of total war, that I became an immediate convert to the idea of limited war, in fact, the more limited the better. After some years of reflection, of course, and as a citizen of the United States and as a part-time Marine officer, I'm less happy about the concept of limited war other than from the standpoint of personal survival.

The idea of limited war, of course, is not new. The phenomenon has been with us for some time, although the exact language is less antique. Limited war is a conflict in which war aims, at least for one of the belligerents, do not involve immediate national survival. This limited commitment is expressed in many ways. It may be a limited commitment in will and lives and resources. The limit may be in geographic area. And the limits may be applied to military means as well. Since World War II, the concept also involves the concept of limited risk, of avoiding escalation to nuclear war of any sort. Limited war, of course, now carries with it a bad odor for many Americans, civilians and military officers. I don't think it is accidental that our conference organizers have selected case studies from Algeria and Vietnam, because this reflects the predisposition to see limited war as synonymous with unpopular war. It's not accidental that we have attached a rather arduous shorthand of "Hearts and Minds" to this session, because the problem of legitimizing limited war in the twentieth century, an era in which the world's military powers could hardly afford any other kind of conflict, is the central dilemma of our time. I think it remains an open question, whether a democratic society of any kind can support limited war.

The gap between effort and results that limited war implies, as I said, is not new. One of the gaps that can open is that between the understanding of the conflict held by those who are fighting it and those who are at home supporting it. This particular problem is, I think, summed up well by the Centurion Marcus Flavinius in a letter written to Tertullus, his cousin and a citizen of Rome, in the second century A.D.: "We had been told on, leaving our native soil, that we are going to defend the sacred rights conferred on us by so many of our citizens settled overseas, so many years of our presence, so many benefits brought by us to populations in need of our assistance and civilization. We could verify that all of this was true and because true, we did not hesitate to shed our blood, to sacrifice our youth and hopes. We regretted nothing. . . . I am told that in Rome factions and conspiracies are rife, that treachery flourishes, and that many in their uncertainty and confusion lend ready ear to the dire temptations of relinquishment and vilify our actions. . . . Make haste to reassure me, I beg you, and tell me that our fellow citizens understand us, support us, and protect us as we ourselves are protecting the glory of the Empire. If it should be otherwise, if we should leave our bleached bones on these desert sands in vain, then beware of the anger of the Legions."

One wonders how long the Roman Empire would have survived if news teams from CBS, that is, the Cataline Broadcasting System, had been with Varus at Teutoburger Wald or with Flavius Silva at Masada. In the most recent issue of *Public Opinion*, Ben Wattenberg speculates, in fact, that TV coverage, rather than the judgment of the battlefield, will decide future limited conflicts, especially when TV crews have access to only half the horror. We have with us an excellent panel today to weigh these problems—waging war with one eye on the enemy and the other on the home front.

Chairman Millett's Introduction of Professor Talbott
Our first speaker this afternoon is John Talbott. He received his undergraduate degree from the University of Missouri and his graduate degrees in 1963 and 1966 from Stanford University. After teaching at Princeton, Jack went to the University of California, Santa Barbara, in 1971 where he is now a professor. He has written articles in *Daedalus, Virginia Quarterly Review,* and *Armed Forces and Society.* He is the author of two books, *The Politics of Educational Reform in France* and *The War Without a Name: France in Algeria, 1954-1962,* published in 1980. He has been a member of the Institute for Advanced Study at Princeton, a visiting professor of strategy at the Naval War College in 1981-82, and a visiting professor at his alma mater.

KEEPING ALGERIA FRENCH: THE WAR ON THE HOME FRONT

John E. Talbott

On November 12, 1954, François Mitterrand, minister of the interior in Pierre Mendes France's government, intervened in the first parliamentary debate on the insurrection that had broken out in Algeria twelve days earlier. "Algeria," he proclaimed, "is France."[1] Earlier in the debate Mendès France had declared that his government would make no compromises with "the sedition."[2] Mendes had sent reinforcements to North Africa as soon as news of the All-Saints Day rising reached the mainland. By year's end, 20,000 additional troops and 20 companies of riot police had been dispatched across the Mediterranean in support of the policy that Algeria was French and French would Algeria remain.

For almost five years Mendès's successors insisted that France would keep Algeria French, until in September 1959 Charles de Gaulle raised the possibility that Algeria might one day be Algerian, independent of French rule. Nearly three years later—in July 1962—the possibility became a reality.

For all General de Gaulle's efforts to portray the outcome as a great French victory, independence marked the defeat of the policy France had pursued throughout most of a long and divisive war. Many explanations for the defeat—or the victory, if you happen to be a Gaullist—have been put forward. At one pole, partisans of the settlers driven from Algeria in the last savage months of the war charged de Gaulle with sabotaging a victory nearly in hand. At the opposite pole, some contemporary observers saw the loss of French Algeria as inevitable; in an era of worldwide decolonization, they declared, nothing else was in the cards.[3]

Between a great man's act of betrayal and the ineluctability of historical forces lie several other explanations for the passing of French Algeria. The one I would like to offer draws on Clausewitz, whose life ended before French rule in North Africa had been established. "No one starts a war—or rather, no one in his senses ought to do so," Clausewitz wrote,—"without first being clear in his mind what he intends to achieve by that war and how he intends to conduct it. The former is its political purpose, the latter its operational objective."[4]

French policy-makers were clear about what they intended to achieve by the war in Algeria: they meant to keep Algeria French. They were even fairly clear

187

about how they intended to conduct the war. From Mendès France's prime-ministership in 1955 to Charles de Gaulle's presidency in 1960, from the Fourth Republic to the Fifth, every French government pursued essentially the same strategy. Each combined repressing the armed insurrection against French rule with reforming the political and economic structure of French Algeria.

But the Fourth Republic failed to make policy and strategy—ends and means—fit together in the manner Clausewitz prescribed. That ill-starred regime failed to do two things, especially, that might have enabled it to reach a more favorable outcome. First, it failed to act swiftly and decisively against the armed forces of the *Front de libération nationale* (FLN). Second, it failed, in a timely fashion, to prevent gunrunners and guerrillas from crossing back and forth over the Tunisian and Moroccan frontiers.

Eventually, both these tasks were accomplished. By 1960 a series of devastating French offensives had rendered the FLN incapable of fielding units larger than company size; elaborate barriers constructed along the frontiers had reduced the flow of men and arms from Tunisia, especially, to a trickle. But by then political events had overtaken military actions. French strategy did not meet the demands of French policy until it was too late to keep Algeria French—until, that is, the policy itself had undergone a fundamental change.

The reasons for the mismatch between policy and strategy are mainly, but not exclusively, to be found in the difficulties of waging such a war in the face of important sectors of public opinion at home. Mainland opinion proved unwilling to pay the price that keeping Algeria French probably demanded.

* * *

From the outset, the Fourth Republic was very hard pressed indeed to pursue a strategy commensurate with its policy. News of the rising of November 1, 1954, came to a mainland that six months earlier had sustained a humiliating military defeat in another corner of the old empire. The fall of the fortress at Dien Bien Phu, although not strategically decisive, had sufficient impact on domestic opinon to force the French government into negotiating in earnest an end to the war in Indochina.[5]

The Indochina experience cast a long shadow over events in Algeria. In the first place, the troubles in North Africa could not have come at a worse time. Large numbers of French troops—the most experienced combat soldiers in the French army—remained in Indochina when the insurrection broke out, and bringing them home stretched well into 1955. Many of the Indochina regiments, victims of heavy casualties, had to be reorganized and reequipped before they could be sent to North Africa.

The Algerian garrison had itself been short-handed for years, stripped of troops and equipment required in Southeast Asia. In late 1954 only one helicopter was to be found in Algeria; virtually no serviceable aircraft of other types were available.[6]

Such troops as could be rushed to Algeria from mainland garrisons had little or no combat experience. And most of the units to which they belonged were in any case designed, equipped, and trained to fight the mechanized, armored war of the North German plain, not the foot-slogging, mountain-hopping war of the guerrilla. Divisions created to fulfill France's NATO mission were as ill-suited to counterinsurgency operations elsewhere as a Royal Navy specializing in antisubmarine warfare turned out to be ill-prepared for amphibious operations in the South Atlantic.

Even had seasoned, properly trained and equipped troops been dispatched to Algeria at the outbreak of the insurrection, their operations would have been hampered by a lack of accurate intelligence. At the outset, French authorities did not know who the FLN was or how great its numbers were. To borrow the famous line from "Casablanca," police arrested "the usual suspects." Jailing the most prominent nationalist leaders did the revolutionaries of the FLN a favor, removing from the scene their chief competitors.[7]

Still, an x-ray photograph of FLN headquarters, a list of names of every last FLN recruit, would have availed little had the mainland been unable to commit sufficient economic resources to the struggle against the Algerian revolution. France's recovery from the material devastation of the Second World War— greater, even, than that of the First—had by the early 1950s been pretty much accomplished. By 1954, the French economy was showing the first stirrings of the rapid growth that later pushed France to the forefront of Western industrial powers. Whether such an economy could have afforded a rapid and massive military response to the revolt against French rule in Algeria is a hard question to answer. Certainly, such a response could not have been made without causing important economic dislocations. Calling up in short order large numbers of reservists and draftees, for example, would have created severe shortages in the labor market, sharply driving up wages and prices. As it was, the French economy didn't escape such war-generated inflationary pressures.[8]

Recovering militarily from the Indochina war and instructing the French army in counterinsurgency warfare slowed the response to the Algerian insurrection; economic bottlenecks impeded the rapid deployment of forces. But the most severe—and in the end most decisive—constraints on French action in Algeria were political.

In the wake of Dien Bien Phu, Pierre Mendes France's threat to send conscripts to join the professional expeditionary force in Southeast Asia quickly brought the National Assembly to see the need for negotiating a settlement. In the light of this experience, not until August 1955 did the French government call up reservists for duty in North Africa; months later it extended active service to twenty-seven months; later still did it become the fate of most conscripted twenty-year-olds to do their time in Algeria.

The government plainly expected recalling reservists to provoke trouble; it chose to announce the measure in August, when most of the French are away on vacation and rulers traditionally disclose unpopular news to the ruled. Elements of one reserve regiment rioted in their barracks. Other soldiers scuffled with police at railroad stations, pulled troop-train emergency brakes, and shouted anti-government remarks at onlookers as they made their way to Marseilles.[9]

Contrary to the hopes of antiwar activists, however, these disruptions did not mark the beginning of the collapse of military discipline over the question of serving in Algeria. The government took steps to deprive reservists of the means of protest; never again did such widespread outbursts take place. Draftees, younger men than the reservists, went more docilely to North Africa than had this first batch of older brothers.

If the French government had less trouble shipping reservists and draftees to North Africa than it feared, the falling-off of protest nevertheless did not encourage it to accelerate the military build-up. Jacques Soustelle, whom Mendes France had appointed governor-general, the government's chief administrative and political officer in Algeria, found his appeals for more troops, dispatched more quickly, falling on deaf ears.[10]

Coming to grips with the insurrection was not, of course, simply a question of pouring an enormous number of troops into North Africa. It was also a question of deploying them. From the outset until early 1959, units composed mainly of reservists and conscripts defended lives and property in the countryside. They essentially performed guard duty. A much smaller force of professional soldiers—paratroopers and legionnaires, for the most part—perhaps 10 percent of the total, conducted offensive operations against the guerrillas. Conscripts may have owed their duty to their lack of military experience. Guard duty was dangerous enough—a grenade rolled through the doorway of a cafe, a bomb exploded in a marketplace, an ambush sprung at night, death by mutilation, were always possibilities to be feared. But such duty was far less risky than hunting down guerrillas in the mountains. It's hard to find a political motive for this division of military labor, but it's also hard to think that one didn't exist. Assigning the conscripts to *quadrillage*, as the system was called, may have been a means of keeping them, at least relatively speaking, out of harm's way.[11]

The costs of this deployment were high. To conduct an essentially defensive war was to play the guerrillas' game. To delay, to hit and run, to avoid decisive engagements, to live to fight another day, to survive until the enemy got tired and went home—nothing could have suited the FLN better.

During the first two years of the insurrection, the FLN was militarily very weak indeed. Fewer than a thousand men took part in the All-Saints rising; their bombs were crude, homemade contraptions, many of which failed to go off.[12] In the months before the flow of weapons across the Tunisian frontier commenced, guerrillas who even bore arms carried mainly ancient hunting rifles and shotguns.[13] For the first year of the war the western half of the country was virtually empty of FLN fighting men. Even in its mountainous eastern stronghold the FLN, out of military weakness, spent much of 1955 lying low.[14] Never, in the entire course of the conflict, did the FLN succeed in organizing the guerrillas of the interior into a conventional army. In this respect, the Algerian war was quite unlike the French and American wars in Indochina, where the final defeats came at the hands of North Vietnamese regulars.

It's true that the French government was unaware of some of the FLN's weaknesses. But it's also true that the predominantly defensive strategy that mainland political considerations seemed to require was not well-suited to exploiting such weaknesses as the government knew about.

* * *

No government of the Fourth Republic could ever be certain that a parliamentary majority cobbled together on one set of issues would survive a challenge posed on another set. In such circumstances, well-placed minorities exerted an influence out of all proportion to their numbers.

This was especially true of the so-called "Algerian lobby," the group of settlers' deputies and senators that had held sway in parliament for three-quarters of a century. Any hint on the government's part of a conciliatory move toward the Algerian insurrection, any whisper of the possibility of negotiating with the FLN, was enough to provoke from the settlers' benches charges of sell-out and treason.[15]

For all their bluster and bombast about keeping Algeria French, conservatives imposed on the Fourth Republic constraints of another kind. They made quite clear that they would not stand for increasing taxes the better to fight the war. This was the issue that brought down Guy Mollet in May 1957; the conservative parties voted against his tax bill even though they supported his Algerian policy.[16]

From another quarter, the government had increasingly to contend with charges arising from the army's methods in Algeria. The most celebrated episode in a lengthy affair was the so-called "Battle of Algiers." In early 1957 the Tenth Parachute Division successfully put down a terrorist campaign in Algeria's capital city at the expense of practices, including the use of torture, that outraged liberal opinion. The Mollet government, which drew much of its parliamentary support from this same quarter, was at least discomfited by the allegations appearing in *Le*

Monde, L'Express, and elsewhere, and appointed a blue-ribbon committee (whose teeth it then carefully extracted) to look into them.

Such a response did nothing to mollify the government's critics; it angered and embittered army officers who saw themselves made into scapegoats for their civilian superiors. In the eyes of the settlers and their mainland allies, of course, these same officers were heroes of whom too much could not be made.[17]

The Battle of Algiers underscored the Fourth Republic's dilemma. By 1957 the fragile consensus on keeping Algeria French that the government hoped to maintain had been shattered. The political leadership found itself having to steer between the Scylla of the left—the minority who believed France should leave Algeria forthwith as well as the growing number of liberals (and a handful of such conservatives as Raymond Aron) who doubted whether Algeria was worth maintaining at the price being extracted—and the Charybdis of the right, the diehards of *Algérie française* who called for ever sterner measures against the insurrection—the strain on the moral and constitutional fabric of the Republic be damned. Between such rocky shores, republican governments had very little room to maneuver. A middle course suggested half measures; neither an all-out offensive against the FLN's ability to wage war, nor a recognition that France had anything to gain from negotiating an end to its sovereignty in Algeria.

And yet . . . the Fourth Republic, unloved during its lifetime and unlamented since its demise, probably deserves more credit than it has received for measures that eventually enabled a way out of the Algerian stalemate to be found. It has been the practice of Gaullists, especially, to stress the discontinuities between the Fourth Republic and the Fifth, to claim credit for post-World War II successes that the Fifth does not exclusively deserve, and to heap the blame for failures on its hapless predecessor. In the realm of economic policy, for instance, it was once fashionable amoung Gaullists to attribute to themselves responsibility for the astonishing growth rates of the 1960s and to ignore that the foundations of economic progress had been laid under the Fourth Republic.[18]

So it has been with respect to Algeria. The continuities between the Fourth Republic and the Fifth have been slighted. Closing the Algerian frontiers, especially the border with Tunisia, had a greater impact on the FLN's war-fighting capabilities than any other measure. Begun in 1957 under André Morice, minister of defense in Maurice Bourgès-Maunoury's cabinet, the barrier sealing off Algeria to gunrunners from Tunisia—and Tunisia to guerrillas slipping across from Algeria—was a formidable construction indeed. A belt several miles deep, laced with accordion wire, festooned with searchlights, strewn with mines, bristling with sensors, patrolled day and night by tanks and other armored vehicles, the Morice Line presented to the FLN a very discouraging obstacle.[19] As I suggested above, had it been in place a year or two earlier, when the guerrillas were not only woefully short of weapons and ammunition, but were also able to hurry into their Tunisian sanctuary any time things got hot on the Algerian side, the war might have gone differently. As it was, the Line contributed to de Gaulle's efforts to negotiate a settlement; both sides knew the FLN was in no position to hold out at the bargaining table in the hope of getting more by means of some battlefield achievement.

The high command that at last took offensive operations against the insurrection was not composed of creatures of the Fifth Republic, but soldiers who had made their reputations under the Fourth. The commander in chief in Algeria was General Maurice Challe, an air force officer whose political opinions, insofar as he had any, were thought to be mildly socialist. Named commander in late 1958, in 1959 Challe directed against the FLN a series of smashing blows that owed as much to World War II as to any manual of counter-insurgency warfare. Sweeping across Algeria from west to east, Challe's offensive hammered away at guerrilla strongholds with air, artillery and infantry, severely diminishing the FLN's capacity to fight.[20] It is hard not to wonder what such an offensive, carried on three or four years earlier, might have accomplished in terms of the FLN's willingness to carry on the struggle. Certainly, a version of the Challe Plan carried out in 1955 or 1956, a Morice Line erected in the same years, would have provided the Fourth Republic with a strategy more in keeping with its policy.

* * *

Nevertheless, it was General de Gaulle who brought the war to an end. What difference did de Gaulle make? Within the context of this essay, the difference he made was to master French public opinion. He alone, among the available political leadership, had both the will and the authority to surmount the clashes of opinion that had torn the Fourth Republic apart and to impose a settlement remote from France's original aims.

The body of opinion that threatened de Gaulle most resided in the army, which was not supposed to have an opinion at all. Worse, the army was prepared to take action on its views, as it had shown in the crisis of May 13, 1958. Conniving with the settler rebels in Algiers, the soldiers had abandoned the Fourth Republic and swung their support to de Gaulle, believing that he represented the best chance of keeping Algeria French.[21]

Before long, it became evident that de Gaulle was not the diehards' man at all. To them, the self-determination hinted at in the General's speech of September 1959 was anathema. On one occasion army and settler activists, in the hope of either changing de Gaulle's course or removing him from power, tried to repeat their tactics of May 13, 1958. The so-called "Week of the Barricades" in January 1960 was far bloodier than May 13 had been; it ended a ludicrous failure. Making masterful use of television, de Gaulle went on the air, denounced the sedition, and recalled the army to its responsibilities. The activists' attempt to rally both force and opinion against him fizzled.[22]

The army's next attempt to force de Gaulle to embrace the policy of *Algérie française* was on the face of it far more serious. This time the army acted alone (on the question of including the settlers, the military conspirators were bitterly divided). In the hope of rallying other commanders behind them, in April 1961 a handful of activist colonels brought their regiments into Algiers. Among the quartet of retired generals who lent themselves to this enterprise was Maurice Challe, the disillusioned former commander in chief. Challe's sense of betrayal had brought him into the conspiracy; his reputation for integrity, it was thought, might induce fence-sitters in the officer corps to join the rebellion against de Gaulle. The "Putsch," as it was called, was a fiasco. Once again de Gaulle appeared on television; once again, he delivered a masterful performance, perhaps the most brilliant, indeed, in a long career of dramatic interventions, ordering the rank and file in Algeria to disobey the commands of the military usurpers. Two days later the Putsch collapsed, whether owing to the resistance de Gaulle had rallied or to the weight of its own internal disarray is hard to judge.[23]

In any event, the failure of the Putsch hastened de Gaulle's search for a settlement. Once the army had been forced to see that it had no right to its own opinions on Algeria, that it was no more—but also no less—than an instrument of the state's policy, negotiations with the FLN steadily progressed. The way certainly did not become easy: the settler activists, wild with anxiety over their future in an Algerian Algeria, joined the military desperadoes, fugitives from the failed Putsch, in the Secret Army Organization (OAS). In the last year of the war, OAS saboteurs and murder gangs hunted down enemies real and imagined in the streets of Algeria and the mainland.[24] Nevertheless, de Gaulle's victory over the army removed the most important obstacle to a settlement.

For in reaching a settlement, de Gaulle had mainland opinion, opinion between the extremes of left and right, squarely behind him. Unlike many things about the Algerian war, we know this with a reasonable degree of certainty. For under de Gaulle's republic, public opinion researchers assiduously studied the relationship between the French and their leader. From 1958 on, de Gaulle's Algerian policy never enjoyed the support of less than half those interviewed, and usually as many as two-thirds.[25] Given the policy's obscurities and ambiguities, deepened by de Gaulle's Delphic pronouncements, such an unvarying expression of support suggests that, with respect to Algeria, the French were content to follow their president's lead.

But their willingness to go along with de Gaulle had limits. A close inspection of the public opinion polls reveals that the mainland French made up their minds about Algeria earlier than the political leadership. As early as July 1957, nearly a year before de Gaulle assumed power, a majority (53 percent) favored negotiations with the FLN with a view to a ceasefire, a position the French government still publicly rejected out of hand.[26] Once the idea of looser ties became admissible, it was but a step to accepting Algerian independence.

This is not the place in which to follow the twists and turns of de Gaulle's course in arriving at independence. In retrospect, at least, one thing stands out. At some point, whether during the lonely years of self-imposed exile on his country estate, as his memoirs imply, or sometime after he returned to power, as seems more likely, de Gaulle made up his mind that France must rid itself of the Algerian obsession. Once his mind was made up, he acted ruthlessly in pursuit of this aim. Everything, in his view, had to be subordinated to France's regeneration. It was time, he often said, that France "marry her century," by which he meant that the nation must modernize, must push itself to the front rank of modern industrial states. In pursuit of this grand ambition, much that belonged to the past must be put aside, regrettable as such losses might be. Foremost among these anachronisms was the empire, Algeria included.[27]

De Gaulle's grand ambition coincided with the far less lofty attitudes of the majority of his countrymen. "Emotionally remote from the settlers, reluctant to spend vast sums of money on their defense, . . . pessimistic about the long-range prospects of the French presence, unenthusiastic about the prosecution of the war,"[28] by 1961 the mainland French were willing to concede the end of empire that withdrawal from Algeria represented.

De Gaulle had the will, the authority, and the ruthlessness to impose a settlement over the objections of the French army and against the wishes of the settlers and the Muslims who had stood by the French. The officers paid with their careers, the settlers with their homeland, the Muslims with their lives. Some things de Gaulle didn't do much differently than the Fourth Republic had done them. The Fifth Republic applied strong military pressures against the insurrection, undertook economic and social reforms, and pursued secret contacts with the FLN. A strategy that, executed early enough and forcefully enough might have put down the insurrection—might even have kept Algeria French— served instead to extricate France from Algeria.

Chairman Millett's Introduction of Mr. Braestrup
Our second speaker, Peter Braestrup, graduated from Yale University in 1951 and did his post-graduate work in the United States Marine Corps in Korea where the People's Liberation Army carried on a number of instructional activities. Peter's active career in journalism started before he went to college, but his earliest writing that I've seen, which he did as a first lieutenant, appeared in the *Marine Corps Gazette*. He and I share that experience. His article was about digging trenches deep. If you are a lieutenant, that is not an inconsequential problem, particularly if you are getting mortared. He later discussed trench digging at Khe Sanh in another series of articles that I can recall. His active career in journalism began in 1953 when he was a staff writer with *Time* magazine. He moved on to the *New York Herald Tribune* where he covered the war in Algeria. He went to Harvard as a Nieman Fellow and spent almost a decade as a correspondent with the *New York Times,* serving in Washington, Algeria, Paris and in Vietnam. He switched to

the *Washington Post* and served there until he left to become a Fellow at the Woodrow Wilson International Center for Scholars. He is now, of course, the editor of the *Wilson Quarterly*. He's had a prolific career as a writer. His best known work, which I think most of you know, is *Big Story*. It is a big book, in fact, two big books, subtitled: *How the American Press and Television Reported and Interpreted the Crisis of Tet 1968 in Vietnam and Washington*. It was published first in 1973 and now is being reissued by the Yale University Press.

A COMMENT ON THE VIETNAM CRISIS IN AMERICA: TET 1968

Peter Braestrup

Almost fifteen years ago, something happened in Vietnam and Washington, and historians and politicians have been arguing among themselves about it ever since.

On January 30-31, 1968, Hanoi switched its strategy and sent 84,000 troops into Saigon, Hue, and a dozen other cities in the South. It was a TV spectacular. A nineteen-man Viet Cong sapper team tried to get into the U.S. embassy in Saigon; two North Vietnamese divisions pressed their seige of the Marine base at Khe Sanh.

But within a week, as the South Vietnamese held firm, the North Vietnamese tide began to ebb with heavy losses; within three weeks, the last city, Hue, was cleared by the allies, and within a month pressure began to ease on Khe Sanh. In the end, it was, as Don Oberdorfer wrote in *Tet!*, a severe military setback for Hanoi even as "the communist claim to moral and political authority in South Vietnam suffered a grievous blow."

But that was not the way the 1968 Tet offensive came across in the news media then or later—leading to a controversy that endures to this day. To varying degrees—and in various ways—the dominant themes in the press and, especially, on television added up to this message in February-March 1968: Disaster in South Vietnam.

Why did this distortion—of a magnitude rare in the annals of American crisis journalism—take place? And what were the consequences?

Tet was an extreme case. Its peculiar circumstances—surprise, melodrama, uncertainty, White House ambiguity—impacted to a rare degree on the peculiar habits, susceptibilities, manpower limitations, and technological constraints of newspapers, news magazines, wire services, and TV news.

In crisis, first reports are always partly wrong, and instant analysis by reporters or TV anchormen represents the hasty reactions of the half-informed. Tet abounds with examples But the failure to convey the changing realities on the

197

ground in February-March 1968 was perhaps the media's greatest sin. As the fog of war lifted and the Communist tide ebbed, the managers of the press and especially TV put the accent on *more* melodrama rather than on trying to update the inevitably melodramatic first impressions—urban destruction, enemy omnipresence, allied confusion—of the Tet surprise. After four weeks, *Time,* the *New York Times,* and the *Washington Post* began to publish a few such recovery stories, but rarely on Page One. Other publications and TV waited even longer. Disaster, real or impending, was a "story"; recovery was not.

The melodrama of Khe Sanh, for example, preoccupied newsmen and their bosses to the exclusion of much else in Vietnam. It was, in reality, a fairly low-intensity siege, only 12 miles from the nearest U.S. forces; and U.S. bombers dumped 100,000 tons of bombs ("five Hiroshimas") to discourage the North Vietnamese besiegers.

But to the eyes of the American reader or viewer, all sense of perspective was lost; Lyndon Johnson's own "leaked" worries about a repeat of the famed 1954 French disaster of Dien Bien Phu only fanned media anticipation of the same climax at Khe Sanh. The seige accounted for 25 percent of all network evening news shows during the Tet period and slightly smaller chunks of newspaper front pages; *Newsweek* put the "Agony of Khe Sanh" on its cover on March 18 (after Communist troops, in fact, had started to withdraw). Khe Sanh was an aberration, an uncharacteristic battle with little military impact on a long war; yet Walter Cronkite and others made it a "microcosm" of the whole war, even as the allies elsewhere began to recover from the Tet onslaught, repair the urban damage, and recapture the battlefield initiative.

The "disaster" occurred not in Vietnam but in Lyndon Johnson's Washington. The Tet surprise led to a political crisis that led to LBJ's own "abdication," the entrance of Robert F. Kennedy into the Democratic race, and as it turned out, to eventual U.S. disengagement from the war.

Why did the crisis take place? Old "doves" said that Tet, exposing the folly of U.S. intervention, suddenly turned the public against the war, and forced LBJ to reject "military victory." This analysis is simplistic, as will be seen below. So is the "hawk" critique—LBJ threw in the towel in the midst of enemy defeat. So is the complaint by Johnson administration alumni that the media treatment of Tet máde the crisis a wound.

The story of the Tet crisis in Washington is complex, and not totally clear, particularly with regard to LBJ's own motives, reactions, and expectations.

But it must be seen in context. Before Tet, Lyndon Johnson was already in trouble on Capitol Hill; his popularity was sagging; and the Democratic party was split on the war, which had gone on for three years at the cost of 16,000 U.S. battle dead. And, as the TV correspondents were fond of saying, there was "no end in sight." Indeed, the administration's limited war policy promised no quick end, only perseverance. In late 1967, the administration had launched a last big propaganda effort, including a much-publicized speech by General William C. Westmoreland, the American commander in Vietnam, to shore up public opinion with assurances that "progress" was being made.

Implicitly, President Johnson promised the press, politicians, and public that no bad news was in store. Although he had warnings from Saigon of an impending enemy effort, he barely mentioned Vietnam in his State of the Union address. Lastly, the Tet surprise caught Washington in the middle of another "crisis"—the January 23 seizure by the North Koreans of the USS *Pueblo,* a Navy spy ship. In short, Washington was caught badly off guard by the big bad news from Vietnam.

The Tet surprise—and the attention thereto— forced LBJ to confront anew the old contradictions of his Vietnam policy. Both the Pentagon "hawks" and the more visible "doves" sought to exploit the Tet surprise to revive old demands for changes (i.e., a bombing halt for the "doves," a reserve call-up for the "hawks"). LBJ hunkered down and sought to buy time. He left the explanations of Tet to subordinates. In effect, the President left a vacuum, which others—senators, pundits, critics—hastened to fill.

Washington newsmen conveyed the White House's "siege" atmosphere and partial echoes of the inner debate over a 206,000 troop increase. But neither newsmen nor their sources understood that LBJ at Tet, as before, always resisted any massive reserve call-up sought by the Joint Chiefs—unless such was needed to ward off catastrophe in Vietnam. LBJ saw such mobilization as fatal to his beloved Great Society programs. In early February, he may have wavered a bit; but Westmoreland soon told him that the allies were going on the offensive without additional troops. Thus reassured, LBJ apparently cast about for ways to quiet the opposition at home, and enable him to pursue his middle-of-the-road war policy as before.

In public, for two months, Johnson gave local sermons but no nationwide TV address—until March 31 when he announced his decision not to seek reelection, another temporary partial bombing pause, and another offer to Hanoi to talk peace. He did not rule out further U.S. escalation, but he spoke of greater efforts by the South Vietnamese. In effect, he again sought to buy time. But to his surprise, Hanoi accepted the offer to talk, and thereafter "peace with honor," not "winning," emerged as the chief U.S. hope.

Did the press and television—through their impact on public opinion—alter the course of the war?

Such claims—made by both critics and champions of the media—are impossible to substantiate. We now know, thanks to Herbert Schandler's *The Unmaking of a President* and other studies, that the White House was shaken not only by the

Tet shock but by its portrayal on TV, and so (as a result?) was the the rest of political and journalistic Washington. Yet, as measured by pollsters, *public* support for the war effort itself remained remarkably steady in February-March 1968, even as LBJ's popularity hit a new low. Scholarly studies have shown that among Democrats who voted for "peace candidate" Eugene McCarthy in the March 12 New Hampshire primary, *anti-Johnson "hawks" outnumbered anti-Johnson "doves"* by more than three to two! Yet the primary results were interpreted by politicians and much of the media as an anti-war protest; Robert F. Kennedy entered the race against LBJ a few days later on a "dove" platform.

My own hunch is that the media's generalized portrait of "disaster" in South Vietnam affected political Washington more than it did the general public. As Oberdorfer suggests, the "disaster" portrait may have impelled many editors, pundits, and "opinion-leaders," long uneasy about the war, to put themselves on record against it. But I would also suggest that election-year politics, and *Lyndon Johnson's own behavior,* did more to aggravate the Washington crisis than did all the alarms of the media.

The election-year pressures—and the underlying contradictions of the Administration's ambiguous, costly "fight and talk," "guns and butter" war policy—would have forced a New Look sometime in 1968, even if the media had come closer to the realities of February-March.

One can speculate, of course, that if the press and television had portrayed the battlefield with more cold light and less black fog, the politicans would have reacted more calmly.

At least the Washington "hawks" and "doves" and Robert Kennedy would not have had a "disaster" to exploit; LBJ might have felt less cornered, less impelled to try (once again) to pacify both sides, more willing to wait for the dust to settle and for Hanoi to make an offer.

The February-March 1968 crisis and LBJ's climactic speech did not end the war, which went on for five more years. They merely made it more difficult for LBJ and his successor to deal from a position of strength with Hanoi in negotiating an end to it. But the ultimate responsibility—for candor and coherence before the crisis and for leadership and coherence in crisis—lay not with the media but with the President. By failing to meet this responsibility, Lyndon Johnson made the Tet crisis and his own humiliation, in large measure, a self-inflicted wound.

Chairman Millett's Introduction of Dr. MacIsaac
Our commentator, Dave MacIsaac, needs no introduction to many of you. I'll tell you what many of you already know. Dave was a long-time and esteemed member of the history faculty at the United States Air Force Academy and served on the faculties at other military institutions until his recent retirement. He is now

boondoggling, happily, down at the Air Power Research Institute at Maxwell Air Force Base where I've had the pleasure to visit and watch him boondoggle. He is doing contract research on a book for the Air Force. He is, of course, a prolific writer, his best known work being *Strategic Bombing in World War Two: The Story of the United States Strategic Bombing Survey,* published in 1976. He's also written articles in *Air Force Magazine, Air University Review,* and the *Naval War College Review.* From August of 1978 through September of 1979 he was a Fellow of the Woodrow Wilson International Center for Scholars at the Smithsonian Institution in Washington. He is a veteran of these meetings. He organized the fourth symposium in 1970, and then edited the proceedings of the fifth in 1972. It is always good to know that Dave is going to be the commentator because that really keeps the other people honest.

COMMENTARY

David MacIsaac

I shall begin by noting that Allan didn't tell you the real reason I was invited back. Namely, the reliably predictable and exceptionally wonderful weather that I always bring to Colorado when I return in the fall. I hasten to point that out lest some of you think it's just a simple fact that the Department of History is afraid to put one of these affairs on without having the "Duke Mafia" adequately represented.

It was mentioned earlier that this is the twentieth anniversary of the Cuban missile crisis. That reminded me of a perverse habit I developed, when I used to teach in these hallowed halls, of going into class in the morning and starting out by asking, "What is this day in history?" And it got to be a pretty good game, once the cadets figured out that they could get an "A" for the day, if they got the right answers. And I would have expected today that it would have been the Cuban missile crisis. But that's at about the "B" level; "B + " level would be Al Millett's birthday. An "A + " level, almost, would be Peter Braestrup's son's birthday. But I would have told them something else that's relevant to a lot of people in this room: that on this date in the year 1746, what is now Princeton University was granted a charter by the royal governor of Virginia; that in the year 1836 on this date, Sam Houston was sworn in as the first President of the new Republic of Texas; and that on the 22nd of October of this year, 1982, a Princeton grad is being sworn in as the President of North Texas State University, and I trust you will all join me in sending him best wishes.*

Implicit in the arrangement in any such session as this one is a conception that, by adopting the techniques of comparative history, some generalizations might emerge that, at best, might lead us to other or new sets of questions that we might otherwise miss in looking at a single instance. Or so I was once taught and have often thought. And at first glance, the Algerian and Vietnam experiences seem to suggest a number of parallels. As I read through Professor Talbott's perceptive, incisive and elegantly written paper, I found myself scribbling the letters "VN" for Vietnam and "K" for Korea in the right margin, time after time.

---

* Ed note: Dr. MacIsaac is referring to the inauguration of Brigadier General Alfred F. Hurley, USAF, Ret., as the President of North Texas State University on 22 October 1982. As Permanent Professor and Head of the Department of History at the Air Force Academy, Brigadier General Hurley organized the First Military History Symposium in 1967 and developed the continuing series of symposia which grew out of that first meeting.

As I got to the end of his paper, though, in the clear revelation of his thesis—that is, as I read it, that by the time the French government found a strategy in tune with its initial policy, the policy itself had changed—that there had been a mismatch between policy and strategy. By the time I got to that point, though, I got to feeling that he was coming close to suggesting, as many of the committed believers have done in writing about Vietnam, that something beyond a temporary victory might have been possible if the French government had just done this or that, earlier or more swiftly, or massively, or whatever. In the end I came, once again, to the conclusion, however, that the two experiences have only minor and superficial resemblances. The presence, for one thing, of the Algerian deputies and senators in the French parliament made so great a difference, it seems to me, that Algeria must be given a nod over Vietnam in terms of its complexity, and for me to say that, that's saying a lot. For all of our difficulties, after all, we did not have to contend with General Thieu and Colonel Ky in the House of Representatives.

With regard to Vietnam, I must openly admit to a rather dire lack of objectivity. I first heard about it in any real sense in 1964, flying home from a three-year tour in Spain, looking through the Paris edition of "The Trib" on the airplane, and finding on page eight or nine, near the bottom, a short column indicating that U.S. strength in Vietnam had reached ten or twelve thousand (I forget the exact number). And I can remember turning to my wife, Charlotte, and saying "My God, that's more people than we had in all of Spain and Morocco when we were running six SAC Combat Support Groups and nine radar posts. Doesn't anybody back there in Washington know what happened to the French?" That was my introduction. Within two months, by August, we had the incident in the Gulf of Tonkin, followed by the Tonkin Gulf resolution. That sort of bothered me; my interpretation was that U.S. warships at sea had been attacked and fired upon, and it seemed unnecessary for me, within my understanding of the laws of war, for the Congress to pass a resolution authorizing reprisals. And so it went. By February of 1965 we had BOQs being blown up and people being killed, and we were answering those with air attacks against others, there being some presumed connection between the terrorists in South Vietnam and the North Vietnamese. And by late 1965, *Time* magazine was writing an unsigned essay about the right war, at the right place, at the right time, and I was starting to retreat into dire thoughts about Nicias and Lamachus and Alcibiades and the expedition to Syracuse.

In his paper this afternoon, Mr. Braestrup begins with the timely reminder that the war in Korea was just as unpopular in its day as Vietnam ever became; that "No more Koreas!" presaged "No more Vietnams!" by a decade and a half. The worry warts among us will gain little solace from remembering that the approved government solution to no more Koreas was a massive buildup of strategic nuclear forces aimed at deterrence via a threat to respond massively at times and places of our own choosing. In a curious way, Mr. Reagan's defense counselors give many the impression that they seek to invoke an update of the 1954-57 solutions(!) in response to America's "Vietnam trauma," so-called conventional forces increases and the RDJTF to the contrary notwithstanding. More, bigger, and better seems unalterably the American way—regardless of the specific military problem we face.

I get the impression now that Mr. Braestrup has moderated his view on the so-called media impact on the home front during Vietnam—or perhaps I misread, or earlier read something into, his superb *Big Story*. With his major points I have no argument: that election year politics and LBJ's own behavior, together with adequate but ignored warnings, made Tet a big surprise for the average American; that the real disasters occurred in Washington rather than in Vietnam; that ambiguous and often contradictory policies had more to do with failure than did the sensationalism of television journalism. With all this I have no quarrel worth mentioning, but I do think we should always remember that Vietnam belongs in that category of situations where there is plenty of blame to go around.

What continues to bother me, though, is the implication that we might have been able to solve the Vietnam problem if we had just done x or y. My own view falls in more closely with that of George Herring. And I'm borrowing this idea from him. "The problem with such explanations," he has written, "is that they are too ethnocentric. They reflect the persistence of . . . the illusion of American omnipotence, the traditional American belief that the difficult we do tomorrow, the impossible may take a while. When failure occurs, [we seem to think] it must be our fault, and we find scapegoats in our own midst: the poor judgment of our leaders, the media, or the anti-war movement. The flaw in this approach is that it ignores the other side of the equation, in this case, the Vietnamese dimension." Herring says that "I would contend that the sources of our frustration and ultimate failure rest primarily, although certainly not exclusively, in the local circumstances of the war: the nature of the conflict itself, the weakness of our ally, the relative strength of our adversary."[1] I want to offer two more ideas, also borrowed.

The next idea I want to borrow from Ernest May. "The general proposition that the Vietnam experience most readily supports is that protracted and inconclusive ground warfare will not for a long period of time command public support [in the United States]. That seems to be a proposition for which one can find many other supporting examples." As Peter [Braestrup] has pointed out as well, ". . . the American experience in Korea supported it, as did the Boer War and, elsewhere, the French experience in Indochina and in Algeria. One can find very few examples that refute that proposition. Where the exceptions exist, they seem to involve objectives that are clearly defensive, and where a fairly high level of idealism is involved, as in the American Revolution or the Irish Rebellion." May went on to argue that "it would be better if the operational inference drawn from Vietnam were somewhat broader. In analyzing a case that might seem to call for the application of military force, an effort could be made explicitly to see the domestic component as one among the set of interests involved. The problem should be cast in those terms, if we have learned anything, and not in terms that characterize these domestic concerns as merely a *limitation* on action that is dictated by external interests."[2]

And the last idea I want to borrow, which I can safely do, given our chairman and his views on life, is from a recently retired Marine Corps lieutenant colonel named David S. Rilling, who speaks very bluntly and in a way comes around full circle to our title for this session. "The Vietnam *War*," says Colonel Rilling, "was lost in the homes of America because it was an undeclared, unconstitutional war called by another name. It is important for this legal status to be firmly established in order to deal with the second fundamental lesson which is yet unlearned. Before American armed forces are ever committed to battle in the future, it must be only after the President has gone to the Congress by some means of communication and that body has exercised its declaratory powers prescribed in the Constitution. Then and only then can the battlefield be censored; treason be called treason and prosecuted as such; and the civilian population brought into the picture as an instrument of policy. The civilian population has a tremendous role to play in the battlefield successes of our armed forces. Whereas this was well understood during World War II, this fact is apparently no longer recognized."[3] Which brings us almost full circle to where we were last night when we *almost* heard how Hollywood went to war.

DISCUSSION AND COMMENTS

Allan R. Millett (Moderator)

Millett: We'll now entertain questions from the audience until about 4 o'clock. I hope that those of you who have real questions to ask will ask real questions rather than make ad hoc speeches, which is the temptation at gatherings like this. And also please identify yourself so that the record of the conference will identify you. You will eventually appear in the text of the proceedings. First of all, while we are getting into position, perhaps our panel would like to comment upon Colonel MacIsaac's comments.

Braestrup: I just would like to say that I think he's forgotten there was a geographical component in America's involvement in Vietnam and part of that was encouraged by the Johnson Administration. There are a lot of self-delusions among the anti-war people, which a number of them have come to recognize, as well as among the Administration people. You may recall that in late 1965, Secretary of State Dean Rusk was saying that North Vietnam was a surrogate for Red China. There were a lot of basic difficulties aside from the policy of intervention, which I think was a noble cause but a bad mistake. We are not quite sure why Lyndon Johnson wanted to intervene in Vietnam in the first place. There was a lack of conviction and a lack of certainty in the Johnson Administration about why we had to go there which was not present among Truman's advisors about Korea. The environment was vastly different and so on and so forth, but there is a good deal of work that still has to be done on the underlying real motivations on the part of Lyndon Johnson for going into Vietnam in the first place. I think the second important thing, or at least I would so argue, was that there was a possibility of a military victory. I mentioned this once to a senior army general. I told him that I thought if we had adopted his plan in 1967 and had cut the Ho Chi Minh Trail and isolated the battlefield, that the war could have been won in a kind of satisfactory way. But then I went on to inquire of the general how long he thought the American people and politicians would have kept 50,000 American troops in Vietnam along a new DMZ against a regime in Hanoi which seemed to have no other goal in life, regardless of cost, than to unify the country under its own colors? You could send in the B-52s once and maybe cool them down, and two years later they'd come again. Do you send in the B-52s again? They care more than we do, I suggested. They would care more than we would. And we would start blaming the South Vietnamese after about the third incursion. I think a military victory, by us, largely by us, was impossible. I think the South Vietnamese, if left in peace, would have developed a fairly reasonable regime by third world standards, certainly by comparison to the North. But they cared more up there than anybody else. They were better organized. And I think that if we'd "won" the war in 1967, somebody would still be fighting there right now. That was my argument.

Millet: May we have questions?

Lt Colonel Joe Guilmartin (Editor of the *Air University Review*): I think we see very clearly, in all our panelists, a keen awareness of the dangers of appearing wise after the fact when dealing with a subject that is so emotionally charged and so near to the present as Vietnam. I believe that what I'm doing is agreeing largely with Dr. MacIsaac's commentary in suggesting that, in fact, large forces were at work and that some of this wisdom, at least, was not after the fact. I'd like to direct your attention, those of you who are turned on by such things, and at the risk of appearing to be self-serving, to a little article which appeared in the *Air University Review* in the spring of 1954. It's a piece by the *Air University Review* staff entitled "The War in Indo-China in light of The Lessons of Korea." It makes rather frightening reading. In essence it said that unless we were prepared to interdict supply lines in southern China, we'd better think very long and very hard about involvement in Vietnam.

Robert Kinsey (Golden High School, Golden, Colorado): I was wondering if we might impose on Arthur Marwick to reflect on the Falkland Islands' situation, and the effect on the hearts and minds of people in Great Britain of an apparently different kind of limited war that was quicker and more successful.

Millett: Arthur shook his head, and my loafers, which were made in Argentina, just squeezed the hell out of my feet. So, we'll pass on that one.

Braestrup: I'll talk about it. The argument has been made, and I have in my hand, as Senator Joe used to say, I have here in my hand Ben Wattenberg's analysis again assigning an enormous role to television's impact. One of the nice things he says about the war in the Falklands was that they censored everything, and that Margaret Thatcher didn't have to worry about that, and so on and so forth. But it seems to me there was plenty of opposition in Britain with or without censorship. The left wing of the Labor party thought this was a terrible thing to do and sufficient word of losses got out so at least I could figure out that some "Brits" were being killed. I think the big thing that helped Margaret Thatcher was that she knew what she wanted and she was going to do it and she made that clear to her countrymen. There were no games. She was straight and she had a good army and they only had some islands to get to. Once they got there, which took a while, they were OK.

There are two other points which I want to make. One is that during the Vietnam war relatively little real battlefield coverage got onto film. The Tet period was special because the war came into the cities and, like the Beirut episode this last summer, it made wonderful film to show all those buildings burning and the refugees weeping and so on. It was excellent melodrama and the TV news organizations loved it. It was almost as good as the Iranian hostage crisis. So at Tet there was this kind of peculiar exercise going on where the actions suited TV. In contrast, most of the normal TV news footage simply consisted of anonymous GIs wandering around in the fields, and the helicopters flying in, and occasionally a wounded guy being carried off. This was accompanied by a very dramatic voiceover by the TV correspondent who made it seem as if you were seeing combat. But very few people died on television in the war. It's too gory. They didn't want to show that stuff at supper time.

The second point is that you ought to realize that the audiences for TV news are very small. The persistent audience is a big audience, but it's very fickle. Only 1 percent of all TV news households watch Dan Rather as often as four nights a week. It's a vast flickering audience that kind of turns on the TV news because it's turning on TV. So this notion of night after night after night the American public was getting bombarded with these horrible images of the war and thereby we couldn't hack it, is false, apparently.

Robin Higham (Kansas State University): I think we've gotten onto an interesting point here, one that Dave MacIsaac started with, and I would like to suggest that we might explore it a little further. I wonder whether, when you are looking at the question of TV coverage, there is any distinct difference that might be commented upon between the United States and, say, France. Certainly with the BBC in wartime, in World War II, it was very easy to provide censorship. The other half of the question is: What if you turn it around the other way? How much of the press in this country would particularly object to having their freedom curtailed if they were told there was going to be censorship and they were going to be restricted or delayed in what they could say in a limited-war situation where we did not have the normal blanket laws that applied in times like World War II?

Braestrup: Again, I think it depends. The press, as Frankie Fitzgerald once pointed out, has the memory of a rabbit. The Israelis have press censorship and employed censorship of various kinds in all of their wars except, really, this last one. They tried it this last time and their efforts were a little clumsy. They ran up against the problem of destruction in Beirut and they couldn't really object on security grounds to that being reported. I think it will be very much dependent on the situation. If we were landing in the Persian Gulf, I think they would clamp on censorship. I would if I were the commander. I would censor everything for the first week or two just on security grounds, because you would be in a non-incremental situation. Two operations in Vietnam were put under censorship. Nothing could be written about them for a week or two. The first was quite successful and was applied when the First Air Cavalry Division went to the A Shau Valley in late April of 1968. There was a blackout on what they were doing for a week or ten days. No one objected; they understood. Similarly, but less successfully, the military command tried to exercise a kind of news blackout when the South Vietnamese army went into Laos in 1971. That was more difficult because Radio Hanoi and others were already talking about it. There was a kind of blurred situation. I think the First Amendment was everything and the most important thing probably through about 1978, but fads change and I think there is a more reasonable attitude today.

Millett: Jack, I wish you'd comment about the practice in Algeria.

Talbott: Very briefly, the growth of French television really came in the 1960s after the war in Algeria was over. Secondly, certainly at that time television was a state monopoly, which meant it was a Gaullist monopoly, which meant it was a marvelous means of conveying the views of the government, ranging all the way from de Gaulle's dramatic appearances, to which I alluded in my paper, to showing American tourists in ridiculous and ludicrous positions when they visited France. The war itself didn't really receive much coverage.

MacIsaac: Excuse me, I cannot speak to this point but I notice that Professor Showalter is up in the back of the room. Would you please share some of your views on this with us?

Dennis E. Showalter (The Colorado College): This is simply a hypothesis, but I suggested when I was down at the Air University that at least part of the American military's almost paranoid "bird toward the snake" attitude towards television reflects a situation that may not be likely to come again. That's simply because ever since Vietnam, television has moved further and further towards the pattern of seeking new stimuli and new sensations. Because of the ability of a military system to complete operations in a relative hurry, the odds are that within two weeks of an event like the Israeli invasion of Beirut, the faithful scribes of the networks would have found something else to attract their attention, some kind of new sensation. I think this process was a bit more difficult in Vietnam, partly because of the ongoing nature of the war, partly because at that point "USA" hadn't quite come to stand for "Universally Stimulated America." As I say, I'm not sure of this. This is simply a hypothesis. But I do have a sense that the media simply tends to shuffle events and to turn events over even much faster now than they did during the Vietnam War. As a parallel, I am impressed, once again, by this almost hypnotized anxiety which the professional military seems to have about television. I mean Walter Cronkite's moustache appears to exercise a great deal of influence even though the man is long in retirement. I know the line you are looking for, Dave, and I think I'll hand it to you, but I also think it appropriate that we all remember that the difference between the television newscasters and a $30 whore is nil. That is to say, these people deliver what they are paid to deliver, no more and no less. And I think it's perhaps inappropriate that, in our concern with the First Amendment, we take the people who deliver the news as damn seriously as we seem to have in the last ten years or so.

Millett: Thank you, Dennis, for being your usual opaque, unopinionated self.

Laura Watson (Washington, D.C.): There were some people on the television news about a week ago who gave a possible explanation of Johnson's policies, or non-policies, in relation to Vietnam by linking them with the circumstances in which he became President after Kennedy's death. They suggested that Johnson was trying to do what he thought Kennedy had wanted to do. He was trying to perpetuate Kennedy's policies and Kennedy's memory, and he was sort of walking on eggs as Truman had done when he came into the presidency under similar sad circumstances.

Braestrup: I don't want to get into this too deeply, but there is an alternative explanation which is that President Johnson was, at that time, surrounded by Kennedy's people. There is one explanation, or one theory, that Lyndon Johnson did what he did in Vietnam out of two fears. One was that if he didn't try to hold Vietnam as his predecessors had done, he would be accused of "losing Vietnam" just as Truman was accused of "losing China." The second fear was that if he did not persevere in Vietnam, if he had, say, decided to cut his losses after he beat Goldwater in 1964, he would have been accused by the Kennedy people of having betrayed the Kennedy mandate, the Kennedy legacy. But it's still a mystery, at least as far as I can tell. No one has really pinned it all down.

James Watson (State Historical Society of Wisconsin): Somebody compared the British experience in the Falklands to the American experience in Vietnam. I really wonder whether the comparison shouldn't be made with the British experience in Borneo where they fought a long counter-insurgency war in about the same time frame. Perhaps somebody in the panel would like to comment on that point.

Millett: I think you mean Malaya, not Borneo. I see—you mean western Borneo in the l960s. I think that the appropriate response is that media coverage, whether in Malaya, Borneo or someplace else, is a reflection of the policies and the conduct of the operations themselves. Whether operations are reported badly or not, they still shouldn't be used to change the policy. I think Mr. Braestrup's point is well taken, which is that media is exactly that, and while one could quibble about the degree of control or censorship, or the quality or quantity of the news, that at least every American military experience in the twentieth century has been shaped by what's really happened. Any regime that believes that by press coverage they can turn bad policy into good policy is asking for difficulty. In the case of Malaya, in handling that long and drawn out affair, the British made some crucial political concessions very early in the business. Basically, they said that Malaya would become Malaysia, an independent nation under local rulers, but only at such time as the insurgency was cleaned up. They asked for Malayan support, particularly Moslem support, to help clean up the insurgency. In short, there were real political goals that isolated the communist movement and allowed the kind of constabulary operations that such a challenge required.

Watson: The confrontation in Borneo was the case I had in mind, and I think it was somewhat different than the situation in Malaya. There was, though, a certain continuity in the military operations between the two, a continuity which involved the troops that were used in the two situations and their experience versus the confrontation forces. That was the question I was raising. In Borneo the British primarily used mercenary units, Gurkhas. I think that's one of the reasons why the war there got so little publicity.

Braestrup: I was in Borneo after the worst of that exercise was over and my impression was that the total casualty toll did not match that of the U.S. highways during the Fourth of July weekend. There was very little fighting between the Indonesians and the Gurkhas. The Gurkhas were there but did not have to do much shooting. It was a much simpler problem for the Malaysian government with its British support than was the problem for the British in Malaya or, needless to say, for the Americans in Vietnam. And the reason it got little attention was that very few people got killed.

Millett: I hope you will join me in thanking our panelists for a very stimulating session.

SUMMARY

EDWARD M. COFFMAN

"BEYOND THE BATTLEFIELD"

Introduction of Professor Edward M. Coffman by Colonel Carl W. Reddel

Professor and Head, Department of History

United States Air Force Academy

I have a very specific and pleasurable task at hand, one that I'm very happy to execute. Someone asked me earlier today why no members of our department are on the program. Well, a visiting member of our department, Professor "Mac" Coffman is indeed on the program. Well known to many of you, Professor "Mac" is the Distinguished Visiting Professor in History at the Air Force Academy this year. He has earned campaign ribbons for nine of our ten military history symposia, a special point of pride for us. I also must inform you that Wisconsonians are not always what they appear to be. Professor "Mac" is, in fact, a Kentuckian. He took all of his academic degrees from the University of Kentucky. However, between his undergraduate and graduate work, recognizing the unreality of academic life, he spent two years in the Army as an infantry officer. And then, having had enough of reality, he began his teaching career at Memphis State University. He has been on the faculty at the University of Wisconsin, Madison, since 1961. He has also served as the Eisenhower Professor at Kansas State and as a distinguished visiting professor at West Point. His two books, *The Hilt of the Sword: The Career of Peyton C. March,* and *The War To End All Wars: The American Military Experience in World War I,* are clearly volumes of great distinction. He is currently writing a social history of the peacetime American army from 1784 to 1940. This afternoon Professor "Mac" has agreed to give his thoughts on the symposium in this summary session.

"BEYOND THE BATTLEFIELD"

Edward M. Coffman

The close relationship between the home front, society as it were, and war is apparently so obvious that one might well ask why make a point of it. The reason is that, too often in the past, historians have either ignored it or created artificial divisions which inhibit recognition of that basic connection. The long lives of the stereotypes which emphasize the differences between the military and the society from which it springs are testaments to this situation. In this country, scholarly specialization shares the blame together with the mutual suspicion with which military historians and those who worked in the fields of social, economic, political, indeed any other area of history, viewed each other. In a session of the second symposium here in 1968, the late Louis Morton addressed this condition. Since those in his audience were mostly military historians, he appealed to them to broaden their interests. "What military historians should be doing more of is seeking the relationship between military institutions and activities and the broadest streams of history in an effort to enlarge our understanding of both."[1] The current symposium and at least three others demonstrate that this appeal was heeded.[2]

As a reader, I have often shuddered at the stark break represented by the word Summary in large block letters at the end of a chapter; yet, when I was a student, I must admit that I welcomed it, particularly if I were pressed for time on the eve of an examination. I suspect that all of you who have listened to these papers have as good an idea of what their essential points were as I do. Once published, they will be even more obvious as well as available. Nevertheless, I happen to be the only one with the task of putting them on paper. So, in the interest of struggling students in the future who may turn to the volume of these proceedings, I shall try to do justice to this assignment.

Before I discuss the papers in the first session on "The Quest for National Unity in the Great War," as one who has studied that era, I wish to express my appreciation for the use of the term "the Great War" because it gives that war its proper due.

In his paper on mobilization in Britain and Germany, Dennis Showalter developed the thesis, in part with the help of the psychological theory of cognitive dissonance, that both nations were ambivalent toward going to war in 1914. This is in contrast to the view that the Germans were enthusiastic while the British were reluctant. The fact that the constitutional state had depersonalized international relations and hence, caused leaders to feel as if they were pawns of a greater power, contributed to the complexity of the problem. Even when war seemed inevitable, these feelings of impotence and ambivalence restrained preparations for the conflict on both sides.

Sandwiched between scholars who talked about countries which paid a terrible price in their participation in the Great War, David M. Kennedy properly acknowledged that the United States did not suffer as much as the other belligerents. This disparity affected the way this nation conducted its war effort. He could have added that it also resulted logically in a different appreciation throughout the past sixty years of the importance of this war by Americans and Europeans. Just as Showalter maintained about Germany and Britain on the eve of war, Kennedy argues that Americans, following the example set by their President, were also ambivalent. This attitude continued even after they entered the war. Although he wanted to win the war, Woodrow Wilson kept the Allies at a distance while at home he tried to restrain the expansion of the power of the central government. In both cases, he hampered a more efficient war effort. Kennedy explains this approach by emphasizing the continuance of pre-war mores developed over the centuries into the few months of war. Without calling on Clausewitz, he corroborates that thinker's thesis that the way nations fight war depends on their "social conditions" as well as other factors.[3]

Gunther Rothenberg wound up this session with a description of Austria-Hungary's wartime experience. The divisions with which this nation was riven were far more crucial to its existence as a state than those differences in attitude toward going to war or carrying on the conflict which the previous authors discussed. Despite the fear that Austria-Hungary could not withstand the pressure of a large-scale war, the diverse peoples responded surprisingly well for the first half of the war. The situation began to change in 1916 after the death of the aged symbol of unity, Emperor Francis Joseph. Eventually, the increasing realization that the war was not going well led to the collapse that pessimists had predicted earlier.

The second and third sessions shifted the focus from nations at war in World War I to the economic and social elements of the home front effort in World War II. In the former, "The Sinews of War: Economic Mobilization in World War II," Wilhelm Deist and Paul Koistinen developed two common themes: that neither Nazi Germany nor the United States were efficient in the mobilization of their economies and that this was the result of conflicting interests and goals of groups within each nation. Diest, who concentrated on the pre-war period, cited in particular Germany's failure to apply the lessons of World War I, the lack of popular enthusiasm for going to war, and the inter-service rivalry which caused the Air Force and Navy to struggle against the coordinating agency for economic mobilization. Koistinen's version of American wartime economic mobilization is more complex. First, he demonstrated that, by comparison with the other warring powers, this nation's economic effort was relatively unimpressive. He then explained this poor showing by building the case that the military leaders ignored not only the World War I experience but also their own pre-war planning when they accepted a partnership with the leaders of some forty major corporations. Since these businessmen had basically a different goal, namely short-term profits rather than winning the war as quickly and efficiently as possible, this hindered the economic contribution to the military goal and put the soldiers in the absurd position of opposition to those civilians who advocated that military goal. Koistinen lays the ultimate blame for this predicament on the President. Rather than it being simply another example of FDR's muddled management, he believes that Roosevelt consciously refused to create a powerful economic agency which would force businessmen to subordinate their interests to the national goal because he wanted to sustain the power elite. To a degree, Koistinen's thesis of the President's responsibility for the situation is similar to that of Kennedy's in regard to Wilson's setting the tone of the American role in the previous war. There is a striking difference, however, in that Koistinen, unlike Kennedy, does not acknowledge the restraints of the social, economic, and political character of the American historical experience.

In the third session, "Social Effects of Total War," Arthur Marwick dealt with the broadest topic of any of the papers in this symposium as he analyzed the effect of the twentieth century's total wars on Britain and other European countries. Fully cognizant that war was only one of many variables influencing social change, Marwick tried to discern its particular role by erecting a model to measure its significance. His conclusion, which was based essentially on the British experience, was that those wars loosened class bonds and led to a better life and a larger participation in government for the working class and women. In his analysis of the closely intertwined relationship of war and society, he also made the crucial point that war is an episode in the continuing evolution of society, but that the nature of such a great challenge and shock speeded up change.

The other two panelists in this session addressed the impact of war on the condition of particular minorities during World War II. Harvard Sitkoff presented a revision of the theory that World War II was the turning point in black consciousness and activism in the United States and led to the civil rights movement of the Fifties and Sixties. During the war, he shows that blacks were generally willing to accept their segregated position and to subordinate their hopes for an improvement of their status to the national war aims. There was, he believes, more protest rhetoric and action in the Thirties than in the war period. He qualified his revisionism, however, with the acknowledgement that the profound changes in society caused by World War II created preconditions which eventually made the civil rights movement not only possible but successful.

Leila Rupp made it very clear that she does not think war is good for people. Not many would argue with that even within the cloisters of a military school. That position established, she embarked on a broad-scale comparison of the effect of World War II on women in Germany, Britain, Japan, Russia, and the United States. In addition to national and racial differences, she recognized that class, age, and type of employment qualified consideration of the feminine experience. Generally, she does not think that women's contributions during this war changed male attitudes enough to foster a revolution in traditional roles although she does admit that, at least in Germany and Japan, women made real gains. In wartime, stereotypes limited the efficient use of women in the United States and much more drastically in Germany and Japan. She also noted that the endeavor of the Germans and Japanese to foster the concept of the master race led to the official encouragement of reproduction which, incidentially, was not reflected in the birth rate, and of rape by their soldiers of foreign, hence inferior in their view, women. Whatever the gain, and she does not think there was much, it certainly was not worth the terrible cost of a war. Of course, nations, as she realizes, do not fight wars with the goal of improving the status of women. Nevertheless, any sensitive student of war can not help but sympathize with those women whom she mentions who deplore the horrors of war.

In contrast with the other sessions which focused on the home front's support of the war effort and the effect of war on society, the last session, "Limited War and the Problem of Hearts and Minds on the Home Front," dealt with the decisive influence on a war by the home front. The similarities between the Algerian and Vietnam Wars are marked. As a historian, I wonder if American planners and policy makers of the Sixties paid any attention to the French experience of less than a decade earlier. Apparently they were too entranced by the abstract beauty of models to notice the grimy realities of recent history. In both wars, the Western power misjudged its adversary and failed to observe the Clausewitzian principle of establishing a clear-cut policy with a matching strategy. Yet they still won military victories. As the basic thrust of this symposium has demonstrated, however, there is more to war than military operations. In Algeria and Vietnam, France and the United States suffered political defeats which resulted in lost wars despite events on the field of combat.

John Talbott surveyed the tortuous twists and turns of the entire Algerian War and concluded that if the French had carried out the strategy early in the war which actually yielded a military victory in the last years, they could have won the political victory necessary to win the war. Those additional years built up a frustration among the French people so great that when it did come they could not accept the victory in the field. Paradoxically, the charisma of de Gaulle enabled many to consider the loss of the war in Algeria a great victory.

In his paper, Peter Braestrup concentrated on the American reaction to the Tet Offensive. He disputed the accepted version that there was a drastic change in public support of the war in the aftermath and believed that the President and his advisors over-reacted in their misperception of the mood of the country. In the end, he blames Lyndon Johnson for the crisis. Johnson's failure to set policy with an appropriate strategy and his lack of candor in explaining the war led to confusion and frustration among the people. He thus agreed with Kennedy and Koistinen in their beliefs that in our major wars of this century the Presidents have wielded their influence to the detriment of the war effort. Braestrup also condemned the media for their failure to give accurate reports and analyses of the fighting. In part this was the result of the reporters and cameramen on the scene being caught up in their particular situation. As Wilmott Ragsdale, who covered D-Day for *Time* and *Life* told me; the eye deceives. In the small part of a battle that any one person can possibly see, horror and chaos dominate, hence it is often easier for an individual removed from the scene, but with access to reports from the entire front, to understand whether the operation is succeeding or failing. At the time of Tet, with television making those immediate scenes of horror and chaos available within hours to an entire nation, all of us who watched the nightly news shows were misled. Braestrup made an even more damaging charge against the media by accusing its practitioners of sticking with the disaster story after it should have been obvious that it was a moral and military defeat for the communists.

I would be remiss if I did not mention David Culbert's stimulating and entertaining banquet presentation: "Hollywood Goes To War." The most striking impression I had of those film clips and analysis is the difference in perceptions of the generations. The meaning and influence of these films on the World War II generation (even a child such as I) understandably differs from their impact on virtually everyone under forty. Attempts to deal with serious matters in the 1940s thus appear to these younger people at best quaint and at worst ludicrous.

When I attempted to discern common themes other than the overall topic of war on the home front in these papers on such diverse subjects, I turned to men who had given much thought to war and to a great novelist whose concern was life itself. The key to understanding war, which after all is a part of life, according to Marshal Maurice de Saxe, the famed French general of the eighteenth century, is: "The human heart [which] is the starting point in all matters pertaining to war." As one would assume, Carl von Clausewitz, who wrote several decades later, agreed: "The art of war deals with living and with moral forces." Appropriately for this symposium which has so amply illustrated the intimate connection of war and society, a civilian, E. M. Forster, as paraphrased and explained by Elting E. Morison, corroborated those two soldiers: "the only true history is the history of human affections." "These incommensurables—a tangle of memories, prejudices, emotional needs, aspirations, common decencies—exert a tremendous and probably always a determining influence upon the real, as opposed to the exposed, nature of a situation."[4] These principles helped me to find what I sought.

In the first session, Showalter explained how the emotional needs and aspirations expressed in nationalism and militarism conflicted with the hopes for peace— —a conflict which caused ambivalence in Germany and Britain as they approached war in 1914. When he searched for a reason for the way the United States fought World War I, Kennedy arrived at the conclusion that the combination of attitudes held by Americans for more than a century and a half was the dominant influence. Rothenberg's analysis of Austria-Hungary's role in the war took into consideration more deep-rooted patterns of attitudes in that multi-national country. Yet, the nation was able to rise above these differences at least for a while. In their papers on economic mobilization, Diest and Koistinen demonstrated that important groups did not rise above what they thought were their particular interests even in the face of extreme crisis.

When Marwick, Sitkoff, and Rupp pondered various aspects of the effect of war on society, they had to address the gamut of Forster's human affections either directly or indirectly. In his general approach, Marwick laid the foundation of any study of war and society by pointing out that society with its inherent attitudes is a continuum in which war is only a temporary episode. The other two authors addressed the experiences of particular groups within societies at war. Both developed Marwick's point with their recognition of the difficulty of eliminating long held prejudices even in times of great pressure on the nation as a whole. In contrast with Diest's and Koistinen's indictments of groups which would not shelve their selfish interests at such times, Sitkoff and Rupp depicted blacks and women as doing just that during World War II.

In the last session, Talbott and Braestrup addressed societies which were not involved in a large-scale war but rather were torn by the problems of limited war. Without the basic threat of total war, society can continue to go on much as in peacetime (Marwick's continuum is thus particularly evident); yet this, in turn, places the horrors of war in more drastic contrast. Against that background, these authors dealt with the expectations and fears of the French and the Americans, and with the efforts of de Gaulle and LBJ to manipulate those perceptions and emotions with different results. In the end, as they show, these intangibles became a force greater than that wielded by the military and determined the outcome of the war.

At several of these symposia in the past, Lou Morton, to whom I referred earlier, performed the role that I am attempting to play today. I believe that he would be pleased with the broad approach toward military history that this symposium has taken. It is not really accurate, however, to refer to this broad approach as "new" military history. Seventy years ago, at the American Historical Association meeting in Boston, academics, army officers, a pacifist editor, and a former President gathered to discuss the state of military history. The consensus was that it was very low indeed and all, even the pacifist, Oswald Garrison Villard, agreed that they should try to bolster the field. Only one of the speakers at that meeting, however, ventured to suggest that military history was anything other than a study of operations. Theodore Roosevelt argued that military historians should blend their studies with other aspects of national history.[5] In his later appeal, Morton was thus following the logic of that argument. During the past decade many historians have responded and broadened the area of military history to provide not only a more balanced image of the military but also new perspectives in the civilian area. They have done much, but they certainly have not exhausted the possibilities.

NOTES

John M. Blum

John M. Blum, V Was For Victory *(New York, 1976), p 3. This essay is based so heavily on that book, and on the works cited in it and so important to its content, that annotation here seems to me redundant. I do want to restate my special debt, for this essay, to two studies cited in the book: Jerome S. Bruner, Mandate from the People* (New York, 1944) and Richard Polenberg, *War and Society, The United States 1941-1945* (Philadelphia, 1972). This essay also draws upon other literature either not relevant or not available in 1976. Each of the works hereafter cited is easily identifiable in the context of the parts of this essay to which it applies: Gordon W. Allport, *The Nature of Prejudice* (Anchor Books edition, Garden City, 1958); Nelson Lichtenstein, *Labor's War at Home: The CIO in World War II* (Cambridge, 1982); Walter Lippman, *Public Opinion* (New York, 1922); Herbert G. Nicholas, ed., *Washington Despatches, 1941-1945: Weekly Political Reports from the British Embassy* (Chicago, 1981); Bradley Smith, *The Road to Nuremberg* (New York, 1981); Alan M. Winkler, *The Politics of Propaganda* (New Haven, 1978).

Dennis E. Showalter

1. The best recent analysis is Paul Kennedy, *The Rise of the Anglo-German Antagonism*, 1860-1914 (London, 1980).
2. A. Von Tirpitz, *My Memoirs* (New York, 1919), I:361 ff.
3. Leon Festinger, *A Theory of Cognitive Dissonance* (Stanford, 1957), is a useful introduction to the concept.
4. Arno Mayer, *The Persistence of the Old Regime: Europe and the Great War* (New York, 1981). For the process of accommodation and absorption in Britain cf. Walter Arnstein, "The Survival of the Victorian Aristocracy," in *The Rich, the Well Born, and the Powerful,* ed. F. C. Jaher (New York, 1973): 203-257, and "The Myth of the Triumphant Victorian Middle Class," *The Historian,* 38 (1975): 205-221. For Germany, cf. Lamar Cecil, "The Creation of Nobles in Prussia," *American Historical Review,* 50 (1970): 757-795, and Otto Graf zu Stolberg-Wernigerode, *Die Unentschiedene Generation: Deutschlands konservative Führungsschichten am Vorabend des Ersten Weltkrieges* (Munich, 1968).
5. The best brief surveys of the process of militarization in Germany are Manfred Messerschmidt, "Die Armee in Staat und Gesellschaft," in *Das Kaiserliche Deutschland,* ed. Michael Stürmer (Dusseldorf, 1970), pp. 89-118; and Wilhelm Deist, "Die Armee in Staat und Gesellschaft, 1890-1914," *ibid.,* 312-329. For the growing public interest in the British army, see Edward M. Spires, *The Army and Society, 1815-1914* (London, 1980), pp. 206 ff.; A. R. Skelley, *The Victorian Army at Home* (Montreal, 1977), pp. 243 ff. and W. S. Hamer, *The British Army: Civil-Military Relations, 1885-1905* (Oxford, 1970), pp. 214 ff.
6. H. R. Moon, "The Invasion of the United Kingdom: Public Controversy and Official Planning, 1888-1918," 2 vols (Ph.D. diss., London, 1968), is comprehensive for its period. I. F. Clarke, *Voices Prophesying War, 1763-1864* (London, 1966), pp. 30 *passim;* and Hugh Cunningham, *The Volunteer Force: A Social and Political History 1859-1908* (Hamden, Conn., 1975), pp. 5 ff; are good for the emotional environment of the invasion scares.

7. Jonathan Steinberg, "The Copenhagen Complex," *Journal of Contemporary History* 1 (1966): 12-46, is an excellent case study of the relationships among fears and realities. Golo Mann, *The History of Germany Since 1789*, tr. Marian Jackson (New York, 1968), pp. 200 *passim*, is among the best general works stressing the Second Empire's *angst*.

8. Ulrich Marwedel, *Carl von Clausewitz: Persönlichkeit und Wirkungsgeschichte seines Werkes bis 1918* (Boppard, 1978), is a good discussion of the degeneration of Clausewitz's work into a source of quotations supporting preconceptions.

9. Jay Luvaas, *The Military Legacy of the Civil War: The European Inheritance* (Chicago, 1959).

10. On the general climate of opinion prior to 1914 cf. particularly Roland N. Stromberg, *Redemption by War: The Intellectuals and 1914* (Lawrence, Kans., 1982); Robert Wohl's superb *The Generation of 1914* (Cambridge, Mass., 1979); and Peter Loewenberg, "Arno Mayer's Internal Causes and Purposes of War in Europe, 1870-1956: An Inadequate Model of Human Behavior, National Conflict, and Historical Change," *Journal of Modern History*, 42 (1970): 628-636. John Gooch, "Attitudes to War in Late Victorian and Edwardian England," in *War and Society*, ed. B. Bond and I. Roy (London, 1975), pp. 88-102, is a useful summary. Alfred Kelly, *The Descent of Darwin: The Popularization of Darwinism in Germany, 1860-1914* (Chapel Hill, N.C., 1981), shows the movement of the idea from an elite to the masses. W. Warren Wagar, *Good Tidings: The Belief in Progress from Darwin to Marcuse* (Bloomington, Ind., 1972), pp. 105 ff., surveys the relationships between theories of progress and theories of violence during the period.

11. The best studies of this relationship are the older ones—not least because of historians' growing dislike for accepting juxtapositions in lieu of connections. Cf. in particular E. M. Carroll, *Germany and the Great Powers, 1866-1914: A Study in Public Opinion and Foreign Policy* (New York, 1940); and Oron J. Hale, *Publicity and Diplomacy with Special Reference to England and Germany, 1890-1914* (New York, 1940). J. F. Scott, *Five Weeks: The Surge of Public Opinion on the Eve of the Great War* (New York, 1927) focuses on the July crisis.

12. Geoffrey F. Best, "Militarism and the Victorian Public School," in *The Victorian Public School*, ed. B. Simon and I. Bradley (Dublin, 1975), pp. 129-146.

13. The essays in *Nationalist and Racialist Movements in Britain and Germany before 1914*, ed. P. Kennedy and A. Nicholls (London, 1981), provide a good comparative overview of these organizations.

14. A pertinent illustration of this problem and its ramifications is Harry F. Young's biography of the German ambassador to Great Britain from 1912 to 1914, *Prince Lichnowsky and the Great War* (Athens, Ga., 1977).

15. A point stressed in Lothar Gall's superb *Bismarck, der weisse Revolutionär* (Frankfurt, 1980). Manfred Messerschmidt, *Militär und Politik in der Bismarckzeit und im Wilhelmischen Deutschland* (Darmstadt, 1975), incorporates a comprehensive survey of the literature on the militaristic aspects of Bismarck's foreign policy. Cf. also Andreas Hillgruber, *Bismarcks Aussenpolitik* (Freiburg, 1972).

16. Kraft Karl zu Hohenloe-Ingelfingen, *Aufzeichnungen aus meinem Leben* (Berlin, 1906), III: 392.

17. Sir John Caldwell, ed., *Field Marshall Sir Henry Wilson: His Life and Diaries* (New York, 1927), I: 105.

18. Nicholas d'Ombrain, *War Machinery and High Policy.: Defense Administrations in Peacetime Britain 1902-1914* (London, 1973); and John Gooch, *The Plans of War: The General Staff and British Military Strategy c. 1900-1916* (London, 1974), can be combined for an excellent description of the process at work in Great Britain. Cf. also L. C. F. Turner, "The Role of the General Staffs in 1914," *Australian Journal of Politics and History*, 11 (1965): 305-323.

19. Robert Conquest, *Present Danger: Towards a Foreign Policy* (Stanford, 1979), pp. 134-136, is refreshingly caustic on the spate of clever books making Harry Truman or Stanley Baldwin the true villains of the twentieth century.

20. Lysbeth Muncy, *The Junker in the Prussian Administration under William II, 1888-1914* (Providence, R.I., 1944), remains useful. Cf. also Karl Demeter, *The German Officer-Corps in Society and State, 1650-1945*, tr. A. Malcom (New York, 1965), pp. 25 ff.; John R. Gillis, *The Prussian Bureaucracy in Crisis, 1840-1860* (Stanford, 1971), pp. 209, 210; and Daniel J. Hughes, "Occupational Origins of Prussia's Generals, 1871-1914," *Central European History*, 13 (1980): 3-33.

21. Such general studies as Bernard Porter, *Critics of Empire* (New York, 1968), and A. P. Thornton, *The Imperial Idea and its Enemies: A Study in British Power* (New York, 1968), can be

supplemented by case histories like John W. Auld, "The Liberal Pro-Boers," *Journal of British Studies*, 14 (1975): 78-101; Arthur Davey, *The British Pro-Boers, 1877-1902* (Cape Town, 1978); and John V. Crangle, "The Economics of British Anti-Imperialism: Victorian Dissent Against India," *Studies in History and Society*, 6 (1975): 60-76.

22. A good overview is Woodruff D. Smith, *The German Colonial Empire* (Chapel Hill, N.C., 1978). Cf. also R. V. Pierard, "The German Colonial Society, 1822-1914" (Ph.D. diss., State University of Iowa, 1964).

23. The best statement of this thesis is Kurt Riezler's *Die Erforderlichkeit des Unmöglichen* (Berlin, 1913). For its influence in general, and on Bethmann-Hollweg specifically, see Wayne C. Thompson, *In the Eye of the Storm: Kurt Riezler and the Crises of Modern Germany* (Iowa City, 1980), pp. 22 ff.

24. See, for example, Moltke's warning of 13 August 1914 to the war ministries and corps districts against doing anything to risk Germany's stability, in *Militär und Innenpolitik im Weltkrieg 1914-1918*, 2 vols, ed. Wilhelm Deist (Düsseldorf, 1970), I: 193-194. Cf. the general analysis in Jürgen Kocha, *Klassengesellschaft im Kriege. Deutsche Sozialgeschichte 1914-1918* (Göttingen, 1973), passim.

25. As in Fritz Fischer, *War of Illusion: German Policies from 1911 to 1914*, tr. M. Jackson (New York, 1975); and Paul Schroeder, "World War I as Galloping Gertie: A Reply to Joachim Remak," *Journal of Modern History*, 44 (1972): 319-345.

26. Adolf Gasser, "Der deutsche Hegemonialkreig von 1914," in *Deutschland und der Weltpolitik des 19. und 20. Jahrhunderts*, ed. I. Geiss and B. J. Wendt (Düsseldorf, 1973), pp 307-339; and "Deutschlands Entschluss zum Proventivkrieg 1913/1914," in *Discordia Concors. Festgabe für Edgar Bonjour zu seinem siebzigsten Geburtstag am 21. August 1968*, 2 vols., ed. M. Sieber (Basel/Stuttgart, 1968), I: 173-224, are the best systematic presentations of the argument that Germany deliberately planned and initiated World War I.

27. As in Gordon A. Craig, *Germany 1866-1945* (New York, 1978), pp. 318-321; or Peter Rassow, "Schlieffen und Holstein," *Historische Zeitschrift* 173 (1952): 297-313.

28. A. Moritz, *Das Problem des Präventivkrieges in der deutschen Politik während der ersten Marokkokrise* (Bern, 1974). Cf. also Norman Rich, *Friedrich von Holstein*, (Cambridge, 1965), II: 696 ff.

29. Particularly in John G. Rohl, ed., "An der Schwelle zum Weltkrieg: Eine Dokumentation über den 'Kriegsrat' von 8. Dezember 1912," *Militärgeschichtliche Mitteilungen*, 21 (1977): 77-134; and "Die Generalprobe. Zur Geschichte und Bedeutung des 'Kriegsrates' von 8. Dezember 1912," in *Industrielle Gesellschaft und politisches System*, ed. D. Stegmann, B-J Wendt, and P-C Witt (Bonn, 1978), pp. 357-373.

30. Cf. especially Wolfgang J. Mommsen, "Domestic Factors in German Foreign Policy Before 1914," *Central European History*, 6 (1973): 12-14; and Egmont Zechlin, "Die Adriakrise und der 'Kriegsrat' von 8. Dezember 1912," in *Krieg und Kriegsrisiko* (Düsseldorf, 1979), pp. 115-159.

31. A good recent survey of this issue is Lothar Burchardt, *Friedenswirtschaft und Kriegsvorsorge. Deutschlands wirtschaftliche Beststrungen von 1914* (Boppard, 1968). P-C Witt, *Die Finanzpolitik des Deutschen Reiches vom 1903 bis 1913* (Lübeck, 1970), is strong on the problems of financing the various armaments programs. Cf. also Alfred Muller, *Die deutsche Kriegsrohstoffbewirtschaftung 1914-1918 im Dienste des deutchen Monopolkapitals* (Berlin, 1955), p. 14; and Gerald S. Feldman, *Army, Industry and Labor in Germany, 1914-1918* (Princeton, 1966), p. 52.

32. Isabel V. Hull, *The Entourage of Kaiser Wilhelm II, 1888-1918* (Cambridge, 1952), p. 250.

33. The best English-language discussion of this issue, despite the author's Fischerite commitment, is John A. Moses, *The Politics of Illusion: The Fischer Controversy in German Historiography* (New York, 1975).

34. The best balanced treatments of Bethmann's pre-war career are Konrad Jarausch, *The Enigmatic Chancellor: Bethmann-Hollweg and the Hubris of Imperial Germany* (New Haven, 1973), pp. 69-184; and Hans-Günter Zmarzlik, *Bethmann-Hollweg als Reichskanzler 1909-1914* (Dusseldorf, 1957). Eberhard Veitsch, *Bethmann-Hollweg, Staatsmann zwischen Macht und Ethos* (Boppard, 1969), is also useful. Egmont Zechlin, "Deutschland zwischen Kabnettskrieg und Wirtschaftskrieg," *Historische Zeitschrift*, 199 (1964): 347-458, is good on the evolution—or degeneration—of Bethmann's policies after August 4.

35. See particularly J. C. G. Röhl, "The Emperor's New Clothes: A Character Sketch of Kaiser Wilhelm II," in *Kaiser Wilhelm II: New Interpretations*, ed. J. C. G. Rohl and N. Sombart (Cambridge, 1982), pp. 23-61.

36. For an opposing viewpoint stressing the army's unwillingness to modernize, see Bernd F. Schulte, *Die deutsche Armee 1900-1914. Zwischen Beharren und Verändern* (Düsseldorf, 1977). Cf. also T. E. H. Travers, "Technology, Tactics and Morale: Jean de Bloch, the Boer War, and British Military Theory, 1900-1914," *Journal of Modern History*, 51 (1979): 284-286.

37. The most familiar work of this type is probably Jacob Meckel, *Ein Sommernachtstraum* (Berlin, 1888). Cf. also two perceptive articles by Joachim Hoffman, "Die Kriegslehre des Generals von Schlichting," *Militärgeschichtliche Mitteilungen*, 5 (1969), 5-36, and "Der Militärschriftsteller Fritz Hoenig," *ibid.*, 7 (1970): 5-26.

38. Schlieffen's growing pessimism is described in Gerhard Ritter, *Sword and Scepter*, tr. Heinz Norden (Coral Gables, Fla., 1970), II: 199 ff. and *The Schlieffen Plan: Critique of a Myth*, tr. M. A. and E. Wilson (London, 1958), pp. 101 ff., 168 ff.

39. Roger Chickering, *Imperial Germany and a World Without War* (Princeton, 1975).

40. Wolfgang J. Mommsen, "The Topos of Inevitable War in Germany in the Decade before 1914," in *Germany in the Age of Total War*, ed. V. R. Berghahn and M. Kitchen (London, 1981), pp. 23-45.

41. A good introduction to this concept is L. L. Farrar, *The Short-War Illusion: German Policy, Strategy, and Domestic Affairs, August-December, 1914* (Santa Barbara, 1973).

42. The best concise statement of this concept remains Eckart Kehr, "Class Struggle and Armament Policy in Imperial Germany," in *Economic Interest, Militarism, and Foreign Policy: Essays on German History*, ed. G. A. Craig, tr. G. Heinz (Berkeley, 1977). pp. 50-75. Jehuda Wallach, *Das Dogma der Vernichtungsschlacht* (Munich, 1970); and Helmut Otto, "Entstehung und Wesen der Blitzkriegsstrategie des deutschen Imperialismus von dem ersten Weltkrieg," *Zeitschrift fur Militärgeschichte*, 6 (1967): 400-414, are more technically oriented.

43. On this issue Gotthard Breit, *Das Staats-und Gesselschaftsbilder deutscher Generale beider Weltkriege im Spiegel ihre Memoiren* (Boppard, 1973), is useful.

44. Cf. Dennis E. Showalter, "The Retaming of Ballona: Prussia and the Institutionalization of the Napoleonic Legacy, 1815-1871," *Military Affairs*, 44 (1980): 57-63.

45. Volker R. Berghahn, *Germany and the Approach of War in 1914* (New York, 1973), pp. 15 ff., is a recent summary presentation of this interpretation.

46. Karl von Einem, Prussian War Minister from 1903 to 1909, suggests the approach in his *Erinnerungen eines Soldaten, 1853-1933* (Leipzig, 1933), pp. 82 *passim*. Cf. the documentary material in Reichsarchiv, *Kriegsrüstung und Kriegswirtschaft*, (Berlin, 1930), Volume II.

47. This particular approach is developed by John Lewis Gaddis in *Strategies of Containment: A Critical Appraisal of Postwar American National Security Policy* (New York, 1982), p. 273.

48. Ritter's *The Schlieffen Plan* can usefully be supplemented by L. C. F. Turner, "The Significance of the Schlieffen Plan," *Australian Journal of Politics and History*, 13 (1967): 47-66; and Gotthard Jäschke, "'Schlieffenplan' und 'Marneschlacht,'" in *Militärgeschichte, Militärwissenschaft und Konfliktforschung. Eine Festschrift für Werner Halweg*, ed. D. Bradley, U. Marwedel (Osnabruck, 1977), pp. 185-189.

49. Heinz Kraft, *Staatsraison und Kriegführung im Kaiswerlichen Deutschland 1914-1916* (Göttingen, 1980), pp. 19 *passim*.

50. A good critical analysis of Moltke's character is Corelli Barnett, *The Swordbearers* (London, 1963), pp. 15-106. Moltke's own *Erinnerungen. Briefe. Dokumente. 1877-1916* (Stuttgart, 1922), are too extensively edited to be useful.

51. I am indebted to Professor Jack Dukes for permission to cite his forthcoming article, "Militarism and Arms Policy Revisited: The Origins of the Germany Army Law of 1913."

52. Cf. F. R. Bridge, *From Sadowa to Sarajevo. The Foreign Policy of Austria-Hungary, 1877-1914* (London, 1972), pp. 310 ff.; and the briefer comments in Schroeder, "Galloping Gertie," pp. 338-343.

53. Cf. P. H. S. Hatton, "Harcourt and Solf: The Search for an Anglo-German Understanding through Africa, 1912-14," *European Studies Review*, 1 (1971): 123-145; and Richard Langhorne, "Anglo-German Negotiations Concerning the Future of the Portuguese Colonies, 1911-1912," *The Historical Journal*, 16 (1973): 361-387.

54. W. Arthur Lewis, "International Competition in Manufactures," *American Economic Review* 47 (1957): 578-587; D. C. Platt, *Latin America and British Trade, 1806-1914* (London, 1972), pp. 99. ff.; and more generally, Platt, *Finance, Trade and Politics in British Foreign Policy, 1815-1914* (Oxford, 1968), *passim*.

55. On the foreign policy functions of the German navy before 1914 see in particular Holger Herwig, *'Luxury' Fleet: The Imperial German Navy, 1888-1918* (London, 1980), pp. 32 ff; Volken R. Berghahn "Zu den Zielen des deutschen Flottenbaus unter Wilhelm II," *Historische Zeitschrift*, 210 (1970): 34-100; and Jonathan Steinberg, *Yesterday's Deterrent* (London, 1965).

56. Cf. in particular Paul Kennedy, *The Rise and Fall of British Naval Mastery* (London, 1976), pp. 208 ff.; R. F. Mackay, *Fisher of Kilverstone* (Oxford, 1973), pp. 319 ff., 383 ff.; Arthur Marder, *From the Dreadnought to Scapa Flow;* Vol 1, *The Road to War, 1904-1914* (London, 1961), and Richard Langhorne, "The Naval Question in Anglo-German Relations, 1912-1914," *Historical Journal*, 14 (1971): 359-370. R. F. Mackay, "Historical Reinterpretations of the Anglo-German Naval Rivalry, 1897-1914," in *Naval Warfare in the Twentieth Century, Essays in Honour of Arthur Marder*, ed G. Jordan (London, 1977), pp. 32-44, surveys the literature.

57. Jonathan Steinberg, "The Kaiser and the British: The State Visit to Windsor, November 1907," in *Kaiser Wilhelm II: New Interpretations*, pp. 121-141, is a useful case study.

58. On this question, see particularly Zara S. Steiner, *The Foreign Office and Foreign Policy, 1898-1914* (Cambridge, 1969), *passim*.

59. The most familiar version of this argument, repeated with some variations in many general histories of twentieth century England, is George Dangerfield, *The Strange Death of Liberal England* (London, 1935). Elie Halevy, *History of the English People in the Nineteenth Century;* Vol VI, *The Rule of Democracy*, tr. E. I. Watkin, rev. ed. (London, 1932), pp. 441 ff., made a similar case as early as 1932. A recent version is Arthur Marwick, *Britain in the Century of Total War* (Boston, 1968), pp. 24 ff.

60. Cf. M. R. Gordon, "Domestic Conflict and the Origins of the First World War: The British and German Cases," *Journal of Modern History*, 46 (1974): 191-226; and Donald Lammers, "Arno Mayer and the British Decision for War," *Journal of British Studies*, 12 (1973): 137-164.

61. This is the thrust of Zara Steiner, *Britain and the Origins of the First World War* (New York, 1977).

62. David French, *British Economic and Strategic Planning, 1905-1915* (London, 1982), pp. 22 ff., capably summarizes this line of reasoning. Cf. in essays in *War and the State: The Transformation of British Government, 1914-1919*, ed. K. Burk (London, 1982).

63. Cf. H. W. Koch, "The Anglo-German Alliance Negotiations: Missed Opportunity or Myth?" *History*, 54 (1969): 378-392; and George Monger, *The End of Isolation: British Foreign Policy, 1900-1907* (London, 1963), pp. 21 ff.

64. Schroeder, "Galloping Gertie," pp. 324 ff., is the clearest brief statement of this thesis. Cf. also *inter alia* Christopher Andrew, *Theophile Delcassé and the Making of the Entente Cordiale* (New York, 1968); P. J. V. Rolo, *Entente Cordiale: The Origins and Negotiations of the Anglo-French Agreements of 8 April 1904* (London, 1969); F. R. Bridge, *Great Britain and Austria-Hungary, 1906-1914: A Diplomatic History* (London, 1972); Horst Jaeckel, *Die Nordwestgrenze in der Verteidigung Indiens 1900-1908 und der Weg Englands zum russischen-britischen Abkommen von 1907* (Koln, 1968); and F. Kazemzadeh, *Russia and Britain in Persia 1864-1914: A Study in Imperialism* (New Haven, Conn., 1968), pp. 44 / *passim*.

65. Trevor Wilson, "Britain's 'Moral Commitment' to France in August 1914," *History*, 64 (1979): 380-390.

66. On this issue Eugen Weber, *The Nationalist Revival in France, 1905-1914* (Berkeley, 1959), remains useful. Cf. also Gilbert Ziebura, *Die deutsche Frage in der öffentliche Meinung Frankreichs von 1911-1914* (West Berlin, 1955).

67. "Memorandum on the Present State of British Relations with France and Germany," January 1, 1907, in *British Documents on the Origins of the War, 1898-1914*, ed. G. P. Gooch, H. Temperley (London, 1928), III: 397 ff.

68. Cf. J. K. Dunlop, *The Development of the British Army, 1899-1914* (London, 1938); and J. E. Tyler, *The British Army and the Continent, 1904-14* (London, 1938).

69. Good overviews of these developments include E. M. Spiers, *Haldane: An Army Reformer* (Edinburgh, 1980); John Gooch, "Mr. Haldane's Army: Military Organization and Foreign Policy in

England," in *The Prospect of War: Studies in British Defence Policy, 1847-1942* (London, 1981), pp. 92-115; L. J. Satre, "St. John Brodrick and Army Reform, 1901-1903," *Journal of British Studies*, 4 (1976): 117-139; and A. V. Tucker, "The Issue of Army Reform in the Unionist Government," *Historical Journal*, 9 (1966): 96-100. On the conscription question see M. J. Allison, "The National Service Issue, 1899-1914" (Ph.D. diss., London, 1977).

70. W. J. McDermott, "The Revolution in British Military Thinking from the Boer War to the Moroccan Crisis," *The Canadian Journal of History*, 9 (1974): 159-177. N. W. Summerton, "The Development of British Military Planning for a War Against Germany, 1904-14," 2 vols. (Ph.D. diss, London, 1970), is comprehensive.

71. A point made by John Terraine in "Somme Myths (1): Machine Guns, 'The Most Lethal Weapon,'" in *The Smoke and the Fire: Myths and Anti-Myths of War 1861-1945* (London, 1980), p. 142. E. M. Spiers, "The Reform of the Front-Line Forces of the Regular Army in the United Kingdom" (Ph.D. diss., Edinburgh, 1974), contains much useful material on specific measures.

72. S. R. Williamson, *The Politics of Grand Strategy: Britain and France Prepare for War, 1904-1914* (Cambridge, Mass., 1969), is the most detailed analysis. Cf. also Michael Howard's stimulating *The Continental Commitment* (London, 1972), pp. 45 ff.; and Gooch, *Plans of War, p.* 279 ff.

73. Douglas Porch, *The March to the Marne: The French Army, 1872-1914* (Cambridge, 1981), pp. 228-229, is the latest authority to argue that the B.E.F. was given a minor role in French planning because British intervention could not be counted on. At operational levels, however, a widespread French attitude toward the British army is best indicated by General Lanrezac's reply to what he regarded as an unbearably stupid question by Sir John French. The Germans, Lanrezac said, had merely gone to the Meuse River to go fishing. Sir Edward Spears, *Liaison 1914*, 2nd ed. (New York, 1968), pp. 74-75 and *passim*.

74. A modern critical study of Wilson would be welcome. Basil Collier, *Brasshat: A Biography of Field Marshal Sir Henry Wilson* (London, 1961), is dated in approach and interpretations.

75. Williamson, *Politics of Grand Strategy*, 369.

76. The quotation is from Michael Howard, "Reflections on the First World War," in *Studies in War and Peace* (New York, 1971), p. 102.

David M. Kennedy

1. Mark Sullivan, *Our Times: The United States, 1900-1924;* Vol V, *Over Here, 1914-1918* (New York, 1933), p. 2.

2. *Ibid.*, p. 32.

3. *Congressional Record*, Senate, 65th Congress, 1st session, April 6, 1917, p. 1148.

4. Wilson's war message may be found most conveniently in Albert Shaw, ed, *The Messages and Papers of Woodrow Wilson*, 2 vols. (New York, 1924), I: 372-383.

5. *Congressional Record*, Senate, 65th Cong., 1st Sess., April 4, 1917, p. 228.

6. Eliot G. Mears to Bureau of Foreign and Domestic Commerce, March 24, 1919, Bureau of Foreign and Domestic Commerce, File 510-UK, Record Group 151, National Archives, Washington, D. C.

7. Herbert Hoover, testimony before Senate Committee on Agriculture, June 19, 1917, quoted in William Clinton Mullendore, *History of the United States Food Administration, 1917-1919* (Stanford, 1941), pp. 52-53.

8. George Creel, *How We Advertised America* (New York, 1920), p. 24.

9. Mullendore, *History of the United States Food Administration*, p. 221.

10. The several quoted remarks in this paragraph are from Grosvenor B. Clarkson, *Industrial America in the World War: The Strategy Behind the Line, 1917-1918* (Boston, 1923), pp. 177, 94, 99.

11. Ray Stannard Baker and William E. Dodds, eds., *The Public Papers of Woodrow Wilson*, 6 vols. (New York, 1925-1927), V: 39.

12. Newton D. Baker to Woodrow Wilson, May 1, 1917, in Ray Stannard Baker, *Woodrow Wilson: Life and Letters*, 8 vols. (Garden City and New York, 1929-1939), VII: 74n.
13. *Second Report of the Provost Marshall General* (Washington, D.C., 1919), p. 277.

GUNTHER E. ROTHENBERG

1. The best discussion of the Compromise is still Ivan Zolger, *Der Staatsrechtliche Ausgleich zwischen Osterreich und Ungarn* (Leipzig, 1911); cf. the critical views in Julius Miskolczy, *Ungarn in der Habsburger Monarchie* (Vienna-Munich, 1959), *passim*.
2. Gunther E. Rothenberg, "Toward a National Hungarian Army: The Military Compromise of 1868 and Its Consequences," *Slavic Review*, 31 (1972), pp. 807-811.
3. Gunther E. Rothenberg, *The Army of Francis Joseph* (W. Lafayette, Ind., 1976), pp. 119-120, 130-131, 144, 146-147, 148.
4. August v. Cramon, *Unser österreichisch-ungarischer Bundesgenosse im Weltkrieg*, 2nd rev ed. (Berlin, 1922), p. 200.
5. Norman Stone, "Army and Society in the Habsburg Monarchy, 1900-1914," *Past and Present*, 33 (1966), p. 103.
6. *Militärstatistisches Jahrbuch für das Jahr 1913* (Vienna, 1914), p. 147.
7. Cited in Arthur J. May, *The Habsburg Monarchy, 1867-1914* (Cambridge, 1951), p. 491.
8. Oskar Regele, *Feldmarschall Conrad* (Vienna-Munich, 1955), p. 491.
9. Rothenberg, *Army of Francis Joseph*, pp. 134-136.
10. Z. A. B. Zeman, *The Break-Up of the Habsburg Empire* (London, 1961), p. 39.
11. Edmund V. Glaise-Horstenau, *Die Katastrophe: Die Zertrümmerung Österreich-Ungarns* (Vienna, 1939), pp. 62-63.
12. Hajo Holborn, "The Final Disintegration of the Habsburg Monarchy," *Austrian History Yearbook*, 3 iii (1967), pp. 189, 205.
13. Joseph Redlich, *Austrian War Government* (New Haven, 1929), pp. 55-63.
14. Christoph Fuhr, *Das k.u.k. Armeeoberkommando und die Innenpolitik in Österreich, 1914-1917* (Graz-Vienna-Cologne, 1968), pp. 19-20; Redlich, *Austrian War Government*, pp. 85-86.
15. Redlich, *Austrian War Government*, pp. 85-86.
16. *Ibid.*, pp. 91-93; Fuhr, *Armeeoberkommando*, pp. 38-46. Redlich also postulates an ideological conflict between the military and the civilian authorities, dating to the pre-war period. Fuhr maintains that this is not proven. Yet, such conflicts clearly existed as attested by the memoirs of Feldmarschall Lieutenant Alfred Krauss, *Die Ursachen unserer Niederlage*, 2nd ed. (Munich, 1920), pp. 69-74, 76-79, and the bitter complaints by Conrad, in Kurt Peball, ed., *Conrad von Hötzendorf. Private Aufzeichnungen* (Vienna-Munich, 1977), *passim*.
17. Rothenberg, *Army of Francis Joseph*, p. 177.
18. Redlich, *Austrian War Government*, p. 93; Fuhr, *Armeeoberkommando*, pp. 46-47.
19. Zeman, *Break-Up of the Habsburg Empire*, p. 251.
20. Fuhr, *Armeeoberkommando*, pp. 49-52. For the defection of the 21st Infantry, see Rothenberg, *Army of Francis Joseph*, p. 185.
21. As Gerhard Ritter put it, "despite their best efforts, the soldiers never assumed the same powers in Austria-Hungary as in Germany." See *Staatskunst und Kriegshandwerk* (Munich, 1956), III, p. 77, and Fuhr's conclusions: "Several authors have described the conditions in Austria during this period (i.e., 1914-1917) as a 'military dictatorship.' However, neither the political powers of the Austro-Hungarian high command nor the course of the dispute between the *Armeeoberkommando* and the government up to February 1917, justify this description." See Fuhr, *Armeeoberkommando*, pp. 181-182.
22. Victor S. Mamatey, "The Union of Czech Political Parties in the Reichsrat, 1916-1918," in Robert A. Kann, Bela K. Kiraly, and Paula Fichtner, eds., *The Habsburg Empire in World War I* (Boulder, Colo., 1977), pp. 6-10. For a traditional view accepting the postwar accounts of unswerving

Czech resistance, see Arthur J. May, *The Passing of the Habsburg Monarchy, 1914-1918* (Philadelphia, 1966), I, pp. 352-361.

23. Mamatey, "Czech Political Parties," p. 24.

24. Zeman, *Break-Up of the Habsburg Empire*, pp.98-99; May, *Passing of the Hapsburg Monarchy*, I, pp. 430-433.

25. C. A. Macartney and A. W. Palmer, *Independent Eastern Europe* (London, 1966), p. 66.

26. For an assessment of Charles, see May, *Passing of the Hapsburg Monarchy*, I, pp. 436-442. Negative evaluations are in Carl v. Bardolff, *Soldat im alten Österreich* (Jena, 1938), pp. 267-268; Karl F. Nowak, *Der Weg zur Katastrophe* (Berlin, 1919), pp. 207-210; and Cramon, *Bundesgenosse im Weltkrieg*, pp. 88-95. A partisan account is that of Reinhold Lorenz, *Kaiser Karl und der Untergang der Donaumonarchie* (Graz-Vienna-Cologne, 1959), while G. Brook-Shepard, *The Last Habsburg* (London, 1968), is far too favorable. See also Peball, *Conrad von Hötzendorf*, pp. 239-240, for Conrad's scathing denunciation of Charles.

27. Rothenberg, *Army of Francis Joseph*, pp. 201-203.

28. *Ibid.*, pp. 204-205; for detail, see Robert A. Kann, *Die Sixtus-Affäre und die geheimen Friedensverhandlunger Österreich-Ungarns im Ersten Weltkrieg* (Vienna, 1966).

29. Redlich, *Austrian War Government*, pp. 110-113.

30. See General Ottokar von Landwehr-Pragenau's memoirs, *Hunger* (Zurich-Leipzig, Vienna, 1931), passim.

31. Redlich, *Austrian War Government*, pp. 110-113.

32. Rothenberg, *Army of Francis Joseph*, p. 204; Zeman, *Break-Up of the Habsburg Empire*, p. 189; Cramon, *Bundesgenosse im Weltkrieg*, pp. 113-115; and Krauss, *Die Ursachen unserer Niederlage*, pp. 279-280.

33. Cited in May, *Passing of the Hapbsburg Monarchy*, II, pp. 666-667.

34. Redlich, *Austrian War Government*, pp. 169-170; Fuhr,*Armeeoberkommando*, pp. 124-125; the memorandum, Kriegsarchiv Wien, Militarkanzlei seiner Majestat 1917 69-2/7 in Rothenberg, *Army of Francis Joseph*, p. 210.

35. Rothenberg, *Army of Francis Joseph*, p. 211; Leo Valiani, *The End of Austria-Hungary* (New York, 1973), pp. 212-213. For a comprehensive treatment of military interventions, etc, on the home front, see Richard G. Plaschka, Horst Haselsteiner, and Arnold Suppan, *Innere Front: Militärassistenzen, Widerstand, und Umsturz in der Donaumonarchie*, 2 vols (Vienna, 1974).

36. May, *Passing of the Hapsburg Monarchy*, II, p. 625.

37. Rothenberg, *Army of Francis Joseph*, pp. 211-212, and Karel Pichlik, "Das Ende der österreichisch-ungarischen Armee," *Österreichische Osthefte*, 2 (1963), pp. 353-356.

38. Holborn, "Final Disintegration of the Habsburg Monarchy," pp. 197-199; Mamatey, "Czech Political Parties," p. 24.

39. Rothenberg, *Army of Francis Joseph*, pp. 209-210; Regele, *Feldmarschall Conrad*, pp. 90-91; and Johann C. Allmayer-Beck, "AOK und 'Armeefrage' im Jahre 1918," *Osterreichische Militarische Zeitschrift*, 6 (1968), pp. 431-433.

40. Rothenberg, *Army of Francis Joseph*, p. 210.

41. C. A. Macartney, *The House of Austria* (Edinburgh, 1978), pp. 268-270.

42. *Ibid.*, pp. 271-272.

43. Peter Fiala, *Die Letzte Offensive Altösterreichs* (Boppard, 1967).

44. Rothenberg, *Army of Francis Joseph*, pp. 215-216.

45. *Ibid.*, pp. 217-218; A. J. P. Taylor, *The Habsburg Monarchy, 1815-1918* (New York, 1975), p. 251.

46. Rothenberg, *Army of Francis Joseph*, pp. 217-219. Cf. Macartney, *House of Austria*, pp. 278-279.

47. Macartney, *House of Austria*, pp. 280-282; May, *Passing of the Hapsburg Monarchy*, II, pp. 805-807.

Wilhelm Deist

My outline of a few problems of mobilization for war within the framework of a totalitarian regime is based predominantly on the following studies: M. Geyer, *Aufrüstung oder Sicherheit: Die Re-*

ichswehr in der Krise der Machtpolitik 1924-1936 (Wiesbaden, 1980); Das Deutsche Reich und der Zweite Weltkrieg, ed. by Militärgeschichtliches Forschungsamt, Vol 1: Ursachen und Voraussetzungen der deutschen Kriegspolitik (Stuttgart, 1979); W. Deist, The Wehrmacht and German Rearmament (London, 1981); for further reading cf. M. Steinert, Hitler's Krieg und die Deutschen: Stimmung und Haltung der deutschen Bevölkerung im Zweiten Weltkrieg (Dusseldorf, 1970); M. Broszat, Hitler's State (London, 1981); T. W. Mason, "Innere Krise und Angriffskrieg 1938/1939," in Wirtschaft und Rüstung am Vorabend des Zweiten Weltkrieges, ed by F. Forstmeier and H. E. Volkmann (Dusseldorf, 1975); The "Führer State"—Myth and Reality: Studies on the Structure and Politics of the Third Reich, ed by G. Hirschfeld and L. Kettenacker (Stuttgart, 1981).

Paul A. C. Koistinen

1. The term "necessitarian" appears first in John Morton Blum, V Was For Victory: Politics and American Culture During World War II (New York, 1976), p. 8. The quotations in the second paragraph are from pp. 13-14. Blum sets forth the basis for his analysis in the Prologue, pp. 3-14, and summarizes it in Chapter 9, pp. 301-332, but the most forthright, brief thesis statement appears on pp. 144-146. Blum's volume is rich and suggestive. At key points, important ideas and material require further development for purposes of clarity and of avoiding apparent contradictions. Labels like "culture" would benefit from more precise definition. Certainly the operations of power in American society could receive additional attention.

Various forms of the "necessity" interpretation are reflected in the works of Blum's students: Allan M. Winkler, The Politics of Propaganda: The Office of War Information, 1942-1945 (New Haven, 1978); Jonathan Foster Fanton, "Robert A. Lovett: The War Years" (Ph.D. diss., Yale University, 1978); and Richard Norman Chapman, "Contours of Public Policy, 1939-1945" (Ph.D. diss., Yale University Press, 1976). The same is true for other publications like: Alan Clive, State of War: Michigan in World War II (Ann Arbor, 1979); Richard A. Lauderbaugh, American Steel Makers and the Coming of the Second World War (Ann Arbor, 1980); and John William Partin, "'Assistant President' for the Home Front: James F. Byrnes and World War II" (Ph.D. diss., University of Florida, 1977).

A variation of Blum's analysis of economic mobilization for the Second World War is exemplified by James MacGregor Burns, Roosevelt: The Soldier of Freedom (New York, 1970). Burns implicitly appears to accept much of the "necessity" thesis, but with many qualifications. He places much greater emphasis on the enormous ambivalance throughout American society about practically all wartime developments; and, by contrast with Blum, he stresses more change than continuity between the prewar and wartime years. This approach is evident in the one most complete surveys of the home front during World War II: Richard Polenberg, War and Society: The United States, 1941-1945 (Philadelphia, 1972). Interpretations similar to Burns' are also found in numerous other scholarly works, including: John W. Jeffries, Testing the Roosevelt Coalition: Connecticut Society and Politics in the Era of World War II (Knoxville, Tenn., 1979); Philip J. Funigiello, The Challenge to Urban Liberalism: Federal-City Relations during World War II (Knoxville, Tenn., 1978); and Donald H. Riddle, The Truman Committee: A Study in Congressional Responsiblity (New Brunswick, N.J., 1964).

Both Blum and Burns back away from emphasizing the positive in the momentous developments of World War II. Eliot Janeway, The Struggle for Survival: A Chronicle of Economic Mobilization in World War II (New Haven, 1951) offers a very different approach: For Janeway, the war years at every level of life were affirmative, restoring the promise of America with the dynamism appropriately coming from the system itself, not the government. In a curious blend of the populist and the neoconservative, a similar interpretation is presented in the journalistic account of Geoffrey Perrett, Days of Sadness, Years of Triumph: The American People, 1939-1945 (New York, 1973). A generally positive view of the war, though without the exuberance of Janeway or Perrett, is offered in George Q. Flynn, The Mess in Washington: Manpower Mobilization in World War II (Westport, Conn., 1979). It should be noted that Flynn's work is rather narrow, being more a rendition of Paul V. McNutt's leadership of the War Manpower Commission than a full-blown study of wartime manpower mobilization.

Bruce Catton's, *The War Lords of Washington* (New York, 1948) presents a negative view of war mobilization. This volume was among the first and early significant publications on the wartime economy. Catton indignantly and passionately indicted industry and the military for thwarting an effort to make the war years serve as a fulfillment of New Deal promises. The author based his indictment on a New Deal, liberal perspective. A similar viewpoint, although with a very different approach, is offered in the popular history of Richard R. Lingeman, *Don't You Know There's A War On? The American Home Front, 1941-1945* (New York, 1970). A much more scholarly, ideological, and systematic critique of the economic mobilization effort, which, unlike Catton and Lingeman, includes the President, was published as a New Left interpretation in 1968 by Barton J. Bernstein, "America in War and Peace: The Test of Liberalism," in *Towards a New Past: Dissenting Essays in American History*, ed. Bernstein (New York, 1968), pp. 289-321.

One of the more subtle and sophisticated liberal defenses of the President and economic mobilization for the Second World War is that of David Brody, "The New Deal and World War II," in *The New Deal: The National Level*, ed. John Braeman, Robert H. Bremner, and Brody (Columbus, Ohio, 1975), pp 267-309. The war years, according to Brody, witnessed a consolidation of a fragmented New Deal under Roosevelt's brilliant pragmatic leadership. Brody had presented a "consolidation" interpretation of organized labor during World War II in an earlier essay: "The Emergence of Mass-Production Unionism," in *Change and Continuity in Twentieth-Century America*, ed. John Braeman, Robert H. Bremner, and Everett Walters (Columbus, Ohio, 1964), pp. 221-262.

The best bibliographic essays on the World War II home front include: Polenberg, *War and Society*, pp. 261-279; and Jim F. Heath, "Domestic America During World War II: Research Opportunities for Historians," *Journal of American History*, 58 (1971): 384-414. Clive, *State of War*, pp. 2-6, outlines the major interpretative approaches to wartime domestic history, but his categories and some of his observations must be treated with caution. Chapman, "Contours of Public Policy," cites in his bibliography various volumes and dissertations involving Congress during wartime (the main subject of his study) which are useful and not often listed elsewhere. Recent dissertations and other literature on the wartime economy will be discussed in the endnotes that follow.

2. I have already published on the subject of economic mobilization for World War II with elaborate documentation: *The Hammer and the Sword: Labor, the Military, and Industrial Mobilization, 1920-1945* (Ph. D. diss., University of California, Berkeley, 1964; reprint ed., New York, 1979); "Mobilizing the World War II Economy: Labor and the Industrial-Military Alliance," *Pacific Historical Review*, 42 (1973): 443-478; and essays that involve the Second World War in *The Military-Industrial Complex: A Historical Perspective* (New York, 1980). In the following pages I will not cite what is in footnotes elsewhere, but I will include secondary or primary material which I have either not used before or which is especially important.

My research in primary material includes: numerous War and Navy Department collections, Papers of the War Production Board and predecessor agencies, the Office of War Mobilization and Reconversion, the War Manpower Commission, the Office of Price Administration, and the Congress of Industrial Organizations, the Papers of Franklin D. Roosevelt, Henry L. Stimson, Bernard M. Baruch, Samuel I. Rosenman, Grenville Clark, William Green, and Phillip Murray, and various privately held collections. Most of the voluminous Congressional hearings and reports have been used, along with many newspapers and numerous unpublished manuscripts. Needless to say, the secondary literature on the subject is legion.

An analysis of economic mobilization for World War II obviously does not involve a limited administrative problem. The entire American political economy, which is exceptionally complex and which includes most aspects of American life, is relevant. Consequently, information and ideas relate to central themes in the paper, but which might distract from them if included in the text proper, have been placed in the endnotes. The notes, therefore, are more a sub-text than simply a citation of sources.

3. Comparative figures on the financing of America's wars are given in Koistinen, *Military-Industrial Complex*, pp. 107-108. Some wartime revenue comparisons between the United States and its allies are contained in: Alan S. Milward, *War, Economy and Society, 1939-1945* (Berkeley, 1977), pp. 105-109.

4. Studies on wartime profits and farm and labor income are still rudimentary, with scholars dependent principally upon contemporary sources. This is a field which cries out for sophisticated, in-

depth analysis. The following quotation from my volume, *Hammer and the Sword,* pp. 283-284, based on sources published in 1945 and 1949, fairly well fills out the points made in the text:

> Certainly the wages of the working population increased during World War II. In 1939 dollars, average weekly earnings in manufacturing rose from $24.00 in 1939 to a high of $36.72 in 1944; average hourly earnings from 64 cents to 81 cents. However, with reduced hours of overtime and downgrading, average weekly earnings skidded to $34.57 in 1945. Rampant inflation in 1946 and 1947 reduced the figures further to $31.46 and $31.39 respectively. But these are gross figures. After taxes and 10 percent war bond deductions—admittedly a saving—the average worker was probably somewhat better off during the war than in 1939 but not substantially. Furthermore, average figures ignore the considerable portion of the population earning below the citations. Compared with war profits, the gains of labor seem slighter. At the peak of production activity during World War II, corporate profits *after taxes* had increased 100.6 percent from the 1939 level; *net* farm income, including government parity payments, went up 181.6 percent; average weekly wages, in unadjusted dollars, *before taxes* increased 84.4 percent, including overtime compensation. Moreover, it must be kept in mind, despite high excess profits taxes, industry was permitted to write off defense plant investments in five rather than the normal twenty years, was permitted to reclaim 10 percent of the excess profits taxes paid during the war at the termination of hostilities, and was permitted to "carry back" or "carry forward" post-war losses to gain tax credits for the war years. In effect, for a limited period, the government would guarantee any industrial losses up to 80 percent in post-war America. Farmers had the security of parity.

See also: pp. 577-584, 664-572, 778-579.

Other useful primary and secondary studies of industrial profits include: "Statement of Col. Maurice Hirsch, General Staff Corps, Chairman, War Contracts Price Adjustment Board, and Chairman, War Department Price Adjustment Board, to the Select Committee on Small Business of the House of Representatives of the United States"—reproduced in U.S., Congress, House, *Congressional Record,* 79th Cong, 1st Sess, 1945, 91, pt 5: 6145-48; U.S., Office of Price Administration, Division of Research, Financial Analysis Branch, War Profits Study 12, *Corporate Profits, 1936-1944, Part III, First Half 1944, Industry Stabilized at Wartime Peak, 1120 Leading Industrial Corporations,* March 1945; Richard C. Osborn, *The Renegotiation of War Profits* (Urbana, Ill., 1948); John Perry Miller, *Pricing of Military Procurement* (New Haven, 1949).

For a recent analysis of labor's wartime gains that is more positive than that presented in the quotation from my study, see: Geoffrey Thomas Mills, "The Economics of Price Control: The OPA Experience 1941-1946" (Ph.D. diss., University of Illinois, Urbana-Champaign, 1979), Chapter 8. As the title indicates, Mills' analysis is derived from an evaluation of the OPA's performance. For a more sophisticated study of the OPA which is based on more extensive work in primary sources, see: Andrew Hudson Bartels, "The Politics of Price Control: The Office of Price Administration and the Dilemmas of Economic Stabilization, 1940-1946" (Ph.D. diss., Johns Hopkins University Press, 1980). Darrel Robert Cady, "The Truman Administration's Reconversion Policies, 1945-1947" (Ph.D. diss., University of Kansas, 1974), also deals with the OPA, but within the larger context of the nation's readjustment to peacetime conditions. While this work provides some useful information and insights on the early years of the Truman Administration, it is based on limited work in primary sources and the organization and development of material and ideas are weak. The author fails to substantiate his positive assessment of the Truman Administration's reconversion program.

Still the most valuable study of the distribution of wartime economic benefits is: U.S., Congress, Senate, *Economic Concentration and World War II: Report of the Smaller War Plants Corporation to the Special Committee to Study Problems of American Small Business,* 79th Cong, 2nd Sess, Doc 206, June 14, 1946. This impressive study was researched and written under the direction of John M. Blair and Dewey Anderson, both of whom served with the Temporary National Economic Committee and drew upon the extensive information of that body for helping to formulate the analysis. Among other observations, the study found that the nation's manufacturing facilities existing in 1939 had cost around $40 billion. Wartime expansion added $26 billion more, two-thirds of which the government financed and most of which had peacetime utility. Furthermore, out of wartime expenditures approximating

$315.8 billion, the War and Navy Departments spent the greater share. Between June 1940 and September 1944, prime contracts went to 18,539 firms, but two-thirds were awarded to the top 100 corporations; 30 percent to 10 corporations. Subcontracting did not significantly change the picture since most of it took place among the large corporations. Expenditures for research and plants and equipment followed a similar pattern.

Concentrating economic power in the traditional sense of mergers and acquisitions did not take place at a significant level during and immediately after the war. But the wealth acquired by corporations and financial institutions during the war no doubt helped create the conditions for economic consolidation which began in the early to mid-1950s and, with varying degrees of intensity, has continued right up to the present day. Moreover, the continued high level of "peacetime" defense spending in the postwar years acted as a stimulus for the growth of conglomerates, as firms heavily involved in munitions production sought to protect their corporations through diversification. See: Samuel Richardson Reid, *Mergers, Managers and the Economy* (New York, 1968), p. 19; Robert Sobel, *The Age of Giant Corporations: A Microeconomic History of American Business, 1914-1970* (Westport, Conn., 1972), pp. 178-235; Ralph L. Nelson, *Merger Movements in American Industry, 1895-1956* (Princeton, 1959), pp. 122-126; and Carl Eis, *The 1919-1930 Merger Movement in American Industry* (New York, 1978), pp. 136-148. The most detailed information about the increase of economic concentration during World War II is presented in U.S., Federal Trade Commission, *The Merger Movement: A Summary Report* (Washington, 1948). While this report concentrates on the years from 1940-47, it also provides an overview of industrial consolidation and the federal government's response to it extending back to the late nineteenth century. For the period 1940-47, the report noted that around 60 percent of all mergers and acquisitions occurred in six manufacturing areas: food and beverages, textiles and apparel, chemicals, nonelectrical machinery, petroleum, and transportation equipment, with the first three categories accounting for 36 percent of activity. Moreover, the commission reported that most consolidations took place during the last three years of the period. See also: Koistinen, *Military-Industrial Complex*, pp. 14-15 and footnotes 11-13 for a brief discussion and citations of sources on the crucial subject of concentrated economic power and its consequences in America. For the latest study challenging the managerialist thesis and proposing that in terms of the control of major corporations by financial institutions more continuity than change has been evident throughout the twentieth century, see: Mark S. Mizruchi, *The American Corporate Network, 1904-1974* (Beverly Hills, Calif., 1982).

A recent study of the Defense Plant Corporation established that industry largely acted as its own watchdog in the operation of government-built plants that cost billions of dollars. See: Gerald T. White, *Billions for Defense: Government Financing by the Defense Plant Corporation during World War II* (University, Ala., 1980). The author contends, but cannot substantiate, that management behaved in a trustworthy fashion. To illustrate the point on discerning with any exactitude corporate profits during World War II, the Senate Special Committee on Investigation of the Munitions Industry (Nye Committee) while examining World War I contracting established that it took twenty-two individuals five years to "audit . . . the income, excess-profits, and war-profits tax returns of the United States Steel Corporation and its subsidiaries for 1917 and 1918." In its most impressive reports, the Nye Committee presented a very sophisticated and thorough analysis of wartime profit controls, including the dangers to private industry and the vicissitudes facing the government. The committee concluded that the government faced insuperable odds when pitted against private industry. These reports are among the best sources on this crucial subject. See: U.S., Congress, Senate, Special Committee on Investigation of the Munitions Industry, *Munitions Industry: Preliminary Report on Wartime Taxation and Price Control*, 74th Cong, 1st Sess, 1935, S. Rept 944, pt 2 (Serial 9882), pp. 1-164 (direct quotation above, p. 38); and U.S., Congress, Senate, Special Committee on Investigation of the Munitions Industry, *Munitions Industry: Report on War Department Bills S. 1716-S. 1722 Relating to Industrial Mobilization in Wartime*, 74th Cong, 2nd Sess, 1936, S. Rept 944, pt 4 (Serial 9884), pp. 1-77.

The distribution of national income and wealth is closely related to the issue of interest-group benefits during war. Those tending towards a more positive view of the home front often assert that from 1939 or 1941 to 1945 there was lessening of economic inequality in that the top 5 percent or 20 percent of the population received less of the national income. That is correct. This type of focus took on new importance and urgency with the publication of the now classic study of Robert J. Lampman, *The Share of the Top Wealth-Holders in National Wealth, 1922-1945* (Princeton, 1962). While it is true that the top 1, 5, 10, or 20 percent of the population saw its share of the national income shrink, several points about this phenomenon need to be made. First, the trend began in 1929, not 1939 or 1941. Second, the redistribution process stopped in 1944 and has held rather consistently until very recently when a turn towards greater inequality apperas to be under way. Lastly, and perhaps most importantly, the beneficiaries of the redistribution in the depression and war years were not the bottom fifth of the population; their gain was minimal. Most of the shift in income went to those in the upper 50 percent of the population. Moreover, when all forms of taxation are taken into account, taxes do not appear to have significantly altered income distribution patterns. Lampman's findings on the distribution of wealth are similar, although he does not give figures indicating who benefitted from the redistribution and he notes that the trend towards greater equality in wealth-holding reversed itself between 1949 and 1956; later studies confirm that that process continued after 1956. The above discussion is based on Lampman and the following: Herman P. Miller, *Rich Man, Poor Man* (New York, 1964), pp. 25-36; Gabriel Kolko, *Wealth and Power in America: An Analysis of Social Class and Income Distribution* (New York, 1962), pp. 9-54; and Ferdinand Lundberg, *The Rich and the Super Rich: A Study in the Power of Money Today* (New York, 1968), pp. 11-37. Ira C. Magaziner and Robert B. Reich, *Minding America's Business: The Decline and Rise of the American Economy* (New York, 1982), Chapter 1, and Lester C. Thurow, *The Zero-Sum Society: Distribution and the Possibilities for Economic Change* (New York, 1980), Chapter 7 and pp. 7-8, 19, 50-54, and 199-200, offer some recent and useful insights and information on income and wealth distribution in the United States. For a differing, rather extreme neo-conservative interpretation of income and wealth distribution matters and citations of secondary literature supporting such a view, see: Barry W. Poulson, *Economic History of the United States* (New York, 1981), Chapter 28. Most scholars studying income and wealth distribution draw heavily from Simon Kuznets, *Shares of Upper Income Groups in Income and Saving* (New York, 1953).

5. Not many scholars have written recently on the mobilization of the labor force during the Second World War. Flynn, *The Mess in Washington: Manpower Mobilization in World War II* is the latest and broadest monograph on the subject. For observations on this volume, see footnote 1. Nelson Nauen Lichtenstein, "Industrial Unionism Under the No-Strike Pledge: A Study of the CIO During the Second World War" (Ph.D. diss., University of California, Berkeley, 1974), in his revisionist assessment of wartime labor developments, contributes some insights relevant to work force policies, although he does not treat with that subject directly.

The most significant work on mobilizing the nation's working population for hostilities involves the participation of women. A rich collection of monographs, dissertations, and articles on the subject is beginning to appear. For some examples, see: Karen Anderson, *Wartime Women: Sex Roles, Family Relations, and the Status of Women During World War II* (Westport, Conn., 1981); Leila J. Rupp, *Mobilizing Women for War: German and American Propaganda, 1939-1945* (Princeton, 1978); Chester W. Gregory, *Women in Defense Work During World War II: An Analysis of the Labor Problem and Women's Rights* (Jericho, N.Y., 1974); D'Ann Mae Campbell, "Wives, Workers and Womanhood: America During World War II" (Ph.D. diss., University of North Carolina at Chapel Hill, 1979); and Eleanor Ferguson Straub, "Government Policy Toward Civilian Women During World War II" (Ph.D. diss., Emory University, 1973). These monographs include bibliographic citations for other work on women and the war effort.

6. Reconversion as a subject has also been neglected of late by scholars. Cady, "The Truman Administration's Reconversion Policies, 1945-1947," focuses on years which still need more attention. See end note No. 4 for a brief critique of Cady's work. A dissertation of William Steinert Hill, Jr. is most relevant to the intense debate over readjusting the economy to peace. Hill's work is discussed at length in endnote 20. Plans and policies for America's fighting forces as part of the process of returning the society to peace are treated elaborately in the following works: Davis R. B. Ross, *Preparing for Ulysses: Politics and Veterans During World War II* (New York, 1969); Bert Marvin Sharp, "'Bring the Boys Home': Demobilization of the United States Armed Forces After World War II" (Ph.D. diss., Michigan State University, 1976).

7. The best source on the Truman Committee is Riddle, *The Truman Committee*. One of the most active members of the Committee, and an astute critic of the entire economic mobilization program, was Harley M. Kilgore (D.-W.Va.). He is discussed briefly in Riddle and at length in the biography of Robert Franklin Maddox, *The Senatorial Career of Harley Martin Kilgore* (New York, 1981).

The idea that the Roosevelt Administration's mobilization policies helped strengthen the conservative opposition is further developed on pp. 107-8 - SESS II and in endnotes 22-25.

8. Civilian Production Administration, *Industrial Mobilization for War: History of the War Production Board and Predecessor Agencies, 1940-1945* (Washington, D.C., 1947), pp. 961-966; Bureau of the Budget, *The United States at War: Development and Administration of the War Program by the Federal Government* (Washington, D.C., 1946), p. 507.

9. The first significant work on the World War II economy, Bureau of the Budget, *United States at War* (1946), did not go in for hyperbole about American production efforts in its very candid and antimilitary rendition of economic mobilization. By reciting statistics, the official history of the WPB (then called the Civilian Production Administration), *Industrial Mobilization for War* (1947), tacitly laid the basis for the "miracle of production" approach. Donald Nelson, *Arsenal of Democracy: The Story of American War Production* (New York, 1946), p. ix, stated it more directly: "American war production . . . I think . . . is one of the greatest stories in human history. . . ." He was seconded by Catton in his brilliant polemic against the *War Lords of Washington*, p. 306: "There is not much use in citing figures, because the figures are all so astronomical that they cease to mean very much. . . . America did the greatest job in the history of the human race." Janeway, *The Struggle for Survival*, p. 361, offered a variation on the theme by labeling the wartime production record as "the Rooseveltian miracle." See Chapter 1 and pp. 360-61 for a full development of the Janeway analysis.

Numerous scholarly works, textbooks, and other volumes either directly or indirectly accept the "miracle of production" thesis, although with vastly ranging levels of sophistication. For some examples, see: Samuel P. Huntington, *The Soldier and the State: The Theory and Politics of Civil-Military Relations* (Cambridge, Mass., 1957), pp. 342-344; Milward, *War, Economy and Society*, pp. 63-75; Sobel, *Age of Giant Corporations*, pp. 162-165; Riddle, *Truman Committee*, p. 97; Lingeman, *Don't You Know There's A War On?*, pp. 110-111; Brody, "The New Deal and World War II," p. 267; Chester Whitney Wright, *Economic History of the United States* (New York, 1949), pp. 794-810; Harry N. Scheiber, Harold G. Vatter, and Harold Underwood Faulkner, *American Economic History* (New York, 1976), pp. 407-409; and Charles Sellers, Henry May and Neil R. McMillen, *A Synopsis of American History* (Boston, 1981), pp. 324-325.

10. The subject of prewar economic potential and wartime performance is examined most thoroughly and from numerous angles by Klaus E. Knorr, *The War Potential of Nations* (Princeton, 1956). Knorr's work contains good statistical material as well as the appropriate caveats about the limitations of any comparative approach. This volume is intended primarily to explain the nature and outcome of World War II. Another work by Knorr, addressed more to the postwar situation, is still relevant to the Second World War and twentieth century warfare in general. See: *Military Power and Potential* (Lexington, Mass., 1970). Two other volumes are valuable for viewing the war from a comparative perspective: Milward, *War, Economy and Society;* and Arthur Marwick, *War and Social Change in the Twentieth Century: A Comparative Study of Britain, France, Germany, Russia and the United States* (New York, 1974).The following tables provide a comparison of prewar and wartime production data for the major combatant nations.

11. Goldsmith, "Power of Victory," p. 79. Of all those writing on the World War II economy, Perrett, *Days of Sadness, Years of Triumph*, p. 182, curiously, in his "pop"-type history, comes closest to making Goldsmith's point.

Table 1
Percentage Distribution of the World's Manufacturing Production (excerpted)

Period	United States	Canada	United Kingdom	USSR	Germany	Japan
1926/1929	42.2	2.4	9.4	4.3	11.6	2.5
1936/1938	32.2	2.0	9.2	18.5	10.7	3.5

Source: National Industrial Conference Board, *The Economic Almanac, 1953–1954* (New York, 1955), pp. 600–601.

Table 2
Volume of Combat Munitions Production of Major Belligerents
Billions of Dollars, 1944 U.S. Munitions Prices

Country	1935–39	1940	1941	1942	1943	1944
United States	11	11	41	20	38	42
Canada	0	0	1	1	11	11
Great Britain	21	31	61	9	11	11
USSR	8	5	81	111	14	16
Germany	12	6	6	81	131	17
Japan	2	1	2	3	41	6

Source: Raymond W. Goldsmith, "The Power of Victory: Munitions Output in World War II," *Military Affairs* 10 (1946): 75.

Note: In comparing manufacturing production before the war with munitions production in 1944, I am assuming a production level of about $100 billion, even though for the six countries listed the total comes to $93.5 billion. The Goldsmith table that follows (Table 3) is a much more accurate gauge of what actually took place.

Table 3
Prewar and Wartime Productivity in Major Belligerent Countries
Production per Manhour in U.S. = 100

Country (1944)	Pre-War (1935–1938)	War
	All Manufacturing Industries	Munitions Industries
United States	100	100
Canada	71	57
Great Britain	36	41
USSR	36	39
Germany	41	48
Japan	25	17

The prewar figures are taken from War Production Board Release TP-178.

The 1944 data are rough estimates based on the figures for total combat munitions production given in Table 2 (increased by estimates of merchant vessels and motor vehicles), number of workers in the metal and basic chemical industries, and average hours per week. The data on number of workers and hours are taken from official sources for the United States, Canada, and the United Kingdom, but based on rough estimates only for the USSR, Germany, and Japan.

Source: Goldsmith, "Power of Victory," p. 79.

Sobel, *Age of Giant Corporations*, p. 177, observes:

> [B]ig business was far stronger in 1938–39 than most contemporaries had realized. Small and medium-sized firms suffered greatly during the depression, but the large concerns emerged without undue difficulty, and often stronger than they had been in 1929.

As pointed out in the text and in note 4, a relatively few huge corporations constituted the basis of the American economic mobilization effort.

12. Goldsmith, "Power of Victory," pp. 78-80—quotation, p. 79. Goldsmith appears to be in error in his assertions involving a labor draft. The proposal was so politically volatile that the implementation of any form of national service would most likely have harmed rather than helped the war production effort unless drastically different war front conditions existed.

13. See above, p. 98 and endnote 3 on U.S. and other belligerent nations' war financing. Other areas which by comparison could cast further light on the American mobilization effort would include interest-group benefits from the war in terms of profits, subsidies, wages, and the like, the amount of private as opposed to public financing of plant expansion, the use of existing facilities before the construction of new plants or the expansion of existing buildings and equipment, and the further concentration of economic power and its consequences. Also of concern would be provisions made for the general public in matters of health, housing, feeding, child care, transportation, recreation, and so forth. From what information is available to me, which is piecemeal and spotty, the United States compares unfavorably with most other belligerents in many of these categories. As noted above, p. 101, however, the nation was almost alone in increasing, rather than diminishing consumer output during the war.

14. That is precisely the point of Huntington, *Soldier and State*, pp. 337-344. Catton, *War Lords of Washington*, argues instead that the prodigious production achievements stand as an indictment of the nation by demonstrating that it did not use the enormous vitality generated by the war to revitalize democracy at home and abroad. Catton's thesis is scattered throughout the volume but is fairly well summed up in the last chapter, pp. 304-313. Many authors fall somewhere between these two polar interpretations and are fairly well represented by the authors and works cited in endnotes 1 and 9.

15. Huntington, *Soldier and State*, pp. 315-344, raises and discusses some of these issues in a most provocative way. The role of an "Advisory War Council," or some similar name, as part of the military's interwar Industrial Mobilization Plans, is analyzed in my volume which will be forthcoming and is tentatively entitled, "The Political Economy of Warfare in America." Magaziner and Reich and Lester Thurow in analyzing the current decline of the American economy, prescribe for today something comparable to a war council in order to devise and implement "a coherent and coordinated industrial policy" required to reverse the nation's failing ability to compete internationally. For a fuller discussion of this theme, see endnote 20.

16. Good information and insights concerning Forrestal and Knox, and indirectly War Department leadership, are offered in the following volumes: Robert Greenhalgh Albion and Robert Howe Connery, *Forrestal and the Navy* (New York, 1962) and Arnold A. Rogow, *James Forrestal: A Study of Personality, Politics, and Policy* (New York, 1963).

17. The Feasibility Dispute laid bare the struggle for power and the issues involving it that wracked the World War II economy. Consequently, an in-depth analysis of that conflict provides many insights about how the nation's industrial system was harnessed for war. The one best source on that controversy is: Committee on Public Administration Cases, *The Feasibility Dispute: Determination of War Production Objectives for 1942 and 1943* (Washington, D.C.: Committee on Public Administration Cases, 1950). The information in this volume is excellent and it is not readily available in other secondary sources. But the author avoids drawing the logical conclusions from his analysis.

18. In the reorganization of the armed services, Roosevelt personally intervened, and continued to do so throughout the war years, to prevent Chief of Naval Operations Admiral Ernest J. King from taking control of procurement operations, but not Chief of Staff George C. Marshall from doing the same thing. Why the President acted in this way is unclear, but experience and knowledge may have made him realize that from twenty years of procurement and economic mobilization planning the War Department was ready for a vastly expanded procurement role while the Navy Department was not and required the civilian talent gathered around Forrestal as Under Secretary.

19. Throughout a good part of 1942 and into 1943, jurisdictional battles were being waged within the War Department over how to coordinate strategy and supply. This created conditions in which the department had less time and energy to even consider, let alone be receptive towards, improving relations with civilian agencies like the WPB. The Navy Department was experiencing similar difficulties, as endnote 18 indicates, but since it was smaller, had fewer requirements, and had been at a higher state of preparedness than the Army at the outset of the war, what the Navy did or did not do was less consequential for mobilization than the Army. Still, the central point remains: Roosevelt did not press the matter of coordinating strategy and production with the military, although proposals for doing

so were constantly being presented to him throughout 1942 by civilians. Had he moved decisively in this area the armed services would have had to respond and display greater flexibility.

Attempts to coordinate strategy and production by having the JCS assign officers to the WPB was only a "gesture" for several reasons: first, the arrangement practically placed the WPB in the position of a subordinate, not a coordinate, let alone a superior, agency to the JCS; and, second, no review of military requirements took place. When the OWM-OWMR was established with Byrnes as director, reviewing military requirements was recognized as imperative, and a program was created for doing so. In the end, the military services and JCS agencies, with some participation by OWM-OWMR personnel, in effect examined and passed on their own requirements with expectably modest results. Herman Miles Somers, *Presidential Agency: OWMR—The Office of War Mobilization and Reconversion* (Cambridge, Mass., 1950) is much more impressed by the Byrnes-directed review of and control over the armed services than is Partin in his more recent study, "'Assistant President' for the Home Front: James F. Byrnes and World War II," (1977). Byrnes' memoirs, if used cautiously, can also be of use in assessing his performance and the record of the offices he headed. See: *Speaking Frankly* (New York, 1947); and *All in One Lifetime* (New York, 1958).

20. The focus of this analysis has been on the government's economic mobilization structure with only general references to the corporate community. To understand fully the wartime economy, an in-depth examination of the attitudes and actions of business, and especially big business, is imperative. Of course, no such presentation is possible in a footnote, but a few general and relevant points can be made. First, during the "Feasibility Dispute," corporate leaders tended to oppose the Planning Committee's approach because they, like the military and the President, favored "incentive scheduling": set the goals high enough so as to force the system to perform maximally. Nelson, Nathan, and associates, according to this viewpoint, were engaged in offering sophisticated excuses for why the WPB was not doing better. Moreover, many business men were simply unaccustomed to and found difficulty accepting the reality of shortages growing out of demand exceeding supply. Additionally, various corporate leaders argued that the armed forces should set strategy and requirements with the WPB created to fulfill their needs. Finally, for some businessmen, operating within a framework of economic analysis and planning involving national production potential, particularly when it was presented and advocated by "academics" and "theoreticians," was both foreign and unacceptable.

Second, these attitudes obviously changed as planning based on finite resources was carried on by the WPB with increasing refinement and sophistication, first, under the Controlled Materials Plan and, later, the Production Executive Committee. But this planning was formulated, advocated, and carried out by those familiar and acceptable to the corporate community. Last, unlike World War I, with the Second World War the industrial giants did not want the planning to continue into the postwar period. Business appeared to believe it could handle its own affairs without the government, or that New Deal-type government was to be contained whenever and wherever possible. In view of the fact that the fear of a postwar depression or a difficult transition to a peacetime economy was justifiably widespread, this attitude and the policies that grew out of it were at best shortsighted, at worst irresponsible.

Mobilizing the World War II economy and the response and role of the corporate giants create some problems of interpretation for the "new business history" which emphasizes an institutional approach. This type of analysis proposes that massive changes in the volume of business after 1840 created conditions for the rise of the modern corporations, with the pioneering efforts first applied to the railroads. By the turn of the century, the modern corporate device had spread from the railroads to industry and was fairly well developed. In the most refined form the new corporation was a multidivisional structure integrated backwards and forwards and directed by professional or professionally-oriented managers. Middle managers ran the process of production and distribution while the top managers were left free to evaluate, plan, and allocate resources for a bureaucratic empire in order to insure balanced, long-range growth. "New business history" scholars deemphasize the role of government in shaping the corporation or the economy and instead stress its role of increasing demand. They similarly downplay the importance of entrepreneurs and a "free enterprise" system. A centralized economy built around the necessarily huge corporation with systematic planning, coordination, and control by detached, farsighted, and clear-headed managers is what counts. What existed before in the nineteenth century was a decentralized system of family firms, partnerships, joint stock companies, and rudimentary corporations, with an interim period, around the turn of the century, in which the giant financial houses like J. P. Morgan and Company exercised widespread influence, if not dominance.

The pioneer, leader, and chief spokesman for the "new business history" is Alfred D. Chandler, Jr. He and his students have trained many or most of those pursuing this line of analysis, and he has incorporated years of research, analysis, and publication in a major work of synthesis: *The Visible Hand: The Managerial Revolution in American Business* (Cambridge, Mass., 1977).

Something is wrong either with the general information available on the corporate community and World War II mobilization, or else with the "new business history." Too many contradictions abound between theory and practice, particularly in the area of what is supposedly the chief characteristic of the modern corporation: the dedication to planning, coordination, integration, balance, and the long, as opposed to the short run. Various reasons can be offered to explain away the paradoxes. For example, it could be argued that the corporate leaders had not and could not achieve over-all planning of the system before the war and did not desire to think it necessary after the war. Consequently, their first objective was to protect the corporate system from an obtrusive government and the vicissitudes of war. Working with the military and quickly dismantling the planning apparatus after the war ended grew out of that protective goal. While this type of explanation might have some validity, it does not suffice. The corporate managers throughout the defense and war years appear too often as parochial, short-sighted, narrow, petty, and fearful in order to fulfill the role of the collective "visible hand," confidently directing industry. Developments during the Second World War may anticipate the present economic crisis the nation faces. With most of the industrial world first in shambles and then rebuilding from 1945 through 1960, the United States had ideal and almost unique conditions for stability and growth. Once belligerents on both sides had fully reconstructed their societies and economies, America's practical monopoly on opportunity disappeared, revealing not a nation with corporate managers setting and implementing a definable industrial policy for the long run, but instead a drifting economic system with business leaders scrambling for short run profit returns with reckless disregard for their own institutions, the government, and the larger social system.

Much current literature probing the decline of American economic power follows this line. An outstanding example of such an analysis is Magaziner and Reich, *Minding America's Business*. One of the best critiques of the "new business history" is presented by Ronald L. F. Davis, "Recent Developments in Business History: The New Determinism," (Paper delivered at the Annual Meeting of the Economic and Business History Association, St. Paul, Minnesota, April 1982). Davis suggests that perhaps the investment bankers of the past were better long-range planners than the short-sighted managers of the present.

A recent dissertation by William Steinert Hill, Jr., "The Business Community and National Defense: Corporate Leaders and the Military, 1943-1950" (Ph.D. diss., Stanford University, 1979) is most relevant concerning the subject of the corporate structure and planning. Hill's work is important because he focuses upon the neglected years from 1945 to 1950 and ties them in well to the World War II and post-Korean periods. During the war and postwar years, the author maintains that businessmen did favor some form of planning once hostilities ended and that planning by necessity included a role for government, albeit a modest one. In analyzing the varying approaches of business leaders, Hill, drawing upon earlier studies, divides them into two categories: the classicalists and the managerialists. The former, best characterized by groups like the National Association of Manufacturers and the Chamber of Commerce, favored as much of an unfettered market as possible; the latter, with the principal spokesmen coming from the Committee for Economic Development and the National Planning Association, accepted the reality of a significantly modified capitalism with a meaningful regulatory role for both industry and government essential. Differences aside, both groups viewed war-induced prosperity as probably their last chance for demonstrating that continued peacetime growth was possible through the operations of a basically privately operated economy.

Hill's principal contribution involves his conclusion, which would be more persuasive if it were based on better primary sources (a fact the author himself recognizes). He concludes that businessmen outside of the aircraft, shipbuilding, and machine tool industries continuously and vigorously fought against military Keynesianism. Indeed, their struggle continued into the late 1950s. The advocates of huge military spending included some industrialists, some military elements, and some non-defense civilian officials, but they mainly involved members of the State Department, Defense Department, and National Security Council who worked out the rationale for massive rearmament during 1949-1950 in what ultimately became labeled NSC-68. Nonetheless, Hill insists that business leaders by acts of omission created conditions which almost inevitably led to military Keynesianism and a Military-

Industrial Complex. In failing to work out with the federal government before the Korean War methods to ensure prosperity and full employment, businessmen lost probably their last chance to combat economic recessions and depressions without relying upon military spending.

Hill's study blends in well with that of Magaziner and Reich. Hill carries out his analysis largely by concentrating upon the policies of business organizations and the ideas of industrial spokesmen; Magaziner and Reich examine carefully not only the strategies of government and business, but also the detailed operations of the business community and its parts. Although he does not use the same terms, Hill would probably agree with Magaziner and Reich on the need for "U.S. companies and the government [to] develop a coherent and coordinated industrial policy" in order to reestablish the efficiency and growth of the American economy and make it internationally competitive (quotation, p. 4). The crux of the matter, however, is whether even the managerial groups that Hill studies would have supported the creation of a "relatively small" governmental organization for formulating and implementing an industrial policy. Ideally, argue Magaziner and Reich, such an agency would be "relatively free from the effects of political changes in government" and based upon interest-group consensus and widespread public support. That would require "significant links with both business management and unions" and other interest groups and modes of operation accessible to the general population (quotations, p. 307). A governmental body of that nature, as reality or as goal, Magaziner and Reich see as practically indispensable for the success of any coherent industrial strategy. These authors appear to be more optimistic than Hill in that they do not view the few years after World War II as the last opportunity for making the American economy and system viable. Indeed, they see the current decline of American industry and its lack of international competitiveness as reversible today and in the future under the right policies and programs and institutions for applying them.

Thurow, *The Zero-Sum Society*, addresses many of the same issues as Magaziner and Reich and reaches many of the same conclusions. Thurow's perspective, however, is considerably broader than that of the other two authors and he is willing to concede the possibility, implied by Hill, that by not facing squarely the numerous economic problems plaguing it, the society may fail like other social systems of the past. For Thurow's view of *Minding America's Business* and further development of some of his ideas, see his review of Magaziner and Reich, "How to Rescue a Drowning Economy," *New York Review of Books*, 29 (April 1, 1982): 3-4.

David P. Calleo, *The Imperious Economy* (Cambridge, Mass., 1982) provides the most comprehensive examination of the nation's diminished and diminishing power. In an intricate and sophisticated analysis, Calleo relates how American economic, political, and military policies have interacted at home and abroad to undermine the nation's economy. Basic to the crisis facing the United States, the author persuasively argues, is the fundamental contradiction between an expansionist economic policy at home and an imperial policy abroad. The nation's leaders of the past twenty years have failed the public by manipulating, instead of trying to resolve, the contradiction between domestic and foreign goals. Any attempt to reverse the nation's decline, Calleo insists, must begin at home with the formulation of "a long-range national economic strategy" which involves major economic interest groups (quotation, p 193). Calleo's analysis is consistent with or complements those of Magaziner and Reich and Thurow. By concentrating upon the nation's international economic policy and especially its relationship to the world's monetary system, the author's approach and conclusions are very similar to those of the New Left, Wisconsin diplomatic school of which William Appleman Williams remains the primary spokesman. For a perceptive review of Calleo's book and another related volume, see: Jason Epstein, "Going for Broke," *New York Review of Books*, 29 (September 23, 1982): 17-22.

21. The subject of a war council relates to the larger issue of the role of the military in the American system of power since 1939. Scholars generally agree that prior to World War II, except for periods of warfare, the armed services did not figure meaningfully into the nation's power relations. A permanently large war and defense establishment that grew out of the Second World War dramatically changed that reality. During and after World War II, and in a few instances even before hostilities, various scholars and other analysts recognized that the modern military had to be incorporated into any analysis of power operations in the United States.

In his seminal volume *The Power Elite* (New York, 1956), C. Wright Mills set the terms for the ongoing debate about the military's changed status. Mills proposed that World War II and the Cold War had elevated the armed services to a position of shared elitest power with the federal executive and the largest corporations. While Mills' thesis was generally recognized as trenchant and provocative, few accepted it totally. Variations of or alternates for Mills' proposal are so numerous and often overlapping as to be bewildering, if not overwhelming. Nonetheless, the varying analyses tend to fall into three general, rough categories. First, the non-Marxist New Left maintains that Mills exaggerated the extent of the military's clout. No doubt its power was greater than in the pre-1940 days, but it was still a secondary, not a primary, power group which was controlled or co-opted by the governmental and economic elites which still basically guided the destinies of the nation. G. William Domhoff, *Who Rules America?* (Englewood Cliffs, N.J., 1967) fairly well represents this approach. Second, the Marxists reject outright the idea that the military has in any meaningful way modified the calculus of power. It is controlled by the capitalist classes and serves their interests at home and abroad. Paul A. Baran and Paul M. Sweezy, *Monopoly Capital: An Essay on the American Economic and Social Order* (New York, 1966), exemplify such an analysis. Third, some liberals tend to view the military of the World War II and the postwar years as the new dominant element in society. Such is the case with Fred J. Cook, *The Warfare State* (New York, 1962). Others of a liberal persuasion adopt a more sophisticated stance by pointing out that the military has emerged as the most aggressive and, hence, potentially the most powerful, element in America's bureaucratic state which has evolved over the course of the twentieth century and which is run by non-elected managers and experts. Seymour Melman, *Pentagon Capitalism: The Political Economy of War* (New York, 1970) presents the most elaborate rendition of this viewpoint. Of course, pluralists look upon even an expanded military as only one more interest group vying to shape national policies and, consequently, only complicating without significantly modifying their concept of what makes the system run. For a conservative and liberal example of pluralism, see respectively: Huntington, *The Soldier and the State*; and Morris Janowitz, *The Professional Soldier: A Social and Political Portrait* (Glencoe, Ill., 1960).

Charles C. Moskos, Jr., "The Concept of the Military-Industrial Complex: Radical Critique or Liberal Bogey," *Social Problems*, 21 (April 1977): 478-512, examines the various interpretative approaches involving the military and power in America, and discusses or cites most works of significance on the issue. His article, however, is quite confused and confusing.

In an earlier publication—*The Military-Industrial Complex*, Chapter 1—I argued that the military, despite World War II and Cold War developments, remained a subordinate rather than a dominant power group. I also pointed out, however, that by seriously eroding the cohesion and authority of the elite, the Vietnamese War had destabilized civil-military relations with uncertain consequences for the future. Sources involving power in general and its relationship to the military in particular are cited and discussed in Chapter 1 of my volume and other parts of the book.

Most theories about the modern military in American society are based on the post-World War II period. The war years should not be neglected. My discussion in the text about the Roosevelt Administration and the military could be recast in the following manner to make it more compatible with the various theories about power in America. Roosevelt passed up the opportunity during World War II to use the military as a rising, although still a secondary, power group to strengthen the more enlightened managerial elements of the business community with the result that the more hidebound classicalists dominated the economic mobilization effort, including the civilian-staffed parts of the armed services. Those developments insured that wartime planning would serve conservative and narrow, as opposed to liberal and broad, interests and precluded needed innovations like indicative planning in the post-war years. An ascendant military could never remain neutral; it would inevitably help to push the nation ideologically to the Left or the Right. While the armed services are traditional by nature, procurement and economic mobilization planning in the interwar years indicated a more flexible, even innovative side to the military which, under the right circumstances, would have favored business managerialists, not the classicalists. By acts of omission and commission, the Roosevelt Administration insured that the armed forces served conservative and restrictive purposes.

Why the Roosevelt Administration proceeded as it did is problematical. Several explanations are possible. First, with war-induced prosperity, the President's own conservative, First New Deal instincts were made manifest. Second, Roosevelt's ideological position may have been actually closer to the enlightened business managerialists instead of the narrow classicalists, but the imperatives of war made it more expedient for him to side with the latter rather than the former. In other words, the President was avoiding confrontation in which the classicalists, much more than the managerialists, were likely to engage. Lastly, the President's limited intellect and understanding prevented him from fully grasping the importance of power systems and what was required on his part to achieve desired goals. In terms of available evidence, the first and the second, not the third, explanation seem to be the more valid with some combination of the first two interpretations providing the most insight into the President's often enigmatic leadership.

22. The most systematic analysis of the 1942 election which concludes that the Democratic losses stemmed principally from "home-front problems and grievances" is found in Jeffries, *Testing the Roosevelt Coalition*, pp. 93-141 (quotation, p. 139). The author contrasts his interpretation with that of Polenberg, *War and Society*, pp. 188-192 and Burns, *Roosevelt*, pp. 276-281. Actually, both of these scholars mention wartime resentment, lack of presidential leadership, and other factors, although the low turnout of Democratic voters as a result of wartime disruption is given prominence. Lingeman, *Don't You Know There's A War On?*, pp. 346-347, goes along with the last two authors. Blum, *V Was for Victory*, pp. 320-334, maintains that low Democratic voter turnout explains the outcome of the election, a claim challenged by Jeffries, but emphasizes attitudes ranging from indifference to resentment over the conduct of the war at home and abroad that kept Democrats away from the polls. Perrett, *Days of Sadness, Years of Triumph*, pp. 247-254, touches all interpretative bases in analyzing the Democratic defeat in a way that can only leave the reader confused.

23. Blum, *V Was For Victory*, p. 244, suggests this point in the following quotation (underlined passage is my emphasis):

> As *Fortune* had predicted, the Congress during 1943 and early 1944 interpreted the election returns of 1942 as a mandate against the New Deal. Roosevelt had read those results about the same way. . . . He had let [his liberal friends] down, though from his point of view with reason. He had not wanted to divert his energy and attention from the necessities of warmaking. He understood the restlessness of his constituents with social reform. He recognized the strength of his opposition on the Hill. In one sense, the "Dear Alben" [Barkley] episode proved that Roosevelt could not have put across liberal domestic measures in 1943 even if he had tried. *In another sense, that episode was something of a self-fulfilling prophecy. Because Roosevelt had not tried, he had built up no reservoir of liberal public and congressional support on which he could call when he needed to.*

The last two sentences appear to contradict the author's necessitarian interpretation.

24. Most authors who have written recently on the World War II home front at least touch on this theme. Blum, *V Was For Victory*, subtly picks up the trend in his Prologue, pp. 3-14, and then addresses it more directly throughout the volume. For some examples, see: pp. 104-105, 222-223, 230-234, 247-248, 256-257, 323-324, and Chapters 5 and 6. See also: Burns, *Roosevelt*, pp. 280-281. As with the election of 1942, the more negative aspects of the public's attitudes are examined most systematically and in depth in Jeffries, *Testing the Roosevelt Coalition*. Clive, *State of War*, adds further details on the subject.

25. Burns, *Roosevelt*, pp. 465-472, so characteristic of his brilliantly written volume which spills over with insights, touches upon the need for the nation's leaders to assist the population through a very trying transition, but he does not develop this key idea. Both directly and indirectly, Jeffries, *Testing the Roosevelt Coalition*, pursues this subject throughout his detailed study of wartime Connecticut.

26. Koistinen, "Mobilizing the World War II Economy," pp. 471-478.

27. The subject of this paragraph is examined in greater depth in endnote 20.

Arthur Marwick

1. Ross McKibbin, *The Evolution of the Labour Party* (1974); H. C. G. Mathew, R. I. McKibbin, J. A. Kay, "The Franchise Factor in the Rise of the Labour Party," *English Historical Review*, 91 (1976): 723-752.

2. McKibbin, *Evolution of the Labour Party*, p. 239.

3. Paul Thompson, *The Edwardians* (1975).

4. Martin Pugh, *Electoral Reform in War and Peace, 1906-1918* (1978).

5. Gail Braybon, *Women Workers in the First World War* (1981). In general, Carol R. Berkin and Clara M. Lovett, *Women, War and Revolution* (New York, 1980).

6. W. J. Reader, *Imperial Chemical Industries: A History* (1970), I: 257.

7. Volume 12 of *Nouvelle Histoire de la France Contemporaine* (1975) (editions du Seuil).

8. Keith Burgess, *The Challenge of Labour* (New York, 1980), see Chapter 5, "1914-1920: A New Social Order?," especially pp. 183-184.

9. Gerd H. Hardach, *The First World War* (1973, English translation 1977); Marc Ferro, *The Great War* (English translation 1973).

10. Keith Middlemas, *Politics in Industrial Society* (1979).

11. Gerald D. Feldman, *Army Industry and Labor* (1966); and *Iron and Steel and the German Inflation 1916-1923*(1977). Charles S. Maier, *Recasting Bourgeois Europe: Stabilization in France, Germany, and Italy in the Decade after World War I* (1975).

12. Philip Abrams, "The Failure of Social Reform: 1918-1920," *Past and Present* (April 1963): 43-64.

13. Henry Pelling, *Britain and the Second World War* (1970), pp. 298-299.

14. R. C. O. Mathews, "Why Has Britain Had Full Employment Since the War?", *Economic Journal* 78 (1968): 555ff.; Pelling, *Britain and the Second World War*, pp. 299-301.

15. William G. Runciman, *Relative Deprivation and Social Justice* (1966).

16. See William E. Leuchtenberg's fascinating article, "The New Deal and the Analogue of War" in *Change and Continuity in Twentieth Century America*, ed. John Braeman, Robert Bremnar and Everett Walters (1966). See also my article "Middle Opinion in the Thirties: Planning, Progress and Political 'Agreement'," *English Historical Review*, 79 (1964): 295ff.

17. J. M. Winter, *Socialism and the Challenge of War* (1974), p. 279.

18. *Parliamentary Papers, 1914-1916*, Cmd 8005.

19. See my *The Deluge: British Society and the First World War* (London, 1965), pp. 232-236.

20. See my *The Deluge*, Chapter 3, "New Women: 1915-1916."

21. Press accounts of the "uppityness" of servant girls cannot, of course, be taken at face value. But a clear picture does emerge from such articles as "Maids and Mistresses Meet Together," *Daily Chronicle*, March 8, 1919, and "Call of the Home Unheeded by Many Girls," *Bristol Evening News*, February 19, 1919, and many, many others. I am indebted to Mr. Bernard Waites for these references. See also Ruth Adam, *A Woman's Place* (1975), pp. 74-75.

22. David H. Colse, "The Collapse of Resistance to Democracy: Conservatives, Adult Suffrage, and Second Chamber Reform, 1911-1928," *Historical Journal*, 20 (1977): 898.

23. *Ibid.*, p. 904, note 49.

24. Millicent Garrett Fawcett, January 1918: "The great searchlight of war showed things in their true light, and they gave us enfranchisement with open hands."

25. James Joll, *Europe Since 1870* (1976).

26. W. H. Dawson, ed, *After War Problems* (1917), p. 7.

27. See M. Dubesset, F. Thebaud and C. Vincent, "Les Munitionettes de la Seine," in *1914-1918, L'autre Front* (1977), ed. Patrick Fridenson, pp. 189-219.

28. *The Journals of Brand Whitlock* (New York, 1936), p. 287. I am indebted to Professor Geoffrey Best for this reference.

29. Jose Harris, "Some Aspects of Social Policy in Britain During the Second World War" in Wolfgang Mommsen, ed., *The Emergence of the Welfare State in Britain and Germany* (1981), p. 249.

30. See my *Britain in the Century of Total War: War, Peace, and Social Change: 1900-1967* (1970 paperback edition), pp. 266-268.

31. For a moving, and disturbing, testimony on the last point, see Marie Paneth, *Branch Street* (1944).

32. Mass Observation: "Report on a Survey of the Activities of Official and Voluntary Bodies in the East End, During the Intensive Bombing, September 7th-27th, 1940" (MO file number 431); *Economist*, October 5, 1940.

33. See especially, in the Imperial War Museum, the diary of William Penny (a London bus driver), the diary of Dr. J. P. McHutchison, the letters of the Reverend J. Mackay, the letters of John Hughes, the diaries of Ernest Kingsbury (a Sidcup policeman), and many other collections. The government also had reliable (secret) information drawn from censored letters, and other sources. See,

for example, "Home Opinion as Shown in the Mail to USA and Eire, Number 11: Britain and the Blitzkrieg," CAB 66/12/W. P. (40) 407 (October 4, 1940); War Cabinet: Civil Defence Report Number 22 for period 1st September 1940 to 29th September 1940, CAB 68/7/W. P. (R) (40) 196 (October 10, 1940); and Air Raids on London, September to November 1940: Memorandum by Home Secretary and Minister of Home Security, CAB 67/9/ (44) (May 5, 1941).

34. E.g., Mass Observation: "Women at Work," M.O. file number 1110, 1944, p 30: "Work after marriage is condemned by the majority of single and by the minority of married women."

35. "Attitudes Towards the Employment of Women, 1946:" appendix 2 *Report on Pensionability of Unestablished Civil Service, Parliamentary Papers, 1945-1946*, XII, Cmd 6942.

36. Mass Observation files 79 and 118; see also Public Opinion Polls, especially in *Daily Mail* and *News Chronicle*.

37. 2nd report from "Mass Observations on Refugees," M.O. file 174 (June 6, 1940).

38. Mass Observation: "Report on Changes of Outlook During the War," M.O. file number 2149 (August 1944).

39. Mass Observation: "The Mood of Britain—1938 and 1944" by Tom Harrisson, M.O. file number 2067 (April 20, 1944).

40. See A. Marwick, *Britain in the Century of Total War* (1970 paperback edition), pp 306-315, and "People's War and Top People's Peace?" in *Crisis and Controversy: Essays in Honour of A. J. P. Taylor* (1976).

41. Lord President's Office: The Beveridge Report, CAB 123/45.

42. W. H. Haslam to J. Winder, March 5, 1943; see also Haslam to Winder June 9, 1942 (Haslam Collection, Imperial War Museum).

43. The "Robinson Charlie" films can be viewed in the National Film Archive, London.

44. Ministry of Health, *About Housing* (1939), p. 16.

45. "Ex-Public Elementary School" and "Non-Ex-Public Elementary School."

46. Sidney Pollard, *The Wasting of the British Economy* (1982).

Harvard Sitkoff

1. Louis E. Lomax, *The Negro Revolt* (New York, 1962); Richard M. Dalfiume, "The 'Forgotten Years' of the Negro Revolution," *Journal of American History*, 55 (1968); Harvard Sitkoff, "Racial Militancy and Interracial Violence in the Second World War," *Journal of American History*, 58 (1971), and "The Detroit Race Riot of 1943," *Michigan History*, 53 (1969).

2. John R. Brooks, *Walls Come Tumbling Down: A History of the Civil Rights Movement, 1940-1970*(Englewood Cliffs, N.J., 1974); John Morton Blum, *V Was For Victory: Politics and American Culture During World War II* (New York, 1976); Richard Polenberg, *War and Society: The United States, 1941-1945* (Philadelphia, 1970); Geoffrey Perrett, *Days of Sadness, Years of Triumph: The American People, 1939-1945* (New York, 1973); Neil A. Wynn, *The Afro-American and the Second World War* (New York, 1975); A. Russell Buchanan, *Black Americans in World War II* (Santa Barbara, Calif., 1977); Lee Finkle, *Forum for Protest: The Black Press During World War II* (Rutherford, N.J., 1975; James A. Nuechterlein, "The Politics of Civil Rights: The FEPC, 1941-46," *Prologue*, 10 (1978); and Peter J. Kellogg, "Civil Rights Consciousness in the 1940s," *The Historian*, 42 (1979).

3. Office of War Information, "Survey of Intelligence Materials," various dates, Record Group 208, National Archives; Ulysses Lee, *The Employment of Negro Troops* (Washington, D. C., 1966), p. 348; Committee on Fair Employment Practice, Report from Special Service Division, "Negro Organizations and the War Effort," April 28, 1942, Record Group 228, National Archives; and Brooks, *Walls Come Tumbling Down*, p. 36.

4. Alfred McClung Lee, "Subversive Individuals of Minority Status," *Annals* of the American Academy of Political and Social Science, 223 (1942) (hereafter cited as *Annals*); Selective Service System, "Selective Service in Peace Time: First Report of the Director of Selective Service," and "Special Groups: Special Monograph No. 10," Record Group 228, National Archives; Louis Martin,

"Fifth Column Among Negroes," *Opportunity*, 20 (1942); A. Philip Randolph, "Pro-Japanese Activities Among Negroes," *The Black Worker*, 11 (1942); and *Chicago Defender*, January 16, 1943.

5. Bernard F. Robinson, "War and Race Conflicts in the United States," *Phylon*, 4 (1943); *Pittsburgh Courier*, August 14, 1943; Lester B. Granger, "Victory Through Unity," *Opportunity*, 21 (1943); Polenberg, *War and Society*, p. 129; and Adam Clayton Powell, *Riots and Ruins* (1945).

6. Granger, "Victory Through Unity"; *Pittsburgh Courier*, October 9, 1943; A. A. Liveright, "The Community and Race Relations," *Annals*, 244 (1946); "Negroes Fight on Four Major Fronts," *Southern Frontier*, 5 (1944); "Programs of Action on the Democratic Front," *Monthly Summary of Events and Trends in Race Relations*, 2 (1944); and National Urban League, *Racial Conflict—A Homefront Danger* (New York, 1943). For a contrary view, see Blum, *V Was For Victory*, p. 215.

7. Finkle, *Forum for Protest*, especially p. 168; Blum, *V Was For Victory*, p. 208; Ralph N. Davis, "The Negro Newspapers and the War," *Sociology and Social Research*, 27 (1943); and P. L. Prattis, "The Role of the Negro Press in Race Relations," *Phylon*, 7 (1946).

8. Polenberg, *War and Society*, p. 106; Virginicus Dabney, "The South Marches On," *Survey Graphic*, 32 (1943); Charles Johnson, et al, *To Stem This Tide: A Survey of Racial Tension Areas in the United States* (1943), pp. 131-139; J. Saunders Redding, "Southern Defensive—I," and Lillian Smith, "Southern Defensive—II," *Common Ground*, 4 (1944).

9. Herbert Garfinkel, *When Negroes March: The March on Washington Movement in the Organizational Politics of FEPC* (New York, 1959). Garfinkel popularized the idea that World War II constituted a watershed in black militancy. The sources cited in notes 1 and 2 above also argue on behalf of that now traditional view. Alan M. Osur, *Blacks in the Army Air Forces During World War II: The Problem of Race Relations* (Washington, D.C., 1977), also closely follows Dalfiume in stressing black mass pressure and protest.

10. Harvard Sitkoff, *A New Deal For Blacks, The Emergence of Civil Rights as a National Issue: The Depression Decade* (New York, 1978).

11. NAACP Board of Director Minutes, April 13, September 14, 1942, Series A, Box 11, and Roy Wilkins to Walter White, July 7, 1943, 270:3, NAACP Papers, Library of Congress; Lester Granger to A. Philip Randolph, September 1, 1942, Series I, Box 28, NUL Papers, Library of Congress; Brooks, *Walls Come Tumbling Down*, p. 34; *New York Times*, February 2, 1944; and Louis C. Kesselman, *The Social Politics of FEPC: A Study in Reform Pressure Movements* (Chapel Hill, N.C., 1948).

12. August Meier and Elliott Rudwick, "The Origins of Nonviolent Direct Action in Afro-American Protest: A Note on Historical Discontinuities," in *Along the Color Line: Explorations in the Black Experiences* (Urbana, Ill., 1976), pp. 387, 344-352.

13. *Ibid.*, pp. 379, 362, 314.

Leila J. Rupp

1. Quoted in the *New York Times*, March 8, 1943.

2. See, for example, the essays in Carol R. Berkin and Clara M. Lovett, *Women, War and Revolution* (New York, 1980).

3. Arthur Marwick, *War and Social Change in the Twentieth Century: A Comparative Study of Britain, France, Germany, Russia, and the United States* (London, 1974), pp. 216-219.

4. Maurine Weiner Greenwald, *Women, War, and Work: The Impact of World War I on Women Workers in the United States* (Westport, Conn., 1980).

5. Raynes Minns, *Bombers and Mash: The Domestic Front 1939-45* (London, 1980), pp. 31-33. For a similar study of British women in the First World War, see Gail Braybon, *Women Workers in the First World War: The British Experience* (London, 1981).

6. K. Jean Cottam, "Soviet Women in Combat in World War II: The Ground Forces and the Navy," *International Journal of Women's Studies*, 3 (1980): 345-357; Bernice Glatzer Rosenthal, "Love on the Tractor: Women in the Russian Revolution and After," in Renate Bridenthal and Claudia Koonz, eds., *Becoming Visible: Women in European History* (Boston, 1977), pp. 370-399.

7. Leila J. Rupp, *Mobilizing Women for War: German and American Propaganda, 1939-1945* (Princeton, 1978); Rupp, "Women, Class, and Mobilization in Nazi Germany," *Science and Society*, 43 (1979): 51-69.

8. Thomas R. H. Havens, "Women and War in Japan, 1937-1945," *American Historical Review*, 80 (1975): 913-934.

9. Karen Tucker Anderson, "Last Hired, First Fired: Black Women Workers During World War II," *Journal of American History*, 69 (1982): 82-97.

10. Rupp, *Mobilizing Women for War* ; "The Life and Times of Rosie the Riveter," directed and produced by Connie Field. See Miriam Frank, Marilyn Ziebarth, Connie Field, *The Life and Times of Rosie the Riveter* (Emeryville, Calif., 1982).

11. William Henry Chafe, *The American Woman: Her Changing Social, Economic, and Political Role, 1920-1970* (New York, 1972). For an excellent discussion of the debate over the impact of the Second World War on American women, see Karen Anderson, *Wartime Women: Sex Roles, Family Relations, and the Status of Women During World War II* (Westport, Conn., 1981), pp. 3-11.

12. See, for example, Paddy Quick, "Rosie the Riveter: Myths and Realities," *Radical America*, 9 (1975): 115-131; Eleanor F. Straub, "Government Policy Toward Civilian Women During World War II," (Ph.D. diss., Emory University, 1973); Alan Clive, "Women Workers in World War II: Michigan as a Test Case," *Labor History*, 20 (1979): 44-72; Karen Beck Skold, "The Job He Left Behind: American Women in the Shipyards During World War II," in Berkin and Norton, *Women, War and Revolution*, pp. 55-75; and Anderson, *Wartime Women*. For a similar analysis of the impact of the First World War, see Greenwald, *Women, War and Work*.

13. Edward R. Beauchamp, "The Social Role of Japanese Women: Continuity and Change," *International Journal of Women's Studies*, 2 (1979): 244-256.

14. Harry G. Shaffer, *Women in the Two Germanies: A Comparative Study of a Socialist and a Non-Socialist Society* (New York, 1981), pp. 55-56.

15. Anderson, *Wartime Women*, pp. 169-171.

16. Gisela Bock, "'Zum Wohle des Vöolkskörpers . . . ': Abtreibung und Sterilisation in Nationalsozialismus," *Journal für Geschichte*, 2 (1980): 58-65; Gisela Bock, "Frauen und ihre Arbeit im Nationalsozialismus," in Annette Kuhn and Gerhard Schneider, eds., *Frauen in der Geschichte* (Düsseldorf, 1979), pp. 113-149.

17. See Harry Wilde, *Das Schicksal der Verfemten*(Tübingen, 1969); and James D. Steakley, *The Homosexual Emancipation Movement in Germany* (New York, 1975).

18. Havens, "Women and War," pp. 927-930.

19. Anderson, *Wartime Women*, pp. 103-111.

20. Madeline Davis, Liz Kennedy, and Avra Michelson, "Aspects of the Buffalo Lesbian Community in the Fifties," Buffalo Women's Oral History Project, paper presented at the National Women's Studies Association conference, Bloomington, Indiana, May 1980.

21. Anderson, *Wartime Women*, pp. 122-153.

22. Minns, *Bombers and Mash*, p. 200.

23. Philip E. Slater, "Social Change and the Democratic Family," in Warren G. Bennis and Philip E. Slater, eds., *The Temporary Society (New York, 1968), pp. 20-52*.

24. Susan Brownmiller, *Against Our Will: Men, Women and Rape* (New York, 1975), pp. 43-78.

25. Quoted in *ibid*, p. 72.

26. Quoted in Janet Bruin and Stephen Salaff, "Never Again: The Organization of Women Atomic Bomb Victims in Osaka," *Feminist Studies*, 7 (1981): 5-18.

27. Magda Menzerath, *Kampffeld Heimat: Deutsche Frauenleistung im Kriege* (Stuttgart, 1944), p. 49.

28. Mrs. William Brown Melony, "Foreword," in *American Women at War, By 7 Newspaper Women* (New York, 1942), p. 6.

29. Hazel Erskine, "The Polls: Women's Role," *Public Opinion Quarterly* 35 (1971): 282-287.

30. Rosenthal, "Love on the Tractor," in Bridenthal and Koonz, *Becoming Visible*, pp. 390-392; and Gail Warshofsky Lapidus, *Women in Soviet Society: Equality, Development, and Social Change* (Berkeley, 1978), pp. 115-119.

31. Betty Friedan, *The Feminine Mystique* (New York, 1963).

32. Ingrid Schmidt-Harzbach, "Die Lüge von der Stunde Null," *Courage*, 7 (June 1982): 32-40.

33. Quoted in *ibid.*, p. 34.
34. Sheila Tobias and Shelah Leader, "An Intelligent Woman's Guide to the Military Mind: What Kinds of Guns Are They Buying with Your Butter?" *Ms.* (July-August 1982): 119ff.
35. Susan J. Pharr, *Political Women in Japan: The Search for a Place in Political Life* (Berkeley, 1981).
36. Shaffer, *Women in the Two Germanies*, pp. 12-13.

John E. Talbott

1. *Le Monde*, March 14, 1954.
2. *Ibid.*
3. Antoine Argoud, *La Décadence, l'imposture et la tragédie* (Paris, 1974); Raoul Salan, *Mémoires: Fin d'un empire*, Vol IV, *L'Algérie, de Gaulle et moi* (Paris, 1974); Alain de Sérigny, *Echos d'Alger*, Vol II, *L'Abandon, 1946-1962* (Paris, 1974); Charles-Robert Ageron, *Histoire de l'Algerie contemporaine*, 4th ed (Paris, 1970), pp. 115-116.
4. Carl von Clausewitz, *On War*, Peter Paret and Michael Howard, eds. and trans. (Princeton, 1976), p. 579.
5. Bernard Fall, *Hell in a Very Small Place: The Siege of Dien Bien Phu* (Philadelphia, 1967).
6. C. A. de Cherriere, "Les Débuts de l'insurrection algérienne," *Revue de défense nationale*, 12 (1956): 1457.
7. William B. Quandt, *Revolution and Political Leadership: Algeria, 1954-1968* (Cambridge, Mass., 1969), p. 94; Michael K. Clark, *Algeria in Turmoil: A History of the Rebellion* (New York, 1959), p. 109; Laurent Theis and Philippe Ratte, La Guerre d'Algérie ou le temps des méprises (Paris, 1974), p. 69.
8. The best book on all this is Jean-Jacques Carré, Paul Dubois and Edmond Malinvaud, *La Croissance francaise* (Paris, 1972).
9. Jean Gardt and Claude Roque, *Service militaire pourquoi?* (Paris, 1960), pp. 47-48; *L'Express*, September 17, 1955; "Une Jeunesse en guerre," *Esprit*, 26 (May 1958): pp. 791-797; Pierre Belleville, "La Guerre et la *'gauche'*," *Perspectives socialistes*, 39-40 (August-September 1960), p. 57.
10. Jean Planchais and Jacques Nobecourt, *Histoire politique de l'armée*, Vol II, *De de Gaulle à de Gaulle, 1940-1967* (Paris, 1967), p. 299.
11. Alf Andrew Heggoy, *Insurgency and Counterinsurgency in Algeria* (Bloomington, Ind., 1972), pp. 189-190.
12. Philippe Tripier, *Autopsie de la guerre d'Algérie* (Paris, 1972), p. 73.
13. Marcel Fèvre, *Petite suite algérienne de guerre et chirurgie* (Paris, 1957), pp. 32, 34.
14. Heggoy, *Insurgency*, pp. 107-129.
15. William G. Andrews, *French Politics and Algeria* (New York, 1962), *passim*.
16. Philip M. Williams, *Crisis and Compromise: Politics in the Fourth Republic* (London, 1964), p. 56.
17. John Talbott, *The War Without a Name: France in Algeria, 1954-1962* (New York, 1980), pp. 90-114.
18. An example of this literature is Louis Terrenoire, *De Gaulle et l'Algérie; témoignage pour l'histoire* (Paris, 1964).
19. Alistair Horne, *A Savage War of Peace: Algeria, 1954-1962* (New York, 1978), pp. 330-338; Tripier, *Autopsie*, pp. 314-343.
20. Maurice Challe, *Notre Révolte* (Paris, 1968), pp. 91-114; Yves Courrière, *La Guerre d'Algérie*, Vol III, *L'Heure des colonels* (Paris, 1970), pp. 472-475.
21. Philip M. Williams, "Death of the Fourth Republic: Murder or Suicide?" in *Wars, Plots and Scandals in Postwar France* (Cambridge, 1970), pp. 144-145.
22. Merry and Serge Bromberger, Georgette Elgey, and Jean-François Chauvel, *Barricades et colonels, 24 janvier 1960* (Paris, 1960) remains the most detailed account of the Week of the Barricades.

23. Talbott, *War Without a Name*, pp. 182-215; Jacques Fauvet and Jean Planchais, *La Fronde des généraux* (Paris, 1961).
24. Paul Henissart, *Wolves in the City: The Death of French Algeria* (New York, 1971) is a good book on the OAS.
25. "Les Débuts de la Ve République: L'Opinion en février 1959," *Sondages*, 2 (1959): 10; "La Vie politique de septembre 1960 à mai 1961," *Sondages*, 1 (1961): 12-18.
26. A table reviewing samplings of opinion between July 1957 and December 1959 is printed in *Sondages*, 3 (1960): 45.
27. Charles de Gaulle, *Discours et messages*, Vol III, *Avec le renouveau, 1958-1962*. (Paris, 1970), *passim*.
28. John Talbott, "French Public Opinion and the Algerian War: A Research Note," *French Historical Studies*, 9 (Fall 1975): 361.

David MacIsaac

1. George C. Herring, "The Vietnam Syndrome and American Foreign Policy," *Virginia Quarterly Review*, 57 (Autumn 1981): 605.
2. Stanley Hoffman, *et al*, "Vietnam Reappraised," *International Security*, (Summer 1981): 4-5.
3. David S. Rilling, "Lessons Yet Unlearned," *Armed Forces Journal International*, 118 (July 1981): 68-69.

Edward L. Coffman

1. Louis Morton, "Commentary," in William Geffen, ed, *Command and Commanders in Modern Warfare: Proceedings of the Second Military History Symposium* (U.S. Air Force Academy, Colo., 1969), p. 32.
2. Although several sessions in other symposia stretch the narrow definition of military history, *Science, Technology, and Warfare* (1969), *The Military and Society* (1972), and *The American Military and the Far East* (1980) stand out in that regard.
3. Carl von Clausewitz, *On War* ed. and trans. Michael Howard and Peter Paret (Princeton, N.J., 1976), p. 76. See also Chapter Three of Book Eight, 582ff.
4. The first quotation is from Stefan T. Possony and Etienne Mantoux, "DuPicq and Foch: The French School," in Edward M. Earle, ed, *Makers of Modern Strategy* (Princeton, 1941), p. 210. The second is from Clausewitz, *On War*, p. 86. The third is from Elting E. Morison, *Men, Machines, and Modern Times* (Cambridge, Mass., 1966), p. 76.
5. "Proceedings of the Conference on Military History," in *Annual Report of the American Historical Association for the Year 1912* (Washington D.C., 1914), pp. 159-197.

PARTICIPANTS

JOHN M. BLUM. Professor Blum received his Ph.D. from Harvard in 1950 and is Sterling Professor of History at Yale. He has held three of the highest appointments in American history at British universities: Pitt Professor at Cambridge, Commonwealth Lecturer at University College, London, and Harmsworth Professor at Oxford. Author and editor of numerous books, his works include *The Progressive Presidents: Roosevelt, Wilson, Roosevelt, Johnson; From the Morgenthau Diaries; The Price of Vision: The Diary of Henry Wallace; V Was for Victory: Politics and American Culture During World War II; and The Letters of Theodore Roosevelt.*

PETER BRAESTRUP. Mr. Braestrup is the editor of the *Wilson Quarterly.* He began his professional career as a local news correspondent for the *New Haven Register.* Graduating from Yale in 1951, he served as a Marine officer in Korea. Following his military service, he held positions as a staff writer for *Time,* an investigative reporter for the *New York Herald Tribune,* and as Saigon bureau chief for the *Washington Post.* He is the author of the award winning two-volume work *Big Story: How the American Press and Television Reported and Interpreted the Tet Crisis of 1968 in Vietnam and Washington.*

EDWARD M. COFFMAN. Professor Coffman graduated from the University of Kentucky in 1951 and served as an infantry officer in Japan and Korea in 1952-1953. Following his military service, he returned to Kentucky and took his Ph.D. there in 1959. A Professor of History at the University of Wisconsin- Madison, he was the Distinguished Visiting Professor of History at the United States Air Force Academy during academic year 1982-83. His major publications include *The Hilt of the Sword: The Career of Peyton C. March* and *The War to End All Wars: The American Military Experience in World War I*. He is currently writing a social history of the peacetime American army.

ROBERT D. CUFF. Professor Cuff received his Ph.D. from Princeton in 1966. He has taught at Princeton University, the University of Rochester, and York University in Downsview, Ontario, where he is currently Professor of History. His publications include *The War Industries Board: Business-Government Relations During World War I* and *American Dollars/Canadian Prosperity: Canadian-American Economic Relations, 1945-1950*.

DAVID H. CULBERT. Professor Culbert received his Ph.D. in 1970 from Northwestern University and has taught at Yale and Louisiana State University where he is currently Associate Professor of History. His numerous awards include a fellowship at the Woodrow Wilson International Center for Scholars, Smithsonian Institution. Dr. Culbert's works include *News for Everyman: Radio and Foreign Affairs in Thirties America; Mission to Moscow; Film and Propaganda in America: A Documentary History;* and a 90 minute film documentary entitled *Television's Vietnam*.

WILHELM DEIST. Dr. Deist is a member of the Military History Research Office in Freiburg, Federal Republic of Germany. He studied at the University of Tübingen and received his Ph.D. from the University of Freiburg. He is co-editor of *Militär-Geschichtliche Miteilungen* and the *War and Society Newsletter*. His works include *Militär und Innenpolitik im Weltkrieg* and *The Wehrmacht and German Rearmament*.

DAVID M. KENNEDY. Professor Kennedy received his Ph.D. from Yale University in 1968 and is presently serving as Professor of History and Associate Dean, School of Humanities and Sciences at Stanford University. He has been a Guggenheim Fellow and Pulitzer Prize runner-up for his *Over Here: The First World War and American Society.* His other works include *Birth Control in America: The Career of Margaret Sanger; Social Thought in America and Europe; Readings in Comparative Intellectual History* (co-editor); *The American People in the Age of Kennedy* (editor); *The American People in the Depression* (editor); and *The American Pageant* (co-author).

RICHARD H. KOHN. Dr. Kohn received his Ph.D. from the University of Wisconsin in 1968 and has taught at Wisconsin, The City College of New York, and Rutgers University. Since 1981 Dr. Kohn has served as Chief of the Office of Air Force History, Washington, D. C. Widely known for his studies in civil-military relations, Dr. Kohn is the author *Eagle and Sword: The Federalists and the Creation of the Military Establishment in America, 1783-1802.* His writings on military history and military affairs have also appeared in such leading journals as the *American Historical Review,* the *Journal of American History,* and the *William and Mary Quarterly.*

PAUL A. C. KOISTINEN. Professor Koistinen received his Ph.D. from the University of California at Berkeley in 1964 and is presently Professor of History at California State University, Northridge. He has been the recipient of research fellowships from the American Council of Learned Societies and Harvard's Charles Warren Center for Studies in American History. His works include *The Hammer and the Sword: Labor, the Military, and Industrial Mobilization, 1920-1945* and *The Military-Industrial Complex: A Historical Perspective.*

DAVID MacISAAC. Dr. MacIsaac is currently serving as a Research Associate at the Air War College, Maxwell AFB, Alabama. A retired Air Force lieutenant colonel, Dr. MacIsaac received his Ph.D. from Duke University and has taught at the U.S. Air Force Academy, the Naval War College, and the Air War College. He was a Fellow of the Woodrow Wilson International Center for Scholars at the Smithsonian Institution in 1978-1979. The author of *Strategic Bombing in World War Two: The Story of the United States Strategic Bombing Survey,* he also edited the companion ten-volume work, *The United States Strategic Bombing Survey.* Dr. MacIsaac's writings on military affairs have appeared in the *Naval War College Review,* the *Air University Review,* and *Air Force Magazine.*

ARTHUR MARWICK. Professor Marwick was named first Professor of History at the United Kingdom's Open University when it opened in 1969. He has been Dean of Arts at the Open University since 1978. He studied at Balliol College, Oxford University, and received the Doctor of Letters degree from Edinburgh University. His publications include *The Explosion of British Society, 1914-1962; The Deluge: British Society and the First World War; Britain in the Century of Total War: War, Peace and Social Change, 1900-1967; The Nature of History; The Home Front: The British and the Second World War;* and *War and Social Change in the Twentieth Century: A Comparative Study of Britain, France, Germany, Russia and the United States.*

ALLAN R. MILLETT. Professor Millett received his Ph.D. from The Ohio State University in 1966. He is Professor of History and Mershon Professor and Director, Program in International Security and Military Affairs at Ohio State. A colonel in the Marine Corps Reserve, Dr. Millett has published *The Politics of Intervention: The Military Occupation of Cuba 1906-1909; The General: Robert T. Bullard and Officership in the United States Army, 1881-1925; A Short History of the Vietnam War;* and *Semper Fidelis: The History of the U.S. Marine Corps.*

RICHARD POLENBERG. Professor Polenberg received his Ph.D. in 1964 from Columbia University and is Professor of History at Cornell University. His numerous works include *Reorganizing Roosevelt's Government, 1936-1939; America at War: The Home Front, 1941-1945; War and Society: The United States, 1941-1945; The American Century* (co- author); and *One Nation Divisible: Class, Race, and Ethnicity in the United States Since 1938.*

GUNTHER E. ROTHENBERG. Professor Rothenberg received his Ph.D. in 1958 from the University of Illinois and has taught at Illinois State, Southern Illinois, and the University of New Mexico. He is presently Professor of History at Purdue University. A Guggenheim Fellow in 1962-1963, his numerous works include *The Austrian Military Border in Croatia, 1522-1747; The Army of Francis Joseph; The Art of Warfare in the Age of Napoleon; The Anatomy of the Israeli Army;* and *The Military Border in Croatia, 1740-1881.*

LEILA J. RUPP. Professor Rupp received her Ph.D. from Bryn Mawr College in 1976, taught for a year at the University of Pennsylvania, and has been teaching history and women's studies since 1977 at The Ohio State University where she is Associate Professor of History. Under a two-year research grant from the National Endowment for the Humanities, she is currently engaged in collaborative research with Verda Taylor on the American women's movement in the post-Second World War period. Her works include *Mobilizing Women for War: German and American Propaganda, 1939-1945* and, in conjunction with Barbara Miller Lane, *Nazi Ideology Before 1933: A Documentation*.

DENNIS E. SHOWALTER. Professor Showalter received his Ph.D. from the University of Minnesota in 1969 and is Associate Professor of History at The Colorado College. He is currently a Trustee of the American Military Institute and serves on the Editorial Advisory Board of *Military Affairs*. His books include *Railroads and Rifles: Soldiers, Technology and the Unification of Germany; German Military History Since 1648: A Critical Bibliography;* and *Little Man, What Now? Der Sturmer in the Weimar Republic*.

HARVARD SITKOFF. Professor Sitkoff received his Ph.D. from Columbia University in 1975. He has taught at Queens College and Washington University and is presently serving as Associate Professor of History at the University of New Hampshire. His major publications include *Fifty Years Later: The New Deal Evaluated; A History of Our Time: Readings on Postwar America; The Struggle for Black Equality, 1954-1980;* and a projected three-volume work entitled *A New Deal for Blacks: The Emergence of Civil Rights As A National Issue. The Depression Decade,* the first volume in that series, was published in 1978.

JOHN E. TALBOTT. Professor Talbott received his Ph.D. from Stanford in 1966 and is Professor of History at the University of California, Santa Barbara. He has been a National Endowment for the Humanities Fellow and was a member of the Institute for Advanced Study at Princeton in 1975-1976. Professor Talbott was a visiting professor at Stanford in 1980-1981 and a visiting Professor of Strategy at the Naval War College in 1981-1982. His works include *The Politics of Educational Reform in France* and *The War Without A Name: France in Algeria, 1954-1967*.

DAVID F. TRASK. Dr. Trask is Chief Historian at the United States Army Center of Military History, Washington, D. C. He received his Ph.D. from Harvard in 1958 and has taught at Boston University, Wesleyan, the University of Nebraska, and the State University of New York at Stony Brook. Before assuming his present position in 1981, he was Director of the Office of the Historian, U.S. Department of State. His major works include *The United States and the Supreme War Council: American War Aims and Inter-Allied Strategy, 1917-1918; Captains and Cabinets: Anglo-American Naval Relations, 1917-1918;* and *The War With Spain in 1898.* Dr. Trask also edited *World War I at Home: Readings on American Life, 1914-1920.*

RUSSELL F. WEIGLEY. Professor Weigley received his Ph.D. from the University of Pennsylvania in 1956. He is Professor of History at Temple University and has taught at the University of Pennsylvania, Drexel Institute of Technology, Dartmouth College, and the Army War College. He has been a Guggenheim Fellow and also has served as President of the American Military Institute. His many works include *Quartermaster General of the Union Army: A Biography of M. C. Meigs; Towards An American Army: Military Thought from Washington to Marshall; History of the United States Army; The American Way of War: A History of United States Military Strategies and Policy;* and *Eisenhower's Lieutenants: The Campaigns of France and Germany, 1944-1945.*

ALLAN M. WINKLER. Professor Winkler received his Ph.D. from Yale in 1974 and is Associate Professor of History at the University of Oregon. He has been a Bicentennial Professor of American Studies at Helsinki University, Finland, and a Mellon Fellow at the Aspen Institute for Humanistic Studies. Professor Winkler's major works include *The Politics of Propaganda: The Office of War Information, 1942-1945*. He is currently completing a new book on the history of the United States since World War II.

INDEX

A Shau Valley: 208
Abrams, Philip: 133, 134
Abrahamson, Col. James: 77
Addison, Paul: 140
Addison Housing Act: 134
Adriatic: 47
Advisory War Council: 103
Afghanistan: 30
Afro-American and the Second World War, The: 131
Agincourt: 33
Agram: 65
Air Force, German: 86
  and rearmament: 88-89
Air Force Academy: 81
  Department of History: 202, 202n
Air warfare
  bombing: 75, 140-141, 158, 163, 164, 198, 199, 206
  and military planning: 21, 76
  and popular thinking: 75, 76
Air University Review: 207
Albania: 66
Algeria
  "is France": 187, 192
  French settlers in: 187, 191, 192, 194, 195
  peace negotiations: 191, 193, 194
  representation in Parliament: 191, 203
  war for independence: 185, 187, 188, 189, 190, 191, 191-192, 192-193, 195, 202, 204, 219
Algerian lobby: 191
Algiers, Battle of: 191-192
Alcibiades: 203
All Saints Day rising: 187, 191
Allied Maritime Transport Council: 50
Allport, Gordon: 10
  quoted: 7
Alsace-Lorraine: 27, 41
Aluminum: 93, 97

America Arms for a New Century: 77
America at War: 170
American Council on Race Relations: 150
American Expeditionary Force: 50.
  See also Army, U.S.
American Federation of Labor (AF of L): 74, 172
American Historical Association: 221
American Revolution: 127, 204
American Revolution Considered as a Social and Economic Movement, The: 127
American Society in Wartime: 172
American Soldier, The: 179
Americanism, 100 percent: 52
Anderson, Karen: 160, 174
Andreski, Stanislav: 132
Anglo-German rivalries: 24, 37-38, 39, 41, 42
Anti-war sentiment: 19-20, 20, 21, 22, 167-168, 190, 198, 199, 200, 203
Armed Forces, British
  professionalism in: 29
  war plans: 29
Armed Forces, French
  strategy and tactics in Algeria: 188, 190, 191-192, 192-193, 195
Armed Forces, German
  High Command: 57, 86
  and para-military organizations: 84, 85
  and political support: 84, 85-86
  professionalism in: 29
  and public opinion and support: 71, 84, 85, 86, 87, 88
  and rearmament: 84-85, 88-90
  War Economic Staff: 83, 88
  during Weimar Republic: 84-85
  World War I and civilian authority: 59
  World War II
    shortages: 83
    use of rape: 163-164
Armed Forces, Japanese: 163-164

265

Armed Forces, South Vietnamese:
   197, 199, 208-209
Armed Forces, U.S.
   Blacks in: 11, 147, 149
   Joint Chiefs of Staff: 199
   and labor: 11-12
   morale: 7-8
   post-WW II occupation duty: 168
   and race riots: 11
   Rapid Deployment Joint Task
      Force: 203
   in Vietnam: 197, 198, 199, 203,
      206, 211
Armistice: 54, 65, 66
Army, Austro-Hungarian: 58, 61, 63
   28th Infantry: 60
   allegiance of: 65-66
   and Charles I: 62
   and civilian authority: 59-60, 229
      (n-16, n-21)
   High Command: 57, 59-60, 62, 63
   and labor strikes: 63
   mutinies in: 63-64
   nationalities in: 58, 60
   returned POWs: 64
   shortages in: 61, 62, 63
   in the Ukraine: 63
Army, British: 27, 41, 43-44, 65,
      65-66
   attitudes and morale: 44
   in Borneo: 210, 211
   continental strategy: 44
   and the French Army: 44-45, 228
      n-73
   General Staff: 44-45
   Imperial commitments: 42-43, 44
   in Malaya: 210, 211
   modernization: 44
   organization: 42, 43, 44
   Territorial Force: 43
   training: 44
   war plans: 44
Army, French: 29, 65, 65-66
   10th Parachute Division: 191
   in Algeria: 187, 188-189, 190
   and the British Army: 44-45, 228
      n-73
   in Indochina: 188-189, 189-190
   and NATO obligations: 189
   and the "Putsch": 193-194
   training: 189
Army, German
   and Austria (1938): 88
   High Command: 83
   pre-WW I expansion: 35-36
   professionalism in: 36
   and the Rhineland: 86
   as a symbol: 27
   training: 34
   World War I: 57, 60, 61, 63, 65
   war plans: 29, 32-33, 36
Army, Hungarian: 58
Army, Indian: 44
Army, Indonesian: 211
Army, Italian: 60, 61, 63, 65-66
Army, North Vietnamese: 191, 197,
      198
Army, Prussian: 29. *See also* Army,
      German
Army, Russian: 60, 61, 62
Army, Soviet: 164
Army, U.S.
   1st Air Cavalry Division: 208
   Blacks in: 11, 176-177
   information films: 123
   and rape: 164
   and social change: 11, 178
   World War I: 49, 50
   World War II economic mobiliza-
      tion: 93, 95, 97, 104, 105,
      107
Army Air Corps: 11, 75, 158
Army-Navy Munitions Board
   (ANMB): 95, 97, 104, 105
Arnold-Forster, H. O.: 43
Atlantic Charter: 6
Atlantic Ocean: 38
Atomic bomb: 164-165
Attlee, Clement: 143
Attorney General, California: 9
Attorney General, U.S.: 10

Attu: 7
Ausgleich, 1867: 58, 59, 62, 63, 64
Austria: 37, 41, 57, 58, 59
   Charles I renunciation of authority over: 66
   civilian morale: 61
   and federalism: 65
   food production: 62
   and Germany (1938): 86
   Reichsrat: 57, 59, 62, 64
   See also Austria-Hungary
Austria-Hungary: 24, 48
   Army. *See* Army, Austro-Hungarian
   civilian morale: 57, 61
   disintegration of: 65-66, 69
   dissenters in: 60
   dualism in: 57-58
   endurance of: 66
   federalism in: 64
   industrial production: 58, 60
   joint budget of: 57, 58
   joint ministries of: 57
   martial law in: 60
   military conscription: 58, 59
   nationalism in: 57, 58, 59, 60-61, 62, 63-65
   parliaments of: 57, 58, 59
   peace negotiations: 62, 63, 65
   revolution in: 57, 59
   Socialists in: 61, 63
   society: 68-69, 221
   strikes in: 58, 59, 63
   war emergency powers: 59, 60
   World War I and empire cohesion: 59, 61, 63, 65-66, 68-69, 217
   See also Dual Monarchy; Habsburg Empire
Austro-Hungarian food commission: 62
Auxiliary Fire Service: 141

B-52s: 206
Badeni, Count Kasimir, quoted: 58
Baker, Newton D.: 73
   quoted: 52

Baruch, Bernard M.: 49, 51, 71, 97, 115, 115-116
   See also War Industries Board
Bastogne: 177
Batt, William: 120, 120n
Battle of Dorking, The: 27
Beirut: 207-208, 209
Belgium: 139
   refugees from in Britain: 142
Berle, Adolf: 174
Berlin: 60, 63, 83, 167
Berlin, Isaiah: 7, 10, 11–12
   quoted: 6, 6-7, 10, 11
Bernard, Philippe: 130
Bernstein, Barton: 112
Bethmann Hollweg, Theobald von: 25, 31, 33, 35
Beveridge Report: 143-144, 145, 171
Bezukhov, Pierre: 24
Big Story: 204
Big Ten: 5
Birmingham, Ala.: 152
Birth rate and population control: 161, 162, 163, 166, 219
Bismarck, Otto von: 27, 28, 33, 42
Black press: 147, 148, 149, 150, 151, 153
   See also News media
Blacks
   gains from war: 154-155, 170, 174, 178
   and the military: 178
      Philippine Insurrection: 176
      Vietnam War: 132
      World War I: 127, 176-177
      World War II: 11-12, 177, 178
   and trade unions: 11, 172
   World War II
      isolationist and pro-Axis attitudes: 147, 148-149
      militancy: 10-11, 147-150, 151, 218
      race relations: 10-11, 14, 147, 148-149, 150-151, 172, 174
      and racial reforms: 154-155, 170, 176, 218

in the work force: 11, 147, 149, 159, 172, 174
    See also Civil Rights movement; Education
Blaisdell, Thomas C., Jr.: 96
Bloch, I.S.: 34
Blockade: 145
Blomberg, Werner von: 88, 89
Blum, John Morton: 1, 69, 113, 127, 148
    Harmon Memorial Lecture: 5-15
    quoted: 91
Boer War: 41, 43, 44, 204
Bohemia: 27, 34, 60, 63, 64
    See also Czeckoslovakia
Bolfras, General: 60
Bolsheviks: 63
Borneo: 210, 211
Boston: 221
Bourgès-Maunoury, Maurice: 192
Braestrup, Peter: 195–196, 203, 204, 210, 219-220, 221
    discussion and comments: 206-207, 207-208, 208-209, 210, 211
    paper: 197-200
    quoted: 204
Brest Litovsk: 63
British Expeditionary Forces (BEF): 29, 44-45, 228 n-73
    See also Army, British
Brno: 60
Brodie, Bernard: 20
Brodrick, St. John: 43
Brooks, John: 148
    on the MOWM: 152
Brotherhood of Sleeping Car Porters: 151
Brown v. Board of Education (Supreme Court, 1954): 147
Brunn: 60
Brusilov offensive: 61, 62
Buchanan, A. Russell: 148
Buchanan, Robert: 73
Budapest: 64, 65
Buenos Aires: 37

Bukovina: 60
Bülow, Count Bernhard von: 31
Burnham, James: 116
Burns, James MacGregor: 174
Burns, John H.: 7
Bureau of Labor Statistics: 98
Bureau of the Budget: 98, 116
Business Advisory Council: 119
Byelorussians: 128
Byrnes, James F.: 95, 98, 99-100, 106, 109
    as Director of Economic Stabilization: 97
    relationship with Franklin Roosevelt: 99

CIO. *See* Congress of Industrial Organizations
CMP. *See* Controlled Materials Plan
CORE. *See* Congress on Racial Equality
CPI. *See* Committee on Public Information
Calder, Angus: 140
California: 9-10
Canada: 43
    industrial production: 102, 236-237n-11
Capitalism: 28, 32, 92
Caporetto: 63
Caribbean: 38
Carnegie Endowment for International Peace
    World War I studies: 128
Carpathian Mountains: 61
Carrington, C.E.: 179
Carsten, F.L.: 84, 84n
Carthage: 24
Casualty rates: 34, 61
Cataline Broadcasting System: 186
Cattaro: 63
Censorship: 48, 71, 146, 207, 208-209
Central Africa: 43
Central Office of Information: 144

Central Powers: 57, 60, 61, 63, 64, 65
Chafe, William: 159, 165
Challe, Gen. Maurice
  and the 1959 offensive: 193
  and the 1961 "Putsch": 194
Challe Plan: 193
Chamber of Commerce: 120
Chan, Charlie: 8
Charles I, of Austria-Hungary: 61-62, 62-63, 64, 66
Chesney, Sir George: 27
Chester, D.N.: 143
Chicago: 153
Chicago Defender: 149, 151
Chicago, University of, Sociology Dept.: 172
Chicanos: 10
China: 14, 43, 164, 206, 207, 210
China-Burma-India Theater: 7
Chinese: 8
Churchill, Winston: 5
Civil Rights League: 152
Civil Rights Movement
  Tactics: 11, 148, 152, 153-154
  World War II
  civil disobedience: 153
  moderation and delay: 11, 148, 149, 150, 150-152, 171, 175, 176, 218
  and racial reforms: 11, 154-155
  See also Blacks
Civil War, U.S.: 27, 109
Civilian morale and durability: 8, 19, 20, 21, 24, 57, 61, 133-134, 141-142, 143, 144, 179-180
  See also Public opinion and support
Clarke, I.F.: 76
Class structure: 1, 5, 11-14, 26, 27, 30, 32, 35, 39, 40, 91, 94, 134, 138, 143, 144, 145, 158, 171, 174, 218
Clausewitz, Carl von: 27, 187, 188, 217, 219, 220
Cleveland: 152

Coal: 13
Coffman, Edward M.: 1, 215
  summary paper: 216-222
Cognitive dissonance: 25-26, 45, 67-68, 73, 216-217
Cole, G.D.H.: 135
Cole, Ron, discussion and comments: 73, 73-74, 74
Collective security: 20
Colons. *See* Algeria, French settlers in
Colse, David H.: 137
Combined Chiefs of Staff: 105, 106
Combined Production and Resources Board: 105, 106
Combined Raw Materials Board: 105
Commerce Department: 50
Committee on Public Information (CPI): 51, 52-53, 55, 70
Common enemy: 1, 5, 6, 7-8, 14
Communism and communists: 12, 14, 39, 74, 149, 153
Comparative Approach to American History: 69
Compromise of 1907: 64
Concentration camps: 14, 163
  See also Internment
Confiscation of property: 127
Congress, U.S.: 12, 13, 48, 98, 198, 203
  and economic mobilization: 50, 96, 100-101, 104, 106, 108, 113
  House: 100, 203
  Senate: 96, 100
Congress of Industrial Organizations (CIO): 13-14, 153, 172, 174
Congress of Vienna: 42
Congress on Racial Equality (CORE): 11, 148, 151, 153, 154
Conrad von Hötzendorf, Gen. Franz: 59, 60, 62
  quoted: 58
Conscription, labor: 158-159

269

Conscription, military: 12, 13, 29, 43, 48-49, 51-52, 53, 58, 59, 135, 137, 149, 158, 178, 190
Conservative Party: 39, 134
Conspiracy law: 9
Controlled Materials Plan (CMP): 97
Copper: 97
Coudenhove, Count: 60
Council of Economic Development: 119
Council of National Defense: 49, 103
Cracow: 65
Cramb, J.A.: 27-28
Creel, George: 51, 52, 73
  See also Committee on Public Information
Crimean War: 27, 39
Cripps, Thomas: 174
Crisis: 150
Crisis management: 28, 30
Croatia: 60
Croats: 58, 60
Cronkite, Walter: 198, 209
Crowder, Gen. Enoch H.: 52
Crowe, Sir Eyre: 42
Crown Council (German), 1912: 31-32, 37
Cuban Missile Crisis: 185, 202
Cuff, Robert D.: 110
  commentary: 111-118
Culbert, David H.: 123, 220
Czech Crisis, 1938: 87
Czech National Council: 61, 65
Czechs, in Austria-Hungary: 58, 60-61, 63, 64-65
Czechoslovakia: 57, 64
  See also Bohemia

D-Day: 220
Dahlerus, Birger: 83
Dalfiume, Richard: 147, 148, 149, 151, 152
Dalmatia: 62
Dawson, W.H., quoted: 138
Darwin, Charles: 27
Darwinism: 27-28, 86-87

de Gaulle, Gen. Charles: 188
  and Algeria: 187, 193, 194-195
  and the Army: 193-194, 195
  and public opinion: 193, 194, 195, 209, 219, 221
Defense Department: 173
Deist, Wilhelm: 71, 82, 112, 113, 118, 217
  paper: 83-90
Demilitarized zone (DMZ), Vietnam: 206
Democratic Party: 13, 14, 54, 108, 112, 198, 200
Denmark: 145
Department of Scientific and Industrial Research: 135
Detroit: 10, 11, 150, 152, 160, 161
Deutsche Volkspartei: 85
Dewey, Thomas E.: 14
DeWitt, Gen. John L.: 9-10
  quoted: 10
Dien Bien Phu: 188, 189, 198
Diplomacy: 28
Disarmament conference, Geneva, 1933: 86
Disney, Walt: 123
Dissenters, treatment of: 6, 7, 14, 48, 60, 86, 127
Draft. See Conscription, military
Dual Monarchy: 57-58, 59, 61, 62
  dissolution of: 65, 66
  See also Austria-Hungary; Habsburg Empire
Durham conference, 1942: 147, 151

Eberstadt, Ferdinand: 95, 97, 115
Economic Development, Council of: 119
Economic history: 81-82
Economic mobilization. See Mobilization, economic; specific country
Economic Stabilization Act, 1942: 98, 101
Economist, on the Blitz and population dislocation: 141

Education: 128, 134, 145, 147, 153
Edwardians, The: 130
Emergency Hospital Scheme: 141
Employment and social change: 132
Ethiopian Pacific Movement: 149
Ethnic rivalries. *See* Prejudice
Eugenics policies: 161, 162, 219
Europe Since 1870: 138
Executive Office of the President: 116

FLN. *See Front de libération nationale*
Facts and Figures, Office of: 6
Fair Employment Practices Commission (FEPC): 11, 153
Falkenhayn, Erich von: 36
Falkland Islands War: 207
Far East: 38, 43
Fatalism: 30, 34-35
Fawcett, Millicent Garrett: 138
Federal Republic of Germany: 160, 168
 See also Germany
Feldman, Gerald D.: 130-131
Feminine Mystique, The: 142
Ferro, Marc: 130
Fifth Republic. *See* de Gaulle, Gen. Charles; France
Fin d'un Monde 1914-1929, La: 130
Finance: 2
 and German rearmament: 84, 88-89, 89-90
 and U.S. economic mobilization: 94, 95, 98, 99, 103, 113
Finkle, Lee: 148, 149
Fischer, Fritz: 31, 36
Fisher, Adm. Sir John: 29
Fisher Education Act: 134
Flanders: 47
Flavinius, Marcus: 185
 on limited war: 186
Food Administration: 49, 50, 51, 53
 See also Hoover, Herbert
Food shortages and rationing: 12, 50-51, 53, 61, 62-63, 71, 72, 99
Forrestal, James V.: 95, 104, 105

 See also Navy Department
Forster, E.M.: 220, 221
Fortune: 12
Four Freedoms: 7
Fourteen Points: 63, 65
Fourth Republic. *See* France
France: 34, 36, 38, 40, 41, 42, 43, 44, 45, 69, 87, 146
 Algerian policy: 187, 187-188, 189, 191-192, 193, 194-195, 203, 219
 Algerian representation in Parliament: 191, 203
 Alsace-Lorraine: 27
 August decisions: 190
 censorship: 209
 Fifth Republic
 and Algeria: 192-195
 and the armed forces: 193-194
 Fourth Republic
 and Algeria: 187-192, 193, 195
 and the armed forces: 191-192
 franchise expansion: 139
 Germanophobia in: 41-42
 Indochina experience
 and Algeria: 188-189, 189-190
 and the U.S. in Vietnam: 203
 labor movement: 139
 military as a cohesive force: 178
 National Assembly: 187, 189
 public opinion and support: 188, 191-192, 193, 194, 195, 221
 Revolution: 26, 127
 World War I
 and break-up of Austria-Hungary: 64-65
 and peace efforts: 62
 and society: 127, 130, 139
 and women: 139
 World War II
 and society: 14, 145
 and women: 163
 See also Armed Forces, French; Army, French
Franchise, expansion of: 137-138, 139, 145, 146

271

Franco-Prussian War: 29
Francis Joseph I, of Austria-Hungary: 59, 60, 63, 217
  death of: 61
French Revolution: 26, 127
Friedan, Betty: 142, 166
Friedrich, Archduke of Austria: 59
Front de libération nationale (FLN): 188, 189, 190, 191, 192, 193, 194, 195
Fu Man Chu: 8
Fuel: 61, 99
Fussel, Paul: 139
Future Outlook League: 152

Galicia: 60, 62
Gallup poll: 166
Gandhism: 154
Garfinkel, Herbert: 152
Garveyism: 147
Gasser, Adolf: 31
Gaullists: 192
Geiss, Immanuel: 31
General Electric Co.: 97
Geneva: 86
George V, of England: 24
German Democratic Republic: 160, 168
  See also Germany
German-Americans: 10
Germans, in propaganda: 8, 9, 52
Germany: 5, 6, 24, 43, 145
  and Austria (1938): 86
  industrial production: 102, 236-237n-11
  liability of Nazi officials: 9
  pre-WW I
    class structure: 35-36
    foreign policy: 26, 27, 31, 32, 33-34, 35, 36, 37, 42, 45
    martial spirit: 26-27, 67
    naval challenge: 38
    relations with the U.K.: 39, 41
    society: 40, 67, 69, 220
  post-WW II occupation: 168
  racial policies: 14, 158, 161, 163
  rearmament: 113
    and the economy: 84, 88, 89-90
    and foreign policy: 87
    and public opinion: 84-87
    Rhineland (1936): 86
    science and technology: 75
    Second Armaments Program: 88
  World War I
    ambivalence toward: 25, 67, 68
    mobilization: 83-84, 85, 130-131, 216, 217
    and society: 130-131, 139
    revolution: 57
  World War II
    economic mobilization: 83-84, 84-85, 88-90, 112, 113, 158, 217
    impact on women: 157, 158, 159, 160, 161, 162, 163-164, 165-166, 166-167, 168, 219
    industrial mobilization and military needs: 81, 83-84, 102
    public opinion and propaganda: 83, 84, 85-88, 90, 161, 162, 165-166
    See also Armed Forces, German; Army, German; National Socialists
Germany and England: 28
G.I. Bill of Rights: 128
Glorious Revolution: 39
Goebbels, Josef: 86, 87
Goering, Reichsmarschall Hermann: 86, 89
Goldsmith, Raymond W.: 102
Goldwater, Barry: 210
Göttingen University: 75
Graham, Otis: 116
Granger, Lester, on race and riots: 150
Great Britain. See United Kingdom
Great Depression: 84, 88, 109, 110, 152, 154
Great Society: 199
Great War. See World War I

272

Great War in Modern Memory, The: 139
Greenland: 7
Greensboro, N.C.: 152
Greenwald, Maurine: 157
Grey, Sir Edward: 25, 39
Guantanamo Bay, naval base: 185
Guerre future, La: 34
Guerrilla warfare: 128, 189, 190, 191, 192, 193
Guilmartin, Lt.Col. Joe, discussion and comments: 207
Guilt by association in law: 9
Gurkhas: 211

Habsburg Empire: 37, 58, 60, 62
  break-up of: 61, 63, 65
  and public support: 60-61
  See also Austria-Hungary; Dual Monarchy
Haldane reforms: 43, 45
Hallion, Dick, discussion and comments: 74-75, 179
Hanle, Paul: 75
Hanoi: 197, 199, 200
Hardach, Gerd H.: 130
Harding, Warren G., on WWI war resolution: 48
Harlem: 10, 150
Harlem Renaissance: 147
Harmon Memorial Lecture, 25th: 1, 5-15
Harrier: 76
Harris, Josie: 140
Harrison, Tom: 143
Harrison and Bachelor, British cartoonists: 144
Harvard University: 5
Haslam, W.H., quoted: 143-144
Hawaii: 10
Henderson, Arthur: 136
Henderson, Leon: 94, 95, 106
  See also Office of Price Administration
Herring, George, on Vietnam: 204
Henry V, of England: 33

Higham, Robin, discussion and comments: 75, 179-180, 208
Hillman, Sidney: 13-14, 94
  See also Congress of Industrial Organizations
Himmler, Reichsführer Heinrich: 87
Hirabeyashi: 10
Hiroshima: 163
Historian, The: 148
Historians:
  as reflectors of society: 171-172
  and war and social change: 172-175
History, military, *See* Military history
Hitler, Adolf: 6, 14, 31, 83, 85, 142, 158
  and propaganda: 85-88
  and rearmament: 85-86, 88-90
  quoted: 85, 86, 87, 90
Hitler-Stalin pact: 149, 150
Ho Chi Minh: 24
Ho Chi Minh Trail: 206
Hofstadter, Richard: 54
Hohenzollern Empire: 57
  See also Germany
Holder, van, Belgian artist: 139
Hollywood: 205
"Hollywood Goes To War": 220
Holocaust: 156
Holstein, Friedrich von: 31
Home Rule, Ireland: 39
Hoover, Herbert: 49, 119
  on legal coercion: 50-51
  See also Food Administration
Hopkins, Harry: 95, 106
Hossbach Conference: 31
Hötzendorf, Baron von. *See* Conrad von Hötzendorf, Gen. Franz
House Select Committee Investigating National Defense Migration. *See* Tolan Committee
Housing: 10, 12, 134, 144
Housing Act of 1946: 144
Housing Act of 1949: 144
Houston, Sam: 202
Howard, Anthony: 140
Howard University: 154

Hue: 197
Hungary: 57, 58, 59
  acceptance of the Fourteen Points: 65
  and Charles I: 61, 64
  civilian morale: 61
  federalism: 65
  food production: 62
  WW I government: 59, 60, 64
  independence: 63, 64
  parliament: 57, 59, 62, 64
  See also Austria-Hungary; Magyars
Hurley, Brig. Gen. Alfred F.: 202n
Hurley, Edward N.: 50

IMP. See Industrial Mobilization Plan
IWW. See International Workers of the World
Ickes, Harold: 13
Imperial Chemical Industries: 130
Imperialism: 27
India: 44
Indochina War: 191, 203, 204
  and Algeria: 188-189, 189-190
  and Korea: 207
  and Vietnam: 203, 207
Industrial Mobilization Plan (IMP): 103, 104, 107, 114, 116
Industrial production, WW II belligerents: 102, 236-237n-11
Industrial revolution: 19, 26, 39
Industry Advisory Committees: 93
Information offices. See Central Office of Information; Committee on Public Information; Office of Facts and Figures; Office of War Information
International conflict, peaceful resolution of: 20, 22
International Workers of the World (IWW): 73, 74
Internment: 9-10, 14, 142, 156–157
Invasion of 1910, The: 27
Iranian hostage crisis: 208
Ireland: 39, 40

Irish Rebellion: 204
Isolationism: 47, 48, 147, 149
Isonzo River: 61
Israel: 208
Istria: 62
Italian-Americans: 10
Italy: 6, 7, 14, 27, 60, 62, 64-65, 65-66, 69, 177
  See also Army, Italian
Ivy League: 5
Iwo Jima: 7

JCS. See Joint Chiefs of Staff
Jamison, J. Franklin: 127
Japan: 5, 6, 14, 38, 43
  industrial production: 102, 236-237n-11
  impact of the atomic bomb: 163-164
  post-WW I occupation: 168
  World War II impact on women: 157, 158, 159, 160, 161, 163, 164-165, 166, 168, 175, 219
Japanese, in propaganda: 8, 9
Japanese-Americans, treatment of in WW II: 9-10, 156-157
Jews, European: 8, 14, 142, 157, 158, 163
Jim Crow: 151, 153
Johnson, Andrew: 174
Johnson, Lyndon B.
  and the Great Society: 199
  and Vietnam: 198, 198-199, 199-200, 204, 206, 210, 219-220, 221
Johnson Administration: 206
Joint Army Navy Board (Joint Board): 104
Joint Chiefs of Staff (JCS): 199
  and WW II economic mobilization: 105, 106
Joll, James, quoted: 138
Jonghe, Count de: 139
Jordan, Robert O.: 149

Journalism. *See* Black press; News media; Press; Radio; Television; Wire services
July Crisis: 45
Junker: 30
Justice Department: 10

Kaiser: The Beast of Berlin, The: 52
Kalahari Desert: 30
Karman, Theodore von: 75
Karolyi, Count Mihaly: 64
Kellogg, Peter: 148
Kennedy, David M.: 46, 68, 69, 74, 77, 176, 217, 218, 220-221
  discussion and comments: 71, 72, 73, 75
  paper: 47-55
Kennedy, John F.: 210
Kennedy, Robert F.: 198, 200
Keynesianism: 110
Khe Sanh: 197, 198
King, Martin Luther, Jr.: 154
Kinsey, Robert, discussion and comments: 178, 207
Kipling, Rudyard: 43
Klein, Felix: 75
Knox, Frank: 104, 105
  See also Navy Department
Kohn, Richard H.: 170
  discussion and comments: 176, 177, 178, 179
  introductions: 128-129, 146, 155, 169
  remarks: 127-128, 181
Koistinen, Paul A.C.: 90, 111, 112, 113, 114, 115, 116, 117, 118, 119, 217-218, 220, 221
  discussion and comments: 119-120
  paper: 91-110
Kolko, Gabriel: 111
Konody, P.G.: 138
  quoted: 139
Korean War: 202, 203, 204, 206, 207
Kotor: 63
Kramar, Czech politician: 60, 63

Krohne, Rudolf, quoted: 85
Kuomintang: 14
Ky, Col. Nguyen Cao: 203

La guerre future: 34
Labor
  in Austria-Hungary: 58, 59, 23
  in France: 139
  gain from war: 132, 136-137, 145, 170
  in Germany: 88, 128, 158
  unemployment insurance: 135
  unions: 11, 12-14, 39, 136, 144, 172
  in the United Kingdom
    World War I: 130, 135, 136-137, 145
    World War II: 133, 142, 145
  in the United States
    discrimination in the work force: 11, 147, 157, 159, 160, 174
    World War I: 74
    World War II: 11, 12, 92, 94, 96, 98, 99-100, 107, 112, 117, 149, 232-233n-4
  wartime strikes: 12, 13, 40, 59, 63, 135, 142, 149
  women and wartime employment: 157-160
  See also Working class
Labour Party: 14, 130, 134, 135-136, 207
La Follette, Robert, quoted: 49
La Guardia, Fiorello: 150
Laibach: 65
laissez-faire: 40, 54
Lamachus: 203
Landwehr, Gen. Ottokar: 62
Langer, William: 68
Laos: 208-209
Law, Anglo-American and European practise: 9
L'Express: 191
Le Monde: 191
Le Quex, William: 27
Leukemia: 165

Lever Act, 1917: 49
Lewis, John L.: 13
Liberal Party: 134
Life: 220
Lindblom, Charles: 115
Lingeman, Richard: 148
Lippman, Walter, quoted: 6
Long, Breckenridge: 171
Lord Chancellor: 9
Lorraine. *See* Alsace-Lorraine
Los Angeles: 10
Louis XIV, of France: 40
Loyalty Leagues: 52
Lubin, Isador: 106
Ljubljana: 65
Luftwaffe. *See* Air Force, German
Lusitania: 48

MOWM. *See* March on Washington Movement
Macartney, C.A.: 61
MacIsaac, Charlotte: 203
MacIssac, David: 200-201, 202n
 commentary: 202-205
 discussion and comments: 209
MacLeish, Archibald: 6
Madison Avenue: 6
MAGIC: 14
Magnesium: 93
Magyars: 57, 58, 60, 61, 64-65
Maier, Charles S.: 130
Malaya: 210, 211
Malaysia: 210
Malcolm X: 153
Malta: 131
Manchester, England: 37
Mann, Golo: 32-33
March on Washington Movement (MOWM): 147, 148, 151, 152-153
Marine Corps, U.S.: 7, 197
Marshall, Gen. George C.
 and integration of the armed forces: 11
 and labor leaders: 12

Martial spirit and militarism: 26-28, 29-30, 31, 33, 37, 67, 83, 85, 86, 87-88, 90, 220
Marseilles: 190
Marshall, S.L.A.: 34
Marwick, Arthur: 128-129, 146, 170, 171, 175, 218, 221
 discussion and comments: 72, 177-178
 paper: 130-146
Marxists and World War I history: 130
Masada: 186
Masaryk, Thomas: 61, 65
Mass Observation documents
 East End Blitz, Sept. 1940: 141
 Mood of Britain, 1939 and 1944: 143
 Changes of Outlook During the War: 143
Mass Observation national panel: 143
Mathews, R.C.O.: 133
Mauldin, Bill, quoted: 7
May, Ernest, quoted: 204
Mayer, Arno: 26, 27, 69
McAdoo, William Gibbs: 50
McCarthy, Eugene: 200
McCormick, Anne O'Hare, quoted: 156
McKibbin, Ross: 130, 135-136, 137
McLaine, Ian: 144
Medical services: 141
Medicine and medical research: 135
Medical Research Committee: 135
Medical Research Council: 135
Meier, August, quoted: 153-154
Mendès-France, Pierre: 187, 188, 189, 190
Metro-Goldwyn-Mayer: 174
Mexican-Americans. *See* Chicanos
Micawber, Wilkins: 37
Michigan, governor of: 11
Middle class: 26, 30, 138, 139, 141
Middlemas, Keith: 130
Milch, Erhard: 88-89
Militär und Innenpolitik: 71

Military and society: 26, 35-36, 132, 133, 177-178, 179
Military historians: 216
Military history: 2, 81-82, 221-222
Military Organisation and Society: 132
Military Participation Ratio (MPR): 132, 133
Millet, Allan R.: 202
  discussion and comments: 206, 207, 209, 210, 211
  introductions: 186, 195-196, 200-201
  remarks: 185-186
Millis, Walter: 2
Mindanao: 176
Ministry of Information: 144
Ministry of Morale: 144
Mississippi: 11
Mr. Roberts: 7-8
Mitchell, Lt.Col. Vance, discussion and comments: 177
Mitterrand, Francois: 187
Miura, Kazue: 164-165
Miura, Maki: 165
Mobile, Ala.: 10
Mobilization, agricultural: 49, 50-51, 53, 62-63
  See also Food shortages and rationing
Mobilization, economic: 2, 217, 217-218
  and inflation: 131
  and limited was: 189, 191
  and military needs: 81, 83-84
  necessitarian conditions: 91
  See also Finance; Labor; specific country
Mobilization, military: 2, 45, 48, 49, 51-52, 58, 59, 68, 189-190, 199, 216-217, 220-221
  See also specific country; specific armed forces
Mobilization, psychological. See Public opinion and support

Modern War: Paintings by C.R.W. Nevinson (1917): 138
MOGUL, operation: 63
Moltke, Gen. Helmuth J.L. von: 31, 36-37
Mollet, Guy: 191
Mommsen, Wolfgang: 34
Montgomery, Ala.: 147, 154
Moravia: 60, 62, 64
Morgenthau, Henry, Jr.: 98
Morice, André: 192
Morice Line: 192, 193
Morison, Elting E.: 220
Morocco: 164, 188
Moroccan Crisis, 1905: 31
Morton, Louis: 221
  on military historians: 216
Muller, Hermann: 84
Munich: 71
Munich Crisis, 1938: 87
Munitions: 32, 83, 93, 94, 95, 101, 102-103, 107, 112, 237
Munitions Assignment Board: 105, 106
Munitions Ministry: 115
Murray Committee: 100, 101, 103
Muste, A.J.: 154

NAACP. See National Association for the Advancement of Colored People
NDAC. See National Defense Advisory Commission
NNC. See National Negro Congress
NRA. See National Recovery Administration
NSC. See National Security Council
NSRB. See National Security Resources Board
NUL. See National Urban League
Nagasaki: 163
Naples: 7
Napoleon III, of France: 28, 42
Napoleonic Wars: 22
Nathan, Robert R.: 96
Nation state, rise of: 19

National Advisory Committee for
Aeronautics: 75
National Association for the Advancement of Colored People
(NAACP): 11, 147, 152, 153
National Association of Intergroup
Relations Officials: 150
National Association of Manufacturers: 120
National Civic Federation: 119
National Defense, Council of: 49
National Defense Advisory Commission (NDAC): 93, 94, 109
National Health Service: 141
National Insurance Act, 1911: 135
National Liberation Front. *See Front
de libération nationale* (FLN)
National Negro Congress (NNC):
152, 153
National Physical Laboratory: 75, 135
National Planning Association: 119
National Recovery Administration
(NRA): 109, 110, 116
National Security Act, 1947: 112-113
National Security Council: 113
National Security Resources Board
(NSRB): 112-113, 113
National Service. *See* Conscription,
military
National Socialists
assume power: 85
eugenics policies: 161, 162
and Nuremberg trials: 9
use of propaganda: 85-88, 161,
162, 165-166
and rearmament: 85-86, 88-90
See also Germany
National unity: 68, 69, 70
See also Public opinion and support; War, as a cohesive force
National Urban League: 152, 153
Nationalism: 28, 30, 39, 57, 58, 59,
60-61, 62, 63-64, 65, 220
See also Front de libération nationale (FLN)

Native Sons and Daughters of the
Golden West: 9
Naval race, pre-WWI: 38
Navy, Austro-Hungarian
mutiny in: 63
Navy, French: 38
Navy, German: 27, 29, 41, 48
and the naval race: 38
and rearmament: 89
Navy, Japanese: 38
Navy, North Korean: 199
Navy, Royal: 27, 38, 39, 41, 43, 44,
189
Navy, Secretary of: 103
Navy, U.S.: 11, 38, 93, 104, 105,
107, 199, 203
See also Navy Department
Navy Department: 13
and WW II economic mobilization:
93, 94, 95, 96, 97, 105, 107
See also Knox, Frank; Forrestal,
James V.
Nazi. *See* National Socialists
Nazi-Soviet pact: 149, 150
Nelson, Donald M.: 95, 95-96,
97-98, 100, 103, 105-106, 109,
120
See also War Production Board
Netherlands: 14
Neue Züricher Zeitung: 83
Neurath, Constantin von: 31
Neutron bomb: 168
New Deal: 6, 14, 91, 108, 109, 110,
111, 112, 113, 114, 116, 117, 148
New Deal for Blacks, A: 152
New Guinea: 7
New Hampshire primary, 1968: 200
New York: 14
New York Herald-Tribune, Paris edition: 203
New York Times: 156, 198
News media
and black militancy: 147, 148, 149,
150, 151, 153
and Vietnam: 197-198, 199-200,
204, 207-208, 208-209, 220

and war coverage: 5, 9, 207-209, 220
See also Black press; Press; Radio; Television; Wire services
Newsweek: 198
Nicias: 203
North Africa: 187, 190
North Atlantic Treaty Organization (NATO): 189
North Korea: 199
North Texas State University: 202
North Vietnam: 24
  and China: 206, 207
  and peace negotiations: 199, 200
  policy and strategy: 197, 206
North Vietnamese: 203, 207
Northwest Frontier, India: 44
Norway: 14, 145
Nuclear deterrence: 203
Nuclear warfare: 2, 22
Nuechterlein, James, quoted: 148
Nuremberg trials: 9

OAS *(Organisation de l'Armee Secrete).* *See* Secret Army Organization
OES. *See* Office of Economic Stabilization
OFF. *See* Office of Facts and Figures
OPA. *See* Office of Price Administration
OPACS. *See* Office of Price Administration and Civilian Supply
OPM. *See* Office of Production Management
OWM. *See* Office of War Mobilization
OWMR. *See* Office of War Mobilization and Reconversion
Oberdorfer, Don: 200
  quoted: 197
Office of Economic Stabilization (OES): 98, 99, 101
  See also Byrnes, James F.
Office of Civilian Requirements. *See* War Production Board

Office of Facts and Figures (OFF): 6
Office of Price Administration (OPA): 95, 98
Office of Price Administration and Civilian Supply (OPACS): 94-95
  See also War Production Board
Office of Production Management (OPM): 93, 94, 94-95, 95, 109
Office of War Information: 70, 159
Office of War Mobilization (OWM): 99, 101
Office of War Mobilization and Reconversion (OWMR): 99-100, 101
Ogburn, William F.: 172
Ordeal of Total War, The: 140
Osaka Association of A-Bomb Victims, Women's Section: 164, 165

PEC. *See* War Production Board, Production Executive Committee
Pacific Theater: 6
Pacifism: 34, 71, 154, 167-168
  See also Anti-war sentiment
Padua: 66
Palmer, A.W.: 61
Palmer, R.R.: 127
Paris: 61
Park, Robert: 172
Parliament and social change: 134
Patterson, Robert L.: 95, 104, 105, 106, 115
  See also War Department
Pearl Harbor: 5, 6, 10, 14, 69, 105, 109, 149, 171
Pearson, Lester, quoted: 116
Peasants, Russian: 139
Pelling, Henry: 140
  and participation and social gain: 132
Pensions: 135
People's War: 140
Perrett, Geoffrey: 148
Pershing, Gen. John J.:
  and Blacks in the military: 176-177
  quoted: 176

279

Persian Gulf: 209
Philippine Insurrection: 176
Piave offensive: 65
Pittsburgh Courier: 150, 151, 153
Police, French, in Algeria: 187
Poland, restoration of: 60
Polenberg, Richard: 113, 148, 168, 168n, 169, 176
  commentary: 170-175
  discussion and comments: 178
Poles, in Austria-Hungary: 58, 60, 63, 65
Polish-Americans: 10
Political Action Committee: 13-14
Politics and Markets: 115
Populism: 48
Portugal: 37
Portuguese Africa: 37
Powell, Adam Clayton, Jr.: 150
Prague: 60, 64, 65
Prandtl, Ludwig: 75
Prejudice: 1, 5, 7, 8-9, 9-12, 14, 14-15, 134, 142, 143, 221
  See also Blacks; Women
Press: 7, 8, 11, 39, 156, 174, 197, 198, 200, 203, 220
  See also Black press; News media
Press, Negro. See Black press
Princeton University: 202
Privy Council: 135
Production Executive Committee. See War Production Board
Progressivism: 48, 54-55, 68, 111-112
Prologue: 148, 174
Propaganda: 11, 51, 52-53, 55, 68, 69-70, 71, 72, 86, 87, 123, 144, 159, 161, 162, 165-166
  See also Public opinion and support
Prussia: 42
Psycho-history: 68
Psychological mobilization. See Public opinion and support
Public opinion: 6, 186
Public opinion and support: 1, 2, 5, 6-7, 8-9, 19-20, 22, 24, 28, 29, 30-31, 34, 39, 45, 47-49, 51-53, 55, 59, 68, 69-70, 72, 83, 84, 85-88, 90, 133-134, 136-137, 144, 186, 188, 190, 191-192, 193, 194, 195, 198, 200, 207-208, 221, 222
  See also Propaganda
Pueblo, USS: 199
Pugh, Martin: 130, 137
"Putsch", 1961: 193
Pyle, Ernie, quoted: 7

Race Relations Institute: 150
Race riots, U.S.: 10-11, 147, 150-151
Radicalism: 74
Radio: 5, 135, 209
  See also News media
Radio Hanoi: 209
Raeder, Gr.Adm. Erich: 89
Ragsdale, Wilmott, and combat reporting: 220
Railroads: 12, 49, 155
Randolph, A. Philip: 149, 151, 152, 152-153, 154
  and communists: 153
Rape, use of in war: 163-164
Rather, Dan: 208
Reader, W.J., quoted: 130
Reagan, Ronald: 168, 203
Reconstruction: 174
Reddel, Col. Carl W.
  introduction: 215
Redfield, Robert: 172
Reichenau, Col. Walter von, quoted: 86
Reichskanzlei: 83
Reichsrat: 57, 59, 62, 64
Reichstag: 83, 84, 89
Reichswehr. See Armed Forces, German
Reichswehr and Politics, The: 84n
Relative Deprivation and Social Justice: 134
Representation of the People Act, 1918: 137
Republican Party: 13, 14, 107

Revolution: 19, 26, 146
Algerian. *See* Algeria
American: 127, 204
Austria-Hungary: 57, 59
French: 26, 127
Germany: 57, 139
Russian: 63, 130
REVOLVER, operation: 63
Rhineland, reoccupation of, 1936: 86
Rhodes, Cecil: 37
Rilling, Lt.Col. David S.
  on legal status of Vietnam War: 205
Ritter, Gerhard: 32-33
Road to 1945: British Politics and the Second World War: 140
Roberts, Field Marshall Frederick S.: 43
"Robinson Charlie": 144
Roland, Alex: 75
Roman Empire, and limited war: 186
Roosevelt, Eleanor: 11
Roosevelt, Franklin D.: 5, 14, 93, 94, 95, 97, 98, 99, 101, 104, 108, 120, 173, 174
  and Blacks: 11
  Hold-the-Line order: 98
  and the Industrial Mobilization Plan: 114
  and Japanese-Americans: 10
  and the military: 103-104, 105, 105-106, 110, 238n-18
  and Smith-Connally: 13
  and the tone of economic mobilization: 92, 94, 103-104, 105, 108-110, 111, 112, 113-118, 218
Roosevelt, F.D., Administration: 92, 93, 94, 96, 98, 101, 103, 104, 109, 113, 120
Roosevelt, Theodore: 54, 221
Ropp, Ted: 19
"Rosie the Riveter": 159, 166, 174
Rostow, Eugene V., quoted: 10
Rothenberg, Gunther E.: 55-56, 67, 68-69, 220
  paper: 57-66

Rubber: 99
Rudwick, Elliott: 153-154
Rumania: 61, 62
Rumanians: 58, 60
Runciman, W.G.: 134
Rupp, Leila J.: 128, 155, 170, 170-171, 171, 172, 175, 176, 179, 218-219, 221
  discussion and comments: 177, 179
  paper: 156-169
Rusk, Dean: 206
Russia: 24, 27, 36, 38, 40, 41, 42, 43, 47, 62, 69, 130, 139
  and Austro-Hungarian POWs: 64
  and peace negotiations: 63
  revolution: 63, 130
  See also Soviet Union
Russians: 128
Russo-Japanese War: 32
Ruthenes: 58, 60

SRC. *See* Southern Regional Council
Saigon: 197, 199
St. Louis, Mo.: 154
St. Stephen, Crown of: 57, 60, 61, 65
  See also Hungary
Salinger, J.D.: 7
Salsbury, Robert A.T.G. Cecil, Marquess of: 39
Saxe, Marshal Maurice de, quoted: 220
Schacht, Hjalmar: 89
Schandler, Herbert: 199
Scheiner, Czech, politician: 60
Schlafley, Phyllis: 170
Schleicher, Gen. Kurt von: 85
Schlieffen, Count Alfred von: 31, 34, 36
Schlieffen Plan: 29, 36, 45
Schmidt-Harzbach, Ingrid: 166-167
Schutzstaffel (SS): 87
Science and technology: 2, 19, 20, 22, 34, 74-75, 128, 135
Scientific and Industrial Research, Dept. of: 135

Searls, Fred, Jr.: 96
Second International: 74
Secrecy and society: 178, 179
Secret Army Organization (OAS): 194
Security Headquarters (SS): 87
Selective Service Administration: 53
Senate Special Committee to Investigate the National Defense Program. *See* Truman Committee
Senate Special Committee to Study and Survey the Problems of American Small Business. *See* Murray Committee
Serbia: 61
Serbs: 58, 60, 65
Shakespeare: 33
Shaw, George Bernard: 170
Sherrod, Robert, quoted: 7
Showalter, Dennis E.: 22-23, 67-68, 73, 216, 217, 220
  discussion and comments: 71, 76, 209
  paper: 24-45
Shy, John: 127
Siberia: 102
Sitkoff, Harvard: 128, 146, 170, 171, 172, 175, 176, 218, 221
  discussion and comments: 176, 178
  paper: 147-155
Silesia: 60, 62, 64
Silva, Flavius: 186
Sixtus, Prince of Parma: 62
Skoda armament works: 60
Slater, Philip: 162
Slavs: 60, 61
Slovaks: 58, 60
Slovenes: 58, 60
Smith, Harold D.: 98
Smith-Connally bill: 13
Spain: 145, 203
Sport, influence of: 28
State, Secretary of: 103
State of the Union address, 1968: 199
Statism: 54-55, 68
Stimson, Henry L.: 95, 104, 104-105, 106, 115

and Blacks in the military: 11
and Japanese-Americans: 10
See also War Department
Stouffer, Samuel: 172
Strategic Air Command, Combat Support Groups: 203
Stresemann, Gustav: 85
Stürgkh, Karl, Count von: 59, 60
Stürmabteilung (SA): 83
Styria: 63
Social Democrats: 84
Socialism and the Challenge of War: 135
Socialists: 58, 61, 135, 154
Solomon Islands: 7
Soustelle, Jacques: 190
South Africa: 30
South Atlantic: 189
South Pacific: 7
South Slavs: 63, 64, 65
South Vietnam: 197, 200, 203, 208-209
South Vietnamese: 206-207
Southeast Asia: 189
Southern Regional Council (SRC): 151-152
Southwest Africa: 30
Soviet Union: 128, 145
  Family Code: 166
  industrial production: 102, 236-237n-11
  World War II
    and ethnic groups: 14, 128
    impact on women: 157, 158, 160, 164, 166, 167, 175, 219
  See also Russia
Subaltern from the Wars Returning, A: 179
Submarine warfare: 48
Subsidies, government: 134, 135
Suffragist movement: 138
Sullivan, Mark, quoted: 47
Supply Priorities and Allocation Board (SPAB): 95
Supreme Court: 10, 147

Sweden: 145, 146
Switzerland: 66, 145
Syracuse: 203

Talbott, John E.: 186, 202-203, 219, 221
 discussion and comments: 209
 paper: 187-195
Tallyrand-Périgord, Charles M. de
 and the use of force: 71
Tawney, R.H.: 135
Taxes: 12, 14
 See also Finance
Taylor, A.J.P.: 140
Technology. *See* Science and technology
Television
 and military news: 186, 197-198, 200, 204, 207-208, 209, 220
 use of by de Gaulle: 193, 194, 209
 See also News media
Tennessee Johnson: 174
Tennessee Valley Authority (TVA): 116
Tertullus: 186
Tet!: 197
Tet offensive: 197, 198
 political reaction to: 198-199, 199-200, 204, 219
Teutoburger Wald: 186
Texas, Republic of: 202
Thatcher, Margaret: 142, 207
Thebes: 24
Thieu, Lt.Gen. Nguyen Van: 203
Thirty Years' War: 33
Thomas, Gen. Georg: 83, 88, 90
Thompson, Paul: 130
Thun, Baron: 60
Time: 8, 174, 198, 203, 220
Tirpitz, Adm. Alfred von: 25
Tisza, Count Stephen: 59, 60, 61, 64
Tolan Committee: 100, 101, 103
Tolstoy, Leo: 24
"Tommy Atkins" and society: 27
Tonkin, Gulf of: 203
Tonkin Gulf resolution: 203

Trask, David F.: 81
 discussion and comments: 75
 introductions: 22-23, 46, 55-56, 66
 remarks: 19-22, 77
Treitschke, Heinrich von: 27
Triple Entente: 40, 61
Triumph of Conservatism, The: 111
Treasury (British): 143
Treasury Department (U.S.): 9, 53, 98
Truman, Harry S.: 101, 115, 176, 177, 206, 210
Truman Committee: 96, 100, 101, 103, 106
Tunisia: 188, 192
Tyrol: 61

UMW. *See* United Mine Workers
USSR. *See* Soviet Union
U-boat. *See* Submarine warfare
Ukraine: 63, 64
Ukrainian unification: 60, 64-65
Ukrainians: 14, 128
Ullman, Richard: 67
Ulster: 39
Unemployment insurance: 135
Unionists, Ulster: 39
Unions, labor. *See* Labor
United Kingdom: 87
 anti-Semitism in: 142
 Beveridge Report: 143-144, 171
 and Borneo: 210, 211
 Cabinet: 39, 40, 103
 class structure: 138, 144, 145
 cognitive dissonance in: 68
 education: 134, 145
 franchise reform, 1918: 130
 government subsidies and pensions: 134, 135
 housing: 134, 144
 industrial production: 102, 236-237n-11
 and Malaya: 210
 medical services: 141
 merchant fleet: 50, 145

pre-WW I foreign policy: 26, 27, 30, 37-38, 39, 39-40, 40-42, 45
pre-WW I martial spirit: 26-27, 67, 220
pre-WW I relations with Germany: 26, 37-39, 39-40, 40-42
pre-WW I society: 39-40, 67, 69, 220
science and technology: 75, 135
war cabinet: 136
Women's Land Army: 132
World War I
   ambivalence toward: 25, 39, 41, 67-68, 220
   and the arts: 138-139
   effects on society: 130, 134-139, 140, 144, 218
   and industry changes: 135-136
   labor gains: 130, 136-137
   military conscription: 135
   mobilization: 216, 217
   use of propaganda: 14, 72
   and women: 137-138, 145, 177-178, 178, 179
   and the working class: 134, 135, 136-137, 218
World War II
   civilian life and morale: 140-141, 141-142, 143, 179-180
   combined boards and staffs: 105, 106
   economic mobilization: 98, 102, 105
   effects on society: 140-145, 171, 218
   impact on women: 142, 157, 158, 159, 162, 171, 175, 218, 219
   internment: 14, 142
   and labor: 142, 145
   use of propaganda: 144
   Washington Embassy observations: 6-7, 10, 11-12, 114
   See also Armed Forces, British; Army, British; Navy, royal

United Mine Workers (UMW): 13
United States: 27, 38, 43
   anti-Semitism: 10, 14
   censorship: 48, 208-209
   civil disobedience: 148, 153
   education: 128, 145, 147, 153
   industrial production compared: 102, 236-237n-11
   Nazi racism, reaction to: 155
   post-WW II economic reconversion: 99-100, 111
   post-WW II occupation influence: 168
   pre-WW I society: 53, 54-55, 69, 75-76, 220-221
   race riots: 10-11, 147, 150-151
   science and technology: 74-75
Vietnam War
   legal status: 205
   policy regarding: 198, 199, 200, 203, 206-207
   political reaction to Tet: 198-199, 199-200, 204, 219
   public opinion and support: 197, 198, 199-200, 204, 208-209, 221
   and World War II: 173-175
World War I
   agricultural mobilization: 49, 50-51
   ambivalence toward: 47-49, 52, 68, 69, 73-74, 217
   domestic violence during: 53
   economic mobilization: 48, 49-51, 76, 115-116, 119, 218
   and labor: 74
   espionage bill: 48-49
   merchant fleet: 50
   migration: 127-128
   military conscription: 48-49, 51-52, 53
   and political and military thinking: 20-22, 218
   public opinion and support: 47-48, 49, 52-53, 69-70

relations with the Allies: 49, 50, 51, 217
use of legal coercion: 49-52, 53-55, 71
use of propaganda: 52-53, 68, 69-70, 71, 72
war aims: 48, 65, 73
and women: 157
World War II
and agriculture: 112, 113, 117
and civil rights delay: 148, 149, 150, 151-152, 154-155, 171, 175, 176, 218
combined boards and staffs: 105, 106
communist opposition to mobilization: 149
consumer goods production: 94-95, 100
economic mobilization agencies: 92-101
economic mobilization and central authority: 96, 98, 100-101, 103-104, 105, 106-108, 112-113, 116-117
economic mobilization and Congress: 96, 98, 100-101, 104, 106, 108, 113
economic mobilization and defense contracts: 93-94, 95, 96, 97, 99, 100
economic mobilization and finance: 94, 95, 98, 99, 113
economic mobilization and power patterns: 108-110, 111, 116, 117
economic mobilization and the corporate community: 12-13, 14, 92, 93, 94, 95, 96, 97, 99, 100, 104, 107-108, 109, 111-113, 115, 117, 118, 120, 218
economic mobilization and the military: 81, 92, 93-94, 95, 96, 97, 98, 100, 103-105, 107-108, 109, 111, 114, 119, 218, 238n-18, 238-239n-19
impact on women: 156-157, 158-159, 159, 160, 161-162, 165-166, 172, 174, 175, 219
internment: 9-10, 156-157
and labor: 11-12, 13, 92, 94, 96, 98, 99-100, 112, 117, 149
price stabilization: 94-95, 98, 113
race relations during: 7-8, 8-11, 14, 147, 150-151, 151-152, 172, 176, 218
rationing during: 8, 53, 98
society: 1, 5, 6-7, 9-11, 12, 14-15, 91, 94, 108-110, 112, 127, 170, 172, 173
use of propaganda: 8-9, 9, 11, 69-70, 159, 165-166, 220
See also Blacks
United States Employment Service: 160
Unmaking of a President, The: 199
Upper classes: 26, 30, 35, 138, 145
Ural Mountains: 102
Urban League. *See* National Urban League

V J Day: 174
Varus, Publius Quintilius: 186
Venereal disease: 161
Versailles Treaty: 84
Victory girls: 161
Vienna: 60, 61, 62, 63, 64, 65, 66
Viet Cong: 197
Vietnam: 24
Vietnam War: 156, 168, 169, 185, 202, 203, 204, 205, 219
interdiction in: 206, 207
Khe Sanh: 197, 198
negotiations: 199, 200
Tet offensive: 197, 198
See also Indochina; United States
Villard, Oswald Garrison: 221
Violence, escalating: 19, 20, 21, 22, 27, 34

Violence, institutional, and women: 163
Virginia, royal governor of: 202
Vittorio Veneto: 65
Voices Prophesying War: 76
Voltaire: 173

WPB. *See* War Production Board
Wabash, Ind., *Plain Dealer,* quoted: 47
Waldersee, Alfred von: 33
Wallace, Henry A.: 14, 95, 114
Walpole, Sir Robert: 30
Warsaw: 14
War
  and the arts: 138-139
  as a cohesive force: 1, 5, 6, 14-15, 57, 58-59, 60-61, 69-70, 127, 130, 134, 138, 143, 173
  as a divisive force: 1, 5, 57, 58-59, 60-61, 134, 138, 173-174
  glorification of: 19-20, 22, 26, 29, 86
  limited: 2, 22, 127, 185-186, 203, 204, 207, 221
  preventive: 31, 33
  and social change, measurement of: 131-134
  total: 2, 20-22, 127, 128, 218
War, Office of the Assistant Secretary of: 103, 107
War, Secretary of: 9, 10, 11, 103, 104
  See also Stimson, Henry L.
War and Social Change in the Twentieth Century: 139
War Department: 9, 13, 93-94, 95, 96, 97, 103, 104, 105, 107
  See also Patterson, Robert L.; Stimson, Henry L.
War Industries Board: 49-50, 51, 53, 115, 116
War in the Air: 76
War Labor Board (WLB): 12, 98
War Ministry, German: 32, 35

War Manpower Commission (WMC): 100, 174
War of American Independence: 127, 204
War Production Board (WPB): 8, 95-98, 99, 100, 105, 105-106, 109, 120n
  Industry Divison: 97, 98
  Material Division: 97, 98
  Office of Civilian Requirements: 100
  Planning Committee: 96-97, 98, 102, 105-106
  Production Executive Committee (PEC): 97-98, 100, 106
  See also Nelson, Donald M.; Wilson, Charles E.
War Relocation Authority: 10
War Resources Board: 104
War Service Act, 1912: 59
War Supervisory Office: 59
Warner, Lloyd: 172
Washington: 10
Washington, D.C.: 1, 13, 14, 197, 198, 199, 200, 203, 204
Washington Post: 198
Watson, James
  discussion and comments: 176-177, 210, 211
Watson, Laura, discussion and comments: 210
Watson, Robert J., discussion and comments: 71
Wattenberg, Ben: 186, 207
Webb, Beatrice: 135
Webb, Sidney: 135
Weber, Eugene: 178
Week of the Barricades: 193
Wehrmacht. *See* Armed Forces, German
Weigley, Russell F.: 21
  discussion and comments: 119, 120
  introductions: 82, 90, 110
  remarks: 81-82
Weimar Republic: 84-85
  See also Germany

Wejerle, Alexander: 64
Wells, H.G.: 76
Westmoreland, Gen. William C.: 199
Whitlock, Brand, American Ambassador to Belgium: 139
White, Walter: 150
White House: 95, 111, 113, 114, 197, 199
Whitehall: 42
William II, of Germany: 24, 25, 28, 31, 33, 37, 38
Willkie, Wendell: 14
Wilson, Charles E.: 97-98, 106, 107
   See also War Production Board, Production Executive Committee
Wilson, Sir Henry H.: 29, 45
Wilson, Woodrow: 50, 61, 63, 65, 73, 115, 217, 218
   and declaration of war: 47-49
   and legal coercion: 53, 54-55
   and military conscription: 51-52
Wilsonian ideology: 5, 20, 48, 50
Winkler, Allan M.: 66, 77
   commentary: 67-70
Winter, J.M., quoted: 135
Wire services: 197
   See also News media
Wirth, Louis: 172
Women
   and the atomic bomb: 164-165
   and childbearing: 157, 160, 161, 162, 163, 164-165, 166, 167, 168
   and conscription: 158-159
   and gain from war: 130, 137 138, 139, 140, 156, 159, 165-166, 167, 168, 170-171, 174, 219, 221
   lesbians: 161, 162
   and military service: 132, 158, 177-178, 179
   and pacificism: 167-168
   and propaganda: 159, 161, 162, 163, 165-166

   public attitudes toward: 12, 39, 40, 157, 165-166, 167, 168, 170, 219
   and reproduction: 157, 160-161, 163, 164-165, 166, 167, 167-168
   self-perceptions: 157, 165, 166-168
   and sex: 157, 160, 161-162, 163, 167
   suffrage: 39, 130, 137-138, 139, 145, 146, 168
   and violence: 157, 163-164, 167
   in the work force: 12, 128, 130, 137, 139, 142, 157-160, 166, 167, 172, 174, 175
   See also specific country
Women's Land Army: 132
Women's Section, Osaka Association of A-Bomb Victims: 164, 165
Women's Volunteer Service: 141
Woodward, C. Vann: 69
Working class: 133, 134, 135, 136-137, 138, 139, 144, 145, 218
   See also Class structure; Labor
World War I: 48, 54, 60, 61, 62, 63, 65-66, 127-128, 130-131, 216-217, 218, 220-221
   Carnegie Endowment for International Peace studies of: 128
   destructiveness of: 20
   reactions to: 20-21
   See also specific country; specific topic
World War II: 1, 6-7, 81-82, 102-103, 127-128, 221
   as an extension of World War I: 21
   attitudes toward and Vietnam: 173-174
   reactions to: 21-22
   See also specific country; specific topic
Wright, Gordon: 140

Yale University: 1, 5

Zagreb: 64, 65
Zechlin, Egmont: 32-33
Zeppelins: 76

287